MASQUERADE

The Feminist Illusion

W. Edward Chynoweth

Hamilton Books
A member of
The Rowman & Littlefield Publishing Group
Lanham · Boulder · New York · Toronto · Oxford

Copyright © 2005 by
W. Edward Chynoweth

Hamilton Books
4501 Forbes Boulevard
Suite 200
Lanham, Maryland 20706
Hamilton Books Acquisitions Department (301) 459-3366

PO Box 317
Oxford
OX2 9RU, UK

This book was previously published by Trafford Publishing.

All rights reserved
Printed in the United States of America
British Library Cataloging in Publication Information Available

Library of Congress Control Number: 2005930464
ISBN 0-7618-3318-8 (paperback : alk. ppr.)

∞™ The paper used in this publication meets the minimum
requirements of American National Standard for Information
Sciences—Permanence of Paper for Printed Library Materials,
ANSI Z39.48—1984

To my mother
Grace Woodruff Chynoweth

With acknowledgements to Nicholas Davidson, Midge Decter, George Gilder, Steven Goldberg, Michael Levin, and William Oddie, on whose research and pioneering work this study builds.
And appreciation to Trafford Publishing for their help in formatting.

Contents

Foreword		*I*
	1. General	*ii*
	2. Civil Rights Act	*v*
Introduction		1
I	Is There a Right Order of the Human Sexes?	13
II	Art and Culture	29
III	Parameters and Pigments, Or Why a Lion Roars	45
IV	Marriage, Or A Lion Roars	61
V	Biblical Paradigms, or How Christianity Deals With the Human Sexes	79
VI	Further Catholic Thought	101
	1. God or Goddesses?	101
	2. The Church and Women, Parts I & II	109
	3. The Church and Women, III, IV & V	119
	4. The Church and Women, Conclusion	128
	5. Is There Precedent for Women as Deaconesses?	130
	6. The National Conference of Catholic Bishops Copes With Feminism – In a Way	132
	7. What Will Happen To God?	145

VII	HISTORY AS A SOCIETY COLUMN FOR LOVELY LADIES – "HERSTORY"	155
	1. Before the Deluge	156
	2. Enter Female Scholarship	159
	3. Brushing the Bloom off the Flowers	164
	4. More Challenges to Society's "Male" Blueprint	171
	5. Toujours L'Amour	176
	6. Flirting With a Feminist Pattern for Society's Mosaic	179
	7. More Women's Liberation	182
	8. Believing More Impossible Things (the White Queen)	192
VIII	"NON-FEMINIST" AND A FEW OTHER FEMINIST WOMEN WRITERS	207
IX	HOW SUNDRY NOTED MEN HAVE DEALT WITH OUR SUBJECT	287
	1. The Bible vs. the Romantic Age: John Knox and Robert Louis Stevenson	288
	2. Right Order Patterned on Adam Smith's Theory of Moral Sentiments	297
	3. The Feminist Goddess Movement	312
X	FROM CLASSICISM TO POSTMODERNISM – ARISTOTLE THROUGH BRYCE AND STEPHEN – TO EGALITARIAN RIGHTS AND DEVOLUTION	317
	1. Aristotle on Men and Women	318
	2. Irving Babbitt	326
	3. Nineteenth-Century Thought on Men and Women	327
	4. A Plea for Liberty	336
	5. Liberty, Equality, Fraternity	339

6. Postmodern Confusions	342
7. The Education of Henry Adams and Richard M. Weaver	345
8. Irreducible Simplicity	352
9. More Contrasting Examples	354
CONCLUSION	363
NOTES	373
BIBLIOGRAPHY	445
Periodicals	451
INDEX	453

Foreword

(T)he "good of a commonwealth" includes the inborn human talents, qualities and potentials, and part of the... justice of power... is the obligation to protect, preserve and foster these capacities.
Josef Pieper[1]

How do we define a truly human life? To ask this challenging question in the midst of all our accomplishments as establish ourselves in this world, to keep this question alive through honest and precise reasoning: this is the fundamental task of philosophy, its specific contribution to the common good — even though, by itself, it is unable to provide the complete answer.
Josef Pieper[2]

Things which are not in their intended position are restless. Once they are in their ordered position, they are at rest.
St. Augustine[3]

Feminists concur that major social structural changes — in the economy, in politics, and in social practices and expectations — are essential.
Claire Fulenwider[4]

1.

*T*he most important challenge for human beings is how to deal with the two sexes — how to adhere to a working arrangement for the common good — a right order. Yet at this juncture, people of the West merely assume sexual fungibility. Philosophy's task is neglected.

What led to crafting this book began over thirteen years ago in a stand against co-ed service academies, followed by an attempted dialogue with the California Judicial Council's "Gender Bias Committee" then "taking testimony" around the state. The ladies' vendetta drew from me letters and research offering reasoned debate, all to no avail. *I seemed the only one offering opposition, which they invited and simply ignored*. The final, voluminous "gender bias" report on instances of ages-old sexual interplay made no mention of philosophical, anthropological, biological or common sense views on the sexes. Benumbed by the litany of "women's issues" (feminism), freedom of expression, right order and human nature were irrelevant. Meanwhile, signs of unrest were appearing in college sports as a result of Title IX, and in society at large due to "sexual harassment," "affirmative action," etc., all revealing a people seriously confused about the role of sex in a "truly human life."

Despite excellent treatises over the past thirty years revealing feminism as a sham, general ignorance of its false message persists. Readers will not fully grasp the subject without first reading these treatises, starting with those of Professors Michael Levin and Steven Goldberg. While most men of above average intelligence could probably understand the "feminine mystique" better than their wives, they fear to speak out, thus lending to the apathy. (They prefer Cal Coolidge's campaign style — avoiding conflict by not talking[5] — although they do resort to platitudes.) But most men haven't bothered to read the evidence. *It is to the wisdom of the past they must answer*. Time will not wait.

Many are on the right track but must go further. Who says A must say B. While George Will sees that family decline "weakens the other institutions of society," he doesn't mention the cause of family decline: statutes fudging the sexes in the name of "equality".⁶ One can't prosecute a homicide ignoring the perp. This book vitalizes the dialectic, which must now include the ravages of the Nineteenth Amendment and other statutes presuming to tamper with sex roles.

Artists' best work often arises from a visual inspiration, of color, form, emotion. For me, it took a photo in the West Point alumni magazine of a lovely young upperclasswoman bracing a taller, manly plebe. For sensible people such a parody should be the final straw, yet it seems not to bother the public conscience. In fact, the public *doesn't seem to notice*. Countless examples followed. Perhaps the most obvious criterion of all — *the timbre of the voices* — is simply ignored.

This book is a further attempt to state the case of the two sexes as comprehensively and convincingly as possible. Despite claims to the contrary (of "inevitable change," etc.), the wisdom of old has not waned. Ordered freedoms allow no simple answer, only guidelines. As with other pilgrimages, there is some repetition, much as an artist might use blue or red in all his paintings, or a wrestler his repertoire of holds and techniques on each of his opponents. Besides, since the sexes involve overlap, so must their study. The gender gap is crucial in numerous ways deserving serious attention, not just morning-after vote-tallying.

As Ptirim Sorokin and others have realized (including epigraphs above), in an integrated culture all the elements are interrelated and interconnected, and alterations in one element alter the others as well.⁷ Neither the people in 1919 as they were working on the Nineteenth Amendment nor Congress in 1963 as its members came up with Title VII gave such thought to the crucial relationship of the sexes. As Wilhelm Roepke, Pope John Paul

II and others have reminded us, however, certain relationships and values exist that take precedence over market mechanisms, freedoms, and contracts.[8] And, one might add, over egalitarian statutes. Such interferences are typical of gnosticism, socialism, and communism, which assure us that government will achieve perfection here and now through their actions.[9] These are not healthy roots.

It is not criticizing women per se to fault the idea of women seeking essentially male employment and activities. It is not chauvinist to appreciate female propensities in their natural milieus. In carelessly accepting androgyny, American males have never been more disappointing. In peacetime, a society faces a tremendous challenge rearing manly males. Care is needed with a son's rite of passage, with the rearing of young men. The difference between men and women's initiation into life are blindly ignored by Title IX in its transmogrification of the playing fields of Eton.

One theme of this book appears often in scholarly literature, as reflected in James Nuechterlein's observation (echoing *The Federalist* writers), "A serious politics requires at all times elements of deterrence, of checking power with counterpower. Realism, Niebuhr said, means that you achieve the common good not just by unselfishness but by the restraint of selfishness. Since power is never in stable equilibrium, so neither is politics: it is an ongoing process, not an achieved end. There can be no dream of perfect justice. Politics has to do with the relatively better, or even the lesser evil."[10] This is undoubtedly true, with Madisonian factions vying with sincere visions of the common good. Since women are more attuned to families and networks than the common good, it becomes an unnatural stretch for those elevated to high office. Rather than "keeping this question alive through honest and precise reasoning," there is only illusive equality talk.

Although we need a full-blown, ethical debate, judging from past experience (aside from the many men and women who will agree with me), responses to this book will be incredulous, scornful, scoffing, irritated, impatient, ridiculing, disdainful, disbelieving, ignorant, or sublimely neutral. Feminists of both sexes lack reasoned arguments. While some will smear this book as Quixotic or a "step back in time," I believe it to be more like the voyage of Wrong Way Corrigan, who was hardly backward looking and did indeed successfully cross the Atlantic, so at least there is hope. Besides, if a step back offers more advantage than where one is standing, one had better take it.

2.

One root of our problem traces to the 1964 Civil Rights Act's Title VII, in which a bemused Congress carelessly enacted a destructive statute on sex that *was not originally intended*.[11] Title IX followed in 1972. Although 1964's "Title VII" and 1972's "Title IX" are considered straightforward measures readily ascertainable (like the Constitution) and digestible by any interested citizen, a reading of their statutory verbiage reveals a veritable bucket of worms. Ironically, these radical exercises in positive law are found in the United States Code in 42 Section 2000e, under the title, "Public Health and Welfare," which two concerns, from the standpoint of the over-all common good, have been severely compromised. Executive orders by presidents of both parties have added to the encroachments. A Republican administration established the "Glass Ceiling Act of 1991," aimed at eliminating "artificial barriers" and "increasing opportunities and development experiences of women." The Reagan administration added its voice in the hopes of "systematic elimination of regulatory and procedural barriers which have unfairly precluded women from receiving equal treatment from Federal activity." Oh? "Unfairly"? Title VII itself, of course, decreed that citizens could no longer discriminate as to sex in matters of compensation, terms, conditions or privileges of employment, except where bona fide occupational qualifications are reasonably necessary to the normal operation of business or enterprise. This was supposed to involve only activities funded by Washington, but inevitably oozed into private enterprise as well. All this ridiculous language came not from philosophers but from feminists, yet our elected representatives bought it hook line and sinker.

One needs no expertise to recognize the profound aspects of human life being casually submerged in such temporizing, with no mention of families, marriage, division of labor, male leadership, historical patriarchy, women's receptivity, testosterone, male aggressiveness, different brain structures and physiques, child rearing and many other facets. It is all to be left up to judges to decide "bona fide qualifications." One can be forgiven for wondering what the congressmen were thinking when this was enacted. Small wonder that courts have usurped our lives; spurious suits proliferate; "political correctness" smothers the delicate framework of our culture; and crime, drugs, and divorce are rampant, largely because napping legislators and a napping executive neglected to read the language of the statutes they were enacting. They forgot their history lessons and left their common sense and courage at the Washington Monument as they voted "aye" to the inane proposition that "women are underrepresented" and need the national government to take away constitutional freedoms in order to "eliminate artificial barriers." Presumably such "barriers" are small matters of "unfairness" like femininity, male strength, greater male risks, importance of childbirth, the more childlike female voice, her attractiveness, male objectivity and athleticity, female sex appeal, and so on." What fools these mortals be!" I would repeal the whole intrusion.

All this is not to say that men invariably have done a good job; far from it. But because men, since Adam, have been far from perfect doesn't mean that we can substitute women for men. When an oak languishes, one doesn't resort to a crepe myrtle; one either revitalizes the oak or replaces it with a new one. Michael Behe defines intelligent design generally as consisting of three things: "a scientific research program that investigates the effects of intelligent causes; an intellectual movement that challenges Darwinism and its naturalistic legacy; and a way of understanding divine action."[12] We have neglected such thinking in our age.

I hope this will shed some light on my aims. While intelligent design will undergo much more debate and analysis, I predict that its ultimate application to the human species will be a revelation, and, although not in so many words, this book is an attempt to stimulate a dialogue toward that end.

Introduction

But, my friend, I said, a measure of such things which in any degree falls short of the whole truth is not fair measure; for nothing imperfect is the measure of anything, although persons are too apt to be contented and think that they need search no further.
Plato's *Republic*, VI, p. 242

And ye shall know the truth, and the truth shall make you free.
The Gospel According to St. John, 8:32

Despite ample clues, much of humanity continues its moral dishabille in the dimorphic sphere of Adam and Eve – i.e., men and women. For examples in the Brave New Western World, there are a "mixed-gender army" and its "Human Sexuality Committee"; girlish voices castigating generals and reporting on war; state-enforced sex equality in sports; state-enforced edicts against Christianity; single-parenting (no father); poor performance levels in state-run co-ed schooling; promotion of homosexuality despite A.I.D.S.; sophomoric entertainment industry; below-replacement birth rate; high abortion rates; males pursuing sports and technology instead of "refining and enlarging the public views"; shortage of nurses; all fueled by perhaps the most critical lapse: a national rhetoric masking truths in enthymemes and politically correct posturing.[1]

The premise of the present book is that our Anglo-American (or Western) Civilization is rooted in church and Bible, long-proven institutions, ancient folkways of civility, Greek philosophy and Roman law, British common law, the Constitution, anthropology – all combining to inform a right order of being – our civilization. Although a considerable heritage, our culture, it is vulnerable without vigilance. At the center are ages-old, distinct roles for men and women in keeping with their natures, abilities, and the common good. The above problems arose from careless neglect of cultural parameters in the rush to equality, individualism and "rights." We shall explore these areas and offer criticism, with representative examples.

Perhaps what is needed is a Voegelinian "leap in being" into "the historical dimension of human nature." Through experience, Voegelin believes, an intelligent people learn their "articulated… order of human existence. This struggle for the truth of order is the very substance of history."[2]

> Human existence in society has history because it has a dimension of spirit and freedom beyond mere animal existence, because social order is an attunement of man with the order of being, and because this order can be understood by man and realized in society with increasing approximations to its truth. Every society is organized for survival in the world and, at the same time, for partnership in the order of being that has its origin in world-transcendent divine Being; it has to cope with problems of its pragmatic existence and, at the same time, it is concerned with the truth of its order.

As we shall see, such thought is a far cry from the writings of male and female herstorians. At the same time, all of the above problems reflect the diminished influence of women along the interior lines they once ruled – adhering to husbands in rearing the young. Too many have surrendered these responsibilities, aspiring to exterior influence "in the gates" aping males.

While other men have probed history, biology, anthropology, theology, and sociology, this book will add art and literature and suggest specific corrections in self-government. Many of the above problems have resulted from unwise actions and judgments of political, judicial and academic leaders. Fortunately we can still take corrective action. While sociologists and anthropologists study the "is," my brief will include the "ought," conducive to the common good. While biology informs the species, will, imagination, reason, and common sense combine to achieve periods of relative sexual peace and accord. While some, like sociologists at an Academy Awards gala, will ask for a "study" or a "commission," the evidence is already in: attractive women have great power over males.

In a more general sense (as with Voegelin), T.S. Eliot in *Christianity and Culture* offers worthwhile insights. The following seriatim excerpts are relevant:

> Thus, what I mean by a political philosophy is not merely even the conscious formulation of the ideal aims of a people, but the substratum of collective temperament, ways of behavior and unconscious values which provide the material for the formulation. What we are seeking is not a programme for a party, but a way of life for a people....[3] And the tendency of unlimited industrialism is to create bodies of men and women – of all classes – detached from tradition, alienated from religion and susceptible to mass suggestion: in other words, a mob. And a mob will be no less a mob if it is well fed, well clothed, well housed, and well disciplined.[4].... but unless we can find a pattern into which all problems of life can have their place, we are only likely to go on complicating chaos.... As political philosophy derives its sanction from ethics, and ethics from the truth of religion, it is only by returning to the eternal source of truth that we can hope for any social organization which will not, to its ultimate destruction, ignore some essential aspect of reality."[5]

The Church has perpetually to answer this question: to what purpose were we born? What is the end of man?[6] Definition

> (of culture): 1. The setting of bounds; limitation (rare) – 1483 – *Oxford English Dictionary*."[7].... It is a part of my thesis that the culture of the individual is dependent upon the culture of a group or class, and that the culture of the group or class is dependent upon the culture of the whole society to which that group or class belongs.[8].... Culture can never be wholly conscious – there is always more to it than we are conscious of ....[9]

While there are no easy, rigid formulas, over millennia there have been better formulations. Club bashers who carve careers attacking male clubs like Lions, Kiwanis, and now Augusta National are impurities in the mix. Families and clubs teach members to submerge individualism in the greater good, much like a well-tuned guitar. In our day, a discordant string needs retuning. We must relearn women's true value and how best they can serve the greater good as well as themselves. As with Mary, heroism for women is not in leading platoons or destroying institutions but in unselfishly helping husbands rear manlier, unselfish sons – and unselfish, womanly daughters. This is no small or limiting responsibility.

Rather than attempting a tight template, the present effort will be a pilgrimage through the literature – a running discourse on each pothole. There undoubtedly are other approaches but, relying on the excellent bona fide studies available, I "will content myself (borrowing from Aimé Georges Martimort) with the reflections suggested to me by a perusal of their inquiry, which extend over several years, and also, especially, with those reflections suggested to me by the history of the subject in general."[10] My approach will also be similar to Manfred Hauke's, who "attempts a systematic review" of his subject (feminist theology) against the backdrop of a historical sketch of its recent history. "While all the themes addressed... will be central, the aim is not to achieve exhaustive coverage... presentation of the relevant ideas and positions will be followed by critical commentary."[11]

J. Budziszewski offers another perspective, with help from Aristotle and C.S. Lewis, discussing "moral excellence and regime design"[12]:

> Although the point is Aristotle's, C.S. Lewis has explained it most clearly. We have spoken of *partnership* in a good life, so Lewis asks us to imagine a fleet of ships sailing in formation. For the voyage to be a success, three things are necessary. First, the ships must avoid collision and getting in each other's way. Second, each ship must be seaworthy, with its engines in good order. Third, they must all know the fleet's destination. "Morality, then," says Lewis, "seems to be concerned with three things. Firstly, with fair play and harmony between individuals. Secondly, with what might be called tidying up or harmonizing the things inside each individual. Thirdly, with the general purpose of human life as a whole; what man was made for; what course the whole fleet ought to be on; what tune the conductor of the band wants to play."

Professor Budziszewski tells of Aristotle's and Aquinas's consideration of the virtues, the soul, the ways in which they operate, and goes on to define the age-old term, the "common good," which should motivate any arrangements between men and women.

In the 40th-anniversary winter 1998 issue of *Modern Age*, the focus is on the "permanent things" (Eliot's original term), "visions of order" and "redeeming the time." Editor George A. Panichas writes, "the need for roots and the need for order have been for *Modern Age* fundamental needs for the inner and outer condition of individual and community... the imperative of standards, for restraint, for limits, for the discriminating faculty, in short, for qualitative life and thought."[13] When did America last benefit from "the discriminating faculty"?

What we are seeking is a reliable public philosophy grounded in what Robert P. Hunt calls "the institutions and virtues that are the lifeblood of any experiment in moral and political governance. – the more profound longings of the human heart, which seek satisfaction in the natural communities, secular and religious, that make for a truly human life."[14] Hunt tells us of John Courtney Murray's concern:

> Murray argued that the only way to recover a truly public philosophy was for the nation to reaffirm the higher truths on which the nation had been founded…. Liberal political philosophy has degenerated into a defense of the unencumbered self, which knows no law higher than that of its own choosing…. To erect a public philosophy only on an economic or contractual foundation is to ignore the more profound longings of the human heart, which seek satisfaction in the natural communities, secular and religious, that make for a truly human life.

This contrasts with the thought of many modern women (and their menfolk) who judge social trends mainly in terms of a woman's being "able to earn her own living." Actually their crucial role in perpetuating the race, instructing the young, and inspiring strong, good men transcends personal ambitions. Such remains the central irony of human order, also involving productive males. Our task will be to convince the reader that the "*natural* communities" must *inevitably* involve rational, natural expectations from the two sexes.

In his turn, Wilhelm Roepke does not explore the sexes other than as another of the "the aberrations of rationalism and liberalism," to decry

> the feminist, demanding complete equality with the male sex while remaining blind to the intriguing circumstance that the sexes were, after all, and not without reason, created different….[15]

Roepke was also searching for "moral foundations" on which to build a sound society. "(E)ven here it is the Spirit which forms the body," he wrote, "….without a correct orientation of the intellect all attempts to achieve a well-ordered and satisfying society are doomed to failure….Were human beings not to possess this gift of Light from Heaven what would they be but pitiful creatures, more pitiful than all the rest in their bodily helplessness and lack of skill?"[16] No room here for, "I did it my way."

Whether or not this amounts to a call to the Church, as Eliot puts it, we are "simply stating a fact… the common tradition of

Christianity, which has made Europe (and the U.S.) what it is, and… the common cultural elements, which this common Christianity has brought with it….It is in Christianity that our arts have developed; it is in Christianity that the laws of Europe have – until recently – been rooted. It is against a background of Christianity that all our thought has significance."[17] (parenthesis added)

* * *

Reflecting our present confusions, in opposition to Eliot we read of sociologists like Robert Wuthnow who claim that "on empirical grounds, evidence from recent research on the role of religion in decisions about work, professional ethics, and money provides reason to doubt that religion plays much of a role in public thinking about these secular issues." With or without "empirical" research, Wuthnow's "doubts" are not persuasive, since he tends to judge people cynically and fails to see that religious norms provide a much-needed paradigm from which to judge morality. Such thought exemplifies the confusions resulting from secular rationalism and mistrust of higher authority.[18]

* * *

In a more helpful vein, according to Ian Garrick Mason in a review of a book by Hilton Kramer and Roger Kimball[19], the authors recognize the present menace to "the moral and cultural achievements of European civilization" and argue that "it is to the future of this European past that we must look, and to the way it is either nurtured or neglected." Since it is wisdom of the past that Americans neglect, the present book will draw on the insights of many (both past and present) *verbatim*. After all, as Mason explains, with relevance for all such endeavors,

> The question is whether we can halt the trend, or whether the costs of doing so are unsupportable. Or perhaps whether a rebuilding is possible at all. – But love for culture and history cannot be reconstructed by executive order…. it is up to each

of us, one by one, to discover and preserve the relevance of our cultural inheritance – and to make sure that the European past has a future.

At times this requires breasting the tide. How we arrange the interaction of the sexes ultimately determines Eliot's "well-ordered and satisfying society" – our well-tuned guitar. As Mother Teresa expresses just one aspect of the discordant string,

> …. if we accept that the mother can kill even her own child, how can we tell other people not to kill one another? …. By abortion, the mother does not learn to live, but kills even her own child to solve her problem. And by abortion, the father is taught that he does not have to take any responsibility at all for the child that he has brought into that world. So that father is likely to put other women into the same trouble…. Any country that accepts abortion is not teaching its people to love one another but to use any violence to get what they want. This is why the greatest destroyer of love and peace is abortion.[20]

Rigorous logic once involved truths avoided by present fashion, e.g., by cloaking abortion as "woman's choice" – a deceptive enthymeme.

Mary Midgley writes of the quarrel between moralists, relativists and subjectivists, and concludes with a defense of "the grandness of morality" and the need for moral standards. As Dean M. Carignan explains, however, we must take Midgley a step further,

> On a social basis, individuals need some common understanding of right and wrong if meaningful human community is to be possible…. Midgley fails to acknowledge an external source of morality. Without such a source morality can ultimately be neither objective nor binding. It becomes a creation of man and thus assumes the status of mere convention…. If skeptics are to be convinced of the validity of moral judgments, they must first be convinced of the reality of objective moral standards that man does not create but rather discovers. Absolute agreement upon the specific standards themselves is not as important as the recognition that such standards exist – and should be sought.[21]

Rather than mining "bills of rights" and new avenues for women, we need to rediscover the old avenues, probing deeply for age-old truths about men and women – a perennial parameter of what we call "morality."

*   *   *

One reads of astronomers, physicists, cosmologists, mathematicians, oceanographers, geologists, etc., pursuing their investigations with determination. Whether it be the disparity between the popular Big Bang theory and the first law of thermodynamics[22]; the dispute between Darwinists, scientists and Creationists; theories on plate tectonics, the formation of Mt. Everest, the eruption of Mt. St. Helens or updates of Einstein; the quest for scientific truth goes on. A worthwhile dialectic needs energetic response to avoid entrenched error. As David Berlinski warns, for their privilege of judging the nature of the physical world, physicists "were to provide an account of the physical world at once penetrating, general, persuasive and true."[23] "This scrupulousness has lately been compromised" and they have felt "free to say anything that pops into their heads. – They carry on endlessly because they can. – Human beings, it would seem, may make scientific theories or they may make myths, but with respect to the same aspects of experience, they cannot quite do both."

Of all modern myths (e.g., Marxism, progressivism, relativism, secular humanism, imperialism, utilitarianism), one not yet unmasked by our dominant culture is the ideology known as "feminism" – the fount of the abortion culture abhorred by Mother Teresa. For the ladies, "morality" needs no understanding; it's merely their scepter – or sledgehammer. (We shall return to this aspect.) It is my belief that the feminist stranglehold is a main cause of the languishing national political dialectic, no less at risk than the formidable regime of physics. Due to feminists weighting down the reform-liberal side of the ship of state, it now lists dangerously to the demagogic left.

One example is a certain female politician's advice not to capitulate, compromise, or abandon "principle" or "conservative values" but to "put a better face on our ideas and go after the gender gap." Be more compassionate without moderating the message, she advises. The problem is she does not understand the message, never having given much thought to ordered freedoms. "It's not enough to be right (right is good enough for brain surgeons)," she says. "In politics you must also be popular." But what value is a "principle" that is not "right"?[24] For her, what matters is appearance, not substance – power, not principle – increasingly familiar themes since 1920. This lady mocks conservative Republicanism as a "diatribe," much like Al Gore's dismissal of constitutionalism as an "ideology." With such women in "politics," resorting to passion and flippancy instead of fact and reason, we no longer refine and enlarge the public views.

It is time to return to a rigorous dialectic. An example, by analogy, was provided in a PBS offering on "The Last Theorem," in which a mathematician devoted several years to discovering "Fermat's Proof," i.e., proof of the equation $X^n+Y^n \neq Z^n$. He struggled through a series of arguments, conjectures and theories based on logic and mathematical concepts, one by one, until he persevered to the logical result. It was of peripheral value and specialized importance, yet it was a path previously unexplored. *Objective inquiry and correction led to truth.*

* * *

Thomas G. West has written a worthwhile treatise in defense of the American founders[25] but, while rejecting historicism, indulges to some extent in historicism himself by endorsing egalitarianism. We shall return to West's book in Chapter I but, for now, we should question his apologetic approach to the roles of men and women: "I regret that I must recite the data – in such a cumbersome way." And then, "much of today's research either proves the obvious in some laborious manner or... distorts the facts...."[26] In fact, however, feminist influence *cries out for scholarly, vigorous rebuttal* to allow our return to a civil society. If it is so obvious, Professor West should not shy away.

It is not that he doesn't offer the right approach. He reminds us that "the great task of statesmanship is to weave moderation and manliness together,"[27] quoting James Madison's admonition on "the vigilant and manly spirit which actuates the people of America" without which "the people will be prepared to tolerate anything but liberty,"[28] He tells of George Washington's calling upon his soldiers "for a vigorous and manly exertion"[29] and that Gouverneur Morris found the 1790s French not masculine enough to muster the kind of vigilant self-assertion necessary to establish and sustain a free government.[30] But then he tempers his remarks with the curious modern fear of being labeled "racist", "bigoted" or unnoble, as he labors to fit "equality" into all things civilized.

If we are to "recover the truth about the founding (as well as about our civilization), to discern its strengths, to acknowledge its defects, and to pass that knowledge along to future generations," we should not shy from "laborious" defense of the "obvious."

For instance, a wise balance between "individual rights" and the order of being deserves more thought from politicians. Edward Shils offers a compelling alternative in his essays on civility:

> Civility is a belief which affirms the possibility of the common good; it is a belief in the community of contending parties within a morally valid unit of society.... Civility is a virtue expressed in action on behalf of the whole society, on behalf of the good of all the members of society to which public liberties and representative institutions are integral.[31]

While Professor West's teaching seems unconsciously to reflect his exposure to liberalizing tendencies since the forties, Professor Shils doesn't hesitate to disapprove of them:

> In a variety of ways, many of the tendencies which have become prominent since 1945 are injurious to civility. The main tendencies of belief and action about society of this period in Western countries are collectivist liberalism, emancipationism, anti-patriotism, egalitarianism, populism, scientism and ecclesiastical abdication. Taken together they form a complex which I call progressivism…. All of these beliefs are in various ways very critical of and hostile to authority. [32]

Those familiar with the teachings of feminism will recognize the disparity between "civility" and the radical claims of the followers of Betty Friedan, Andrea Dworkin and Germaine Greer. Although Dr. West sees the disparity, he doesn't go far enough to correct it. This book will add its voice to those who wish to do so.

I

Is There a Right Order of the Human Sexes?

And the Lord God said, It is not good that the man should be alone; I will make him a help meet for him. ... but for Adam there was not found an help meet for him. ... And the Lord God ... made he a woman, and brought her unto the man. ... male and female created he them.
Genesis 1,2, Authorized King James Version, 1:27; 2:18,22.

Thou shalt govern thyselves under God, through the deliberate sense of the community, of the generality of the men amongst thee; thou shalt respect certain procedures necessary for that purpose;... thou shalt try, above all, to be a virtuous people, made up of virtuous individuals, because only a virtuous people can do justice, remain untyrannical, as it governs itself through deliberation about the general good.
Willmore Kendall and George W. Carey[1]

While the mystery of sexual right order can be daunting, the clues are everywhere. Our childhood, our parents and siblings; our school days and lessons; our adolescence and adulthood – life's experience; our families, our work, loves, and passions; literature, daily news, science, chemistry, biology, physiology; traditions and customs: culture. Despite recent latitudinarianism, the Bible offers probably the most sensible teaching on the subject. (We shall cover this in Chapter V.) With all the trendy excursions over the centuries, underlying human nature remains the same. A wealth of evidence awaits the diligent detective.

"To me it appears indisputable," wrote Albert Jay Nock, "that out of all peoples, nations and languages, male writers of every sort and size have committed themselves to more damneder fiddle-faddle on the subject of women than on any other subject under the sun."[2] Despite such whimsy, Mr. Nock would certainly acknowledge that by his own man-of-letters participation, albeit stylishly skeptical, he joins an esteemed literature involving the Bible, Plato and Aristotle, kings and princes, elders like John Knox, statesmen, poets, and in modern times Orestes Brownson, Alexis de Tocqueville, James Fitzjames Stephen, Henry Adams, Richard M. Weaver, and others. Since Sappho, distaff offerings also have abounded, too often with a rebellious feminist twist, though sometimes worthwhile as with Jane Austen, George Eliot, and more recently Midge Decter, Florence King, Phyllis Schlafly and a few others.

After discounting the major omission by Nock to include *both* human sexes in the discussion, the two most surprising aspects of the "fiddle-faddle" are that there hasn't been more of it and that recent manifestations ignore biblical lessons as well as the "general good."

It is all probably what God intended when he created man and woman in such different molds; even for the honest atheist, the irony blares its continuous challenge. As Morris Dickstein discussed Van Wyck Brooks' finding of a "starved and abstract quality" in Emerson,

> Brooks may also have been influenced by John Jay Chapman's brilliant account of the "anaemic incompleteness of Emerson's character," with its astonishing peroration: If an inhabitant of

another planet should visit the earth, he would receive, on the whole, a truer notion of human life by attending the Italian opera than he would by reading Emerson's volumes. He would learn from the Italian opera that there were two sexes; and this, after all, is probably the fact with which the education of such a stranger ought to begin.[3]

Though evolutionists see only randomness, the human sexes offer a definite dichotomy. How should we maintain its best balance, its intrinsic design?

Steven Goldberg cautions, "moral-political analyses must take into account the empirical realities that they hope to affect if they are to be relevant to anything other than unattainable utopias."[4] He makes the point that "the reader who remembers that all statements about males and females are *statistical* statements will avoid wasting time on criticisms that ignore this fact and render all discussion of males and females incoherent." Such evidence of the "is" certainly establishes a base, although Chapman's insight is not reducible solely to statistical evidence.

While science and statistics contribute greatly, so must morality and ethics, God and religion. (Nor can we ignore intuition, artistic insight, common sense, custom, the heart, etc.) As Wolfhart Pannenberg suggests, "For most of history, unity of religion was deemed essential to the unity of society and culture...."[5] Religion lies at the root of our social norms, giving life to statistics, as with the Ten Commandments, Saint Paul, or the Catechism. As Pannenberg reminds us, "Historical experience demonstrates that, for societies and individuals, the autonomy of reason cannot replace the authority of God." Which, of course, is why feminism inevitably fails – along with other reasons.

Of significance to the dialogue are the many others like Mr. Nock who avoid the appearance of taking sides while wavering from one side to the other, another result of discomfort with ultimate truths, or a supreme being. While, like many "progressives" of the Teddy Roosevelt-Woodrow Wilson era Nock welcomed the idea of women's "advances," he then wonders why they used their newfound liberty merely to act more like men. He believes that women can do just about everything as well as men but then he reverses course to declare that men are better teachers than women. Of course, he manages later to qualify his casual remarks as the spirit moves him and ultimately to take refuge in being merely "a superfluous man making aimless reminiscences." His are the thoughts of Adam after the fall, rendered even more superfluous by recent experience.

Hegel's remark, "women are the eternal irony of the community," reflects the inadequacy of offhand opinions on the subject. Steven Goldberg sees a "final irony":

> ...(T)he physiological factors that underly women's life-sustaining abilities – the qualities most vital to the survival of our species – preclude them from ever manifesting the psychological predisposition or the obsessive need of power, necessary for the attainment of significant amounts of political power.[6]

Professor Goldberg has contributed exhaustive research, mainly into the evidence of inevitable male dominance in societies throughout history. His final Chapter, "Male and Female," is compelling, and may well sum up the entire issue in his closing lines (echoing Alexis Carrel; see Notes, Chapter VIII):

> A true feminist movement that genuinely believes in the uniqueness of women yearns to discover rather than deny the biological factors within women which make them unique. – I believe the evidence indicates that women follow their own psychophysiological imperatives and that they would not choose to compete for goals that men devote their lives to attaining. Women have more important things to do. Men are aware of this and that is why in this and every other society they look to women for gentleness, kindness, and love, for refuge from a world of pain and force, for safety from their own excesses. In every society a

basic male motivation is the feeling that the women and children must be protected. But a woman cannot have it both ways: if she wishes to sacrifice all this, what she will get in return is the right to meet men on male terms. She will lose.[7]

Similar insights appear also in the writings of various theologians (see below). Unfortunately, thanks to feminism, too many women aspire to have it both ways. As for other authority, Professor Michael Levin's *Feminism and Freedom* is a scholarly study of feminism and its effects on society. Nicholas Davidson[8] and George Gilder[9] each have also offered valuable research and exegesis on the subject of male and female roles, effectively rebutting feminism's claims while reminding us of sane and healthy norms. For scientific, sociological, anthropological, or technical evidence, one may refer to these writers.

* * *

We meet a recurring paradox: A respected women's group spokeswoman acknowledged my criticism of sexual politics as "informative" and added innocently that her "colleagues are all very committed to equal *opportunity* not equal *proportions*" which is a bit faint with damned praise. In reality, "equality of opportunity" for biological sexes is no more ordainable by God, the Constitution, the Magna Carta, the Bill of Rights, or any all-powerful law of nature than the concept of "equality" itself. The differences between men and women are so profound (though sometimes infinitesimal) that talk of "equality" is as practical as Icarus' flying to the Sun to demonstrate "equal feathered opportunity." While most bodies in the cosmos enjoy a tentative *equilibrium*, they are hardly "equal." One cannot casually rearrange the cosmos without regard for the interacting tensions, like tampering with a house of cards.

The fact seems to be, as Roger Kimball and others remind us, that the current wave of feminism was born in the same years that brought a destructive cultural revolution – the 1960s. He rejects the possibility that the changes amounted to any sort of "genuine political revolution" because of the period's essential "hyperactive sterility" and "infantilization" rather than creative innovation. In fact, the whole subject is colored by this one aspect, namely, that "women's liberation" and "advances for women," even if presently the fashion, have neither been beneficial to society nor arisen from any natural, organic shift in values or achievement as much as by mob action and a *misguided act of Congress*. In view of diminished male leadership and declining social institutions involving both men and women, the idea of "advances for women" is pure pretense. Political leaders have been strangely close-minded on such questions.

Kimball's judgment holds as true for government-mandated "women's lib" as it does for the other 1960s manifestations he blames on a "combination of vacuousness, self-infatuation, and political grandstanding" amounting to a "wholesale attack on the very idea of standards."[10] Resort to female police captains, judges, lawyers, detectives, preachers, military masters of the sword, and the like, did not occur because women were better suited to these jobs or brought improvement but because men didn't know how to resist political pressures and stumbled into foolishly revisionist laws.

Wolfhart Pannenberg traces the decline in importance of religious belief to our shared values to Kant's belief that "God and immortality only play the role of reconciling the demands of the moral law with our natural desire for happiness, (which) looks an awful lot like eudaemonism – the theory that the highest moral goal is happiness – which was otherwise abhorrent to Kant."[11] Thus appears another aspect of feminism – its utter eudaemonism – elevating the "rights of women" above all else.

* * *

Francis Fukuyama reminds us of a credible sexual order when he compares us to the two industrialized Asian nations that have yet to succumb to feminism – Japan and Korea. There, increased crime, illegitimacy and divorce rates, and breakdown of the nuclear family did not occur. While he acknowledges that any number of factors could be adduced, the most important, in his view, "has to do with the role of women. Here, indeed, is an example of a social value with large effects both in economic life and in politics":

> To a much greater extent than in the West, women in Japan and Korea, not to mention in other, less-developed Asian societies, continue to be treated differently from men both in social custom and in law.... When Asian spokesmen (at least the male ones) say they do not like Western values, what they often mean is that they do not like Western sexual roles; the individualism that is problematic for them includes not only freewheeling political protest but freewheeling protest within the family. And no wonder: family structure has implications for education, for economic performance, for public safety, and for government investment in such things as crime prevention and health care. Through the selective application of "Asian values," Asian societies have so far preserved the coherence of the nuclear family and have spared themselves the social disruption that has attended economic change in the West.[12]

No doubt many will resist the idea that the U.S. should emulate Japan or Korea in retrieving traditional roles for men and women so as to revive the nuclear family, fight crime, drugs, divorce, illegitimacy and in general bolster our values, but the option does beckon. Chet Gottschalk offers an endorsement of Francis Fukuyama's report in a letter to *Commentary*.[13] As a resident of Sagamihara City, Japan, he states that women are not found in the halls of power in politics or business, where men must labor. "Japanese women... are supreme in other, more important areas.... What we find in Japanese society, therefore, is a clear delineation of the roles of men and women, with the latter's role often superior to that of the former. This gives Japanese women a high stake in preserving and maintaining the status quo and will, I believe, continue to spare the country what Mr. Fukuyama calls 'the social disruption that has attended economic change in the West.'" It bears considering that in adhering to their customs for the sexes, Japan and Korea have maintained a more enduring order than our *Novus Ordo Seclorum*. (I do not include the Republic of China in this comparison.)

*   *   *

Let us consider three more guideposts before visiting other fronts. Hillel Halkin offers a telling account of the feminization of Jewish Studies (a new canon born in the same revolution as feminist, or women's, studies) in the same issue of *Commentary* as Professor Fukuyama's essay and with a similar theme – another community's "suffering from a loss of boundaries and a deep confusion about its identity; a decline of the family as its core unit; a low birth rate and a high rate of exogamous marriage; falling participation of men as compared with women...." Mr. Halkin tells of (1) scholars teaching the usual feminist rubric of "misogyny" and (2) a female complaining of "exclusion" from the world of male pursuits. He suggests, however, that her husband might not have been any better off. Such women overlook "the power often wielded by women in the home, refusing to grant the slightest dignity or satisfaction to traditional female lives while wildly glamorizing the lives of working men." He closes as follows:

> No one can predict the outcome of the sexual revolution that America is now in the throes of, and that dwarfs any of its predecessors in its concentrated assault on fundamentals of male and female behavior that have been taken for granted by nearly all human beings until now. No one can say whether men or women are built to withstand this assault, or what the results may be if they are not. And no one knows what a world lacking firm notions of masculinity and femininity or the distinctions

between them, would be like. But it is chilling for custodians of the history of a people who taught mankind that it was created, male and female, in God's image to join the serpent of delusory omnipotence in whispering in our ear that we can become like gods, and that we can with impunity remake our pasts and ourselves, sexually and in every other way, as we please.[14]

While this is quite a moving statement, I believe his fears can ultimately be avoided.

*   *   *

Peter Augustne Lawler offers help in a review of Thomas G. West's *Vindicating the Founders*, mentioned above. Lawler rightly commends West for "boldly aim(ing) to transform American education by defending the American founders from the charges of ignorance and negligence" and resisting the current effort to "reduce the study of history, politics, and even literature to the issues of race, class and gender," in which, according to present calumnies, our forefathers are maligned as unprincipled bigots. Lawler believes that West convincingly rebuts such aspersions and shows that the founders were primarily committed to the common good… "to create wealth and improve the condition of all."[15] They sincerely believed, with much reason, that women would be better protected by strict laws on divorce, familial responsibility, mutual dependency, distinct roles and moral codes for the sexes in keeping with their natures and long-accepted customs adapted thereto. Whether they were right or wrong from our 2000s perspective is immaterial if such ideas were generally held at the time, which seems the case. And they worked! Thus it is probable that their pattern would serve us well in our own time. Restrictions on women (as well as men) were considered natural in view of the greater public and private responsibility of males, which in turn set appropriate limits.

While Professor West doesn't go deeply into why women did not vote, he makes a good start. In those pre-industrial times, the founders took for granted that "marriage and children create a community of love and interest that protects women far more effectively than the right to vote." They were "virtually represented" in ways that the Americans who considered themselves taxed by the British "without representation" were not. The idea of the "general good" permeated the founders' thought. It was commonly understood in the past that the vote should not be considered merely as a "right" as much as a duty – a responsibility requiring a broader, less subjective viewpoint than most women are aware of. (We shall touch on this again.)

Recent evidence of the effect of the "gender gap" on national voting patterns would probably have shocked the founders. Certainly one aspect of this gap serves to highlight the significance of the family unit by revealing that married women vote more conservatively than single women, which suggests a more subjective, personal, or benignly self-centered motivation in the fair sex than in men, which one suspects the founders understood better than men do now. It is a peculiarity of our times, despite clear-headed reports on the "gender gap" and historical analyses like Thomas West's, that scholars have yet to study the effects on the nation of the Nineteenth Amendment to the U.S. Constitution.

Unfortunately, as mentioned above, Professor West's dedication to the equality principle inevitably tends to confuse his hermeneutics. It is fruitless to try squeezing the square peg of the "founding principles" into the round hole of the "modern movement of equal political rights for women." (That Dr. West's book doesn't mention Goldberg, Levin, et al, vis-à-vis patriarchy leads to unavoidable gaps.) Cloaking ones rhetoric in the drapery of "genuine equality," much like political-campaign talk, never washes in serious discussion. How could it? As West quotes the earthy but purely impulsive Camille Paglia, "We have what they want. I think woman is the dominant sex. Men have to do all sorts of stuff to prove that they are worthy of a woman's attention."¹⁶ (Western literature is brimming with examples that should dispel the chimera of "sex equality," as does West's own brief coverage, but utopias die hard.)

As a result, West gets tangled in such webs as, "This ideological equality (the social scientists' urge to prove the sexes similar in every respect), which denies and tries to destroy natural differences, is totally opposed to the natural equality of the Declaration of Independence, which recognizes and protects the equal rights, and therefore the natural differences, of all. The purpose of a government based on equal rights, as Madison said in Federalist No. 10, is 'the protection of… the different and unequal faculties' or abilities of each citizen. This diversity, Madison believed, is 'sown in the nature of man.' A free society will therefore be built on a division of labor, not only among individuals of different talents, but also between the sexes, insofar as each sex has its typical talents and inclinations." West simply reads into the Declaration a meaning – a "protection" for "natural equality" – that is not there. (For one thing, Madison was not writing of women in the sense that we do today – "sex equality" was far from his mind.)

In fact, I find no reference in Federalist No. 10 to Madison's use of the term, "a government based on equal rights." Federalist No. 10 is his famous discussion of the advantage of an extended republic in moderating disparate factions, obviously a far cry from equality. Of some pertinence here, he comments, by reason of the desired larger number of representatives in an extended republic, "the suffrages of the people being more free, will be more likely to centre on men who possess the most attractive merit, and the most diffusive and established characters." Not only does such reasoning go against any idea of "equality," but it also defuses the idea of subjecting one's wife or daughters to the rigors of the electoral process. As West quotes founder Benjamin Rush, sounding remarkably like

Margaret Mead, "To be mistress of a family is one of the great ends of woman's being."[17] Alas, we have strayed from that course.

One can learn much about the idea of "sex equality" from the teachings of the Catholic Church, generally that men and women are "equal before God" (which will be discussed below) or Tocqueville's somewhat similar version that "Americans... think of men and women as beings of equal worth, though their fates are different."[18] Despite drawing us into this endless cave without much illumination, Professor West does offer an excellent summary of how the family benefits women and children, the value of incentives for men to behave responsibly, the degradation of women caused by a decline in previous customs and beliefs, the fact that modern Americans "no longer understand that the good things in life require effort, love, and postponement of immediate gratification," and that feminist charges of societal abuse or disrespect for women are almost entirely false.

But returning to Professor Lawler's review of West's book, Lawler makes a salient point in remarking that

> West makes a convincing connection between traditional (I wish he had said religious) morality and natural rights. So he shows that legal understandings of rights that erode the family are empirically untenable, as are those that understand the individual as fundamentally an asocial, irresponsible being. But in emphasizing the interdependence of traditional morality and the effective exercise of rights, West obscures the fact that it is still the doctrine of rights that has been largely responsible for dissolving that morality. He does admit that the founders' severe morality was oppressive for extraordinary women who could not find fulfillment within the family. It was much harder for women than for men to flourish as unconventional individuals. Women's rights were surely violated, and so it is more true to say that there is a tension between rights and traditional, familial morality. The original American regime embodied that invigorating tension through federalism, which left state law free from national, rights-oriented supervision. The Court, through

the Fourteenth Amendment, seeks to eradicate that tension, at the cost of both the exercise of rights and moral responsibility. West's instructive and intelligent book would have been even more illuminating had he acknowledged that the doctrine of natural rights has its human limits.

Indeed, this is a helpful synopsis for our project of ordering the human sexes for the general good, mainly because it suggests that *there is a right order for the common good*. Professor Lawler sees clearly that there is a tension and that it needs dialectic to sustain it for healthy ends. Perhaps we can shed light on the limits he seeks.

Despite his call for religion, Lawler's judgment that men and women are merely equal contestants in life's arena, both seeking to "flourish" as either conventional or "unconventional individuals" leaves much to be desired. That the founders' practices should now be considered as "tough" and "discriminatory" despite their acceptance by both men and women as appropriate for their more rigorous lives will not sustain scholarly study. His agreeing that women were better protected when marriage was a strong, respected institution does not square with his pronouncement that "women's rights were surely violated," especially when he recognizes "rights" as a nebulous recent concept that has limits. Actually, the crucial factor most often ignored in such discussions is the benumbing sex "non-discrimination" law of the mindless 60s, which essentially squelches West's, Lawler's, and my ideas on men and women.

* * *

Another perspective on our right order is that of the Reverend William Oddie, a Fellow of St. Cross College at the University of Oxford. An Anglican, he is a regular speaker on British television and radio, and a press commentator. In his book, *What Will Happen to God?* (1984), he suggests that those who try to impose our attitudes on customs of another age may be giving us the short end of the stick. He cites the sinking of the Titanic as an example of how highly women were valued in earlier times, dispelling in dramatic fashion feminist claims to the contrary. "To Charles H. Lightroller, one of the sailors put in charge of the lifeboats full of women and children, their priority over the men in such a situation seemed, quite simply, 'the law of nature.'... Even more, we may ask whether, some seventy years later, such distinctions of sex would still be asserted: and if they would not, whether such a development towards an androgynous society genuinely represents an advance for human civilization, or a regression into barbarism." We shall return to Dr. Oddie for more thought on the order of the sexes.

As one learns from Gilder's book and others, as well as Thomas West's, women are "fulfilled" in far different ways than men, usually involving a family or friends, caring and sustaining. There have long been the Clara Bartons, Helen Kellers and Florence Nightingales and there is ample literature on the experiences of women in medieval and other times serving not as paradigms as much as examples of a lack of male leaders. (Some are discussed below.) "Talented" women are not prevented by marriage from using their talents. Broad claims for "unfulfilled talented women" wrongly imply that the male world should be their milieu. But Gilder says it best: "Nothing that has been written in the annals of feminism gives the slightest indication that this is the role that women want or are prepared to perform. The feminists demand liberation. The male role means bondage to the demands of the workplace and the needs of the family.... The men's role that feminists seek is not the real role of men but the male role of the Marxist dream in which 'society' does the work."

> "Women's liberation" entails a profound dislocation. Women, uniquely in charge of the central activities of human life, are exalting instead the peripheral values – values that have meaning only in relation to the role they would disparage or abandon.

In addition, sexual liberals ask society to give up most of the devices and conventions by which it is ensured that women perform their indispensable work and by which men have been induced to support it. As a result, in many of the world's welfare states that have accepted the feminist vision, the two sexes are no longer making the necessary sacrifices to sustain society.[19]

In Captain Frederick Marryat's early-19th-century stories, fathers lecturing on fads like "equality and the rights of man" inspired comical fancies in their children. In our own time, the comedy of "sex equality and the rights of woman" powered by government-mandated employment in the courts, the military, industry, and the corridors of power presumably of "extraordinary women finding fulfillment" is yet unnoticed by most. Men are too busy defending themselves against charges of "chauvinism" and "sexism" to see the humor. Inevitably, a right order must include a focus, in Wade C. Mackey's words, on "adhering biological and social fathers to the mother-child dyad."[20] We shall take a closer look at what religion tells us in later chapters. For now, let us consider an artistic approach.

II

Art and Culture

And art itself may be defined as a single-minded attempt to render the highest kind of justice to the visible universe, by bringing to light the truth, manifold and one, underlying its every aspect. It is an attempt to find in its forms, in its colors, in its light, in its shadows, in the aspects of matter and in the facts of life, what of each is fundamental, what is enduring and essential – their one illuminating and convincing quality – the very truth of their existence. The artist then, like the thinker or the scientist, seeks the truth and makes his appeal.

Preface, The Nigger of the Narcissus

And if our youth are to do their work in life, must they not make these graces and harmonies their perpetual aim? – And surely the art of the painter and every other constructive art are full of them, – weaving, embroidery, architecture, and every kind of manufacture; also nature, animal and vegetable, – in all of them there is grace or the absence of grace. And ugliness and discord and inharmonious motion are nearly allied to ill words and ill nature, as grace and harmony are the twin sisters of goodness and virtue and bear their likeness.

Plato's *Republic*, III, p. 104

Studying the human sexes involves as much art as it does science and religion, yet in the area of men and women, the prevailing artistic sense is about as perceptive as the Goths' or Huns' in the Roman Forum. By this I do not mean art's perversion in some quarters since the 60s (although this did accompany the reemergence of emancipated women) but the classic artistic sense as a lens for our own study. It pervades our subject and will appear throughout this book, generally as limned by Conrad and Plato in the above epigraphs.

Father Chad Ripperger reminds us with regards to the Latin Mass, "(T)he argument from aesthetics is actually one of the most cogent of the arguments in favor of the old rite."[1] He discusses how aesthetics relate to culture through "the attributes of beauty, viz. clarity, symmetry and completion or perfection."

> Since these attributes of beauty constitute whether the *thing* is beautiful or not, then something is objectively beautiful or it is not, if it possesses the attributes or not. The aesthetic sense, which we develop regarding those things that are beautiful, must therefore be in conformity with the beauty of the things as they are, since the aesthetic sense must be based on truth.
>
> Truth is defined as the conformity of intellect and thing. This means that ones ideas are true when they are in conformity with the way things are in reality.

It is basic to the order of being that the two sexes conform to these attributes. Adapting a syllogism from Father Ripperger, if a man thinks that a man can substitute for a woman, he does not have truth in his mind since his mind does not conform to reality. And vice versa, i.e., substituting a woman for a man. For instance, how ignore Edmund Burke's words on his future wife, "'tis all the sweetness of temper, benevolence, innocence and sensibility which a face can express, that forms her beauty."[2] Or G.K. Chesterton's for his wife-to-be, Frances Blogg,

> God made you very carefully,
> He set a star apart for it,
> He stained it green and gold with fields

And aureoled it with sunshine;
He peopled it with kings, peoples, republics,
And so made you, very carefully.
All nature is God's book, filled with his rough
sketches for you.³

For Chesterton, Frances was

> ….a harmony in green and brown. There is some gold somewhere in it, but cannot be located upon examination. Probably the gold crown. Harp not yet arrived. Physically there is not quite enough of her to carry all that temperament: she looks slight, fiery and wasted, with a face which would be a Burne-Jones if it were not brave; it has the asceticism of melancholy. Devouring appetite for sensations; very fond of the Bible; very fond of dancing. When she is enjoying herself thoroughly, one has a sense that it would be well for her to go to sleep for a hundred years. It would be jolly fun for some prince too.⁴

The point is not so much that these are the words of a starstruck lover as that there will always be star-struck lovers – young men passionately in love with young women – a central parameter of human existence. While trying to put "an orderly frame around disorderly humanity"⁵ man must deal with this truth in pursuance of his life's art. But, since men and women are not uniformly cut out for each other, it's not always a bed of roses, which is why the subject deserves more thought.

*　*　*

Thomas Jefferson knew well that "Women are formed by nature for attentions, not for hard labor. A woman never forgets one of the numerous train of little offices which belong to her. A man forgets often."⁶ Mr. Jefferson commented on customs in France in noting that

> The women here, as in Germany, do all sorts of work. While one considers them as useful and rational companions, one cannot forget that they are also objects of our pleasures; nor can they ever forget it. While employed in dirt or drudgery, some tag of a ribbon, some ring, or bit of bracelet, earbob or necklace, or

something of that kind, will show that the desire of pleasing is never suspended from them. It is an honorable circumstance for man that the first moment he is at ease, he allots the internal employments to his female partner, and takes the external on himself. And this circumstance, or its reverse, is a pretty good indication that a people are, or are not at their ease.

* * *

The challenge is to maintain a felicitous balance of sex roles so that perversions are rare. One sees in England and America today the extreme perversion of "sex integration" in the military, leading petite young females with girlish voices to exercise command over large males capable of flooring them in an eye-blink. Male officers used to be taught to lead by example never by using their rank; now female officers are told, "use your rank." In no way does this conform to art, except perhaps in parody.

* * *

Jean Jacques Rousseau and Mr. Jefferson apparently agreed at least on the subject of women, the former believing that "To please, to be useful to us, to make us love and esteem them, to educate us when young, and take care of us when grown up, to advise us, to console us, to render our lives easy and agreeable – these are the duties of women at all times."[7] It is known that both Jefferson and Rousseau liked the ladies, so such views are not surprising. They were true to their natures and spoke their minds, a refreshing contrast to the 2000s public male trained in "equality" and "opportunity," afraid that anything else might lose female votes, contributions, subscriptions or caresses. Equality has vanquished quality.

* * *

Great artists offer pointers. When Robert Henri gave us *The Art Spirit*, he chose a fragmentary format similar to the present book: "No effort has been made toward the form of a regular book. In fact the opinions are presented more as paintings are hung on the wall, to be looked at at will and taken as rough sketches for what they are worth. If they have a suggestive value and stimulate to independent thought they will attain the object of their presentation. There are many repeats throughout the work, many times the same subject is taken up and viewed from a different angle or seen in relation to other matters.... If they irritate to activity in a quite different direction it will be just as well. The subject is beauty – or happiness, and man's approach to it is various."[8]

Henri starts out, "Art when really understood is the province of every human being. It is simply a question of doing things, anything, well. It is not an outside, extra thing. – he opens ways for a better understanding – he can work in any medium – where there is the art spirit there will be precious works to fill museums. Better still, there will be the happiness that is in the making. Art tends toward balance, order, judgment of relative values, the laws of growth, the economy of living – very good things for anyone to be interested in."[9]

> Why do we love the sea? It is because it has some potent power to make us think things we like to think. – The great artist has not reproduced nature, but has expressed by his extract the most choice sensation it has made upon him.[10]

"Painting is the expression of ideas in their permanent form. It is the giving of evidence. It is the study of our lives, our environment." This is not to say that art should be the only pillar of our culture but that it can be a reliable guide. While Henri was not a philosopher, his ideas merge philosophy, art and poetry and help illuminate our grasp of reality. "It is harder to see than to express," he wrote of artists[11], but a philosopher finds both hard. And Henri knew the difference between men and women: "Berthe Morisot learned a great deal from Manet, but she expressed her own, a woman's vision."[12]

> There are men who admire women's dress. They do not know what the material of the dress is.... He paints what and as he

sees. He has found it beautiful and it is beauty he has sought to render. The garments of a woman may be fine – rare – expensive – a certain kind, but to the artist the dress may be only part of the woman.[13]

Henri made no such observation about a man's suit, since a woman is a separate artistic category, as she is for all artists – and people, except for Orwellian "non-discrimination" politicians. As Lord Byron saw her,

> She walks in beauty, like the night
> Of cloudless climes and starry skies;
> And all that's best of dark and bright
> Meet in her aspect and her eyes:
> Thus mellow'd to that tender light
> Which heaven to gaudy days denies. [14]

"The sense that everything is poetical is a thing solid and absolute; it is not a mere matter of phraseology or persuasion. It is not merely true, it is ascertainable."[15]

> Your eyes have set man's heart ablaze"
> And you have had your will of him.
> Are you not weary of ardent ways? ...
> And still you hold our longing gaze
> With languorous look and lavish limb!
> Are you not weary of ardent ways?
> Tell no more of enchanted days.[16]

While in this poem James Joyce does not choose to address it directly, George Gilder's perception is apparent (as well as Henry Adams' and many others', not to overlook pagan cultures), that a woman's sexuality is at the core of human society. Classical artists were not constrained to paint and sculpt otherwise and poets have drawn regularly from this fount. I suggest that we can use art and poetry as a *supplement* to religion, since ideas of "total perfection," "tact," "higher truths and seriousness" are not incompatible with a higher authority and in fact quite subservient to it.

Art, Science and Religion have many guises in which thoughtful men seek an optimum balance. Feminists ignore the power of poetry, despite Shelley's thought that "Poets are the unacknowledged legislators of the world."[17] Matthew Arnold enlarges on this:

> Arnold's point in his essay ("The Study of Poetry") is that, due to the breakdown of dogma and the loss of evidence for the supernatural which occurred through the rise of modern science and the Darwinian theory and explication of evolution, Shelley's role of the poet will more and more come to be acknowledged. Poetry will now provide the consolation and inspiration, the sense of purpose and guarantee of values that religion had previously embodied. Arnold states: "More and more mankind will discover that we have to return to poetry to interpret life for us, to console us, to sustain us. Without poetry, our science will appear incomplete; and most of what now passes with us for religion and philosophy will be replaced by poetry."[18]

Professor John S. Reist Jr. relies on several noted sources, such as Samuel T. Coleridge, Rudolph Bultmann, Cleanth Brooks, Shakespeare, Chaucer, T.S. Eliot, and Donald Howard, in urging:

> That poetry has a primary value and function in society is obvious; by its imaginative and mimetic ordering of the spray of contingency called experience, it provides a seizure of life, a representation of life, which at its best provokes reflection about the basic issues and questions of humanity.[19]

"What is needed for literary study is a hundred percent of formalism and a hundred percent of critical intuition – There are many ways to transcend formalism, but the worst is not to study form."[20]

Leo Tolstoy discussed the definitions of art offered by a number of authorities and reached his own conclusions. He too believed in the great value of art for mankind, as ruled by religion. He opposed the view of "art for art's sake," no less than Joseph Conrad and Maritain, and believed that art played a definite role in civilizing humanity. Whether this amounts to a "political" art need not divert us from its important hermeneutical function:

> Art is not a pleasure, a solace, or an amusement; art is a great matter. Art is an organ of human life, transmitting man's reasonable perception into feeling. In our age the common religious perception of men is the consciousness of the brotherhood of man – we know that the well-being of man lies in union with his fellow men. True science should indicate the various methods of applying this consciousness to life. Art should transform this perception into feeling. The task of art is enormous. Through the influence of real art, aided by science guided by religion, that peaceful cooperation of man which is now obtained by external means – by our law courts, police, charitable institutions, factory inspection, etc. – should be obtained by man's free and joyous activity. Art should cause violence to be set aside.[21]

> The estimation of the value of art (i.e., of the feelings it transmits) depends on man's perception of the meaning of life. And what is good and what is evil is defined by what are termed religions.[22]

"The poets stand in a dialectic relationship to history," wrote Hans Urs von Balthasar in his treatise on Reinhold Schneider[23]. "… they must be judges. 'For the poet is closest to the spirit that composes the poem of history,… The idea becomes the conscience of the world.…" Von Balthasar goes on to discuss "the image" of the poet:

> In the tragic world, the image remains the only meaning…. The image is not a concept abstracted from reality, for it is not possible to deduce anything eternal from what is contradictory and declining; nor is it without any relationship to reality (in the sense of the symbolism of "art for art's sake"), since it comes from the power of the imagination, the fundamental power of the soul.…"[24] The entire being of the world has the quality of an image, a reflection of the Divine Being.[25]

One need not belabor here the many ingredients of art, such as form, texture, shape, color, mood, spirit, design or composition, sound, even smell. Critics like Tolstoy make constant use of such essentials in their commentary on truth, beauty and reality, even as they expound on the art of living as related to science:

But science, true science – such science as would really deserve the respect which is now claimed by the followers of one (the least important) part of science – it is not all such as this: real science lies in knowing what we should and what we should not believe, in knowing how the associated life of man should and should not be constituted; how to treat sexual relations, how to educate children – and much more that is important for the life of man.[26]

The following comment by Claes G. Ryn is along the same line:

The great art of the past sometimes reacted against degradations and indignities in the present, and it conveyed man's true humanity in some way, but, unlike so much romantic art, it was not a denial of historical reality. It affirmed life's higher potential in often acute awareness of the limits of our existence.[27]

In all of this, it should be noted that art is neither a "masculine" nor a "feminine" construct but a *human* "great matter." In *The Republic*, it was apparently agreed between Socrates, Adeimantus, and Glaucon that family life and "the right or wrong management of such matters (as the community of women and children) will have a great and paramount influence on the State for good or for evil."[28] Some have argued that in Plato's paradoxical Book V, Socrates even went to the extreme of arguing for androgyny and sexual egalitarianism. Because of such ideas, Plato has been characterized by Jeffrey Hart as "the first socialist," whose "city governed solely by intellect would have a totalitarian potential."[29] He "cared nothing for freedom," writes Llewellyn H. Rockwell, Jr., quoting Ludwig von Mises, "It is no accident that the proposal to treat men and women as radically equal, to regulate sexual intercourse by the State, to put infants into public nursing homes at birth and to ensure that children and parents remain quite unknown to each other should have originated with Plato."[30]

At the same time, one cannot ignore the possibility of an intended irony in the dream-like aspects of those passages from *The*

Republic, which in so many ways are at odds with much else in Socrates's dissertations on justice and reality, harmony and discord. From all reports, his wife Xanthippe's proverbial nagging certainly didn't lend support to utopian dreams of men and women living in communal harmony. Elsewhere, Socrates seems to believe that the arts contributed much of value to the republic, whether in the way of governing, medicine, music, or "the essential forms, in all their combinations."[31] Although he stumbles in remarking, "the good of each art is especially confined to the art," he also values the effect of graces and harmonies on the work of life, as becomes evident in the following exchanges with Glaucon:

> And if our youth are to do their work in life, must they not make these graces and harmonies their perpetual aim?
>
> They must....
>
> Let our artists rather be those who are gifted to discern the true nature of the beautiful and graceful; then will our youth dwell in a land of health, amid fair sights and sounds, and receive the good in everything; and beauty, the effluence of good works, shall flow into the eye and ear, like a health-giving breeze from a purer region, and insensibly draw the soul from earliest years into likeness and sympathy with the beauty of reason.
>
> There can be no nobler training than that, he replied.[32]

Surely we may apply such parameters as "grace and absence of grace" or "ugliness and discord and inharmonious motion" to the contrast of male or female voices in public arenas or over the airways, as well as to the distinct physiologies? Joseph Conrad would agree with Socrates that art helps us "discern the true nature of the beautiful and graceful," as seems evident in the following excerpt from his preface to *The Nigger of the Narcissus*:

> A work that aspires, however humbly, to the condition of art should carry its justification in every line. And art itself may be defined as a single-minded attempt to render the highest kind of justice to the visible universe, by bringing to light the truth, manifold and one, underlying its every aspect. It is an attempt to find in

its forms, in its colors, in its light, in its shadows, in the aspects of matter and in the facts of life, what of each is fundamental, what is enduring and essential – their one illuminating and convincing quality – the very truth of their existence. The artist, then, like the thinker or the scientist, seeks the truth and makes his appeal....

* * *

As if to demonstrate the application of art to government and "civil rights," Edmund Burke penned the following letter with regards to *habeas corpus*, prudence and civil liberty, demolishing modern pretenses of human "equality":

> Civil freedom.... is a blessing and a benefit, not an abstract speculation.... Far from any resemblance to those propositions in geometry and metaphysics which admit no medium, but must be true or false in all their latitude, social and civil freedom, like all other things in common life, are variously mixed and modified, enjoyed in different degrees, shaped into an infinite diversity of forms, according to the temper and circumstance of every community.... Liberty, too, must be limited in order to be possessed. The degree of restraint it is impossible in any case to settle precisely. But it ought to be the constant aim of every wise public counsel to find out by cautious experiments, and rational, cool endeavors, with how little, not how much, of this restraint the community can subsist; for liberty is a good to be improved, and not an evil to be lessened.[33]

It is their shame that 1964 U.S. legislators ignored such wisdom. The artistic perspective is apparent every day in "arts" sections of most publications, peddling colorful, descriptive adjectives for those familiar with the genre. "Depraved, moronic, grotesque," writes Roger Kimball in reference to "the current art scene," which includes the actual name of one show at the Gallery Stendhal in New York in early 1998.[34] "Trendy"; "philistine"; "tedious"; "futile"; "unpleasant"; "depressing"; "boring"; "nasty smell"; "sorry spectacle"; "feelings of pity and irritation"; "terribly sad"; "fatuousness"; "studied perversity"; "obsession with novelty"; "various clichés"; "shocking or repulsive"; "stylistic, moral, political" (radical leftist, I should add); "lacking any guiding aesthetic imperative"; "encroaching futility"; "faddishness"; "a shift away from beauty as the end of art"; all describe with remorseless gusto the predicament the avant-garde has brought on itself. Somewhat analogous to Berlinski's Darwinist physicists and "sex equality" androgynists, followers of the avant-garde lack discipline, as Mr. Kimball's peroration makes clear:

> The problem is that the avant-garde has become a casualty of its own success. Having won battle after battle, it gradually transformed a recalcitrant bourgeois culture into a willing collaborator in its raids on established taste. But in this victory were the seeds of its own irrelevance, for without credible resistance, its operational gestures degenerated into a kind of aesthetic buffoonery. In this sense, the institutionalization of the avant-garde spells the death or at least the senility of the avant-garde.

Such concerns as a "guiding aesthetic imperative" apply inevitably to "texture" and "harmony" of the male and female voices and figures, and their roles in public life. Each sex has a highest and best use neglected when we let fathers play mothers or vice versa, much like Jerry Rice playing tackle, or Monet painting a Mondrian.

* * *

Classical ballet, opera, long-ago musicals with their beautiful duets, or big bands blending male and female both artistically and passionately, realistically, naturally, and inspirationally, all show how our two sexes best function together. If the ballet dancer fails to support the ballerina's undulating body, complementing her lovely feminine grace with firm, strong resolve, he fails. Her femaleness makes the dance beautifully artistic with his male guidance. Neither role can be "over-valued." Great literature adds its patterns of passion, irony, turmoil, sacrifice and love. One can only play one's role on stage with the script at hand and the attention it deserves. Unfortunately, we have progressed from Shakespearean males playing female roles out of deference to the purity of womanhood, to women playing male roles out of ignorance of manhood. Thus, the artistry fails. The public drama does not *cause wonder*, the pageant *inspire*, or the music *sing*. Even political conventions are neutered to frills and placards without the old gutsy, masculine honesty.

The ballerina now supports and guides the male in enticing convolutions across the stage, laboring to control his heavier body as he labors to express erotic ecstasy, reinforced by her muscular care to his alluring grace and loveliness. Because it does not reflect life, it is not art but comic relief – bumbling, hilarious mischances like an Abbot-and-Costello ladder-and bucket routine, or an Oliver-and-Hardy farce. Or like the town's dogs all walking on their hinder legs, unable to sniff hydrants, deprived of their basic instincts, their skills, their mobility – their doggishness. Thus we toy with the human sexes. Thinking she as been "excluded" from his art, in wanting to play both the delicate female and the strong male the ballerina soon learns that *he has been judged all along on how well he complements her*.

It reflects a diminished cultural awareness when sports commentators look on the "crossroads of the sixties" as a time, not of upheaval in our universities or the advent of feminism, but "when Cuban baseball players began to join American ball clubs." With her shapely, feminine figure, a female ice dancer trying to play the more muscular male would shock the consciousness, yet female "reporters" grace men's locker rooms and sidelines and chirp of war on hourly news broadcasts. It's as convincing as an African lioness taking over the pride.

* * *

As Irving Babbitt urges in his *Democracy and Leadership* (1924),

> If the individualist ... is to have standards, he must rely on the critical spirit in direct ratio to the completeness of his break with the traditional unifications of life.... For it is obvious that standards cannot exist unless there is an element of oneness somewhere with which to measure the infinite otherwiseness of

> things.... The failure of criticism to attain to any center of judgment set above the shifting impressions of the individual and the flux of phenomenal nature is a defeat for civilization itself, if it be true, as I have tried to show, that civilization must ultimately depend on the maintenance of standards.[55]

Artistic perception would have helped preserve such standards. Like technology, androgynization suffers from dehumanization, rationalization, self-augmentation, aculturality, ahistoricism, and independence from settled norms. Drawing a parallel with John Paul Russo's metaphorical explanation of technology, despite women's supposed liberation, the "principle of least effort or efficient ordering" with its "standardization, minimalism, linearity, speed and segmentation" rules them with an iron hand.[56] Unlike technology, however, androgyny can be met with intelligent masculine resistance, acting as a counterforce and, if exerted distinctly and effectively, suffusing the feminist impulse. Adam should have done no less! As Saint Thomas Aquinas taught, referring to Aristotle "the Philosopher,"

> The usage of the multitude, which according to the Philosopher is to be followed in giving names to things, has commonly held that they are to be called wise who order things rightly and govern them well. Hence, among other things that men have conceived about the wise man, the Philosopher includes the notion that "it belongs to the wise man to order."... The arts that rule other arts are called architectonic, as being the ruling arts.... The name of the absolutely wise man, however, is reserved for him whose consideration is directed to the end of the universe, which is also the origin of the universe. That is why, according to the Philosopher, it belongs to the wise man to consider the highest causes.[57]

Left unchecked, feminist women oblivious to "the highest causes" will continue to indulge their own vision of mistaken "progress" in a state of "spiritual blindness." This makes for poor public leadership. As Babbitt puts it, "... material progress, so far from assuring moral progress, is, on the contrary, extremely difficult to combine with it. This progress has been won by an almost tyrannical concentration on the facts of the natural law. Man's capacity for concentration is limited, so that the price he has paid for material progress has been an increasing inattention to facts of an entirely different order – those, namely, of the human law. The resulting spiritual blindness has been an invitation to Nemesis."[38] (Here, he is referring to "natural law" as the law of physics, science, technology and so forth, and not Burkean-Christian natural law, which probably comes closer to his "human law.")

* * *

For now, however, immune to art and any law but their own fancy, adherents of feminism continue their misguided way. When confronted with the fact that men's and women's brains and driving skills differ, women retort, "male chauvinist pig" and continue on their way. As a lady recently demonstrated after passing her driver's test on the eighth try and was told of such differences, instead of inquiring further, she joked that the man reporting such disparities "should go back to his tree." Of course, men aren't the best drivers, especially when young, but her attitude hardly exemplifies a "capacity for concentration."[39] There is no room for real learning in such minds; yet, as reported by columnist Widget Finn chipping away at the patriarchy in British industry with the dull hatchet of "equal opportunity," attention is continually distracted towards "gender issues" as women are encouraged to compete "in a male world" while males are diverted from competitive excellence.[40] We are toying with the world without concern for the art of life, much as if "virtual reality" now rules the Western ethos.

III

Parameters and Pigments, Or Why a Lion Roars

She can bring no more to living than the powers that make her great
As the Mother of the Infant and the Mistress of the Mate;
And when Babe and Man are lacking and she strides unclaimed to claim.
Her right as femme (and baron), her equipment is the same.
  "The Female of the Species," Rudyard Kipling

It sheds light on our confusions to know that the above real-world excerpt from Rudyard Kipling first appeared in *The Ladies Home Journal* decades ago but is now described by a Dover Publishing editor as "devastatingly misogynist."[1] However, like Kipling, we are discriminating enough to know that the male and female of the human species are different in significant ways. As Michael Levin writes on "methodological preliminaries," reviewing "some of the literature on innate sex differences drawn from evolutionary biology, neurology, the controlled observation of children, and social anthropology. Each line of evidence is individually persuasive, and, taken jointly, they establish beyond rational doubt the existence of socially determinative sex differences."[2] The logical conclusion from this is that distinct natures warrant distinct roles.

Assuring its inevitable demise, feminism is based on the idea that sex differences are either nonexistent or inconsequential. As Professor Levin comments, "Indeed, the accessibility of the immense volume of material on sex differences makes the continued respectability of feminism no less than a scandal."[3]

More prosaically, we note that the human male and female are characterized by different size, shape, texture, smell and sound, with interesting results best epitomized by Jefferson's remark that women are "formed for attentions." Not only do women attract male attentions but also young children's, whereas "attention" to males is of quite a different sort. The respective modes of dress seem to bear this out, with adult males generally garbed in subdued, utilitarian clothes and women generally choosing more seductive, attractive, revealing garments (at least since the 1920s).

Films of rutting animals suggest analogy with the power of nubile young women to attract males. Sexual motivation is common to human and animal existence, although for the former the powerful image of motherhood has a stronger and more lasting sway. Whether this is "over-hasty generalization" seems immaterial. In the words of Samuel Johnson, "Nature has given women so much power that the law has very wisely given them little."[4] Holbrook Jackson backs this up with his own aphorism, "Women cannot be impersonal; that is why they are irresistible – and detestable." To which G.K. Chesterton replied simply, "yes."[5] Regardless of whether or not such attributes developed solely as a result of the female's physiology, the fact remains that females now possess them. Whether God created them or they happened by chance, the symptoms are ours.

Hegel's remark, "women are the eternal irony of the community," is nowhere truer than in the paradox of their irresistible sexual power in a world of male dominance. Male dominance is attributed to genealogical characteristics rather than to culture, i.e., nature, not nurture. Professor Steven Goldberg observes that there is "a high degree of certainty that sexual differences in dominance are a function of testosterone and the hormonalization of the fetal brain."[6] As he explains further, "... at this point the tightening web of evidence allows no escape from the conclusion that human sexual differences in aggression are strongly related to irreversible differences in the central nervous systems of men and women that are generated before birth."[7] How this effects marriage in terms of "equality," we shall discuss below.

Other results are apparent both in literature and individual experience, yet it needed rather sketchy research by Carol Gilligan to remind feminists that the two human sexes possess distinct moral senses. These are generally defined as the female's being uniquely "rooted in webs of relationship and responsibility, in intimacy and caring, rather than in (the) rules and abstractions" more typical of males.[8] Or, as Gilligan might say, men adhere to an "ethic of justice," women to an "ethic of caring."[9]

In other words, women tend to enjoy groups, communal reinforcement, sharing and combining resources, togetherness, "long talks and long walks"; whereas men tend towards individual struggle, marching to distant drummers, personal challenge and achievement for social and marital acceptance. As Rudyard Kipling saw it, "'til a man is built like the angels, with hammer and sickle and pen, he will work for himself and a woman, forever and ever, Amen." Or, according to Theodor Reik, "Women love men, but men love work." Dr. Joyce Brothers tells us that men have two basic needs, "Neither of them, no matter what they say, is sex. They need love and they need work. The work takes priority over love. If a woman could know only one fact about men and work, it should be that work is the most seductive mistress that most men ever have." Thus, Nietzsche's Zarathustra's claim that "The man's happiness is: I will. The woman's happiness is: He will," which suggests that women know how to tap into the male work ethic for the benefit of both. There is an abundance of lore defining men and women, most of which is ignored by "sex equality" advocates.

So, for those who reject the idea of distinct moral senses, the evidence of centuries proves them wrong. David Blankenhorn reminds us that, while a father's love is conditional on acceptable behavior, a mother's is unconditional. While her life tends to be concentric, a man's is more peripheral, circumferential, extended, understandably so, since she bears and nurtures the indomitable life force for which he serves as guardian. Why Eve as help mate ended up with this powerful force instead of Adam is yet to be explained, so the paradox remains. That the same dichotomy in the arachnid species leads to a murderous, dominant female as opposed to a more benign human pairing offers a striking lesson for our species. One explanation is probably Charlotte's web, by which she is self-sufficient and independent of a male hunter-gatherer, who thus becomes a mere suicidal impregnator. With such an analogy, it is small wonder that C.S. Lewis would write, "in the hive and the anthill we see fully realized the two things that some of us most dread for our own species – the dominance of the female and the dominance of the collective."[10]

One must credit feminism at least with having forced us to study men and women more deeply, with enlightening results – at times humorous or endearing, at times ridiculous as almost any account of "women's studies" will show. It reminds one of King Arthur's lament in *Camelot*, "All you can do with a woman is to love her, love her – love her," which is probably why God formed her for attentions and not for hard labor – or abstract thought.

Despite having "discovered" the difference, Gilligan doesn't know what to make of it. She sidesteps the complementary function of the two sexes to assume we should all think like women – a disquieting thought. As evident in "women's studies," the ladies seem to love to talk and talk and never really resolve or teach anything, reminding us of Ben Franklin's quatrain,

> When man and woman die,
>   As poets sung!
> His heart's the last part moves,
>   Her last, the tongue.[11]

I for one have no quarrel with the ladies' delightful communicative skills, and in fact consider them charmingly endearing in the appropriate milieu. Misapplied in angry revisionism or "power" seeking, however, they remind one of Edmund Burke's comment on Richard Price's "harangues from the pulpit" extolling the virtues of a bloody revolution, "Those who quit their proper character, to assume what does not belong to them, are, for the greater part, ignorant both of the character they weave, and of the character they assume. Wholly unacquainted with the world in which they are so fond of meddling, and inexperienced in all its affairs, on which they pronounce with so much confidence, they have nothing of politics but the passions they excite."[12] "Caring," after all, doesn't require knowledge or honesty as much as feelings. As Michael Weiss elaborates:

> An essential duplicity pervades feminist pedagogy – feminists want to expose all presuppositions to examination, even their own. Beneath the surface, however, an intellectually shallow agenda is ruthlessly enforced. To be sure, there is vigorous debate, both within a given feminist class and among feminist scholars; but the parameters of that debate are narrowly drawn. Its dynamic is to see who can top whom in exposing oppression. And the very looseness of feminist classroom decorum functions in reality to constrain debate within those limits.

Typical of the genre is an article that Morrison Torrey, then an assistant professor of law at DePaul University, wrote with two of her students. Appearing in the 1990 *Harvard Women's Law Journal*, "Teaching Law in a Feminist Manner: A Commentary from Experience," is filled with tortuous windings, as Torrey and her students attempt to sort out their various feelings – Nevertheless, this article presents an admirably clear and concise, but otherwise representative, account of feminist law school pedagogy: "The four basic methods to achieve a feminist approach that we offer, and which we frequently referred to and relied upon in class, are: [1] consciousness-raising, [2] destruction of artificial dichotomies, [3] rejection of abstraction, and [4] perpetual questioning. – The validity of knowledge gained through consciousness-raising is established through the corroboration of other women in the group."[13]

Echoing this coelenterate brand of learning, Professor Susan Arpad, Director of Women's Studies at California State University, Fresno, offers this synopsis: "Women's studies classes have an essential life component that more theoretical oriented courses do not – Students discuss frankly the issues of relationships, career, and cultural institutions such as religion. This can touch a lot of raw nerves."[14] And make for unprincipled self-government.

Such collegiate oddity will be a continual target in these pages. Meanwhile, human sex differences should ever remind us of the value of the Adam and Eve story. After God had created night and day, earth and water, hot and cold, gravity, and all the other dualities in precarious balance, he created man and woman. Whether we rely on creation or natural evolution to explain man and woman, they do appear in a world with all this tension, which includes other areas as well – good and evil, large and small, ugliness and beauty, red and green, high and low.

Men of our day have become intimidated by such matters, as J. Budziszewski explains: "The American republic was long the beneficiary of this tension; it was like a string pulled tight between the cult of the individual and the cult of the state. Unfortunately the public philosophy of our own century has made the string go slack. It glues the two cults together rather than keeping them apart: it distends the individual in some ways while diminishing him in others. The lesson for those who love the tradition is that we can no longer rely on a balance of errors. From now on, nothing less than the truth will suffice."[15] This applies especially to 2000s men and women, who need to recover their old, charming independence and throw off the shackles of androgyny and the state. Then might Adam finally reach his potential in wisdom.

Wilhelm Roepke also recognizes the "problem of maintaining a healthy balance between the individual and the state in its full implications...."[16] He was no believer in equality of the sexes. According to William F. Campbell, Roepke realized that "nature, sex, religion, beauty, and politics are all meaningful as part of the whole. When they are considered to become the whole, then there is mischief."[17] Perhaps this is why Roepke commences his Part III with a quotation from Shakespeare's *Troilus and Cressida*, Act I, Scene 3:

> Take but degree away, untune that string,
> And, hark! what discord follows; each thing meets
> In mere repugnancy;...
> Then everything includes itself in power,
> Power into will, will into appetite;
> And appetite, an universal wolf,
> So doubly seconded with will and power,
> Must make perforce an universal prey,
> And last eat up himself.

"Individual rights" have transformed us into herds of animals, vying for territory, entertained by women like Erica Jong declaring, "Men and women, women and men. It will never work." In contrast, Roepke writes of the need for a three-dimensional society, "necessarily pyramidal and hierarchical in a sense which can be no longer be misunderstood or misinterpreted as a relationship involving oppression and arbitrary force.... These individuals who have been blown out of their community are finding themselves exposed to a chaotic lack of any relationship to anything and are becoming lost nomadic herds who no longer know where they belong, what their place in society is, and where they have become more and more divorced from the ties of family, occupation, neighborhood, nature and society. – (They have become a) *simple aggregation of individuals dependent now upon themselves alone....*"[18] This echoes Henry and Brooks Adams's lament in 1920 regarding modern women: "The woman, as the cement of society, the head of the family, and the center of cohesion, has, for all intents and purposes, ceased to exist. She has become a wandering isolated unit, rather a dispersive than a collective force."[19]

Weakening of the former healthy order of the sexes traces back to the age of individualism, when "the older view of the free self as a tense equilibrium of countervailing forces had been replaced by the romantic and holistic injunction to 'trust thyself' – the very advice a Jonathan Edwards would have strenuously cautioned us against. That our present-day sages would be more likely to warn us against Edwards than against Emerson speaks volumes about the place where we have now arrived."[20]

While faith on a higher plane is needed, individualism has fostered an entertainment industry now driven by faith in explicit sex display, with artistic restraint lacking. T.S. Eliot re-emphasizes the importance of a higher "common faith" in his definition of culture:

> ... it would seem that a constant struggle between the centripetal and centrifugal forces is desirable. For without the struggle no balance can be maintained; and if either force won the result would be deplorable.... it is only by the struggle against constantly appearing false ideas that the truth is enlarged and

clarified.... the culture proper to each area and each class may flourish; but there must also be a force holding these areas and these classes together. If this corrective force in the direction of uniformity of belief and practice is lacking, then the culture of each part will suffer.... And without a common faith, all efforts towards drawing nations closer together in culture can produce only an illusion of unity.[21]

For the sexes this will require a return to more refined roles – ladies and gentlemen – civility, responsibility. Adam must lead the way.

In other words, again, a healthy tension characterizes human society, and physical, genealogical and moral differences between the human sexes play a principal role in ordering the countless areas that make up our culture. The age-old "battle of the sexes" is no petty squabble or flapdoodle. It served as a natural sociocultural preservative until we deferred to the dull-witted state. A fondness for equality has subjugated us to state-mandated "individualism, the unencumbered self, and egotistic autonomy."[22] David M. Rasmussen warns, "the decadence of modernity: public morality, social responsibility, even the motivational foundation for public democratic action must be sacrificed at the altar of human rights." This is largely the result of the female moral sense run amok – free rein for Eve without response from Adam, as she enlists Nero in her rebellious, "compassionate" cause.

*   *   *

As the reader will see, there is a wide range of women's voices on our subject. Those who come close to the truth are often as charming as the few who hit the bullseye, while showing generally why total objectivity is lacking. Eve will always be an enigma. One example is offered by Dale O'Leary, who, although a staunch pro-family advocate and aware of contrary trends and practices, misses the point. In her book, *The Gender Agenda*:

Redefining Equality, as reviewed by Patricia Lança in *The Salisbury Review*[25], she rightly attacks the anti-traditional-family "gender feminists," her main complaint being semantic: the faddish use of the term "gender" when we mean "sex." "Feminism," she doesn't mind, but "gender feminism" is subversive and countercultural. While she is certainly right in her assessment of the lesbian "gender feminists" who promote homosexuality, like so many others she doesn't realize that the root of the "anti-traditional-family" problem is feminism itself, an ideology of group statism and sexual separatism. In any event, her concluding call to action is a call to Adam: ".... it will take calculated rudeness. The feminists have relied on the politeness of men. They have demanded that dangerous nonsense and utter stupidity be treated with respect. The Gender Agenda cannot be defeated until people are willing to stand up and say, 'No more inclusive language, no more politically correct speech.' We must refuse to say 'gender' when we mean 'sex'. Those who are offended by reality and human nature will just have to live with it."

Typical of the gender gap, or Eve's focus on intimacy and caring rather than robust tension and rightness, is columnist Ellen Goodman's complaint that "constant combat in political issues is wearing on the public."[24] Here stems the familiar cry of "gridlock" whenever the right resists the left's favorite causes, as if they had never heard of Madisonian "factions." (It is never applied to the left's intransigence but that is another story.) In argument, Goodman cites linguistics professor Deborah Tannen and law professor Lani Guinier as authority for her lament against "gladiator politics," "polarization," "pitched battles," "wrangling." As alternatives to her supposed horrors of political "combat," "winning and losing," "battles," and "spoiling for a fight," she and the others suggest "conversation," "serious talk," "study circles," "engaging people in creating solutions," and "coming together." Aside from the obvious tendency here to prefer ladylike "togetherness," she forgets that by her very suggestions she is playing the gladiator no less than the culprits she condemns. In fact, her solution of top-down "dialogues" on whatever cause her group favors at the moment is more centrist, authoritarian and tyrannical than, for all its faults, Madison's *Federalist* approach could ever be. If women ruled, all would be peaches and cream, *or else*. Unfortunately, Republicans have given much ground to such middlingness and the republic tends toward "the metaphysics of an undergraduate."

Goodman's own combative bias shows in her sympathy for Lani Guinier as a "victim of drive-by politics when her nomination to the head civil rights job was derailed," never mind that Guinier's ideas of degenerative Balkanism were too radical to deserve general approval. Perhaps open discussion for the Ellen Goodmans of the world becomes "wearing" or "tone-deaf" only when they see their side losing, as in Jim Rockford's comment to his lady friend in T.V.'s *Rockford Files*, "Whenever anyone disagrees with you, you accuse them of 'shouting'." As Chester E. Finn, Jr., tells us of Guinier's views, however, "Those ideas, though expressed perhaps less radically, remain influential in law-school lecture halls, in the grant decisions of giant foundations, in the personnel departments of major corporations, and in the cubbyholes of Washington. But that is why even the boring stretches of Guinier's book, when she is not vividly describing how her friend the President stabbed her in the back, warrant attention. Although she is profoundly wrong about nearly everything, we ignore her at our peril."[25] Which, unfortunately, can also be said for the Ellen Goodmans – like enemy submarines, we should keep 'em hemmed in.

One must make distinctions, of course, between Madison's extended-republic factions and Guinier's separatist ethnic groups.

Perhaps the main differences are, [1] his operated more organically by natural law, and hers by edict and post-1960s individual-rights activism; and [2] Madison assumed, "In the extended republic of the United States, and among the great variety of interests, parties, and sects which it embraces a coalition of a majority of the whole society could seldom take place on any other principles than those of justice and the general good."[26] For Guinier, such fundamentals are immaterial. The feminist Achilles heel is the rejection of our heritage as "male-oriented."

* * *

But God's higher authority is a boon to women as well as men of all peoples. As Matthew Berke explains "God and Gender in Judaism,"

> Feminist critics and modern liturgy revisers often assume that God's awesome patriarchal aspect is merely an idolatrous projection of the male image, which it can be and sometimes is. At the same time, God's lordship is the only plausible check on the predatory tendencies of wicked men and nations, from Pharaoh to Haman to Hitler (and one hopes of wicked women also). The feminist argument that traditional God-language stresses power, fear, rules, and hierarchy is essentially correct (as Goodman and Guinier complain) but it misses the point that these things are required for the good of women as well as men. It is precisely His capacity as a warrior-judge that enables Him to be a God of justice who frees the captive and releases the oppressed, who answers the cries of the poor, the widows, the fatherless. "King" and "Lord" are the most convincing symbolizations for this aspect of divine action. Re-imagings that magnify characteristically feminine traits undermine the plausibility of God's ultimate power to overcome evil.[27] (parenthesis supplied)

* * *

With all this in mind, the feminist-inspired fad of denigrating the male (as, for example, in the collection, *What Women Say About Men*", see below) is countercultural. While in certain company such barbs titillate and entertain, their shortsightedness inevitably dulls the senses. Columnist John Leo has grasped the essence of the risk in suggesting that "pervasive male-bashing isn't good for society."[28] He tells of greeting card companies, magazine ads, 3M, Inc., and female teachers who indulge in such humor intended to please the mass of women, despite its inevitable double standard. Men have long been known to resort to off-color humor about women *in limited male company* but public display would have been unthinkable. As Leo quotes Christina Sommers, "There used to be a certain level of good-natured teasing between the sexes. Now even the most innocent remark about women will get you in trouble, but there's no limit at all to what you can say about men." But Leo points out that "commercial attempts to increase the amount of sexual antagonism in America are never a good idea. And if you keep attacking men as a group, they will eventually start acting as a group, something we should fervently avoid... the worst impact of all the male-bashing is on the young."

Another example of the wages of female rule appears in a typical response to a complaint about Eve's misbehavior: "Poor, sensitive Adam," as if irrelevant ripostes had meaning other than to justify Florence King's appraisal that feminization "gives equal importance to anything as long as it's personal,"[29] echoing Holbrook Jackson's remark, "Women can't be impersonal." John Leo writes, "The double standard is rooted in identity politics and fashionable theories about victimization: Men as a group are oppressors; jokes that oppressors use to degrade the oppressed must be taken seriously and suppressed. Jokes by the oppressed against the oppressors, however, are liberating and progressive. So while sexual harassment doctrine cracks down on the harmless jokes about women, very hostile humor about men keeps expanding with almost no objection." The risks from empowering one who claims past "oppression" are considerable.

* * *

The tension between our classical, pagan heritage (Rome, Greece, Socrates, Aristotle) and our religious heritage (Jerusalem, Moses, Jesus) has served to give us what we call Western Civilization, which, as Jeffrey Hart reminds us, "emerged through a combination of two powerful impulses…. the philosophic-scientific aspiration to understand the universe through the intellect…. (and) the aspiration to spiritual perfection."[30] One without the other would have bred only tyranny, discord and poverty. "But in their Western combination, the two aspirations interact and 'correct' one another," much like the former positive, healthy interaction between men and women.

Hart tells us of the seminal actors in this great story, including Dante, who "holds together a vast synthesis of the classical and the Christian. He also adds a powerful and third inspiration to Athens and Jerusalem: the idealization of women that emerged suddenly and mysteriously in southern France in the 11th century. It spread throughout Europe and continues to affect manners in the West. As regards women, Western manners differ from those of the ancient world and also contemporary Africa and Asia. Romantic love, in other words, was invented in the 11th century in southern France."

Some romantic tendencies have led to unnaturally "advanced" women's roles, while others have possibly led to regression. Westerners who scorn Islam's extremism as to the sexes seem themselves no longer to comprehend the sexes at all. A middle ground seems justified, that is, a continued interaction of men and women according to their distinct natures and long-accepted patterns, balancing a healthy version of "romantic love" and an "idealization of women" with a Judaeo-Christian-Buddhist division of labor, rather than Westerners' utilitarian reversion to androgynous fungibility. In any case, Hart joins others in rebutting the feminist claim that women have been excluded or brutalized in Western civilization.

* * *

Any such interaction requires earnest input from both sides, admittedly a lack in 21st-century America. Reflecting the imbalance is the flood of books by women on women. Periodicals defer to female authors no matter how young or unproven, and public attitudes languish. As a recent example, conservative columnist Mona Charen writes of F. Carolyn Graglia's 1998 book, *Domestic Tranquility: A Brief Against Feminism*, and claims that "there is a backlash against feminism.... it isn't to be found among men.... The voice of anti-feminism is a female voice."[31] She first mentions a yet unpublished book by Danielle Crittenden... an analysis of the way feminism has steered women into unhappiness," and then reviews Graglia's book in glowing terms. She seems unaware of the scholarly literature of the past twenty-five years. From all appearances, women are now plentiful in the publishing industry and the available scholarly literature reflects the result.[32] Graglia's book will be discussed in a later chapter.

Should it all depend on how women feel, as Charen and others seem to assume? A productive balance of views would seem better, requiring also a reasoned, knowledgeable stand by men in other than an obedient fatherly-husbandly-loverly posture. A Catholic husband admits ignorance of the Catechism's teaching on Saint Mary, despite its cogency for womanhood and opposition to his wife's feminism. Yet, with their ability to make abstract judgments, men could be relied on more often to have the interests of both sexes at heart, if only they exercise it. Who says A must say B: Since the odds of a wife's singing the praises of "masculinism" are slim, so "feminism" is incongruous unless one feels women are inadequate and need a movement. This is hardly a compliment.

* * *

In the light of such perspectives, Lani Guinier's reformist proposals against settled customs inevitably summon visions of political radicalism, another outgrowth of the rebellious 1960s which conjures up comparisons with the French Revolution, of which Roger Scruton writes, "the decisive feature of the revolutionary credo – is its provision of a criterion of legitimacy that no actual institution can ever pass."[33] Roger Kimball quotes this passage and goes on to write,

> The Polish philosopher Leszek Kolakowski summed it up neatly in his essay, "The Death of Utopia Reconsidered" (1983): "Utopians, once they attempt to convert their visions into practical proposals, come up with the most malignant project ever devised: they want to institutionalize fraternity, which is the surest way to totalitarian despotism.[34]

Similarly, feminists would lead us to despotism by institutionalizing sorority.

How Adam and Eve help resolve our puzzle: As a parable on how to minimize the dysfunction naively invited by Guinier and Goodman. One need only imagine what it would be like today if Adam had merely told Eve, "No!" and explained why. Or if his ancestors will tell Betty Friedan, Germaine Greer, and their angry sisters, "No!" and explain why. Inevitably the story involves the subject of marriage and the family – probably the most important "little platoon" of all – which deserves its own chapter.

IV

Marriage, Or A Lion Roars

I should like to know what is the proper function for women, if it is not make reasons for husbands to stay at home, and still stronger reasons for bachelors to go out.
George Eliot

Getting along with men isn't what's truly important. The vital knowledge is how to get along with a man. One man.
Phyllis McGinley[1]

A young man enters the decisive phase of his life when he resolves on marriage and career.... At this point, economic incentives and bureaucratic rules alone are impotent to make him a useful citizen.... It is the sexual constitution, not the legal one, that is decisive in subduing the aggressions of young men. The outcome is set by work and women. If he finds work that affirms his manhood and a girl who demands that his sexuality succumb to hers, he is likely to become a valuable and constructive citizen. If, on the other hand, he sees long-term employment and marriage as a woman's world, he will tend to exploit both jobs and women as short-term ways to money and pleasure.
George Gilder[2]

1.

No institution can teach these lessons better than the family, which requires both a mother and a father. James Q. Wilson has suggested that remedies for present "social disorders" will arise from its recovery. "Cultures grow out of the countless small choices of millions of people. To restore a culture, we must do it retail, not wholesale. – When a culture changes, policy can rarely change it back. – Most people wish to be part of a family and one nation. If we wish to be one nation again, we must make the second one part of the first. We have tried almost everything to do this except the one thing that matters most – rebuilding the family. However difficult, it is what there is left to try."[3]

"To be more specific," Francis Canavan suggests, "public policy may and ought to take the monogamous family as the basic unit of society, and should support and encourage it in its culture-transmitting function. To aid the family in this function, and to support the different religious and cultural communities to which families belong, the educational system ought to become more open and flexible than it now is. We need to rethink the notion that the secularized public school is the rock on which the republic stands."[4]

That the question transcends "individual rights" should be the West's guiding principle. As Canavan explains: "Those who do not love their families, their kinsmen, their 'own kind,' their neighborhoods, or their churches are not likely to love a merely political unit or the democratic system. Edmund Burke again puts it well: 'to be attached to the subdivision, to love the little platoon we belong to in society, is the first principle (the germ as it were) of public affections. It is the first link in the series by which we proceed toward a love to our country and to mankind.'"[5]

For this reason, God's creation of the two sexes serves not only as the epitome of tension and paradox (as if God knew Eve would give Adam the apple and inevitably unleash the human tragicomedy) but also as a template for the human species with its ability to reason. In this ironic pairing, the lesson of love becomes central, and even if one considers sexual dimorphism an accidental happenstance, the challenge remains of maintaining a semblance of productive coherence. As Allan Bloom describes the human pair bond, "The arrangement implicit in marriage, even if it is only conventional, tells those who enter into it what to expect and what the satisfactions are supposed to be. Very simply, the family is a sort of miniature body politic in which the husband's will is the will of the whole. The woman can influence her husband's will, and it is supposed to be informed by love of wife and children."[6] Those who scoff at this approach do not understand the true power of womanhood (as other than caviling). Again, we use Adam and Eve as a parable since they offer an instructive pattern.

Many have dealt with the perplexing challenge with all sorts of insights, which we are only sampling while setting the stage. As an atheist, Friedrich Nietzsche had his prophet Zarathustra declare that "marriage is promised to many, and more than marriage – to many that are stranger to one another than man and woman: and who has fully conceived *how* strange man and woman are to one another!"[7] On the other hand, the Reverend James Dobson comments, "The natural tendency of everything in the universe is to move from order to disorder.... Not surprisingly, human relations also conform to the principle of disintegration. The natural tendency is for husbands and wives to drift away from each other unless they work at staying together.... If they don't take the time for romantic activities and experiences that draw them together, something precious begins to slip away."[8] Here is our friend tension again.

Despite Adam's original high status, his descendants have fared less well, as, for instance, D.H. Lawrence's protagonist Rupert

Birkin in *Women in Love*, for whom his lady fair Ursula Brangwen "felt such a poignant hatred – that all her brain seemed turned into a sharp crystal of fine hatred. Her whole nature seemed sharpened and intensified into a pure dart of hate."[9]

Birkin's own approach was somewhat more benign: "And he wanted to be with Ursula as free as with himself, single and clear and cool, yet balanced, polarised with her. The merging, the clutching, the mingling of love was becoming madly abhorrent to him.[10]

Surely God realized the risk of having two sexes so different but, had it been otherwise, familiarity would have bred contempt. As C.S. Lewis wrote in *A Grief Observed* after the death of his wife, "There is, hidden or flaunted, a sword between the sexes till an entire marriage reconciles them." God also knew the ramifications of the color wheel with its various potentially discordant colors needing organization by certain rules to achieve desired harmonies of nature. The beauties of form and color don't happen accidentally but need rational combinations to give masterpieces. By the same token, if every man and every woman were compatible or mutually attractive, the human race would have long since become a mob. Instead, they are challenged by the tensions of dissimilarity and compatibility to be selective. "How to get along with a man. One man," becomes the challenge for a woman, and vice versa for a man, so that children may be nurtured in perduring two-parent environments. As Charles Williams reputedly replied to a suggestion that "marriage becomes in time a bond of quiet understanding," "Well, there's not all that much understanding, and it's not at all quiet, but it's close enough and will have to do."

While, like the arachnids, human propagation in itself is biological, human offspring differ in needing more than a brief period of motherhood. The world's tensions are introduced to the human being in his formative years when parents must teach and guide the young, especially the mother, leading Chesterton to comment, "No one, staring at this frightful female privilege, can quite believe in the equality of the sexes."[11]

Once past Birkin's prenuptial trauma and the threshold of marital bliss, he enters fatherhood with its distinct function. As Matthew Berke explains (echoing others), analogous with the Judeo-Christian God's paternity, "Maternal care arises more or less naturally, and mother love tends to be unconditional. Fatherhood, by contrast, is largely a socially constructed phenomenon, and it is far more conditional and hierarchical than motherhood – demanding obedience, threatening punishment, and setting standards in return for love and approval. In families without fathers or strong male authority figures, order tends to break down, particularly among the male children, who become wild and predatory."[12]

Berke expands it to a higher level with a helpful analogy, "The God of Israel introduces Himself into history as a kind of adoptive parent, in particular as a father figure who steps in to bring order to a chaotic and violent world. At times He exhibits the gratuitous love and tender care associated with femininity and motherhood – but more often our broken, unredeemed world calls forth from Him a specifically *paternal* form of authority, implemented over and against His human children, especially His sons. While women, in their own fashion, may sin as much as men, it is the pride and willfulness and violence of men that most radically disrupt the world's peace and order. Feminist reformers may have no trouble in recognizing this fact, but they seem not to notice that breaking the arrogance and power of men requires a God who is, among other things, the judge of Nations, the Lord of Hosts, the 'King of glory –mighty in battle.' [Psalm 24:8]."

Most traditionally oriented women sense this truth, that the male of the species stands for something above the mundane human existence with his capacity for broader and higher reaches, his larger size and deeper voice, his physical strength and proneness to mischief as well as protection of the weak, all suggesting a greater potential for life's more utilitarian work. One might consider the female a specialist[13], the male a generalist. This gives rise to part of the paradox, that females with their gift of speech and perception, their caring and aspirations, must ultimately depend on the male for full and optimum realization of their own higher goals. Irony also rules in Dr. Dobson's law of "the natural tendency to move from order to disorder," with the result that the male of the species doesn't ordinarily reach his God-given potential without traditional training, and most women know it, although they differ as to ways to achieve this goal. Women can step in and do much that men do but the substitution is unnatural, much like using a wood post to pound nails. It is essentially a misuse of tools. And wise women know this too. One doesn't use a Porsche to negotiate rocky mountain roads. Allan Bloom offers a titillating twist to this paradox in his discussion of "love" and "relationships":

> A man was to make a living and protect his wife and children, and a woman was to provide for the domestic economy, particularly in caring for husband and children. Frequently this did not work very well for one or both of the partners, because they either were not good at their functions or were not eager to perform them. In order to assure the proper ordering of things, the transvestite women in Shakespeare, like Portia and Rosalind, are forced to masquerade as men because the real men are inadequate and need to be corrected. This happens only in comedies; when there are no such intrepid women, the situation turns into tragedy. But the assumption of male garb observes the proprieties or conventions. Men should be doing what the impersonating women are doing; and when the women have set things right, they become women again and submit to the men, albeit with a tactful, ironical consciousness that they are at least partially playacting in order to preserve a viable order.[14]

Such is our central irony. But whether Eve realized that Adam let them both down has, to my knowledge, never been fully explored. Instead, in contrast to men's generally objective and often bawdy comment on the opposite sex, women often resort to cute, cutting and catty barbs about men not only because men often deserve (and perversely enjoy) them but also because women possibly realize that straightforward criticism risks harridanism and ineffectiveness. Or perhaps their different brains simply resort to different methods! "Woman is not undeveloped man; but man is," as Holbrook Jackson suggested and Chesterton agreed.[15]

Henry Adam's dinner partner certainly would have endorsed this appraisal, as he relates in *The Education of Henry Adams*, "Sometimes, at dinner, one might wait until talk flagged, and then, as mildly as possible, ask one's liveliest neighbor whether she could explain why the American woman was a failure. Without an instant's hesitation, she was sure to answer: – 'Because the American man is a failure!' She meant it."[16] More recent women resort to witticisms, mostly shorn of ontology but – cute. Some examples from *What Women Say About Men*[17]:

> "Behind every great man there is a surprised woman." (Maryon Pearson)
>
> "As long as you know that most men are like children, you know everything." (Coco Chanel)
>
> "A man's home may seem to be his castle from the outside; inside, it is more often his nursery." (Claire Boothe Luce)
>
> "I insist on believing that some men are my equals." (Brigid Brophy)
>
> "I like men to behave like men – strong and childish." (Françoise Sagan)
>
> "The trouble with some women is that they get all excited about nothing – and then marry him." (Cher)

"I've yet to hear a man ask for advice on how to combine marriage and a career," says Gloria Steinem. She exaggerates here, of course, as suggested by James Q. Wilson's observation, "No parent, whether father or mother, can 'have it all.' Choices must be made between family and work. The first must take priority over the second."[18] In all honesty, however, both Steinem and Wilson may be over-simplifying, if we can agree that the bacon brought home is a top priority for most families. This is the point of a man's working in the first place, as Kipling, Brothers and Reik have realized, while a wife's home making is equally demanding and important.

"'We must find happiness in our work, or not at all.' So wrote a twentieth-century admirer of (Edmund) Burke, Irving Babbitt. In the sense that he was perpetually busy with concerns of high – often enduring – importance, Burke was a happy man."[19] There is also the unavoidable reality that partners in each marriage must coordinate priorities and, as long as the working father remains dedicated to the home, his authority can be effective even when absent. There is often a delicate balance in a male and female partnership but, as Wilson and others make clear, it is far better than single parenthood. And with two such partners, the division of labor over untold centuries has brought civilization and economic well-being. But all this is too serious for the witty ladies. "I marry beneath me – all women do." (Lady Nancy Astor)

All of these quotations and many more may be found in *What Women Say About Men*. They tell us less about men than about how women think. For instance, Lady Nancy Astor remarks that "the first time Adam had a chance he laid the blame on women," as if Eve had no share in the fall. There's a touch of denial at work here. Of course these women are only trying to be witty but perhaps that's the point: seriousness is ultimately a male responsibility and, when he doesn't measure up, he deserves their scorn. If they were actually as much in charge as they pretend, women would not resort to comedy. By a quirk of the publisher, an anonymous aphorism was also included: "A woman who strives to be like a man lacks ambition," which, as Portia and Rosalind understood, demolishes the whole idea of "career equality."

It is worthwhile to note that women actually don't have that much to complain about, considering that thanks to the advance of our materialistic age and its enterprising males their lives have been considerably eased. As remarked by Herbert Spencer over a hundred years ago, when men seemed to speak more forthrightly than most men do today,

> (T)he more things improve the louder become the explanations about their badness. In days when the people were without any political power, their subjection was rarely complained of; but after free institutions had so far advanced in England that our political arrangements were envied by continental people, the denunciations of aristocratic rule grew gradually stronger, until there came a great widening of the franchise, soon followed by complaints that things were going wrong for want of still further widening. If we trace up the treatment of women from the days of savagedom, when they bore all the burdens and after the men had eaten received such food as remained, up through the middle ages when they served the men at their meals, to our own day when throughout our social arrangements the claims of women are always put first, we see that along with the worst treatment there went the least apparent consciousness that the treatment was bad; while now that they are better treated than ever before, the complaining of their grievances daily strengthens: the loudest outcries coming from "the paradise of women," America.[20]

Intelligent women in more savage days didn't consider their share of labor as "bad treatment," thanks to the security and protection the men afforded them in those barbarous times. We shall take up the views of other nineteenth-century writers in a later chapter.

Jean Kerr is quoted in the book of women's witticisms for a quirky truism that might reveal the whole secret: "Women speak because they wish to speak; whereas a man speaks only when driven by something outside himself – like, for instance, he can't find his clean socks." In other words, men have an external, at least *potentially* broader motivation than the female's more biological and centered sphere. In a better world, "clean socks" might become, as they have for many great men in the past, the search for truth and justice, better mousetraps, more durable systems of government, peace and order. As we shall explore below, this male trait can also have the advantage for a family of keeping an eye on external matters. Women of the past no doubt have served as inspiration even for clean socks, and will probably continue to do so, since we cannot separate the two sexes nor overlook the gifts of either. It seems probable, for instance, that Marilyn Peterson could find ways to inspire more effectively than with barbs, "if it wasn't for women, men would still be hanging from trees." That two such diverse sexes can be melded into a human pair bond is indeed a miracle.

2.

No less than "the subject of women," the subject of marriage also elicits ample instruction from writers in periodicals and on the Internet. Unless such teachings include the nuanced lesson of Adam and Eve, however, they are inadequate. To understand marriage, one must understand the sexes. Otherwise it is a roll of the dice. For instance, more women than men think that life doesn't really begin until marriage and assume that only parents understand babies. This reflects a woman's more centered perspective, requiring a male's to complement and sustain her gifts.

As an example, despite her commendable motives, Elizabeth Powers shows this in her article on "Table Manners and Morals,"[21] telling of her original entry into marriage, "I marvel now at my failure to consider what is involved in building a common household, forming common friendships and interests, strengthening the ties that bind – ties that come, for a start, from sitting down every morning to coffee together." Personally, I believe most (not all) men know such ties either instinctively or experientially or both, which is probably another reason why men prefer marriage. In contrast, Ms. Powers tells us that "Perhaps because I had never been married, and perhaps because I could not cook, I was somewhat naïve about what goes into making a life together... Parents who do the necessary work have obviously acquired a little starch in their own outward habits, if only by dint of *being* parents." Perhaps this is why single women often seem so attractive to men, exuding an insouciance for their gifts that defies reason, or an innocence that cries out for complement. We shall return to Ms. Powers in Chapter VIII.

Marriage for a man can be a sinecure with a status previously unrealized. His natural instincts – to hunt, to gather, to work, to defend, or to reconnoiter – which result in a heightened awareness of the world outside the family – the broader horizon – can easily become submerged and atrophied in marriage, especially in these days of the denigrated male. Younger men need to resist this lapse and maintain their manhood within the parameters of marriage so as to make themselves better fathers as well as citizens "in the gates." Parents should learn to instruct their children in the important roles they'll play in the crucial institution of marriage.

George Sim Johnson writes, "couples about to marry are embarking on a great adventure"[22] and, as Pope John Paul II has written, "the future of humanity passes through the family."[23] However, while the Pope and the Church make a commendable effort to instruct the young in the profound mysteries and realities of marriage, their teachings should not be construed as discouraging husbands from being *men*. Remember, our purpose is to find a right order outside of marriage as well.

3.

Should marriage be based on equality or hierarchy? A flat structure or a pyramid? Since geometric terms are inadequate, other options are more helpful. For instance, there is God's Genesis 3:16 mandate to Eve, "and thy desire shall be for thy husband and he shall rule over thee." While obviously hierarchical, God's scheme of love, duty and faith was no sanction for tyranny, but a simple pattern for our biological natures. Tocqueville's American men and women lived by it, as men and women had for centuries while there was still relative harmony between the sexes, which is why he credited the "superiority" of American women as they enjoyed both respect and authority. Many years later, George Gilder would still consider women the "hub of the human community," although "liberated" women scoff at the idea, being programmed like robots to assume men and women are identical. A strange negative psychopathy! Until we recapture an understanding of Genesis 3:16, sexual harmony will continue to show symptoms of schizophrenia.

Ephesians 5:23 seems to reinforce Genesis 3:16 by actually specifying that "the husband is the head of the wife, even as Christ is the head of the church…." Unlike more recent apologists for watered-down versions of the marriage bond, C.S. Lewis had a way of explaining marriage roles which gets down to basics: "If there be a head, why the man? … The relations of the family to the outer world – what might be called its foreign policy – must depend, in the last resort, upon the man, because he always ought to be, and usually is, much more just to the outsiders. A woman is primarily fighting for her own children and husband against the rest of the world. Naturally, almost, in a sense, rightly, their claims override, for her, all other claims. She is the special trustee of their interests. The function of the husband is to see that this natural preference of hers is not given its head. He has the last word in order to protect other people from the intense family patriotism of the wife."[24]

William Oddie reinforces this view in reference to the biblical passage from the book of Proverbs (31:10-31), worth repeating verbatim:

> The portrait of the perfect wife in the book of Proverbs vividly evokes an essential human archetype. She is tireless; weaving; buying food from a distance; feeding the household and giving orders to the servants; buying land and planting vines with her earnings; giving to the poor and the needy; clothing her household. She is a powerful and dignified figure, in no way her husband's drudge; and the clear delineation of their spheres of action cannot be seen as implying any superiority of the public over the domestic arena:
>
> Her husband is known in the gates.
>   when he sits among the elders of the land.
> She makes linen garments and sells them;
>   she delivers girdles to the merchant.
> Strength and dignity are her clothing
>   and she laughs at the time to come.
> She opens her mouth with wisdom,
>   and the teaching of kindness is on her tongue.
> She looks well to the ways of her household,
>   and does not eat the bread of idleness.
> Her children rise up and call her blessed;
>   her husband also, and he praises her:
> 'Many women have done excellently,
>   but you surpass them all.'
> Charm is deceitful, and beauty is vain,
>   but a woman who fears the LORD is to be praised.
> Give her of the fruit of her hands,
>   and let her works praise her in the gates.
>
> This familiar passage strikingly conveys the most obvious traditional distinction between men's and women's roles. The husband constantly leaves and returns to the domestic sphere, and is the link between the home and the wider world in which his activities unfold. He is known "in the gates"; the wife "looks ... to the ways of her household".[25]

Gilbert Meilaender, in contrast, deals with the subject in a more conciliatory vein, referring, for instance, to Genesis 3:16

as a "curse," and labeling C.S. Lewis's approach "wooden," as though somehow the subject should be more pleasant for wives after all these centuries.[26] At the same time, he agrees somewhat with James Dobson that "marriage is... a sphere of life in which we must struggle to enact our faithfulness." In other words, he extends the matrimonial experience from its natural melding of differences into the sphere of faith in God, in the process, however, probably trying harder than Tocqueville to render the two sexes "equal" in more than mere value. But if it is a "struggle," it follows that there are tensions needing better resolution than pretensions of "equality" (in itself, a disputatious brier patch). In any event, Professor Meilaender prefers Helmut Thielicke's somewhat defused version of the "headship" idea: "And even if it does come to the point where the borderline situation exists, and the father exercises his right to make the final decision, it is important that the responsible person is one who is constantly aware of the other person in the marriage itself and must accept the consequences of his decision while continuing to live with the other partner."

Each is right, of course, but Lewis's more direct style is refreshing in this day of political correctness (the culture of hypocrisy) and probably still leaves room for Meilaender's middleness. Like Lewis, David Blankenhorn makes no bones about the father's position, when he tells us, "Historically, the good father protects his family, provides for its material needs, devotes himself to the education of his children, and represents his family's interests in the larger world. This work is necessarily rooted in a repertoire of inherited male values: historically and socially mediated understandings of what it means to be a good father. These values are not limited to toughness, competition, instrumentalism, and aggression – but they certainly include them. These 'hard' male values have changed and will continue to change. But they will not disappear or turn into their opposites. Nor should we wish them to."[27]

The reader can see the point: like it or not, men make better public leaders than women; and, ineluctably, women are better matured – more lovable – in roles other than leadership, etc. Meilaender's essay is helpful but why shy from robust expressions of reality, especially when we realize that distinct responsibilities tend to push a man towards his full potential, and a woman towards hers? Instead of accepting this Aristotelean, teleological concept, Meilaender and Thielicke both flirt with relativism, probably like other modern males out of deference to the ladies. They anticipate the modern, resistant woman, forgetting that relativism or consensus politics inevitably leads to confusion lacking an accepted, common standard of justice. As Francis Canavan explains the morass, "a people who increasingly disagree on basic moral principles may be able to agree only on procedures.... (such that) the freedom of the individual (becomes) our highest national value, but it is a freedom that must be guaranteed to all equally, without distinction of race, religion, morals, sex, or sexual preference."[28] (This recalls Goethe's "mountebanks or psychopaths" promising both equality *and* liberty.) Ultimate male authority requires by its very nature the self-restraint and sense of responsibility that Meilaender and Thielicke envision. A Tocqueville lady would understand completely the delicate balance of roles and the nature of responsibilities, and men must always realize that Lewis is not promoting crude, coercive domination.

Still another approach is offered by William Oddie, who comes closest to C.S. Lewis while taking the subject to a different level, also deserving quotation at some length (as he in turn quotes St. Paul's Letter to the Ephesians):

> Within such a dispensation, the authority normally exercised by men in society and within the family is transformed from the crude, coercive domination it can be in a fallen and disordered world, into an entirely new principle of human relationship: the authority of

the crucified Christ, now mediated by his Church, and within the Christian family particularly by the father. But no one is exempt from Christ's own subjection; we are to accept a kind of mutual subordination. The wife is subject to the husband; and the husband, if necessary, is to die for the wife. Ephesians 5.21ff, a key Pauline passage here, should be quoted at some length:

> Be subject to one another out of reverence for Christ. Wives, be subject to your husbands, as to the Lord. For the husband is the head of the wife as Christ is the head of the church, his body, and is himself its Saviour. As the church is subject to Christ, so let wives also be subject in everything to their husbands. Husbands, love your wives, as Christ loved the church, and gave himself up for her ... Even so husbands should love their wives as their own bodies. He who loves his wife loves himself. For no man ever hates his own flesh, but nourishes and cherishes it, as Christ does the church, because we are members of his body. "For this reason a man shall leave his father and mother and be joined to his wife, and the two shall become one flesh." This is a great mystery, and I take it to mean Christ and the church; however, let each one of you love his wife as himself, and let the wife see that she respects her husband.

Undoubtedly, this balance of love, obedience, obligation and sacrifice has not, within Christian civilization, always been observed. What is perhaps more striking, however, is how unquestioned in practice its acceptance has often been. The sinking of the *Titanic* remains as a kind of modern icon of the assertion of sacrificial and Christ-like male authority over the female within the Christian dispensation: perhaps some of the successful and powerful male "supremacists", who died so that their wives and daughters might live, remembered as they calmly awaited death, the prayer (based on Ephesians 5) which the parson had read at the marriage ceremonies of many of them: "Look mercifully upon these thy servants, that both this man may love his wife, according to thy word (as Christ did love his spouse the Church, who gave himself for it ...) and also that this woman may be loving and amiable, faithful and obedient to her husband ...."[29]

This is the message that postmoderns of both sexes are deaf, dumb, and blind to. Trying to force such human drama into the mold of "sex equality" is futile. It is reassuring that, despite the confusions of trying to balance a desired equality in marriage, Professor Meilaender still agrees with Karl Barth, "husband and wife submit not so much to each other as to the order itself – that is, to Christ." For here we find the verities of Christ's order grounded in the remarkable physical differences between the sexes.

As Harold O.J. Brown has reminded us, "The Psalmist asks, 'What is man, that Thou art mindful of him?' When we forget the divine Thou that is mindful of us, we soon cease to be mindful of ourselves." The main problem for feminists, with their fungible men and women; or for enthusiasts about "women's liberation" and "advances in the market place"; or Robert Hefner's "freedom, equality, and tolerance in plurality" arises from the delightful female voice and physiology, forever linking childhood with an intriguingly biological adulthood. They are more specialized and compatible, even authoritative in family milieus of relationships and caring, but tend to pall and wax screechy in male arenas where the male's more utilitarian voice and physiology can serve us best. Much like the baby and child, the female is smaller, cuter, cuddlier, "formed by nature for attentions," for a reason. As a baby's cry attracts a woman's instinctive protective reaction[30], so a woman's cry attracts a man's. That neighbors failed to act in defense of rape/murder victim Kitty Genovese was a sign of social dysfunction, not "a new idea for the good accommodating new interests."[31] Like it or not, a child is more attracted to the mother's smoother, rounder texture than to the father's hairier, harder body and deeper, gruffer voice, which in its turn, serves its own function as ultimate strength and authority in the family. Such parameters cannot be ignored even as women migrate to corridors of power.

Primarily suited to the family relationship, the distinctly feminine moral sense plays out its role of healing, nurturing, caring and sheltering, while the father takes care of his extra-marital chores. Because of their ultimate, ineluctable destiny as the core of families – the fountainhead of humanity, much like prehistoric Lucy who with child and a male escort trod through ancient mud beds – women are accorded high esteem and power in intimacy and personal relationships. However, it is misguided to assume that such a role plays naturally out into the public arena – where intimacy and nurturing give way to objective judgment, honesty, rules and brute force. Ancient Lucy was not a tribal leader.

The thought of those like Jutta Burggraf who argue, "equal obligation and responsibility of man and woman fully justify the woman's access to the public domain"[32] can only be considered bizarre. It defies reason to contend that two sexes of such unequal, dissimilar natures can be so carelessly rendered fungible, all while fellow theologians take great pains to offer carefully crafted, nuanced versions of distinct sex roles and functions in the eyes of the Church.[33] Frau Burggraf seems to be writing in a promotional vein rather than for pastoral edification.

In realizing, as above, that marriage is such a difficult challenge despite being central to civilization, we learn two things: (1) We need far more sensible public policy in support of marriage than presently enacted. (2) We should dispel all notions that women are readily adapted to, and that men and women naturally complement each other in the public domain. From the evidence, the very opposite is true.

We need now to consider how biblical authority sheds light on our subject, an area that materialists and individualists sadly neglect.

V

Biblical Paradigms, or How Christianity Deals With the Human Sexes

Men are too well inclined to sit at home, instead of stirring themselves to inquire whether a revelation has been given; they expect its evidences to come to them without their trouble; they act not as suppliants but as judges.... No inquiry comes to good which is not conducted under a deep sense of responsibility, and of the issues depending upon its determination.

John Henry Newman[1]

The very fact, I should say, that there is a Creator, and a hidden one, powerfully bears you on and sets you down at the very threshold of revelation, and leaves you there looking up earnestly for Divine tokens that a revelation has been made.

John Henry Newman[2]

1.

Theologians and clerics offer excellent treatises on the subject of men and women as servants of God. Full ministerial treatment is not my aim – but more that of a concerned layman who appreciates the value of religion and the Church. That some clerics have chosen to accept women as priests obviously conflicts with the God-given male potential for authority and the God-given female propensity for nurturing. In contrast, the Catholic Church chooses to ground her teachings in inspired dogma on Mary and other long-held precepts. I include a more earthly approach grounded also in common sense, as I believe Aquinas would approve. It seems inconceivable, for instance (as mentioned above), that any human organization can ignore the human voice and stature, of which the male's is so obviously best suited to duties of public authority and the female's for intimacy and caring. This is why my treatment has led, if only cursively, through considerations of art, science, music, poetry, science and civil order. In ancient times, in the time of Jesus, in the middle ages, in the voyages of discovery, the conquests, the time of empires, such verities were taken for granted. That we must now review their former natural acceptance in order to clear our present confusions is remarkable but necessary, much like one's returning from foreign lands to learn again one's native tongue.

In discussing the role of religion in our historical arrangements between men and women one should start with further examples from the Bible, since Judeo-Christianity and its powerful, majestic prose has played a crucial role. Usually this is where people do start, for, as Wilfred M. McClay has urged, "The fact remains that our civilization's most effective pattern for ordered liberty, whether in matters religious or matters civil and constitutional, rests upon the constraining force of foundational texts, such as the bible and the Constitution…. it is infinitely…. naive to think that a liberal and democratic order can continue to exist as such when its laws become unintelligible to its citizens…. and the moral or religious principles upon which their constraining function depends are left without the support of generally accessible and authoritative texts."³ We have already mentioned some words of Genesis as they applied to previous chapters. Let us look at other references, without trying to include all:

> As for my people children are their oppressors, and women rule over them. O my people, they which lead thee cause thee to err, and destroy the way of thy paths. Isaiah, 3:12.
>
> Let your women keep silence in the churches: for it is not permitted unto them to speak; but they are commanded to be under obedience, as also saith the law. I Corinthians 14:34.
>
> But I suffer not a woman to teach, nor to usurp authority over the man, but to be in silence…. Notwithstanding she shall be saved in childbearing, if they continue in faith and charity and holiness with sobriety. I Timothy 2:12, 15.
>
> Likewise, ye wives, be in subjection to your own husbands; that, if any obey not the word, they also may without the word be won by the conversation of the wives; … Likewise, ye husbands, dwell with them according to knowledge, giving honour unto the wife, as unto the weaker vessel, and as being heirs together of the grace of life; that your prayers be not hindered. Finally, be ye all of one mind, having compassion one of another, love as brethren, be pitiful, be courteous: I Peter 3:1, 7, 8.
>
> But speak thou the things which become sound doctrine: That the aged men be sober, grave, temperate, sound in faith, in charity, in patience. The aged women likewise, that they be in behaviour as becometh holiness, not false accusers, not given to much wine, teachers of good things; That they may teach the young women to be sober, to love their husbands, to love their children, To be discreet, chaste, keepers at home, good, obedient to their own husbands, that the word of God be not blasphemed. Young men likewise exhort to be sober minded. Titus 2:1-6.

Such colorful, direct language takes us back 2000+ years to a time of great import and charming lessons for our more advanced, luxurious age. One detects a distinct drift toward restraining the ladies even then in their acknowledged natural powers. At the same time, in keeping with the age-old need to shape and mold the human male for his role in life, the men warranted admonishment and instruction to pursue manly ways, patterns that one suspects were better understood and appreciated in those ancient times. Despite many modern voices, whether they can be safely ignored in our times seems dubious.

One can speculate why Saint Paul or Saint Peter felt the need for such intriguingly quaint patterns of living for men and women – rules of social etiquette – for those aspiring to the teachings of Jesus Christ, but reflection suggests that the word of God, properly understood, is indeed all-encompassing. Congregations, after all, hope for guidance in worldly matters as well as spiritual, since, as Cardinal Newman often made clear, the two are quite properly related. That modern autonomous man has tended to separate the spiritual from worldly desires is not a sign of improvement. While many now fault certain biblical passages on their face, these nevertheless offer much wisdom. Their message need not be "subjugation," "subordination," or "demeaning," as much as "responsibility," "caring," "relationship," "service to God," and other aspects which, at least the female moral sense is reputed to favor. That modernists often miss the implications of these teachings in Genesis or Saint Paul's letters is more a sign of obtuseness than wisdom.

And there are more examples worth considering, laying a basis as it were:

> This is a true saying, If a man desire the office of a bishop, he desireth good work. A bishop then must be blameless, the husband of one good wife, vigilant, sober, of good behaviour, given to hospitality, apt to teach; Not given to wine, no striker, not greedy of filthy lucre; but patient, not a brawler, not covetous; One that ruleth his own house, having his children in subjection with all gravity; For if a man know not how to rule his own house, how shall he take care of the church of God?... Let the deacons be the husbands of one wife, ruling their children and

their own houses well. I Timothy 3:1-5, 12.

Children, obey your parents in the Lord: for this is right. Honour thy father and mother; which is the first commandment with promise; That it may be well with thee, and thou mayest live long on this earth. And, ye fathers, provoke not your children to wrath: but bring them up in the nurture and admonition of the Lord. Ephesians 6;1-4.a

It is better to dwell in the wilderness, than with a contentious and angry woman. Proverbs 21:19.

A prudent man foreseeth the evil, and hideth himself: but the simple pass on, and are punished. By humility and the fear of the Lord are riches, and honour, and life. Thorns and snares are the way of the froward: he that doth keep his soul shall be far from them. Proverbs 22:3-6.1

Give not thy strength unto women, nor thy ways to that which destroyeth kings.... Proverbs 31:3.

Such excerpts alone convey a sense that, for reasons other than subjugation of women and more of preserving God's people, followers of Christ adhered to customary standards of the day in a time much given to conflict, poverty and – yes, sinful ways. Demands on women were no more strenuous than those on men. A distinct ordering of sex roles was felt appropriate for realization of civil harmony. It is regrettable that modern (simpler?) descendants of these people of long ago have succumbed to "contentious and angry" distortions of historical accuracy giving rise to charges of "systematic exclusion" of women. It is also doubtful that women living during Christ's lifetime considered themselves shortchanged in any way, so as to crave "emancipation" or "liberation." One doubts that savants in those virile times had the leisure to construct querulous systems of government based on elusive abstractions of "equality." Yes, slavery and other peculiar practices were accepted and are no longer, but such unrelated change cannot substantiate a newfound androgyny for the sexes.

For now and always, the above examples will speak for themselves. It is interesting, however, to see the various ways that biblical scholars apply such precepts to the role of modern men and women. We have already looked at the Meilaender-Thielicke-Lewis treatment of marriage, probably the most frequent subject for discussion. Psychiatrists, of course, will tell us of many types of marriage, some far from Saint Paul's version, and more's the pity. The fact that material wealth has multiplied the risks and variety of orderly marriages should remind us of the continual need for conscientious effort and understanding of marriage's essential meaning and value. As Cardinal Newman would say, it requires work to succeed.

To that end, one sympathizes with Newman's struggle against both liberalism and Anglican views on the Catholic Church. Space precludes a full-scale justification for Catholic orthodoxy here. For this, one must turn to the *Catechism of the Catholic Church*, apostolic letters, von Balthasar, von Hildebrand, G.K. Chesterton and many others, as well as to Pope John Paul and Chapter VI below. It does seem true, however, that the Catholic Church appears to be the single-most, staunchest defender of right order in the Western world, which in itself says much for the power of Jesus Christ and His Church. (The Church's coping with claims of "inevitable change," abortion and celibacy are beyond our scope here.) I am mainly concerned with the Church's teachings on women, as, for instance, the issues of female priests, Mariology and feminism.

2.

An example of disoriented Anglican or Protestant thinking on such matters is offered by Britisher Andrew Brown, "Because Pentecostals make their own clergy and are radically decentralized, they respond to a market economy in religion much better than the command structure of an established church can do. Though they seem extremely patriarchal, they offer women better treatment and, often, more responsibility than can the Catholic Church, which is writhing in knots around feminism like a worm impaled on a hook."[4] Mr. Brown's preference for "democracy" in the Church shows the battle lines clearly. He would take an apple from a modern Eve in a whisk, ready for any change regardless of the consequences, oblivious to the meaning of God and nature. For him, life is mostly going with the tide and avoiding conflict on matters of lasting value. Some Anglo-Americans harbor an aversion to permanencies no matter how vital, preferring instead more facile adaptations to liberalism's demands, e.g., Tony Blair's "New Way" or John Kennedy's "New Society."

Besides Mr. Brown, one reads David Barrett's review of a book by Peter Stanford attempting to prove the existence of a 9th-century she-Pope Joan. Despite inconsistencies in the story, Mr. Barrett is a fan: "Ever since reading Lawrence Durrell's *Pope Joan* over a decade ago, I've wanted to believe, on the grounds that even if the story isn't true, it's so wonderful that it ought to be."[5] Although he finds insufficient proof, in an odd lapse of rationality, he amuses himself with the idea anyway: "Could a woman have reached the highest office in male-dominated Christendom?... for a Church which still denies women the right to be priests or even the wives of priests, Stanford (largely quoting Joan Morris) confirms that in the early Middle Ages several women held quasi-episcopal powers as abbesses, and going back to the very earliest centuries of Christianity, that there were even women priests. Whether Pope Joan lived or not, Stanford, who is something of a radical Catholic, is clearly suggesting that she has a message for today's ultra-conservative Pope."

Here is a prime cut of postmodern male befuddledness. Since God is far from dependent on human inventiveness, one surmises that Barrett is a non-scholar. For the new man – a puppet for feminism – anything goes to please the ladies or smear the Church. But Barrett's and Stanford's airy visions have been thoroughly debunked, so their views are worthless. (See Eamon Duffy, discussing the same book below, Chap. VII; also Aimé Georges Martimort's *Deaconesses*, Chapter 6.)

Such traces of the influence of feminism are also seen in the thought of Martha Nussbaum, of whom Ralph McInerny writes, "She seeks to enlist the Pope in her neopagan vision of education aimed at world citizenship."[6] Ms. Nussbaum apparently outstrips Eve, Brown, Barrett and Stanford in finding that Notre Dame University is behind the times in adhering to Catholic precepts. Oblivious to the great history of universities in general and Notre Dame in particular, she would rather the University admit to being a product of modern liberalism and accommodate the various destructive aberrancies plaguing society today such as homosexuality, multiculturalism, relativism, nihilism, even while adopting the appearance of opposing them. As McInerny tells us, Nussbaum seeks to apply to Notre Dame "the liberal ideals that obtain in the wider society," or "to replace an outlook and principles devised over centuries with the latter-day liberalism that presides over the chaos around us." One cannot ignore the womanliness of Nussbaum's approach to so profound a topic, reducing great history to the persons and relationships of her moment. It is lax, unconditional, maternal tolerance without the moderating force of paternal conditional love. At least the Catholic Church endeavors to preserve our ties to enduring, proven precepts, realizing, as Nussbaum does not, that we are not self-anointed.

3.

It is again indicative of the eternal irony of the subject, however, that even the Catholic Church does not enjoy full accord on matters involving men and women. For instance, in November, 1988, Richard John Neuhaus briefly discusses Pope John Paul II's 1988 response to the Roman Catholic bishops of the United States in which the Pope criticizes the bishops' first draft of a "pastoral response to women's concerns for church and society."[7] While Neuhaus suggests that the draft "bore all the markings of having been written in the woodshed where Catholic feminists spanked committee members for the church's 'sin' of sexism," both Neuhaus and the Pope also show signs of being spanked. Neuhaus tells us that the Pope "agrees with the Second Vatican Council that the hour has come 'when the vocation of women is being acknowledged in its fullness, the hour in which women acquire in the world an influence, an effect, and a power never hitherto achieved.' The Biblical teaching of mutual service between man and woman, he writes, 'must gradually establish itself in hearts, consciences, behaviors, and customs.' This has not yet happened. Not by a long shot." One suspects that such hopeful visions of powerful females is more for the benefit of Neuhaus's female readers than the pursuit of truth.

Neuhaus quotes the Pope as saying, "True Christian feminism" must be grounded in "the immutable basis of Christian anthropology," despite the glaring oxymoron, as a thorough study of the feminist literature should show (e.g., see Levin, et al, mentioned above). A recurring theme of the present book is that "feminism" (whatever its guise) is a separatist ideology of either resentment or gynocentricism incompatible with history, human nature, Christian teaching or anthropology. When one considers the conscientious efforts of church spokesmen through the ages to deal with the always challenging subject of men, women, their *mutual* service in Christ as well as more mundane daily relationships, the fact that the Pope and Neuhaus feel that a separate, distinct canon on women is appropriate seems incomprehensible. In fact, at least from my reading of the Pope's eventual apostolic letter, "On the Dignity and Vocation of Women," there appears no such statement, so perhaps the Pope had second thoughts.[8]

While the Pope apparently agrees with the bishops in anticipating "power never hitherto achieved" for women, he also suggests, according to Neuhaus, that the Church must resist "criteria of understanding and judgment that do not pertain to her nature" and he rightly adheres to the reality of manhood and womanhood, as well as the principle of a male priesthood. Put more basically, however, once we grasp that "power" and leadership have always been quite naturally a male function and not female, how can the Pope both "deplore the masculinization" of women as denying the "originality" of the feminine and at the same time welcome a new era of "power" for women without contradicting himself? Also, one might ask, how will women achieve any more "influence" or "power" in the world than they already have, and have had for millennia? In other words, after thousands of years of generally acceptable peace under a patriarchy, what will suddenly give more "power" to women, and why, or for what general improvement? Is the natural function of sexual dimorphism so easily shed?

Pope John Paul obviously has given the subject of men and women much thought, probably under the pressure of demands for greater female power in the Church hierarchy. As if to rebut Andrew Brown's above claim that other churches "offer better treatment than can the Catholic Church," he offers uplifting language and ingenious prose (often suspiciously abstract) to express his insights on women's quite elevated calling without resorting to vernacular versions of "submission," "master," "head," and the like. Perhaps this is the accepted religious thought these days instead of the more Pauline directness. However, the Pope does attempt to accommodate contemporary ideas of "non-discrimination" and "equal rights," which, as always, leaves more doubt than certainty due to the essential abstractness and banality of such terms. To my knowledge, Jesus Christ didn't teach them during his ministry.

In the end, however, to his credit, the Pope never strays far and always returns to woman's femininity, gift of love, responsibility for the young, and receptivity, and takes great care to emphasize the contributions of brave and loyal women over the centuries. What people like Andrew Brown expect beyond this, while still maintaining the integrity of the word of the Lord Almighty, is a mystery if not rank Philistinism.

Furthermore, while Pope John Paul is more gentle with Eve than the present writer, he echoes the underlying tension characterizing human existence when he writes, "Is not the Bible trying to tell us that it is in the 'woman' – Eve – Mary – that history witnesses a dramatic struggle for every human being, the struggle for his or her fundamental 'yes' or 'no' to God and God's eternal plan for humanity?"[9] And the Pope's passing reference to *incidental* "exploitation" is not the same as Neuhaus's implication of a general exploitation of women by men.[10]

Given their unease at more commonplace utterances on men and women, it is not surprising that both Neuhaus and the Pope (like Meilaender and Thielicke) in somewhat differing degrees, have a problem with Saint Paul's Ephesian teachings on the implied "subordination" of the wife to the husband's natural "headship," which, despite their fears, is actually quite appropriately inspired "to serve Christ." Instead of adhering to this commendable formulation, they both opt to focus on the Christ-inspired husband's "self-surrendering service," and the husband and wife's "equality not in the rights they claim against one another but in the service they render one another." But what do they find unholy in timely spousal "subordination" to serve God, or Saint Paul's idea of husbandly "headship"? Why get stuck on the tar baby of "equality"? The risk in God's having a more dominant male and a smaller, more attractive yet quite expressive female is bound to be substantial, yet it appears basic to God's arrangement and cannot be side-stepped by delicate flapdoodle to make it more palatable to the fair sex. Males must be given the responsibility of being gentlemanly and it is doubtful there can be such a thing as male responsibility without taking the bold step of accepting their Christly role of service in *headship*. Criminal laws protect against the "brutalization" which most people harp on when they discuss this subject. In the end, God knows best in relying on the human male to measure up to his design. (Most honest women sense this in their sons.)

There is something powerful yet inherently receptive in the human female that the Pope expresses better than the bishops or the feminists, yet he disappoints by apparently, and inconsistently, endorsing the bishops' rather un-Pauline call for "more power for women." (Of course, in merely quoting the bishops, he may not have actually intended such an endorsement.) Again, one cannot honestly overlook the immense potency and influence that women have wielded all along, as Samuel Johnson saw and one suspects the Pope sees also. As John Paul probes the mystery of womanhood,

> The woman's motherhood in the period between the baby's conception and birth is a biological and psychological process which is better understood in our days than in the past, and is the subject of many detailed studies. Scientific analysis fully confirms that the very physical constitution of women is

naturally disposed to motherhood – conception, pregnancy and giving birth – which is the consequence of the marriage union with the man. At the same time, this also corresponds to the psycho-physical structure of women. What the different branches of science have to say on this subject is important and useful, provided that it is not limited to an exclusively bio-physiological interpretation of women and of motherhood. Such a *"restricted" picture* would go hand in hand with a materialistic concept of the human being and of the world. In such a case, what is truly essential would unfortunately be lost. Motherhood as a fact and phenomenon is fully explained on the basis of the truth about the person. Motherhood *is linked to the personal structure of the woman and to the personal dimension of the gift*: "I have brought a man into being with the help of the Lord" (Gen 4:1). The Creator grants the parents the gift of a child. On the woman's part, this fact is linked in a special way to "a sincere gift of self." Mary's words at the Annunciation – "let it be according to your word" – signify the woman's readiness for the gift of self and her readiness to accept a new life.

The eternal mystery of generation, which is in God himself, the one and triune God (cf. Eph 3:14-15), is reflected in the woman's motherhood and in the man's fatherhood.[11]

Such lucid explication of a central reality is offered by others like Levin, Gilder, Davidson, and Alexis Carrel, although with a perspective more bio-sociological. That the Pope engages it even with a theological twist shows its importance. As Walter Kasper writes of the Church's struggle to deal with feminism, "Ultimately, behind the problems of ecclesiology, lie the problems of anthropology, a crisis and a radical change in women's self-understanding, or rather in the self-understanding of man and woman."[12] Unfortunately, most fail to grasp that the "crisis" is more an elusive mirage than a true anthropological change. The true crisis lies in society's attention level. The idea of "new power for women" should have been laughed out of existence, or finessed by just saying No! As Nicholas Davidson puts it so well,

> In addition, the role of men in the feminist revolution is often over-

looked. Without the promotion of unisexism by thinkers like Franz Boas and Richard Hofstadter and the hippie rejection of traditional masculinity, feminist arguments would have found singularly little purchase in American thought. Feminists were often simply acting out a program already laid out for them by John Stuart Mill, Friedrich Engels, or their own fathers, husbands, or lovers....

Many men feel that to critically evaluate feminist positions would be a bit ungallant. Misplaced chivalry is a major reason there has been so little critical discussion of feminism outside the movement itself. The Feminist Era witnessed a veritable abdication of masculine responsibility for gender issues.[13]

Women are not blind to the inherent fallacy in "women's emancipation." Although for many it is merely a path to a supposedly easier life, some are more objective than others, as for instance, Florence King, a gifted wordsmith, who tells of an advanceman for our ills, Henry Ward Beecher, an 18th-century champion of women's rights who called God "Mother": "Rejecting harsh Calvinism, he concocted a 'feminized, romantic conception' of religion as a warm, indiscriminate bath of love. To be truly religious, he told his flock, you must sin, since Christ can't very well save you if you don't."[14] Here, Ms. King is reviewing a book on Victoria Woodhull that apparently offers her life as a stellar exemplar of womanhood, to which Ms. King retorts, "Sorry, but Victoria Woodhull is eccentric and aberrant any way you slice her." From King's treatment, one gathers that Beecher and Woodhull were an early "weak man and disorderly woman."

While reinforcing the Pope's acceptance of "the personal structure of the woman," Barbara Albrecht writes of the ways in which a woman is different. Her "being-in-relation" is well known by women (e.g., Margaret Mead and George Eliot) although for some reason now camouflaged:

.... real, earthbound, directed toward persons, above all, toward children. For she was created as "the mother of all the living" (Gen. 3:20) to be a physical as well as a psychological and spiritual mother, not an autonomous virgin, as Catherina Halkes wishes us to believe.... This quality endows woman with a particular intensity vis-à-vis life and human beings; it makes her "intact" as a person and able "to participate constructively in providing a future." She goes about this not so much by aggressively shaping things, discovery, by research and control of the world, not by constant mobility, often at the price of flexibility. For women are as a rule more tied to a home, to a permanent place to which they can belong – be it family, school, a hospital, a firm, a parish, or a convent. On the whole it can be said that women, particularly, suffer from any form of relocation.[15]

This being so, it becomes even more incomprehensible why she, the Pope, and other women repeat the familiar call for more public power for women, which is totally inconsistent with the above analysis. However, and more to the point, Ms. Albrecht has this to say, reinforcing other thinkers mentioned herein:

Equality of personhood in the order of creation and redemption, however, does not mean equality and uniformity in ones human existence. Quite the contrary, God, in his limitless imagination, created two models, two archetypes of man, distinct in every cell – "to the roots of the hair" – distinct in anatomy and in the blood corpuscles as well as in psychological and mental constitution. Although men and women are equal in their immediacy toward God, they are distinct and not interchangeable on the plane of their human nature.

.... The Swiss scientist N. Bischof comes closest to my point of view. During a conference of the Catholic Academy in Bavaria entitled "Emancipation of Woman: Between Biology and Ideology" (1978), he drew attention to the sexual differentiation on the plane of the gamete. "The selection of sperm cells by mobility" (to travel the longer distance) and the egg cell by vitality at the price of immobility ... determines that the egg-producing organism becomes the receiving one. This, in all likelihood, is the most momentous factor in the genesis of sex differentiation", the determining clue to all differentiation within that which men and women possess in common.[16]

Thus, "equality" talk is futile. By itself "mutual subjection in

Christ" is a workable formulation extraneous to any sterile "equality," and to contend that "the equality of woman and man is not in the rights they claim against one another but in the service they render to one another" is stretching it.

Returning to Pastor Neuhaus, his misinterpretation of the Pope's message in an attempt to link history's treatment of women with the institution of slavery is surprisingly clumsy, especially when one considers the flourishing of women throughout history as opposed to the unfortunate treatment of most slaves. The Pope's comment seems more to address the slowness of man's development through the ages than to imply the specific comparison Neuhaus claims.

The Pope's treatment suffers from inconsistencies such as regretting "serious social discrimination" of the past, while himself exercising excruciating social discrimination in the present. Serious social discrimination, as with St. Paul, is his job! Whether the God-ordained natural human practice of "discrimination" is "for" or "against" is victimology's main weakness, and susceptible more of demagoguery than of truth. Also, the Pope misses the incongruity of professional women and all it entails[17] alongside a woman's dignity in her more natural vocation: *"the dignity of women is measured by the order of love,* which is essentially the order of justice and charity."[18] This renders the Pope's approach somewhat strained – very careful and commiserative with women, (although not as obsequious as many who over-exalt women not as Mead's "wives and mothers" but as somewhat mannish female patriarchs!), yet all in all, a superb treatment of the subject. He attempts to transcend popular misconceptions in order to establish a higher, more profound significance to worldly realities. What he portrays in this apostolic letter is a theological version of the Victorian ideal of the Lady and the Gentleman, as well as a drastically revised Pauline discourse, both of which need reviving.

4.

In all fairness to the Pope, we shall consider examples below of the feminist litany he has to deal with. Many women, even while abjuring feminism still emulate its disruptive teachings. Like liberalism, as Flannery O'Connor might have said, feminism is a bad seed, capable of influencing many well-intentioned but ill-informed people of both sexes. For instance, it has been popular to dwell on the aspect of male violence as though a defining issue in the discussion when in fact the issue of violence not only cuts both ways but also highlights the benefits of a well-functioning patriarchy in which violence is atypical: Families without fathers tend to rear the more violent males, a fact which should forever convince us to maintain families and rear ladies and gentlemen rather than "powerful women," which gets us back to the Pope's teaching and to mutual service in Christ. As Manfred Hauke expresses it albeit with his own lapse into "oppression" rubric, "A true note is struck by those criticisms that are directed against an aggressive, hyper-masculine desire to dominate, which finds one outlet in destruction of the environment. There are also real links here to the oppression of women. But even feminists such as [Catharina] Halkes, must admit that this mentality is a product of the modern age, which has thereby broken with the ancient and medieval view of creation."[19]

However, despite such an overview, it's quite popular to adopt the more narrow-minded approach attributed by Nancy M. Cross to Edith Stein, that "the relationship of the sexes since the Fall has become a brutal relationship of master and slave."[20] As with others like Allan Bloom and Father Neuhaus, this tendency to use terms of "victimization," "slavery," "exploitation," and "objects" (even while decrying the feminism responsible for such aspersions), seems to be referring to various third-world customs or to certain American Indian tribes' former treatment of women rather than to general Western society. We cannot emphasize too much what William Oddie points out in the following passage:

> The sense of grievance which underlies the assumptions of the 'Women's Movement', both inside and outside the Church, becomes in the end one of the most fascinating and enigmatic characteristics of feminist utterance. It is not so much that the resentment exists (though it can be of a virulence quite startling to men and women unfamiliar with hard-core feminist literature). It is rather that feeling aggrieved appears to be itself a necessary primary objective. It is a state of mind, almost a spiritual condition, which seems at times not so much a natural reaction to perceived injustice as itself a means of perception, a kind of lens through which familiar landmarks can take on horrid and undreamed-of shapes. "How", asks Paula Fredrikson Landes, "could feminist consciousness have developed without anger? ….
>
> Many feminists, of course, are quite well aware of this. They simply see it as further evidence for their claim that women have been degraded to the point where they are no longer able to see how degraded they are.[21]

Perhaps this is the source of "victimology" talk. Feminism has managed to subvert our rhetoric. To help recover our integrity, Manfred Hauke urges women to use caution: "What is required today is not to run breathlessly after the banners of androgynous or gynocentric feminism. The real need is a new self-assurance on the part of women, which should take its direction from Mary. According to Vatican II, Mary concentrates 'the greatest mysteries of the faith in herself and radiates them out again'."[22] Among women, Midge Decter seems to be especially aware of Mary's way, in contrast to the "libbers – who were militant, angry, and in the grip of a curious but lethal combination of galloping self-pity and driving ambition."[23] Ms. Decter has been a pioneer in the fight against feminism starting with her essay, *The New Chastity and Other Arguments Against Women's*

Liberation, in which she suggests that feminists are merely those who, in times of plenty, tend to fear adult womanhood.

And, lest we reject entirely the entire Anglican community as androgynous aspostates, it would be fitting to consider the story of the Reverend John Pelling of the Church of England, as told by Byron Rogers in *The Sunday Telegraph*[24]:

> Mr. Pelling, like many Anglican priests, is opposed to the ordination of women. But while others have rushed into print (in particular, the letters columns of the broadsheets), or even left the Church, he has chosen a unique form of protest. …. (He) has turned to paint and to canvases of a size rarely seen in England since B.R. Haydon in the early 19th century. …. His paintings are part abstract, but abstraction goes out the window when he gets among women. Great thighs kneel, the outline of smooth muscles …
>
> The Intruder was bought by the great Italian actor Vittorio de Sica. Other people who have bought his work include Prince Rainier and the Kuwaiti royal family, so John Pelling – one of whose nudes the *Sunday Mirror* beadily calculated even 30 years ago fetch almost three times his monthly stipend – now lives in some style in a house in Chelsea. At 67 he is retired from the ministry, a distinguished white-haired figure in denim walking through corridors where nudes hang next to the odd crucifix … He works in a garden studio, his wife in one at the top of the house. … "I don't think there's necessarily anything sexy about using a nude figure to carry an idea through, whether it is just rage or happiness. It is just more expressive than a bowl of flowers….
>
> "I met one of these women-as-priests, as I call them, and she said, 'Well, I *was* a Deacon for 10 years…' and it was as though she thought she deserved promotion. What would she be after now? A bishopric? Oh dear… " I love women, that's my trouble, that's probably why I feel so strongly about this. Feminists don't see the woman's role as being any different from that of a man. But it is, that's why they're so wonderful, and that's why I painted them over and over again.… " The bones of a bishop turn in his tomb, church towers topple and candles gutter as women, the whacking big women with ginormous bazoomas, celebrate the mysteries of the church. Over these he has written in capital letters: *DIES MAGNA ET AMARA*. Oh great and bit-

ter day. "There will be a lot of trouble over this," said the Rev. Pelling happily.

It would seem, after all, Thank God, that there is indeed a backlash. The female ear is very selective, blocking out realities involving other than ones own activities, friends, family and children. And rightly so. As Mr. Pelling might agree, that is why they can be wonderful, especially if a man is fortunate enough to come within their cozy ambit, the focus of their eyes and tongues, perhaps as Dante longed for Beatrice's. In its own way, the Rev. Pelling's artistic expression says it all – amplifying the use of art to convey a message long ignored by political spokesmen for the West. What kind of pastoral leadership, or any other kind of leadership, can one expect from a person, male or female, who wears blinders to woman's basic sexual unsuitability for leadership over males? Or the incongruity of "whacking big women with ginormous bazoomas" ponderously pirouetting and dictating their way through the corridors of power, at Captain's desks or judges' and senators' benches.

*　*　*

Considering specific examples as we go along, there is the strange case of Britain's First Lady, Cherie Blair, who caused an uproar for dealing through a con man to obtain a Bristol flat. The stress and strain was devastating – a woman beyond her depth – with the "bloom off the flower." And yet she occupies a seat on the British bench, with gray wig and all. A soft-hearted Germaine Greer gets to the jugular wondering, "if this wild-eyed woman with the scarlet mouth racing all over her face is quite sane…. (wearing) a face we had never seen before, sweetened and saddened, with pearly pink lipstick and lilac eye-shadow mask…"[25] In her hatchet job, Ms. Greer claims that Cherie (with four children) should have her career without the inconvenience of having to be a wife to a Prime Minister and putting up with all this guff. A high-profile feminist, Greer is a prime example of disorderly womanhood.

In any event, Ms. Blair reminds us that a dialectic of "equalizing power" is vacuous. Instead, there are different kinds of power, male and female. It is not so much a question of women acquiring more influence as it is their being true to the nature they now own, and men to theirs, while both do a better job of understanding and respecting *each other's*. For, in reality, men and women are going to enjoy their respective natures for a long time to come, inseparably configured, like the yin and the yang, and it were best we got used to it. As for additional Church teachings on women and the Church, we shall resort to the next chapter.

VI

Further Catholic Thought

As I write, events are unfolding which may take the Episcopal Church of the USA down the path it has chosen beyond the point of no return. For others, it is still not too late to draw back.
                                    William Oddie (1984)[1]

The Virgin Mary cooperated through free faith and obedience in human salvation. She uttered her "yes" in the name of all human nature. By her obedience she became the new Eve, mother of the living.
                    Catechism of the Catholic Church, ¶ 511

1. GOD OR GODDESSES?

Since the Catholic Church has been a staunch defender against many aspects of feminism, we shall probe her thought in greater depth. It appears well reinforced in the Vatican and several other thinkers but, as seen above, shows signs of wavering in the ranks of American bishops and lesser battalions. No less than Anglican Reverend Pelling in his artistic voice, writers for the Catholic Church have contributed erudite, compelling writings overriding the claims of the regiment of feminists. While we cannot cover their full thought here, pertinent treatises convey their message. To start with, Manfred Hauke's excellent 1993 study, *God or Goddesses?* adheres to a judicious approach and thoroughly dissects "feminist theology," analyzing the radical ideas of worldwide feminist stalwarts like Mary Daly, Rosemary Radford Ruether, Christa Mulack, Elisabeth Moltmann-Wendel, Catharina Halkes, Hedwig Meyer-Wilmes, and others.

Hauke, a German Catholic priest and theology professor, summarizes, "Along with all the concern for the role of women in the Church, we should not forget, of course, that spiritual care aimed specifically at men also deserves our attention.... At the world synod of bishops on the laity in 1987, after the topic of women had been extensively illuminated, Thomas Forrest – one of the leading personalities in the charismatic revival movement.... spoke up, warning of the dangers of exclusive obsession with women's issues. Women often played so large a role in the congregations that priests no longer knew how to approach pastoral dialogue with men.... It is necessary, then, to avoid one-sided focus on the topic of women. The kind of responsibility specific to men is also important, especially that of a head of a family, in which self-confident authority is combined with devoted solicitude. Neither a 'feminization' nor a 'masculinization' is the need of the moment but, rather, the distinctively contoured natures of both man and woman in mutual support."[2]

For this reason alone, one questions Dr. Hauke's (and possibly the Pope's) acceptance of Barbara Albrecht's call for "full-time service by women in the Church," which by now we should recognize as an invitation to another Trojan Horse similar to that of the Episcopal Church as well as the professions, the military, sports, politics and other areas. As William Oddie points out with regards to American Bishop Robert Terwilliger's warning of the dangers of the Episcopal Church's ordination of women in 1976, "Twelve years later, his words have come true: the ordination of women priests in ECUSA has brought about, not a reform of the ordained ministry but an ecclesiological and theological revolution."³ He further quotes Bishop John Shelby Spong, who supported the change, as now saying that it "is too shallow a judgment" to "see the women's movement ... primarily in terms of justice and human rights.... (Instead) it is a fundamental break with history and tradition ... much of what we Christians think of as crucial to the life of the Church will not survive the revolution."

While Hauke and Albrecht aren't advocating ordination of women, they agree that "spiritual care is not a matter for priests alone," with implications for an expanded official role for women unless we consider "spiritual care" here as nurturing, succoring, hospitality, and not the pastorate. While they may not increase the role of women in the hierarchy, like the ECUSA they are flirting with it. Instead, they should remain steadfast with the model of Mary, whose role was hardly so bureaucratized as a "responsible coworker in the area of spiritual care" as much as a courageous, receptive, accepting source of inspiration and strength for congregation members. As Hauke says, "there is a superabundance of tasks for women in the Church ... that require a large and varied wealth of talents and charisms" but competing with or acting as mere adjuncts to priests is not one of them.

Albrecht's rather dictatorial view that larger roles "would have to be accepted by the Church" does not square with Marian service in Christ, any more than Albrecht's authoritarian promotion of areas of "appropriate competence, on the basis of baptism and confirmation" for women to assume more priestly duties. The Church should ask, "Why should increased roles be accepted?" "What are the benefits of women's more active roles in the hierarchy?" It is analogous to the field of medicine, where nurses are needed as much as doctors. (From reports, expanded women's roles in male occupations such as doctors are inevitably resulting in a shortage of nurses. And, like it or not, females are more naturally, ideally adapted to nursing than males.) As increasing examples like Cherie Blair show, one cannot mandate "expanded roles" per se without thought for physiology, any more than one would mandate that the Corps must accept expanded roles for women marines. (The as yet incomplete file on PFC Jessica Lynch seems to bear this out. Her ordeal in Iraq was such as to cause amnesia, hardly a selling point for more female soldiers near the front lines.) Feminism has forced too much artificiality down our throats, even in the Church.

As Hauke notes, traditional theology is basically a study of the word of God, while *feminist theology is the work of human beings* – not at all reassuring. "Above all, it must not be forgotten when evaluating feminist theology that its basic anthropological starting point, which influences its stand on all more philosophical issues, is irreconcilable with Christian faith. God did not create humans as androgynous, or the male as an imperfect satellite-being to the female, but as man and woman, equal in value but not in kind."[4] "Like liberation theology, theological feminism understands itself as 'contextual theology', that is, theology that is to be developed in relation to a quite specific kind of social context. ... (Catherina) Halkes formulates this perspectival aspect even more clearly: 'You, rebellious women, are the theme and subjects of this theology, and you make your relationship with God and the divine the central object of your theology.'"[5]

Hauke points out incisively that the "The universal Church aims to include all men of all times and cultures. Such an all-embracing ('catholic') communion is grounded in a mission that goes much deeper than any grouping of people based merely on shared sympathies. Will the often contradictory feminist circles, with their group-centered orientations, be able to measure up to that?"[6] While Barbara Albrecht has criticized feminist theology[7], in her demands for greater service for women in the pastoral Church she nevertheless shows its influence.

Hauke distinguishes between male and female administering when he tells of the American Anne Carr, who "is initially critical of the androgyne model: 'While it is an attractive vision, it has problems as well, for it ignores the importance of human embodiment….' But she then goes on to align herself with a report issued by the Catholic Theological Society of America in 1978. This asserts that even though one-nature or single anthropology, which disregards the difference between men and women, can be criticized, it provides a sounder basis for theological debate than the dual anthropology. Is not logic replaced by pragmatism here?"[8] In other words, the female moral sense inevitably will take over and the Church would never be the same. In more appropriate situations, a woman's great gift of pragmatism, though incompatible with Christology and the meaning of Church dogma, is indispensable in caring for her family and others.

Pastoral words must speak of raw truth – a more masculine credibility, beyond the siren song of murmuring caresses or screeching harpies. Mark Twain once remarked when he heard his wife swearing, "You know the words, my dear, but not the tune!" A woman understands the intimate power of her voice intuitively – affectively, if not cognitively – and is not above taking advantage of it, as one might suspect, e.g., listening to the ladies during national public radio's fund-raising "quiet campaign," which is far from quiet. She uses her voice accordingly – it's her art – intending impact by its sheer passion and tonality, not from serious, well-thought-out truths. The problem is that, in time, too many "intimate" voices in public milieus begin to wax screechy and to pall.

This fact of life is often ignored when women complain of not being respected as women. One lady remarked that she was not a feminist but felt hurt when at a meeting no one would listen to her, she assumed because she was a woman. Actually, her voice was a tiny, gentle soprano and not given to oratory, so it was not a question of her being a woman per se, but of *her voice*. A similar occurrence is related by feminist theologians Carol P. Christ and Judith Plaskow, in a seminar at Yale: "'I said so and so about Tillich in a seminar today,' one of us would say, 'and everyone ignored me. Was I wrong, or am I stupid?' 'No. You aren't stupid. That's an important point', the other would reply. 'they didn't hear you because you're a woman.'"[9] As William Oddie comments, "It is not entirely insensitive to comment that those without the special handicap of belief in a conspiracy are better able to adjust to the rough and tumble of academic life, in which" one's own special interests or "*idée fixe* dominating a student's mind so as to imbalance his or her understanding of a while subject" are not more important than universal truths. Their tendency to ignore the truth of their voices while complaining of discrimination is not evidence for greater female leadership in the Church – or anywhere.

Appropriate "spiritual care" perhaps can be compared with the care of a nurse, who administers to patients in ways of comfort, caring and firmness after doctors have prescribed cures. It's not so much that female nurses are incapable of learning the same cures as it is that the female of the species, although quite apt to claim authority, carries less of it by voice and stature than the male. It has less *value* than the marian spiritual career. Mary didn't exercise her power through physical authority but through her abiding presence and spirit. Whether or not the Pope, Albrecht, Hauke and others maintain honesty about such limitations in their calls for more women's involvement may decide the future of the Church. As the Pope has wisely suggested, it is not within the Church's authority to change human nature or God's biblical strictures.

As with all such conscientious studies of feminism, one gains from Manfred Hauke's tales of feminist theology a vivid picture of feminist solipsism, designed willfully to impress postmodern academics and each other – as G.K. Chesterton would have put it, a veritable "nightmare, a Bacchic orgie, a Witches Sabbath.... For in all legends men have thought of women as sublime separately but horrible in a herd."[10] As mentioned earlier, Michael Weiss considers that "an essential duplicity pervades feminist pedagogy and is its hallmark... feelings are not sacrificed on the altar of facts and logic."[11] It is all delightfully exciting but not a rock on which to build His Church.

* * *

As already mentioned, it is no small coincidence that the present strain of feminism took root in the sixties along with the likes of Timothy Leary and his psychedelic erosion of sanity. Roger Kimball provides an example of Leary's "amateur solipsism" that is surprisingly reminiscent of feminist thought:

> Among other things, such credulity reminds one of how elaborate are the excuses one can generate and embrace for the sake of a hedonistic evasion of reality.... In any event, histrionics, not to say melodrama – not to say outright hucksterism – played a prominent part in Leary's activities from the beginning.[12]

* * *

One senses that, after his experience on the lecture circuit, Manfred Hauke tends to temper his feelings and adapt them for his audiences, which, for all his careful scholarship, unavoidably results in occasional fence straddling. For instance, although he claims, "That it seems sensible today for women to participate more widely in tasks formerly thought suited only to men need not be disputed here," he then demurs as to whether it is "really auspicious to identify the redemption of mankind with gaining totally equal and undifferentiated access to every sort of task."[13] He agrees with the Pope's encouragement of women to assume a greater public role, and considers it "certainly sensible" that "women should have opportunities for greater responsibility in positions of leadership, even within the Church" yet then remarks that "the strident demand for a fifty-fifty (or, for [Christa] Mulack, a seventy-thirty) 'quota arrangement' could, in the longer term, provoke male counteractions not likely to help the female cause."[14] Here, much like misguided legislators, he indulges in policy talk best left to the market place. Or perhaps he favors female "leadership" as long as it does not involve him? As with socialism, there is no way he or anyone could rearrange *de novo* a workable division of labor for the sexes. Jesus never taught specific public *re*arrangements of the sexes, nor, for all his wise advice on manners and morals, did Saint Paul. Feminism has had an insidiously erosive effect on the dialectic.

Thus, Hauke acknowledges too many feminist claims, such as the past "disadvantaging and suppressing of women," "rightly struggling for full recognition of your dignity and your rights," "women devalued," or "deaconesses," all of which unavoidably compromise the integrity of his own, the bishops', and the Pope's scholarship, since he implies that everything done before has been wanting, which, aside from individual cases involving either sex, is untrue. It is an inevitable sign of disrespect for women of the past that we should now seek all these "improvements" for women. Hauke even asks, "To what extent can feminist theology be integrated into existing theological scholarship?"[15] Why, indeed, *to any extent*? In wrestling with the enigma of sex equality, the Church can only lose sight of higher truth. In the end, as Hauke's own evidence indicates, feminists simply don't belong in the Catholic Church.

* * *

In passing, one notes that, besides Connaught Marshner's National Pro-Family Coalition, Beverly LaHaye's Concerned Women of America, and Phyllis Schlafly's Eagle Forum, other organizations of avowedly non-feminist women are engaging in their own reinforcement of Christian activities, as for instance, "Chosen Women," a revivalist ministry founded in Orange County, California, in 1995, "to give women an opportunity to take inventory of their relationship with God and participate in a spiritual renewal movement." As one participant explains, it offers a woman "reinforcement and new ideas in her quest to be 'an obedient, humble woman who lets God be in control.'"[16] The Catholic Church might do well to orient her apostolic thinking to such women rather than to feminist ideology, with which, one hopes, Chosen Women would differ strongly.

* * *

Manfred Hauke would do well to adhere to his more down-to-earth insights, such as this paragraph: "Regarding the way that Christians should deal with feminist theology, it would be a pity if the old saying were to apply: Whoever remains ignorant of history is condemned to repeat it. The Church cannot do justice to the challenge of feminist theology by demonstrating a naive 'openness' and allowing – with well-meaning forbearance – all the aberrations of this theology to infiltrate the Church's educational work and the universities."[17] Indeed.

2. THE CHURCH AND WOMEN, PARTS I & II

Ignatius Press has published an interesting compendium entitled *The Church and Women*, representing responses from other German thinkers to the same feminist theology analyzed by Manfred Hauke, whose book's English translation is also published by Ignatius. After reading these discussions on "feminist theology," one begins to wonder why the Church hierarchy has tolerated for so long what amounts obviously to a heresy. Though there is little substance in the thought processes of these militant ladies, theologians seem generally powerless to "just say No," reminding one of Lycurgus's attempt to bring the Spartan women within the ambit of his laws but "they opposed him and he had to abandon the attempt."[18] Right order deserves better.

To add depth, we shall consider each of these writers, as briefly as possible to avoid the doldrums. Karl Lehmann, who is currently the Bishop of Mainz and head of the German Bishop's Conference, seems to lack full convictions on the subject, judging from his seeming recognition of distinct sex differences yet failure to follow through with clear-headed guidelines.[19] He shows little evidence of having read Goldberg or Levin (no date is given but he may have written his piece before more recent research was disseminated) and flounders in the familiar morass of equality talk. Perhaps his translator erred in this confusing sentence: "…. beyond sexual characteristics and functions, there is biological-psychological evidence for a substantial difference between the sexes which cannot reduce to socially enforced or historio-culturally developed 'roles'."[20] In fact, the contrary would seem true. "Sexual characteristics and functions" are at the root of human society, and sound stereotypes are essential to foster healthy norms. Yet he finds that "the appeal to biology must not thereby mean the fixation of an inalterable fate," sounding much like J.S. Mill (see below), and then turns around and declares emphatically, "If one ignores this (the differences) in its significance, then women themselves must pay the price." (parenthesis added) Such ambiguity seems to be abdicating his responsibility to offer women sound Pauline advice on living in Christ.

Frankly, one senses that Lehmann is afraid to antagonize the feminists whom he must see as representing legitimate social interests rather than Lear's angry daughters. His writing reflects the familiar defensive posturing against "tendencies in the air" and fails to rise above the faddish rhythms of strident feminism. He ignores woman's powerful sexuality and unwittingly encourages a very un-Marian Lady MacBeth, with only lip service to the risk to society of women's emergence as mere competing integers in the male market place. Most earnest talk of new approaches for women tend to get bogged down in abstraction, as does Lehmann and also Margaret Meade in her call to "build a whole society only by using both the gifts special to each sex and those shared by both sexes – by using the gifts of the whole of humanity"[21], as if they were on the campaign trail. Lehmann carries this further in promoting his "polarity model," trying to relate the human sexes in a mathematical context but only ending in a confused apologia for a utopian system. Again, his odd rhetoric might be the fault of the translator.

* * *

Barbara Albrecht's essay, for the most part, offers a clear-headed analysis of the feminist claim of autonomy and a convincing rebuttal based on her own views.[22] As mentioned above, she recognizes the receptivity of women and centers her teaching on Mary, "the most important woman in the history of the world." Dr. Albrecht uses Christian doctrine, while appreciating the full significance of biology (what others refer to as "anthropology"). Drawing on the thought of metaphysician J. Kentenich, she considers the Holy Spirit to be "the feminine dimension of God" and Mary, "in her graced femininity, the instrument of the Holy Spirit silently serving the loving union of God with man, man with God, and men with each other," surely reflective of a woman's bent for relationships, caring and responsibility.

Albrecht does suffer feminist error in assuming the Holy Spirit to be feminine, when the *Catechism of the Catholic Church* refers to the Holy Spirit as the "Spirit of the Son," and "with the Father and the Son he is worshipped and glorified" as one of the Holy Trinity.

Otherwise, Dr. Albrecht seems to grasp the truth that rather than mere autonomous integers, men and women are joined in a "being-in-relation" with God, which, as quoted earlier, for a woman is "real, earthbound, directed toward persons, above all, toward children," and so forth. For she was created as 'the mother of all the living' (Gen 3:20) to be a physical as well as a psychological and spiritual mother, not an autonomous virgin," as some feminists wish us to believe. Finally, echoing Manfred Hauke (above), Dr. Albrecht cuts to the practical core with this asseveration:

> As men and women we should be aware of the meaning of fidelity to being and to all it involves. I am quite concretely in agreement with C. Meves when she says: "The true psychological-spiritual emancipation has not yet begun; for it would presuppose that women develop a consciousness of their own specific attributes; that they would recognize that assimilation to men, in whatever form, will never liberate them from 'slavery'; whereas a concept which will help develop their potentialities will. Only in this way, by becoming increasingly aware of their self-worth, and by realizing that there exists no future for humanity without their psychological and spiritual contribution, could ways to emancipation be discovered. It would then clearly emerge that women have to take different educational paths than men, and that their realization should be sought in special education institutions."[23]

While one doubts that women before feminism were not already well aware of their "self-worth," this statement resounds with truth.

* * *

Next, Walter Kasper takes a somewhat different tack, at times a bit confusing, as when he pays homage to feminist theology or the "woman's movement," which is self-defeating. As a result, his rhetoric is dense and conflicting, as when he warns against pursuing "uncritically the slogans of emancipation," and yet suggests that "on the basis of the Christian understanding of the personal dignity of man and woman, (we) give a genuinely Christian response to the challenge of the woman's movement. It must be a response that points forward. Now it is our Christian conviction that you can point forward only by pointing upward and by being fed by faith in God's order in creation and redemption." Does one sense here an escape into theological rubric to avoid a more frontal testing of the "women's movement"? Not very biblical, really.

Kasper is another of those who seem not to have fully thought out the ramifications of "equality" vis-à-vis the realities of human nature. From all appearances, he understands our natures and woman's vocation "to the service of life," yet he avoids taking a stand against its antithesis – feminism. After making some good points, he then states that, "The proposition that women are different must not be interpreted to the disadvantage of women – as many, not just feminists, fear – and not without reason. What it does entail is the task of creating conditions, in society and the Church, in which women can fulfill their being and their vocation in the best possible way. This means ultimately the renunciation of a one-sided orientation toward the so-called male ideals. In the past these have led not only to the exploitation of women but also the over-exploitation of nature and the destruction of the environment as a humane world in which to live." Here we see not only a strong dose of 20th-century liberal guilt but also a decided anti-male as well as anti-female mindset, as if Mary, the apostles, the saints, traditional gentleman, and the whole Christian idea of good husbands and wives were all "male ideals." Like Karl Lehmann, Kasper straddles the familiar fence of "increased autonomy for women" despite the "considerable burdens and disadvantages." Although well intentioned, Kasper seems over his head in this area.

* * *

On the other hand, Joseph Cardinal Ratzinger, to this layman's eye, seems far above the crowd in his essay on mariology. Generally speaking, it appears that in her focus on ecclesiology, christology, soteriology and mariology, the Church elevates doctrine to a level certainly well above the "rhythm of history" and almost beyond the ordinary believer's grasp. At the same time, Cardinal Ratzinger's treatment does obey Dietrich von Hildebrand's rule of "attempting to awaken and develop a sense of mystery and reverence in his pupils."

Cardinal Ratzinger's basic premise is that, "As against the masculinist, activist, and sociological approach of the 'People of God' there is the fact that Church – Ecclesia – is feminine."[24] "This brings out a dimension of the mystery that points beyond the sociological aspect; only here can we see the real basis and unifying power that ground the Church. Church is more than 'people,' more than structure and action: in her lives the mystery of motherhood and of that spousal love which makes motherhood possible." With soaring theological prose exploring the fundamental mystery, his teaching implicitly makes relevant the *sexual duality* of the human race, as reflected in the image of Christ and the Church as "Head and Body," metaphorically the masculine and the feminine, administered by God through the Holy Spirit. As if addressing male torpor as well as the solipsistic "rights of woman and sexual equality," he offers this passage:

> In her believing response to the call of God, Mary appears as the prototype of a creation which is likewise called to respond; she manifests the freedom of the creature, a freedom which is not dissolved, but comes to its fulfillment, in love. But it is precisely as a woman that she exemplifies saved and liberated mankind, that

is, in the physical specificity which is inseparable from the human being: "male and female he created them" (Gen 1:27). The "biological" is inseparable from the human, just as the human is inseparable from the "theological". On the one hand all this is intimately connected with the dominant trends of our time, and on the other hand it contradicts them head-on.

Where the biological aspect of humanity is eliminated, humanity itself is obliterated. So we have the issue of whether men are allowed to be men and women to be women – the issue of the creature as such. Since human specificity can be avoided least in the question of motherhood, any emancipation that denies the *bios* attacks women in particular, rejects her right to be a woman.[25]

Cardinal Ratzinger probes the depths of the human sexual dichotomy. "Marian spirituality," he writes, "will always be in tension between theological rationality and faith's affectivity. This tension is of its very essence; neither pole must be allowed to fade. Where the emotions are involved, we must not forget the sober mean of reason, but on the other hand the sobriety of a faith which seeks understanding must not stifle the heart, which often sees more than reason," a metaphor reminiscent of Burke and Pascal. In the raw light of such teaching, 2000s entertainment trends with nubile kick-boxing females and seductively clothed female attorneys are incongruous.

Ratzinger knows it is the heart that ultimately guides behavior in sexual right order, as was so poignantly evident the night the *Titanic* went down and the men gave priority to the women because it was "the law of human nature." The emancipated woman is like a church without God, a mother trying to play the ecclesial role without a father, essentially rudderless. Instead of appreciating the supererogation of the men in their behalf according to Victorian custom at probably the apex of Western Civilization, are not the feminists now coveting an asocial and unnatural advantage to excess? In light of the *Titanic* tragedy, the Equal Rights

Amendment seems utterly petty. Cardinal Ratzinger's peroration should stir the lawyers to more study: "If it is modern man's distressful fate increasingly to fall apart into mere *bios* and mere rationality, marian spirituality could counteract this 'decomposition' of the human being by helping him to rediscover unity in the center, by attending to his heart."[26] Is he up to it?

* * *

Next, Leo Scheffczyk, currently emeritus professor of dogmatic theology at the University of Munich, adds his thoughts on "Mary As a Model of Catholic Faith." Cardinal Ratzinger's essay, of course, is a hard act to follow, but in his acceptance of the "deep mysteries," Scheffczyk deals with his subject in a delicate, comprehensive way helping us understand mariology. His and Karl Barth's insight are good guides – that the doctrine of salvation through devotion to Jesus Christ is grounded in a new birth brought about through Mary's receptivity to God, "a reality-filled symbol of pure grace and a sign of the absolute sovereignty of God."[27] Scheffczyk believes that Mary's role "in the order of salvation imparts to the Church, which is the outstanding place of continuing salvation, in a totally special way, profoundly sensitive, deeper human maternal and even mystical characteristics," thus suggesting a womanly paradigm worthy of emulation by all women. He then provides this interesting insight, quoting Hans Urs von Balthasar's *Klarstellungen. Zur Prüfung der Geister*:

> Without mariology Christianity is in danger of becoming inhuman. The Church becomes functionalistic, without a soul, a hectic enterprise without resting place, alienated by over-planning. Because in this male-masculine world one new ideology replaces another, everything becomes polemical, critical, bitter, humorless, and ultimately boring. People desert such a Church in droves.
>
> These consequences for the Church with an atrophied faith in the Virgin Mother are also confirmed occasionally by protes-

tants' awareness of their faith and are applied self-critically to their own situation when it is said: "When in the Church the attention which one pays to Mary declines, then.... the Church as successor to Mary becomes more or less unfeeling." Then to all that is human, which is part of all that is Christian, something crucial is lost. "The loss of this (marian) devotion appears.... to be a far-reaching step resulting from the Reformation...."[28]

Of interest, Scheffczyk makes clear that mariology goes beyond mere "sociological-democratic models" (such as "sex equality and the rights of woman"), while like Augustine making certain to ground Mary's role "in the bodily element" rather than pure spiritual theology. In other words, as a faithful woman who gave birth to the Son of God and sustained Him as His mother in His lifetime and now serves as our mediator with Him. This does not include female priests or sermonizers.

*   *   *

In contrast, Jutta Burggraf's essay leaves one unconvinced.[29] While she understands the differences between men and women; their creation for the service of God; appreciates the humble, courageous and obedient example of Mary; and recognizes our call to worship God; her thought is marked by our friend, "equality and the rights of woman." Despite her hoeing the line on general doctrinal matters, she reveals a defensive mindset in resorting to familiar charges of past degradation, exclusion, misjudgment as "deficient" or "unintelligent," etc., never mind all the examples to the contrary, including Mary herself.

Unfortunately, even though she pays lip service to duties and distinctions, this trait influences most of her essay, which tends to set man vs. woman, rather than seeking a delicate balance of shared responsibilities. For her, there is a nagging need to resist the idea that a man's or a priest's service inevitably involves authority because for her, no matter how politely disguised, males need females more than the opposite. She seems to aspire to an unlikely androgyny in believing that holy men's "true kindness and care for souls" must be "motherly," and that a holy woman's "courage, firmness, and decisiveness" must be "manly." Such overreaching rhetoric becomes too contrived.

This is not to say that Dr. Burggraf has nothing worthwhile to say, but only that her feminist leanings against "our present male-dominated society" confuse her hermeneutics considerably. This becomes apparent especially when she welcomes the Pope's remark on "the entry of women into public life," which deserves much, much more thought if not outright rejection. For example, the United States Military Academy at West Point, founded in 1802 to train officers for the defense of the nation in times of war and converted to co-education in 1976, now boasts a "Consideration-of-Others Officer." Physical standards have been lowered to accommodate the girls. Sexual harassment, as in other areas of the public domain entered by Burggraf's sensitive ladies, has increased noticeably, often to the detriment of business as usual. A "Human Sexuality Committee" promulgates "goals" and establishes "sexual knowledge and attitudes tests" and coordinates dutifully with "the Sex Information and Education Council of the United States."[30] In light of such developments, Tocqueville, Huxley and Orwell would have been skeptical of Burggraf's roseate visions of a "more humane atmosphere in the workplace." Her expectations for women outside the home while also demanding "that the values of motherhood and family be clearly acknowledged" do not wash.

* * *

Not only the Church but also lay research offers guidelines, as for instance frequent findings that male and female brains are too different for ready accommodation in many markets. As Rod

Little writes on Chris Babcock's research in *The Spectator*, "there are two distinct types of cognition – male and female. They are, he argues, essentially 'non-commensurate' and incompatible. This should give the liberal social scientists fun. They will have to face the idea that we are different, men and women, and that legislation designed to negate those differences will be worse than useless."[31]

As farmers stricken by drought who do not prepare their soil lose it to winds and later floods, feminism makes inroads because few have prepared themselves to resist its trespasses. Women with their generous, liberal, unconditional love would tend to give away Christ's Church through sheer lack of resistance to the winds of fashion – like changing dress styles each year. When people learn feminism's true character and impede its advance, it will become a passing fancy.

3. THE CHURCH AND WOMEN, III, IV & V

Another aspect of women's roles involves the question of women as deaconesses or priests. Contributors to Parts III and IV of *The Church and Women* offer an excellent treatment of this subject. The writers approach their topic with the idea of allowing both men and women to live as men and women and not as a gerrymandered construct. There is the lurking inconsistency of acknowledging women's past history of "inferiority," although also "elevated," but even so, these writers present convincing evidence and exegesis for the impossibility of having women priests or deaconesses. Generally, since the reason is not to subordinate women as much as to assure proper use of men in accordance with nature and the teachings of Jesus Christ, we can applaud them enthusiastically.

Manfred Hauke appears again, to examine the historical evidence and concludes that "the sacramental ordination of women (is) theologically impossible, and the (non-sacramental) diaconate (is) pastorally lacking in meaning. What is urgently needed, however, theologically and pastorally, is the committed service of men *and* women in the Church, where the charisms of all Christians complement each other in a wonderful way. Particularly at a time such as this, which in so many ways utters the *'non serviam'* – 'I will not serve' – we all need the mind of Christ, who said of himself: 'the Son of Man came not to be served but to serve, and to give his life as a ransom for many' (Mark 10:45)."[32]

Bruno Kleinheyer approaches his subject feeling "obligated to argue the theological implications carefully and without emotions"[33] and explores the issue admirably, relying extensively on the research of Aimé Georges Martimort, as presented in *Deaconesses: An Historical Study*, which will be considered below. Kleinheyer finds the evidence on past "deaconesses" non-supportive of the idea: "According to Martimort, in a discussion of the actual practice, this means that anybody who might try, in our own day, to invoke historical realities in order to (re-)create an Institution of Deaconesses, would only come up, after so many centuries, with another practice which would have merely the name in common with things of the past." This means that historical evidence of "deaconesses" only shows subsidiary functions of temporary, non-apostolic ministrations subject to male ordination and primacy. Again, as all these writers make clear, this did not mean derogation of women but merely their respected functioning in separate roles.

Hans Urs von Balthasar similarly examines the evidence on the intricate subject of the sexes – dabbling in the familiar "equality of both sexes in essence and value" – and wisely offers no definitive exposition on Jesus's sacrifice and resultant "participation of the apostolic office in this all-sexuality-transcending male fertility...."[34] Far from devaluing the female, he remarks on the man's inferiority in his dependency "on the woman as nurturing and model of completion," even while noting his being more than himself as "the 'head' of the woman, and in the Christian context... mediator of God's gifts." He finds such concepts "very difficult to formulate. If this dimension could be fully brought to light, only then would the previously latent inferiority of the man in relation to the woman be somehow be overcome. It must suffice here to have hinted at this concept."

It is apparently not von Balthasar's favorite subject, since he usually has more transcendent concepts to deal with. However, he closes by commenting, "The Church's tradition, then, as becomes evident from all this, has roots much deeper than a first glance would lead to believe. It reaches way down into depths which cannot fully be plumbed. And still, what little we are able to catch and form into stammering words, shows us that this tradition is justified and immune to the changes of time and opinion (including opinions about the proper role of the sexes)."

* * *

Helmut Moll commences his essay with a fanfare for the various parameters influencing our discussion: equality of the sexes, feminist theology, increasing shortage of priests, ecumenism, doubting Thomases, and the human sciences themselves.[35] He quotes Cardinal Ratzinger on feminist theology, in a stunning restatement of one of the main points of the present book: "Behind the mask of emancipation, of the finally accomplished equality, hides total assimilation and the denial of the right to be a woman, and thus be human...; this is all the more threatening because what is perfectly justified can easily become the vehicle for what is destructive and untrue." Although he repeats the faddish charge of "discrimination against women" (ironically, even while acknowledging women's calling), he emphasizes the "shining example" of Mary "for the Christian woman and mother" and quotes Mother Teresa's response to why women cannot be priests: "because Mary was not".

Of significance for our purposes, while Moll calls for a "thoroughly Christian attitude" to help "diminish the still existing undervaluation of women in professional and public life" (circa 1988), he considers that "a total equalization of the sexes cannot be encouraged. The apparent victory which they would win in such circumstances, far from assuring them of their heart's desire, would be its veiled defeat. The French theologian L. Bouyer analyzes the increasing loss of orientation and direction of woman by pointing out that both extremes would result in a loss of female identity: either she falls into complete dependence on man, or she is assimilated in him." Unfortunately, some churchmen have yet to realize that in the process of her "emancipation" a concomitant *feminization* also occurs for men not generally beneficial to his headship.

* * *

As Father Joseph D. Fessio observes in his essay, "the impression has often been given that the main or only reasons against (possible admission of women to the non-ordained ministries of acolyte and lector, etc.) are of a cultural, pastoral, or psychological nature. In particular, some have said there seem to be no intrinsic reasons of a doctrinal or theological character against such admission."[36] He then proceeds to argue on philosophical and theological grounds that indeed such reasons exist – that the two-thousand-year tradition of the Catholic Church could hardly be based merely on "contingent or culturally conditioned foundations." He does not intend an exhaustive treatment, however, but primarily one derived from "philosophical anthropology, trinitarian doctrine, christology, and ecclesiology," all of which are obviously seminal and intrinsic to the Church.

In the process, Father Fessio takes us again through Catholic theology and doctrine, which forms the basis for his discussion of the "Man-Woman Relationship." He touches on the physiological differences which are the basis for the woman's receptivity and the man's activity in forming the "mysterious but profound spiritual complementarity between men and women," acknowledging that it is "difficult" to "describe this complementarity in adequate language." However, he sees it "from the vantage point of the marital act or the reproductive act, as characterized by equal dignity and equally active participation but diversity of role." From there he proceeds to the important role of Mary as an expression of "the perfection of all material creation raised to the personal…. Mary, who is the symbol of all creation, becomes at that moment (of receptivity) the symbol of the Church as Bride of Christ."

One infers from his incisive exposition that the assault on the settled order of the Church exhibits all the radical presumptuousness with which we are already familiar. The feminists simply want, ahistorically, unscientifically, irrationally, and selfishly, to "eliminate all sex-based distinction of roles between men and women, including motherhood and priesthood." In view of this evidence that feminists do not respect Christian doctrine based on truth and objectivity, the Church should simply excommunicate them. To attempt to find room in the Church for radical discontents can only lead to weakened doctrine.

* * *

There is a point at which a stand must be taken to avoid erosion of proven principle. As Hans Urs von Balthasar explains the thinking of his Protestant contemporary Karl Barth,

It might well be that the common need for making common

cause against some anti-Christian threat can reawaken this original alertness to the meaning of dogmatic divergence. But it should not lead to a false irenicism, to overhasty compromises, but to a relentlessly earnest theological testing of one's own confessional beliefs. The move from a divided to a united confession must happen without compromise and above all without resorting to forms and formulas of unity that try only to cover up rather than to overcome disunity.[37]

Revealing the basic incompatibility of feminist thought with either Catholic doctrine or Fessio's "complementarity between men and women," William Oddie tells of a feminist's erecting "a completely private, even 'secret,' spiritual life; one with an entirely personal origin, and which has no point of contact with the tradition with which she nevertheless remains uneasily affiliated." He goes on to elaborate:

> The psychological difficulties of the attitude to faith, for the "feminist consciousness", are clear enough. We have already seen how, in different ways, the various strains of secular feminism are based on the quest for freedom from dependence. In the first place, this means dependence on the male sex; and we can see that in this context "dependence" often means "interdependence", since the woman's rejection of her own dependence will also, where it is recognized, involve a rejection of the man's complementary dependence – emotional and otherwise – on her. Broadly speaking, this shows itself in two ways. Some feminists look toward an androgynous society, in which males and females would be independent of the opposite sex for emotional completion: the new androgynous personality which would in such a society develop for both sexes would already contain within itself both masculine and feminine; thus women would be freed from the shackles of "complementarity". Others, as we have seen, have asserted a full separatist and matriarchalist feminism, in which male "domination" is bypassed or even in theory reversed, by asserting female values within a feminist alternative society.[38]

With such a contrast, the feminist theology can never have a home in the Catholic Church. In attacking a millennia-old tradition they have the burden of proof, and sheer anger and rebellion

– the power of a woman scorned – are inadmissible evidence.

Women writers like Albrecht and Burggraf show signs of the "women's studies" parallax, which creates an image of women as something they can never be. They set about applying their immense powers to force a roseate world by coloring women as if they were something else – powerful creatures of exquisite feminine charm yet performing like men in a woman's world: Like all other ideologies, it is only a chimera. For instance, as mentioned, while their delightful sexual voices on the airways can charm, they are being overused and misused in areas inevitably best voiced by the male of the species.

While the reason for male priests is cultural as well as theological, and therefore pastoral and psychological, Church spokesmen have not yet resorted to this argument, although it is compelling. They apply theological rhetoric, which they do admirably, with the same result: it is no benefit for women or society to try to play male roles. As Fessio realizes, "While it would not lead to the invalidity of the Sacrament for a woman to act as acolyte, it would be in serious disharmony with the very nature and character of the whole order of grace and redemption, the mediation of the priest, and the symbolic character of men and women." Here he sees the artistic quality in "harmony" as he goes on to add, "It would be a confusion of the role which is specifically that of the woman as representative of creation and the Church."

* * *

Barbara Albrecht appears again, expounding "on women priests," and provides an example of a female Catholic defending Church doctrine without grasping the full biological-psychological implications – that is, our natures.[39] One senses that she would gladly adapt to "sociologically and culturally conditioned arrangements which keep changing according to circumstances" were it not for the "decrees of God," which one accepts "at best with gritted teeth." No matter how apt her argument, one finds a womanly ambivalence reminding us of the need for a male "head." Although she comes close, Albrecht knows the words but not quite the tune. It is hard to square her call "to let us women become and be real women" (presumably, after millennia of not being "real"?) or "to become genuine women, virginal persons, and mothers" with her later idea that women should also be welcomed into the market place to compete with aggressive males.

Despite her general adherence to Church rubric, Albrecht adopts a rather untheological woman's perspective in contending that, "If the official Church rejects the priesthood of women, we must have demonstrated that in the end this rejection stems from consideration for woman, not against her. The Church upholds the right of woman to be 'herself,' namely, a woman, and that means 'to be human in the highest way.'" There is something in such rhetoric which reflects a "religion of self-realization," of which William Oddie writes, "Human 'self-realization' on mankind's own terms has always been seen in mainstream Christian tradition as a profoundly dangerous aspiration, and it is only a theological tradition which denies or weakens the Church's doctrine of sin and the fall of man which could suppose that it is anything else."[40] As Oddie remarks, "It has been, of course, a recurring theme throughout the century," and typical of many like "the liberal Anglican Bishop Paul J. Moore Jr., who recalls that, when he was considering whether it was right to ordain women to the priesthood, he strengthened himself with the dictum 'whenever you are faced with a difficult choice, go with the future, not the past'."[41] Against this line, and as if refuting Albrecht's demand that Church doctrine must be geared to "consideration for woman, not against her," Oddie draws on Protestant Karl Barth "who rigidly insisted on the vital need for theological orthodoxy, based on submission to God as he has revealed himself, and not from our idea of God deriving from our own understanding of human needs and human society."[42]

* * *

Desmond Connell then takes his turn at wrestling with the feminist schism by creative resort to Catholic doctrine.[43] It is not unrewarding to rely on such concepts as the "sacramental symbolism"; a "common priesthood"; "marriage of Church, the new Eve, and Christ, the new Adam"; "redeemed Eve"; and such, while also recognizing as Connell does the significance of the differences between the sexes, but again, why not simply accept the latter as given? For example, "sex equality" can never transform a woman's voice into "headship"; or, if male "headship" is crucial to the marriage sacrament, how can it be ignored in public life? How is a role reversal in *public* arenas possible? (Rumpole of the Bailey's "she who must be obeyed" was his own wife, not his neighbor's!)

Connell does make some telling points that should lay to rest frivolous feminist claims. "I do not say that a woman cannot represent Christ: every baptized person, man or woman, is *alter Christus*. What I do say, however, is that a woman cannot be a sacramental image of Christ in the act that is proper to him precisely as the new Adam. The symbolism of the new Adam and the new Eve expresses the relation between Christ and the Church which is profoundly involved in the Eucharist celebration. Now the distinction between Adam and Eve is the sexual difference between man and woman, the primordial distinction universally present wherever human beings are to be found."

It is a wonder the Church must devote any time at all to narrow-minded feminist demands. Connell points out that "woman has a higher vocation and destiny. Her sex symbolizes the finality of human existence.... Deprived of the interiority symbolized by woman, our being in the world is rootless, deprived of its inner purpose, without heart.... Created nature has nothing more eloquent of its mystery than a woman's love."

After explaining a woman's "interiority," Connell closes with this instructive message:

> Lastly there is fruitfulness. Like Mary, the Church is the fruitful virgin, the virgin whose fruitfulness derives not from man's sexuality but from the gift of the Holy Spirit. She is blessed because she believes that there will be a fulfillment of what was spoken to her by the Lord. Open to God through this virginal faith, she receives from the Holy Spirit the fruitfulness that makes her mother of all the living. In her they are born not to a perishable life but to everlasting life. And the abiding fullness of that life is charity.

Certainly, such a destiny presents no easy challenge; however, it is nevertheless a challenge that life and the Church offers to women, because it conforms to the plan of God Almighty. Whether it be a "higher vocation and destiny" than men's is pointless, since men's challenge is no less demanding. That women, however, with their capacity for love, might have to accept their destiny without as much understanding of it seems highly probable, which in no way renders it any the less remarkable – and lovable.

4. THE CHURCH AND WOMEN, CONCLUSION

In the final chapter of *The Church and Women*, edited by Helmut Moll, he and Jutta Burggraf offer closing comments on "The Challenge of Feminism." Although mistakenly praising the original "women's movement" as a benign phenomenon, Dr. Burggraf offers a telling critique of feminist theology, a modern-day heresy of anti-Church malcontents who have published profusely for a gullible public and garnered undeserved attention. But, again, one doesn't argue with angry daughters; one only excises them. In their turn, although marian women (always receptive to male "headship") should have been able to rely on strong men, in the age of watered down education and "women's liberation" men let their women down (like Johnny of the 1920s' song "Frankie and Johnny"). They still do.

Helmut Moll offers a concluding essay on the "challenge" of Catherina J.M. Halkes's feminist theology.[44] Here again is an obvious case of a woman's heretical, essentially anti-Christian "protest against an androcentric and therefore unilateral theology of several centuries duration," and yet Father Moll suggests that "whoever attempts to evaluate the different currents of feminist theology should suspend judgment for the time being, for this new movement (he was writing in 1983) is still in a state of development and at the present time presents anything but a uniform structure. Consequently, apodictic as well as conclusive evaluations are premature." Considering that the late 20th century version of feminism had been around since the 1960s, and that its premises – revolutionary deconstructivism, androgyny and rejection of male objectivity – were already apparent in 1983 and quite well publicized by Catholic writers themselves, Father Moll's tolerance seems remiss. Thus Norman Podhoretz's severity:

> Anyone paying attention to these matters over the years was bound to have become aware that the feminist's success in infecting our culture with their ideas of the relations between men and women owed an immeasurable debt to the supine acquiescence of most men themselves in the sisterhood's assault upon the entire male sex as nothing but oppressors and predators. And I mean supine: scarcely a male voice was raised in protest when feminists issued such proclamations as this by Susan Brownmiller: "Rape is nothing more or less than a conscious process of intimidation by which *all men* keep *all women* in a state of fear" (the italics were *all hers*).[45]

While the Church obviously endeavors with its "ecumenical dialogue" to achieve for Christ as wide as possible a universality, at times this is like walking a tightrope without a balance rod. There is precedent for strong defense, as when Augustine "triumphantly defended Catholic universality by exposing the Donatist church as merely an African outpost: that famous *pars Donati*, which died out precisely because it was only a part." Hans Urs von Balthasar shows how difficult this path is in his discussion of the subject in regards to Protestant Karl Barth's thought. He argues that Catholics cannot assume supremacy but must engage in a dialogue to avoid "the yawning chasm over which no dialectical or analogical method can leap, the bloody wound that cannot be healed with the plaster of theological formulas!"[46] Yet he apparently sides with Newman in finding that "the Catholic Church can see herself as the embodiment of wholeness and totality only when she has done all in her power actively to incorporate the riches of all partial points of view." In light of the radical agenda of feminist theology, however, the possibility of such "riches" is slim.

For now, let us continue our survey of the religious dimension by a summary of the work of Aimé Georges Martimort and William Oddie, along with another look at the thought of the National Conference of Catholic Bishops.

5. Is There Precedent for Women as Deaconesses?

Having presented in as complete and objective a fashion as possible the history of deaconesses in their various concrete manifestations in history, I think it necessary to confront, at least in a modest way, the theological controversies that the institution of deaconesses in the Church has inspired in our own day. I will content myself with the reflections suggested to me by this inquiry

–Aimé Georges Martimort[47]

From the cover comments for his book, *Deaconesses*, one gathers that Fr. Aimé Georges Martimort is considered "one of the foremost French authorities on the Liturgy" and has authored numerous works on Liturgy and Ritual in Church history. "The present book on deaconesses is considered one of (his) most significant and valuable works." It is an excellent work of scholarly research, with thorough footnotes, and can be considered the last word on the subject – the definitive work – a skillful, invaluable reference work. In the process of his endeavor, no less than Goldberg, Levin, Davidson and Gilder in their more socio-biological research, Fr. Martimort "reviewed all of the sources known today that could throw any light on the subject."[48]

In general, Martimort found that the roles played by women through the centuries resembling the role of deaconesses were mainly ceremonial or honorific rather than consecrative, sacramental or authoritative. Apparently, other theologians have agreed. The facts speak for themselves:

> Of course, it is always possible to attribute these kinds of restrictions to some kind of sociological prejudice, but that changes nothing with respect to the facts, and, especially, nothing with respect to the very nature of the facts: namely, that during all the time when the institution of deaconesses was a living institution, both the discipline and the liturgy of the churches insisted upon a very clear distinction between deacons and deaconesses.[49]

"Attributions of prejudice," of course, issue mainly from demands for greater authority for women in the Church – from those caring less for historical accuracy and systemic continuity than for their own ideology of androgyny. As Martimort suggests in his peroration, the true role of women can be considered far more important than mere serving as functionaries:

The real importance and efficaciousness of the role of women in the Church has always been vividly perceived in the consciousness of the hierarchy and of the faithful as much more broad than the historical role that deaconesses in fact played. And perhaps a proposal based on an "archeological" institution might even obscure the fact that the call to serve the Church is urgently addressed today to *all* women, especially in the area of the transmission of Faith and works of charity.[50]

6. THE NATIONAL CONFERENCE OF CATHOLIC BISHOPS COPES WITH FEMINISM – IN A WAY

We offer this message, then, as one moment in a developing dialogue, with the hope that all women and men of the Church will receive it as such and continue as participants in what can be a sacred conversation for all of us....

With Pope Paul VI's words in mind, we consider these points: leadership in the Church, equality of women and men, and diversity of gifts. Confident that the Holy Spirit will guide us in the way of peace and justice, we invite all women and men in the Church to join in this dialogue.

The United States Catholic Conference[51]

What makes it difficult to digest the Catholic Bishops' pastoral teaching on women is perhaps that their teaching should never have been attempted in the atmosphere that prevailed. In the end it is simply unsuitable – jamming a square peg in a round hole, or a pianist's teaching football. It never used to be necessary to talk of nuts and bolts regarding men and women *defensively* because everyone had the common sense to appreciate what was involved – an ingredient which was long Christianity's most effective tool – love. As mentioned above, we can easily accept Saint Paul's or Saint Peter's quaint patterns of living for men and women – rules of social etiquette for those aspiring to the teachings of Jesus Christ – because reflection tells us "that the word of God, properly understood, is indeed all-encompassing. Congregations, after all, hope for guidance in worldly matters as well as spiritual, since, as Cardinal Newman often made clear, the two are quite properly related." In fulfilling this responsibility in that more sensible time, Saint Paul was undistracted by self-centered deconstructivists and adhered to common sense, human nature, truth, and his inspiration from God. One wishes the bishops had also.

In these days, no less than in St. Paul's, a human being senses that young, single women are not looking for gentle, faceless, sexless males "in Christ" marching for "the bonds of peace" as much as for masculine goers, doers, builders – and, of course, also civil, thoughtful, gentlemanly, and one hopes, loving men. To use theological rhetoric for such mundane parameters seems over-reaching, and, although Saint Paul managed it brilliantly, the bishops do not. Again, one has to read the pertinent literature to comprehend feminism and whether the bishops have done this appears dubious. Instead, they courteously and "meekly" heed the "dialogue with representatives of various women's organizations" and arranged their respective responses to "address the concerns and issues that have been raised." Inexplicably, they have bent to the complaints of Lear's angry daughters.

We have already covered some aspects that bear repeating if we are to accept the invitation to join in the bishops' dialogue. In their more abbreviated pastoral refection, "Strengthening the Bonds of Peace," the bishops reveal a surprisingly docile and ill-informed grasp of their subject. Without belaboring each misstep, suffice it to say that in writing "a pastoral letter that would capture the vast range of concerns expressed by women," they have not convinced this writer that they are aware of what those concerns are. The process is heavy with subservience to complaining activists and shows no sign of a scholarly study of twentieth-century men and women. In pursuing a dialogue of "clear, understandable language, peaceful and patient meekness, trust between speaker and listener, and sensitivity to the situation and needs of the hearer" while steering shy of the word "truth," they sound much like Uriah Heep.

Peppered with tiresome banalities of "equality," "past suffering," "sexism," "just remuneration for women," "discrimination against women," and so forth, this pamphlet lacks substance. The idea of "peace" becomes obscurantist, with men mentioned primarily as perpetrators and not as actual peacekeepers. As often as not in myth and history, however, women have been the cause of war and riot. As a recent letter writer, the Dowager Marchioness of Reading, recently wrote to *The Spectator*: "I would like to join with Alan Clark's recent remarks defending the English soccer fans in France. We are a nation of yobs. Without that characteristic how did we colonize the world? And our fame as fighters is second to none. Now that we don't have a war, what's wrong with a good 'punch-up'?"[52] But, of course, some will say, "That's Anglicanism for you!" whose adherents don't appreciate "our sister peacemakers" as much as Catholics do. And then again, it may be that the bishops are missing something in human nature. Unfortunately, the Pope might have instigated this exercise by choosing as the wistful theme for the 1995 World Day of Peace "Women: Educators for Peace."

While the ladies certainly could help by raising sons who don't litter, paint graffiti, commit crime, and who are gentlemen, we might be asking too much from our womenfolk to saddle them with the job of keeping the peace, a task which, if one recalls Joan, Thatcher, and Madeleine Albright – not to overlook Helen of Troy – they seem not particularly suited for unless it means having their men knock the lights out of the local bully. The best way to "keep the peace" is with a strong, intelligent man, very well armed, which happens not to be very marian.

In inviting a dialogue that "will make us wise," the bishops also tip their hand badly in calling us to "draw upon the insights of contemporary scholarship in a wide variety of disciplines – Scripture, anthropology, history, women's studies, and systematic theology." For anyone who has kept abreast of such matters, inclusion of women's studies here is laughable. Amplifying the examples discussed above, *The New Criterion*'s "Notes and Comments" for June, 1998 reminds us, "no feature of the contemporary university is more destructive than these women's studies 'sites' (to use the favored jargon) of politicized 'transgression' (ditto)." Such "canons" regularly indoctrinate young students in very un-Catholic practices such as "Lesbian and Gay Studies," "sexual and erotic desires and orientations," and "transgressive sexual indoctrination." As *The New Criterion* editor suggests, "such courses are examples not of serious scholarship but of serious indoctrination.... But the more immediate question is whether most of what goes on under the name of women's studies really qualifies as serious scholarship at all." That, in seeking "wisdom," the bishops wish to "draw on these insights" seems overly "meek."

The bishop's pamphlet appears to have been an attempt to placate the women who "found acceptance difficult" of the Pope's letter, *Ordinatio Sacerdotalis*, "reaffirming the teaching and practice that priestly ordination is restricted to men." Unfortunately, instead of adhering to higher truths, the bishops choose to offer untruths to appease the malcontents. As a result, some hypocrisy appears, mainly in overtures toward "women exercising leadership" in "alternate ways," despite the fact that mariology is not "leadership" at all (unless we include, say, women like Russia's carping "citizenesses", which seems unlikely).

Thus, the bishops' proclaiming benefits from "women holding positions of exacting leadership, as heads of government, judges, research doctors, symphony conductors, business executives, presidents of Catholic colleges, chief executives, theologians, school superintendents," and so forth, is obsequious posturing. While one may agree that "women's gifts have tremendously improved the quality of parish ministry," one must ask, "But haven't they always?" Samuel Johnson adds a touch of humor with his famous remark to James Boswell, "Sir, a woman's preaching is like a dog's walking on his hinder legs. It is not done well; but you are surprised to find it done at all." (Today, the network would have fired him.) We do no service to mankind to abjure such honesty and pretend that women are cut out for leadership.

* * *

Let us next look at the 1992 report of the Ad Hoc Committee for a Pastoral Response to Women's Concerns, also under the aegis of the National Conference of Catholic Bishops (NCCB).[53] This is a longer treatise than "Strengthening the Bonds of Peace" and reflects more than one train of thought, which is possibly why the Pope chose to offer his own treatment. (See Neuhaus above) Again, the main thesis assumes roles for women unrelated to Mary's experience and thus condemns us to unnatural relationships. "Less recognition for women's labors" in male arenas could reflect a healthy rejection of women straying out of their jurisdiction – into areas where they are inevitably compromised. Ample reports are available of women's different work schedules and habits, so the growing literature on such details will not be belabored here.

The irony of womanhood is incontrovertible, as was evident recently when a well-known female public figure agreed that men and women cannot be considered fungible (as the bishops tend to do when they get into talk of "equal recognition"), yet contradicted herself by claiming, "women should be willing to compete equally with men because they are just as smart, except for jobs involving strength, risk, and unpleasantness." Was this perhaps the same thinking that led Eve to get us into this fix?

When applied to men and women, "equal pay for equal work" is simply a dishonest use of an otherwise plausible truism. For one thing, men and women generally *don't do equal* work. Another crucial aspect long neglected is demographic: As Wade C. Mackey among others has warned, the trend toward working women and single parenthood is driving our population rate below replacement levels with the inevitable result that cultures having greater father and mother involvement will simply out-populate our culture and take over. (See Chapter I, Note 20.)

Where do the bishops discover ideas on "equality" in Christ's teaching? How will "commissions on women" over-ride the husband's "headship" prescribed in Ephesians? How "collaborate with women in leadership roles" and adhere to Proverbs, Isaiah or Ephesians? How assume that the larger, more aggressive male will docilely accept female leadership without changing God's plan? Why would the Church endorse "changing roles and relationships between the sexes" when the "changes" are neither natural nor an improvement? Why is it "not a simple matter to identify what it means to be feminine or masculine"? (The Bible certainly doesn't waffle on this!) On what basis can the Church believe that "society errs in defining men principally by their work"? (Since age-old, productive custom is involved and natural stereotypes are crucial to a healthy society, aren't the bishops overreaching here?) The bishops seem to need much more thought on Caesar's world before they venture into his territory, if they should at all.

This Ad Hoc Report invites target practice. The bishops' treatment of women's sexuality seems beyond their capacity, as they flounder in disclaiming a woman's sexuality as a principle consideration and then, later, acknowledge its considerable importance. They stumble in endorsing the tiresome pretense that "with respect to fundamental rights of the person, every type of discrimination, whether social or cultural,… based on sex, is to be overcome and eradicated as contrary to God's intent," unaware that this mundane Democratic-GOP platform amounts to raw egalitarianism (which they themselves later condemn and which conflicts with much that they have been struggling to do in this pastoral response). We actually need *more* discrimination as to sex in order to maintain a healthy Christian society.

In other words, the bishops are not very convincing in their assessment of women's sexual vulnerability as having "its roots in original sin" and their ascribing "a significantly greater share of the blame" to men. Before politicization by pulpit and party platform, the female of the species herself, with all her charm, power, and wisdom (or lack thereof), served as the single most effective agency in either causing or minimizing not only "original sin" but also "sexual harassment." With so-called "emancipation," they gave up this marian power and became mere prey. All the bishops need is a return to ladies and gentlemen.

All in all, the bishops show little logic or understanding in accepting the feminist litany of troubles. That the marketplace by its very nature is *competitive* is a given, so how complain of women being treated *"as competitors or threats"* as if when the paint washes off in the first rain, its promoter can complain of unfair conditions? It seems ridiculous that we should be asked to change the nature of the marketplace to please ambitious, timorous ladies of "energy and talent".

It would seem schizophrenic to promote lofty visions of "the dignity and equality" of women for some eighteen pages and then launch into a down-to-earth defense of "hierarchical reality" of the Church and her undemocratic tradition abjuring "simplistic egalitarianism", yet that's what the bishops do. Like others, they try having it both ways! Even then, their closing list of recommendations could have been lifted from a leftwing political platform: "to ensure that all preaching, catechizing, and practice promote the dignity and equality of women"; "to adopt language and behavior that foster attitudes of mutual respect, appreciation, acceptance, and collaboration between men and women"; "to advocate legislative efforts that will respond to the needs of women, especially the poor, the elderly and those requiring special care."

The bishops' final proposal invites disaster: "to implement these initiatives… each diocese (should) consider establishing a commission on women in church and society or some comparable body or council that will promote the just and equal treatment of women and men on a continuing basis. To facilitate this process, we further call upon the NCCB Committee on Women to assist dioceses in carrying out these recommendations and in developing new initiatives as new needs arise." It is surprising that the bishops are not more wary of committees, which have a way of obeying Parkinson's Law by expanding their work to fill the allotted time. DACOWITS provides a good example, as reported by the Center for Military Readiness, headed by Elaine Donnelly. "Most members of the committee are civilians, nearly all women, who constantly make recommendations that promote the goals of radical feminism at the expense of military culture and readiness."[54] The Trojan Horse has been let in and the Pentagon sleeps. And now the bishops would follow suit.

* * *

Other examples abound of the mummery of "sex equality." Michael Lewis, a repentant liberal professor fed up with higher education in America, has written a book on his disgust with the modern university, *Poisoning the Ivy*, which Edward E. Ericson, Jr., reviews in *The University Bookman*. As if to alert the bishops to the sins of women's studies, Ericson discusses an example from the book, showing the morally ambivalent atmosphere generated by the whole feminist project and markedly reminiscent of some of the bishops' complainers:

> Lewis devotes the bulk of Chapter Three to telling three tales out of school. In one, a newly hired feminist told the few male students who enrolled in her course that they were unwelcome. The dean, to whom they complained, agreed that the university could not deny students access to any course. The professor, defiant, explained that the course was designed to develop "self-understanding among women." When the dean sought support from various department heads, they advised him to drop the matter. After all, the feminist professor had not flatly required the males to withdraw; she had merely suggested (very forcefully) why they should want to do so. Thus are traditional academic arrangements subverted.[55]

Then, regarding the all-powerful sexuality factor that escapes the bishops, we see an example of why sensible administrators prefer separate schools for the two sexes rather merging them and relying on the purity of males and liberated women of energy and talent:

> If no principles are worse than bad principles, the other two tales are yet more scandalous. The local "deconstructivist guru" wrote a take-home exam (and more) for a female doctoral student. "The rules? Screw the rules" of the "faculty Neanderthals." Yes, as you guessed, he was bedding her. Eventually guilt-stricken, the student told her roommate, who told a respected professor, who told the department chair. But how could he act on hearsay evidence, the chair objected? Nor could the roommate go public, since she needed a dissertation director from among the guru's friends. So here we have an actionable offense, widespread rumors about it, but no action – just what the guru calculated. Equally shocking is the professor who turned over almost all his teaching assignment to his graduate assistant, appeared on campus seldom, and pulled down his fifty thou.[56]

Such cases crop up in almost every conceivable milieu, as, for instance, the current trial for treason of an Israeli paratrooper in holy Jerusalem, in which a defense attorney is claiming his female associate "maintained an intensive personal relationship with the judge during the trial and gave him confidential information about the case." The ramifications are intriguing at this stage in which the defendant awaits sentence after having been found guilty of selling chemical and biological weapons to Iran. One can never be certain of the honesty of today's lawyers but the suspicion works both ways when the presumably attractive legal lady in question claims, "the allegations that I had erotic relations with the judge are a lie and aimed at humiliating me and discrediting the judge." She says a former boyfriend is engaged in a vendetta against her. Which is right? *When the weaker sex is involved, one never knows*. The eternal, ubiquitous triangle takes on bizarre forms.

Whatever the truth in the Israeli case, one doubts the dignity of the court has been enhanced. Nor for that matter has the dignity of womanhood when allowed to permeate such serious proceedings and call into question the whole legal process which once provided respectable resolution of human conflict. The bishops might no doubt say that, if everybody involved were "servants in Christ" and purified their hearts before the Lord, there would be no occasion for sexual interaction, but then Jesus never suggested we check our common sense at the courtroom door. It is all very well to condemn "sinning in our hearts" by the mere appreciation of female beauty but, at the same time, it shows no great intelligence to forget that there were sound reasons for distinct roles and separate arenas for men and women where the masculine and the feminine were allowed to thrive while both enjoyed a higher value, back when we had a better grasp of such matters, that is, before feminism strummed its siren song and gullible males swooned.

Thus, there is a strong element of public misconception in all the talk of "women in expanding public roles" without care for the consequences. A credible Fourth Estate would be above fads "in the air" and seek higher rhythms but instead offer news reports like the July 11, 1998, *Fresno Bee* item headlined "Latinas encouraged to succeed." It reported the Third Annual Latina Women's Conference, which was intended "to motivate and educate" Mexican-American women to "succeed in business, politics, and their personal lives." Apparently, not much thought had been given to what "success" means for a woman, but one gathers that it involves having a lot of conferences, usually sponsored by eager politicians and bishops; making a lot of money and achieving power or fame; becoming surgeons, lawyers, engineers, combat soldiers "being all they can be," and so on. No mention of nurses, mothers, wives, or other more marian pursuits, which one hopes also measure up to the "success" these ladies are seeking with their "entrepreneurial spirit." Of course, care was taken to stress the "value of education" and "the importance of Hispanics reaching their goals"; "they need to be inspired and raise expectations about themselves." Naturally, the National Small Business Administration was represented and President Clinton would guarantee up to $5 billion in loans to Hispanic businesses, which will probably spell many more votes for the Democratic Party.

We certainly hope for the best for our fellow Hispanics and wish them well. But why all the fanfare? More committee work? Mary merely went about her business, which, after all, most "successful" people do, including many Latinas in the many agricultural-marketing jobs the valley offers. Much of it is hand labor and essential. Are there "conferences" spotlighting such women akin to the bishops' similar materialistic focus on women and "equal pay for equal work"?

Work used to be something men did outside the camp and women inside, by training and nature without much hoopla about making it "competitive." Now, if the aspiring female worker under the bishops' helpful wing doesn't make the grade, it is the enterprise's fault, not hers. And if she does make it, she merely exemplifies the "power of women," or becomes a candidate for Congress.

It warrants consideration whether co-education and sex equality level vigor and character down to a neutered stratum where there are few heroes except in crisis, who then are forgotten until we blunder into the next war. The bishops' resort to committees and programs of consciousness-raising with materialistic goals is reminiscent of Russian Communism and demagogic politics. As Matthew Parris recalls, speaking of Tony Blair's regime, "Our Prime Minister has come to resemble the creatures Alice met through the looking-glass, and in Wonderland.... Children do not, on the whole, like Lewis Carroll's writing because they do not know if it's supposed to be funny, or what – and nobody in the book seems to know either. It's like a rather unpleasant dream. I feel the same about New Labour. Like Carroll, it's creepy."[57]

However, Humpty Dumpty knows what it all means, as he declares scornfully, "When *I* use a word, it means just what I choose it to mean – neither more nor less." When Alice raises the question whether "you *can* make words mean so many different things," Humpty replies, as if laying the cornerstone for feminism, "The question is which is to be master – that's all."[58] Later, when Alice quite sensibly declares, "one *can't* believe impossible things," the White Queen, as if foreseeing women's studies, declares, "When I was your age, I always did it for half-an-hour a day. Why, sometimes, I've believed as many as six impossible things before breakfast."[59]

Of course, the ladies will remind us that, since Carroll was a man, he naturally misrepresented women, yet herstorians definitely improve on the White Queen's technique. This is not to say that men do not also have their Humpty Dumpties, as is apparent in the thought of Bill Clinton, Tony Blair and even the bishops, the first having redesigned the English language on the subject of truth, and the second having conceived of a New Order for Great Britain, much like the White Knight's own invention – the upside-down box designed to keep the rain out but unable to hold anything.[60] For his part, Parris, who is parliamentary sketchwriter and a columnist for the London *Times*, represents postmodern man stripped of intrepid initiative, unable to offer corrective measures other than a somewhat apologetic suggestion "to report the speech straight." Again, one suspects that all of this in large part is a result of incorporating the ladies' "receptivity" into the political and academic dialectic, thereby benumbing males into gentlemanly avoidance of pointed Johnsonian metaphor and Burkean wisdom. Such hoary input would be too – hmm – manly.

* * *

Despite such breakdown in thinking, there are signs of life in the Church, as we see in a July 1, 1998, newspaper item on the Vatican's latest reaction to dissenting liberal voices within the Church.[61] It reports that, in an apostolic letter, the Pope strongly reinforces the Church's profession of faith and teaching on male ordination, against euthanasia and sexual intercourse outside marriage. The Holy Father declares deviations from Catholicism's "definitive truths" to be a violation of Church law. Supplementing the Pontiff's statement, Cardinal Joseph Ratzinger adds that dissenters would be subject to punishment ranging from a warning to full excommunication. All prelates, parish priests, Catholic theology teachers and religious superiors are bound by the edict. In light of this announcement, one gathers that despite recent ecumenical rhetoric of solicitude even for feminist theologians the Vatican realizes that certain precepts are impregnable and will defend them. At least, we can hope so.

7. What Will Happen To God?

(T)he feminist movement in the Church is the very opposite of prophetic. All its theological principles are constructed by human hands: "It is from the tortured and angry world of the secular feminist struggle that the 'feminist hermeneutics of suspicion' has been directly called so that it may scatter its dragon's teeth of resentment and distrust into the fertile soil of the Church's life." He argues his case from a wide and detailed knowledge of the literature of feminism coupled with a profound theological understanding, and as such his book has importance in its own right as a piece of constructive theology.

Rear cover synopsis of William Oddie's
What Will Happen To God? (1984)

With his book, *What Will Happen to God?* William Oddie has given us the most unequivocal, "pungently written" treatise I have read on the pernicious inroads of feminist "theology."[62] As an Anglican (a Fellow of St. Cross College and its Priest Librarian of Pusey House, the Theology Faculty Library at the University of Oxford), Dr. Oddie writes for "the Christian Church"; thus his work should be relevant to the Catholic Church as well as to Protestant denominations. His book is a refreshing antidote to the Catholic bishops' pastoral letter on "women and the Church" and can stand alongside those of Goldberg, Levin, Davidson, and Gilder as impeccable authority. Some excerpts have appeared above. That almost twenty years later (long after midnight) the ladies still indulge in the masquerade says little for the savvy of their menfolk.

Oddie first tabs the feminist anger that motivates the feminists. Their complaints, one-sided distortions, and excuses are familiar, so I shall minimize repetition. It is refreshing to see Oddie pull no punches in his comments: "But the 'injustice' under which women suffer in the Christian tradition is not merely ignored by Christian men, but entirely imperceptible to most Christian women too."

Dr. Oddie tells of the advance of "women's studies," "women's liberation workshops," "almost universal awareness of women's problems and demands in western Europe and the United States," "women's rights," and the general disdain for traditional sex roles and Church teachings propagated by disenchanted women of the 60s and 70s who, according to Arianna Stassinopoulos Huffington, amount not to "a people's movement ... (but to) an eclectic sect drawn from the trendier section of the middle classes."[63]

Finding "male bias" in every corner, as well as frequent rejection of their entirely woman-centered concerns, the newly-aroused young women aspiring to "scholarship" of their own choosing, found sufficient cronies to nurture each other with "support, encouragement, and intellectual comradeship" out of which the bonds of contrived feminist theorizing was forged. Naive politicians were swept up in the onrush of wronged, prosperous young females claiming their share of 60s-inspired power, fame and fortune and in 1964 decreed "substantial changes in social policy" which plague us to this day. Dr. Oddie warns, however, that "the Woman's Movement will not be assuaged by any such reforms; it is not a reformist movement but a revolutionary one. The radical feminist fights the battle of the sexes in deadly earnest. She profoundly *believes* that she lives in a culture which for millennia has been expressly fashioned for her degradation. The aim, no matter how ill-defined, is revolution and nothing less, a revolution involving more than a mere assertion of women's rights. Quoting Kate Millett's words,

> As the largest alienated element in our society, and because of their numbers, passion, and length of oppression, its largest revolutionary base, women might come to play a leadership part in social revolution, quite unknown before in history.

(Which has all the veracity of a stray cat howling at midnight.) Dr. Oddie adds, "It is clear that for the Christian women's movement it is secular feminism which provides the initial impetus and, to some extent, the ideological nurture for its own revolutionary objective: the substantial reconstruction of the Christian religion itself."[64]

Actually, there has been no real "battle" because late-twentieth-century men proved surprisingly unfit to resist with the many sound precepts of long-proven healthy male-female arrangements. Most professors and politicians have drifted along like Paul Johnson's depiction of Stephen Spender, "It is true.... that he was sentimental and easily influenced, but that was all part of his warm, spontaneous and soft-hearted character. He was an exceptionally nice man, one of the few to emerge from the 'low, dishonest decade' of the 1930s, and the even lower ones which followed it, the 1940s and 1950s, with a degree of innocence, enabling him to survive into a serene and guiltless old age."[65]

Thanks to such men (who are the norm), the activist angry women have been allowed almost free rein, whether in the schools, the military, the courts, the corridors of power, or even some churches, despite the feminist ideology itself being much like the posturing Wizard of Oz, who, when confronted with a strong counter-argument, stood revealed as a laughable imposter.

Thus Kate Millett's predictions acquire status because the faculty does not expose them for fraud, college administrators fall meekly in line, and young, far-from-wise students think they are enjoying the uplifting refinement of higher education. They aspire to better grades by having the "right answers" which they then repeat outside of class without objection because few people know anything about feminism. One is struck by the similarity of feminists with former Marxist sympathizers of whom historian Paul Johnson offers a telling epigram:

> Orwell was too generous to some people: Walter Duranty, for instance, the odious apologist for Stalin, who worked for the *New York Times*, and the ridiculous Anna Louise Strong, who wrote a pamphlet applauding Stalin's use of slave labor, and who had, according to Malcolm Muggeridge, "an expression of stupidity on her face that amounted to a kind of beauty". Orwell rightly guessed that it was stupidity rather than depravity which led most of the pro-Soviet stooges to do what they did. Thus Sean O'Casey is dismissed as "very stupid" and Solly Zuckerman as "political ignorant" (though he later acquired more savvy). Poor Stephen Spender emerges as, "Sentimental sympathizer, and very unreliable. Easily influenced." All this, written in 1949, was soon to be out of date....[66]

Rather than "progress," qualification of women as "iron ladies" in the long run will prove quite the contrary. The "worth and dignity" of women would seem to deserve better.

To continue with Dr. Oddie's book, he discusses the thought of feminists Catherina Halkes, Elizabeth Fiorenza, Una Kroll, Rosemary Radford Ruether, Naomi Goldenberg, Mary Daly, Carol P. Christ, Susan Dowell, Linda Hurcombe, Betty Friedan, Sara Maitland, and others, not to overlook the surprising number of men like Anglican bishop Kenneth Woollcombe who believes that priestly ordination should be a question not of theological impact but of political "equal opportunity" legislation, hardly a sign of savvy on the good bishop's part. Ignoring human nature, the ladies like the idea of a female god, despite its radical heresy. But, as Oddie's passage instructs us, quoting from C.S. Lewis: "... the Church's understanding of the masculine and feminine principles in creation, and the roles fulfilled by men and women in the Christian tradition, are not our own to adjust at our whim,

> ".... for there we are dealing with male and female not merely as facts of nature but as the live and awful shadows of realities utterly beyond our control and largely beyond our direct knowledge. Or rather, we are not dealing with them but (as we shall soon learn if we meddle) they are dealing with us."

> Lewis was writing in the late nineteen-forties: nearly forty years on, his words have a chilling and increasingly unmistakable ring of prophetic truth. Whether, for the Anglican communion at least, the sound will be heard for generations to come as a warning note or as a funeral knell may depend on future events as yet only half guessed at.[67]

Oddie next explores the significance of men and women's biological differences and the correspondence of these "to clear differences of spiritual identity." "At this stage,... the most salient fact to register, simple but of overwhelming importance, is that however it may be observed, all known human societies without exception have assumed a clear distinction between 'masculine' and 'feminine' personality, behavior and social roles."[68] In contrast, the feminists strive to show some form of social determinism as the cause but invariably come up short. Oddie calls this their "great dilemma," which they confront with contrived sophistry having limited success only because grounded in general public ignorance. It is "crude, even silly," suggests Oddie, to believe feminist claims that, despite all the evidence to the contrary, there are no distinct personality differences or that men and women are not opposites to each other but merely adaptable integers whose qualities can be diffused through society by practice.[69] Faculty senates, college trustees, and politicians have proven timorous and ignorant in surrendering to such nonsense.

It is often claimed that the Bible stands for misogyny in our inheritance, yet Oddie shows this to be false. "The ideal of the good wife in Hebrew and Jewish tradition is clear enough, and it is one by no means either falsely romanticized or demeaning to women: it is both tender and realistic."[70] Shakespeare too has been maligned as "ephemeral or culture-bound," as has Saint Paul, but Oddie contends that close attention to the historical background "leads us further into the universality and massiveness of scale of (their) particular understanding of the human condition."[71] While Oddie feels Paul's teaching on women's covering in church (1 Cor. 11.5ff) and her silence in assembly (1 Cor. 14.33ff) were only addressing "particular and ephemeral pastoral situations, and their authority *as practical advice* has clearly now lapsed," he nevertheless defends the "principles with which Paul is truly concerned here, within the context of re-establishing right order within an actual congregation (as) more important." Frankly, it is not clear what he means by "lapse," since he does go on to emphasize the importance of man's and woman's distinctness by quoting Karl Barth's forthright advice: "As Karl Barth puts it, commenting on these two passages,"

> The essential point is that woman must always and in all circumstances be woman; that she must feel and conduct herself as such and not as a man; that the command of the Lord, which is for all eternity, directs both man and woman to their own proper sacred place and forbids all attempts to violate this order. The command may be given a different interpretation from that of Paul, for it is the living command of the living Lord. Yet if it is to be respected at all it cannot be even for a moment or in any conceivable sense be disregarded in this its decisive expression and requirement.

> "And in directing the sexes to 'their proper sacred place', Barth says of 1 Cor. 14.33ff, 'appearances must be very deceptive … the command of the Lord does not put anyone, man or woman, in a humiliating, dishonorable or unworthy position. It puts both man and woman in their proper place.'"[72]

Responding to feminist claims of "irrelevance" for any authority conflicting with their ideology, Dr. Oddie continues in this vein:

> We need, then, to be very careful when we dismiss teachings which may seem to be irrelevant and culturally limited or even unjust, but which may be so only to minds confined within a civilization like our own, in which human beings appear to themselves enlightened and increasingly free, but in which they are in fact in so many ways enthralled in a profound ignorance about the very basis for human dignity and freedom; an ignorance all the darker for seeming to be knowledge.[73]
>
> But to understand equality in *this* way, it is necessary entirely to distance ourselves from any merely human or ephemerally political understanding of the word. Our relationships are "in Christ"; and to *prefer*, or give priority to, any non-theological understanding, rooted in twentieth-century western culture, is not to be *more* radical but to be infinitely *less* so.[74]

Oddie makes clear that "in all societies it is the domestic sphere that women's particular aptitudes and instincts have been seen as especially necessary, and that the tasks and functions associated with this have not been regarded as degrading or as having less intrinsic worth than those traditionally performed by males until comparatively recent times." If we do not study these differences fully, we shall flounder. (See similar findings of Goldberg, Levin, Davidson, Gilder et al. Oddie's summary is especially on point and is included in the Notes herein.[75])

In the face of profound sexual differences, which underneath the feminist rhetoric of discontent rule our lives every day, discordant claims of "exclusion," "male brutalization," "female victimization," or "more leadership roles for women," pale in insignificance. Far from acting the "oppressors," the human male has his own cross to bear. As Arianna Stassinopoulos Huffington puts it, feminists are so obsessed with the "wrongs" of women that neither they nor their fans ever come to terms with the question of what life is like for men:

Men are just as emotionally vulnerable; indeed, Stassinopoulos goes on, in most ways they are more vulnerable than women. There are more male miscarriages and stillbirths. Infant mortality is higher among males, and male mortality is higher throughout childhood. More boys than girls are referred to child psychiatric services, and the more severe the disorder the higher proportion of males. Above all, women today live longer, often very much longer, a fact which Stassinopoulos sees as especially telling: "If it is the result," she says, of "innate differences between the sexes, the Women's Lib thesis that all sex differences are culturally determined collapses; if it is the result of environmental factors, then men are more harshly treated than women and it is their myth of the downtrodden woman that collapses."[76]

Such gerontological hardship comparisons are only relevant, however, to the more important goal of an *over-all* disposition of roles to effect societal harmony.

Betty Friedan's discovery that life has its ups and downs reflects an age-old truism not peculiar to women alone. As Oddie puts it, "The Christian answer to the conundrum has always been clear: our *lives* are not what they should be because *we* are not what we should be. And for Christians this is not in the end a pessimistic answer, since through Christ's incarnation, death and resurrection we have been given the means to overcome our human limitations and to attain at last what all human beings long for, whether they know it or not: the vision of the glory of God in the face of Jesus Christ. 'O God, thou hast made us for thyself,' prayed Augustine; 'our souls are restless until they rest in thee.' From a Christian perspective, then, the cardinal error of feminism is to ask an essentially religious question, 'is this all there is? What is wrong with my life?' and to give it a merely secular answer."[77] The feminist lexicon of political complaining is symptomatic of an inferiority complex.

Dr. Oddie's closing pages deserve a wide reading.

The effect of this distorting lens, applied by religious feminists to their perception of the Christian tradition, has been to produce a reversal of understanding of an extent unavailable to any merely secular feminism. ...

Is it really to be guilty of androcentric bias to suggest that such blind and loveless apprehension of the reality of Christian teaching is so grotesquely and so evidently far from the truth as it has been lived through the ages, so clearly the product of a distorted "historical imagination" formed in bitterness and resentment, that our main problem is no longer the apologetic one of reasoned counter-argument, but the more urgent pastoral task of judging how influential such writing may be, and containing the hatred and destruction it can surely cause?[78]

Indeed, and the appropriate solution would be not to accommodate but to expunge such thought from "Catholic" dialogue.

The stakes are high for civilization itself. As Philip Vander Elst writes on the tragic twentieth-century consequences of atheism – with connotations equally dire for feminist "theologians" – their "philosophy which denies the objectivity of moral values implicitly removes a crucial barrier to tyranny and evil.... (I)ts spread is therefore bound to be destructive of our civilization."[79]

The resulting decline in quality of women's writing will become evident in the next two chapters.

VII

History as a Society Column for Lovely Ladies – "Herstory"

Why should a democratic people dedicated to equality not applaud the attention now given to the roles in history of women, African Americans, working people, religious denominations, and other groups relatively powerless in the formal political sense? ... Is this the voice of "political correctness" or a recognition of the link between a democratic society and a more historically complete and accurate rendering of the past? ... That American history textbooks until recently left out the record of common folk seems extraordinary in a democratic society where we live by the motto "of, for, and by the people."
      Gary B. Nash, Charlotte Crabtree, and Ross E. Dunn[1]

Most people who read history books did so because they wanted to know why their society took the form it did and how it responded to its major challenges. Historians usually answered this demand in terms of how authority had been determined and deployed, and they invoked causes of a political, military and legal nature. The "common folk" and most of the now familiar sexual and ethnic identity groups played only intermittent roles in this account.... This was because for most of the time most of the people were not causally effective: they were the objects rather than the agents of history; they were on the receiving end of major historic events, not their instigators.

Keith Windschuttle[2]

1. BEFORE THE DELUGE

We could learn much from Fyodor Dostoevsky's "burden of vision," in which "he identified the major theme of his time as religious. It was the problem of faith and unbelief, in their confrontation and conflict."[3] "For Dostoevsky the burden of vision must include the vision of evil, for evil, as Claude Tresmontant says, 'is the work of man, and not of matter,' (it) 'is the work of created freedom.'"[4] It is a striking twist of fate that twentieth-century feminists with their "bitter harvest of division, anger and suspicion" have taken over the role of Dostoevsky's Satanic male protagonists in broadcasting their false claims: In its destructive campaign, feminism is on the side of Satan. Again, men must assume the larger responsibility for this phenomenon, since, as our nation drifted away from biblical precepts, it was their choice to encourage the "women's movement," which would probably still be languishing harmlessly had not men offered sustenance.

In his impressive study, *The American Commonwealth*, James Bryce tells of the general ambivalence prevailing in the late nineteenth century as many people believed "that to bring women into politics might lower their social position, diminish men's deference to them, harden and roughen them, and as it is expressed, 'brush the bloom off the flowers.' This feeling is at least as strong among women as among men, and some judicious observers deem it stronger now than it was formerly…. Of the many American ladies whose opinion I have from time to time during forty years inquired, the enormous majority expressed themselves hostile ... "[5] Although we shall return to Bryce, one should note his mention that the main impetus for women's suffrage came [1] from England and Europe, [2] the socialist and labor movements, [3] the tendency to exalt "democracy" and abstract "rights" over more practical and expedient representative government, and [4] the hope that the women's vote would further social reforms. In the event, none of these led to "inevitable forward progress"; instead, they only show that "progressive" males have dealt carelessly with the delicate balance of sexual power.

Although, to give them credit, they lived more ordered, circumspect lives, most men and women in 1890 were not very knowledgeable about our sexual constitution (any more than today!), nor for that matter was James Bryce, despite his intelligent survey of our country. People lived according to respected custom that proved vulnerable to calamitous waves of unrest. Thanks to the single-minded obsession of a few disgruntled women, the siren song of "equality and the rights of woman" exercised its allure over our vaunted *novus ordo seclorum*. Lack of serious, responsible thought led both Europeans and Americans eventually to ignore God's intricate pattern – our "sociocultural supersystem" [to use a term from Pitirim Sorokin's *The Crisis of Our Age*[6]] – and to succumb to "women's liberation," with the result that Bryce's listed fears came true and the social fabric withers. As with many other human pillars, standards of scholarly value have in many cases fallen by the wayside. (The above epigraph by Crabtree, Nash and Dunn is an example.)

Modern feminism has played no small part in this process, for, as William Oddie noted, there is a basic "incompatibility between the Christian tradition as it has been understood from the beginning, on the one hand, and a radicalized feminism, on the other."[7] Feminists had two options: either leave the Church or "find ways of transforming Church tradition." Since feminism is avowedly revolutionary, the ladies chose the latter and set about to "reconstruct" allegedly "androcentric" Christian origins to suit their own preferences. Feminist Elisabeth Schüssler Fiorenza adheres to the strange litany, "It is crucial, therefore, that we challenge the blueprints of androcentric design, assuming instead a feminist pattern for the historical mosaic, one that allows us to place women as well as men into the center of early Christian history. Such a feminist critical method could be likened to the work of a detective insofar as it does not rely solely on historical 'facts' nor invents its evidence, but is engaged in an imaginative reconstruction of historical reality."[8] Such dishonesty characterizes the "feminist transformation."

As Fiorenza urges, "it seems helpful to conjecture female authorship for early Christian writings in *order to challenge the androcentric dogmatism that ascribes apostolic authorship only to men.*" As Oddie suggests, "The issue has become, now, not whether or not such suggestions are *true*, but which of the various possibilities is most useful to the feminist case. According to Fiorenza, "the suggestion of female authorship…. has great imaginative-theological value because it opens up the possibility of attributing the authority of apostolic writings to women and of claiming theological authority for women." Oddie paraphrases this to mean, "What we need to know is not what actually was the case, but what should have been the case. The purpose of scholarship has become, not the discovery of truth, but the nurture of feminist consciousness…." While one can acknowledge that "history is more than 'what actually happened',… (this) is not to say that it is quite independent of what has happened, or that the values and interpretations of the historian may ever be so evidently unassailable as to warrant a conclusion being reached as to historicity *primarily* on ideological grounds. This appears, however, to be Fiorenza's basic assumption."[9]

Oddie's 1984 interpretation of feminist "scholarship" is amply reinforced by the later findings of Michael Levin and others.[10] One would like to think that, in view of such blatant disdain for the truth, in keeping with the well-known rules of evidence, people would reject out of hand anything the feminists stand for. Oddly, this is not yet the case. Their "ought" is not the "ought" sought by philosophers but the "ought" of Eve.

2. ENTER FEMALE SCHOLARSHIP

Which leads to the present fad of recasting history with women as the key actors, often referred to as "herstory." We shall consider several samples. One is Régine Pernoud's *Women in the Days of the Cathedrals* [1989], a rather one-sided discourse promoting certain women in history on the premise that "a feminine solution is.... necessary in order to put an end to the general injustice of our rational and controlled universe, where two beings out of three do not have enough to eat."[11] Anyone wanting to know how alleviating world hunger or injustice will result from retelling history to include more mention of women, or why a particular "society took the form it did and how it responded to its major challenges" will not find it in Pernoud's book. Yet, as the cover synopsis claims, "no feminine activity in the course of the feudal and medieval periods is neglected," which raises the question why Ignatius Press chose to publish this gyno-narrative in the first place – gossipy anecdotes about women that neglect the Church itself.

As if to camouflage the book's confused boundaries of legitimacy, Mme. Pernoud is described as "a highly regarded French author and archivist, and an experienced medievalist with some thirty years of archival work." Furthermore, as if her subject deserved nothing more, or perhaps because she merely prefers the freedom of creative writing to give form to her feminist urges, she disclaims any pretensions to scholarship, remarking that "this book is not intended for scholars." Thus the pretense of "women's studies," which delight in such works involving "an essential life component that more theoretically oriented courses" do not have.[12] Confirming this, author Donna Steichen adds her rear-cover bouquet to the project by gushing, "Intelligent readers with a taste for history will find this book a delight. It should be required reading in every Women's Studies department, and is highly recommended for anyone else who, for any reason, thinks women were not considered full human beings until Betty Friedan grew up." Such putdowns of women of the past are standard fare for feminist ladies – code words taken for granted by loyalists and never substantiated. So much for the supposed "scholarly" credentials of "women's studies."

Pernoud's book is like a prolonged Dear Abby column on the nuances of European society for the Sunday Women's Section, offering endless examples of woman's predilections for intimacy and caring, responsibility and relationships. History is simply retold from the angle of women – an example of what the world might be like as a matriarchy – a diffuse amalgam of sexless humanoids curtseying through a life of beauty and sameness in the most horrible of times and in the most delightful company. All is a bland panorama of pretty women engaged in incidental behavior with mighty monarchs as if civilization were being forged without power or bloodshed, adventure or risk. "I could be reproached for having sometimes oversimplified," acknowledges Pernoud at the outset, and one must agree. Her aim in this "historical" offering is to place her feminist spotlight solely *on women* and only incidentally on their male contemporaries. Her version would have us believe that "before the advent of the bourgeoisie," "the place of women in society" was far more influential, less "diminished," less "eclipsed," and more important than those coming after the French

Revolution. The latter (our great-great-great grandmothers, mind you) became "totally eclipsed from the scene" and subject to "the disillusioned personal self-obliteration that was demanded of them"[13], which, judging from their rather well fed, lovely twenty-first-century progeny, hardly seems likely. In fact, to reassure her readers, she lets them know that modern women have managed to emerge gloriously from their great-great-great grandmothers' "eclipse" presumably to resume women's former power and influence. One hears often this torch song, which has fortunately not yet reached the extreme of marching women belting out the Marseillaise or a Soviet working chant.

One wishes Pernoud had given the subject the "proper study" she says it was denied and which she leaves up to her feminist sisters-in-arms but then that would have required her to be more studious or – manly. It is a striking example of the pervasive irony of the "canon," that she is allowed by her male peers to pretend "that the question of the history of women holds attention and has already produced theses, studies, and research that will certainly lead later to a richer and more complete synthesis than mine. And would we ever write, especially in the field of history, unless we were already reconciled to being incomplete?"[14] Well, one must question such gauzy resignation to "incompleteness," which is hardly conducive to "completing" a studious effort of any value at all. While Michael Oakeshott considered education an "endless conversation" and Voegelin also saw the incompleteness of history, one doubts they meant to emphasize the "endless" or "incomplete" aspect as much as seeking the *truth*. Pernoud is misapplying a profound truth to excuse fictional scholarship.

Mme. Pernoud et al represent our current society's aversion to forthrightness and objectivity of which they and their ideology are largely the cause. As David Gelernter sees the general trend, "We are in the habit nowadays of looking only at the part of the picture that pleases us, the pretty part."[15] Herstory has a way of leaving out the best part.

Characteristic of much feminist writing and its love of self-expression, women often hit upon a persuasive truism – an apt turn of phrase – as if by accident, but then revert to solecism. After prolonged celebration of her Joans and Catherines, Pernoud's insight that women's "copying" the opposite sex only leads to "failed men" not only makes for inconsistency in her gyno-centric tale but also pinpoints the illusion of feminism itself.[16] Yet she hews to her theme that women can do it all on their own, if only by being more like women, thus challenging "the rigorously masculine world of the French classical and middle-class civilization."[17]

Feminists seem unaware of their kinship with the Furies, flooding the public arenas where men doggedly persevere in life's pageant, while either consciously or unconsciously aping male ways and squandering their own best resources. As a result, for all the political favoritism, female protagonists end up half-male and half-female, like gryphons or satyrs. Kipling found the bullseye in his poem, "The Female of the Species":

> And Man knows it! Knows, moreover, that the Woman that God gave him
> Must command but may not govern; shall enthrall but not enslave him.
> And *She* knows, because She warns him and Her instincts never fail,
> That the female of Her species is more deadly than the male!

Meanwhile, Pernoud lapses into a fantasy world with twisted metaphor introducing the enchanting Clotilda – the love of Clovis, King of the Salian Franks: "This book encompasses a millennium or thereabouts, with, as a starting point, a surprising change, which began the movement of the wheel of fortune; and is not fortune traditionally pictured as a woman?"[18] Such stuff is nectar to the canon, plying "no better apparatus than the metaphysics of an undergraduate, and the mathematics and metaphysics of an exciseman."[19]

In her final word on Joan of Arc, Pernoud brushes up against the truth: "Is there any need to say that Joan's mission would have been impossible in the nineteenth century? At any rate it was then unthinkable in the strict sense of the word." Indeed it was, primarily because the Church was no longer paramount, not because of male chauvinism or a supposed suppression of women, but because of the Enlightenment and its elevation of the self over the sacred — the same sensate culture that informs Pernoud. There were no Joans in 1830 because women were less devout unto death and the word of God carried less weight. At that, the nineteenth century sustained the era of Queen Victoria, possibly the acme of secular Western Civilization, when men were men and women women, against which feminists rail. Pernoud uses Joan to fabricate a false expectation for women. (Much like the Fresno Bee sportswriter who promotes a female pugilist as a "role model for young girls.") Joan's was a singular martyrdom — all she wanted was to return to her village — hardly a model for young girls seeking careers, fame and fortune. In stark contrast to feminist pretensions her life stands forever as a model of humble obedience to God.

In the end, one sees no improvement from Pernoud's women resurrected to "power and status." The fact that the Church has defended the institutional values reflecting human nature goes unnoticed in Pernoud's vision. A feminist trying to dissect the age of chivalry is like a toddler baking a cake, fumbling the ingredients without knowing the recipe. To center history around selected miniatures of women's lives in castles, boudoirs, monasteries and guildhalls instead of calamitous, seminal or mundane events that actually shaped history defies an orderly sequence of events. When Pernoud finally suggests that women change the world by – well, being more like women, she has come full circle, since this is what her foremothers were all along!

3. Brushing the Bloom off the Flowers

Let us leave Mme. Pernoud and struggle with another lady's effort, *After Suffrage: Women in Partisan and Electoral Politics before the New Deal*, by Kristi Anderson. This offering by The University of Chicago Press is classified as "women's studies/politics" and announces itself (rear cover) as "a compelling account of both the accomplishments and disappointments experienced by women in the decade following suffrage." If you get the impression this is going to be another women-centered effort, you are right. "This revisionist history traces how, despite male resistance to women's progress, the entrance of women and their concerns into the public sphere transformed both the political system and women themselves." Here again is a transformation of government and right order into a solipsistic exercise centered on the selfish interests and perceptions of women. Instead of a healthy tension between two balanced forces, it decomposes into "us" against "them" in an assault on all balance. "Gaining the right to vote, campaign, and run for office transformed women's citizenship; at the same time, women's independent partisan stance, their focus on social welfare concerns, and their use of new political techniques such as lobbying all helped to redefine politics." Indeed; and gone are the days of responsible constitutional government, now superseded by bossy reform liberalism and the welfare state.

With the loss of rigorous dialogue geared to objective truth and long-term issues, we are now saddled with the breezy back-cover nonsense of female "political scientist" Eileen L. McDonagh of Northeastern University, who promotes fellow Professor Anderson's

> .... lucid and insightful book (as) a valuable addition to the literature on women's rights in general and the relationship between political rights, political participation, and policy outcomes in particular. It addresses a key dimension cutting through many subfields in political science – how the entry of new groups into the electorate in the twentieth century contributes to a complex configuration of political change that transforms nineteenth century partisan politics into contemporary nonpartisan politics.

So, the untapped wealth of "political science" and its ability to demote sex to just another political "group"! National judgments are now based on "how men treat women," with those earlier concerns for the Ten Commandments, Magna Carta, and the like now dismissed as male pond scum. Accompanying the emergence of women's "new influence," few consider whether it is any more or beneficial than Eve's.

Like Pernoud's flirting with truth she doesn't see, Anderson's publisher offers a preview on the front cover – "Suffragettes celebrate victory, 31 August 1920 (detail)" courtesy of UPI/Corbis-Bettmann. The Trojan Horse has entered the gates and the gentle Greeks are romping; as yet there's no pillage, since the subtle ambivalences work only gradually to undermine rather than to shatter. These always entertaining creatures are now in charge – or so it would seem. Depicted are two subdued token males, one in the background with dour if not grim face and noncommittal expression, wearing a broad-brimmed hat and dark suit with bow tie slightly askew. Well he might wonder what the sages had wrought in this "progressive" era. His fellow male, the chauffeur, wears a uniform hat, white tie and dark suit, and sports a jaundiced grimace and half grin – the perennial male indulging the fair sex in their fancy, this time with implications serious for all the world. The precious "vote" – the all-powerful franchise – has been diminished to an exercise in female cavorting. The old days of male rousting, boozing and fighting on Election Day at least had basic nuts-and-bolts issues in mind, not primping, coquetry and display. Male objectivity has surrendered to female finery and giggles with no more thought than a passing compliment and bow on the boardwalk. For the ladies, it's a party – they love parties – a gathering, a togetherness, a flocking to wherever their compassionate world-peace-justice-utopia will lead, regardless of whose lives, fortunes and sacred honor are at stake.

Are not these women merely cavorting in male shoes and thus shedding their feminine dignity and influence, falling into the trap of Pernoud's "failed men"? After announcing that "Woman suffrage was said by its detractors to be a failure,"[20] Anderson assays to disprove this with an impressive torrent of facts and figures easily shaped to satisfy feminist absorption with "women's issues," i.e., retelling history to show women "coming out on top" in a much "more influential" position than their great grandmothers. But the deeper question, e.g., how the vote has improved the lot of women or society in general, she ignores. Anderson stabs at the question, "was it a failure?" from the perspective of *women*, hardly a comprehensive study, although certainly profuse; from start to finish, her tale offers another example of the fallacy of the Nineteenth Amendment.

Anderson contends that the "slow process of shifting boundaries… continues today," ignoring evidence that married women still tend to vote more conservatively with their husbands, earlier signs of which she tabs a "myth."[21] She pays no attention to our distinctive sexual natures (which Pernoud at least nods at in passing) in her rush to transform women into political creatures. She brushes aside the "boundaries that delineated appropriate male and female behavior" to reveal women who could "rise to a leadership position" as though science fiction ruled and males were neutered automatons in dark suits. (Regrettably, many now are.)

It would be interesting to hear her explanation of why women are so interested in political power but have written so little on political philosophy or government. The consequences from such lack of conscientious reflection will prove disastrous. After all, as the Founders took for granted, the goal was to assure the most knowledgeable electors, not universal minimal input from every Tom, Dick and Mary. (Aside from the founding literature, they might read James Fenimore Cooper's *The American Democrat* to understand what is involved.)

What has women's suffrage brought? "Relief and social services… emerge as basic objectives in framing public policy."[22] Before, "the central issues of male politics" were more limited "to tariff, finance, internal improvements, foreign relations."[23] Women's party loyalties were less established and their behavior was more "independent than men."[24] Anderson ingenuously argues that women had "an impact on political decision-making and on the shape of the political agenda" with the effect that "visible women in parties and in public offices were able to use their connections with women reformers to preserve, if only partially and precariously, the progressive impulse through the unfriendly twenties,"… transforming "the act of voting from a male ritual to a good citizen's obligation"… with "the organizational innovations pioneered by women's groups, helped to solidify the movement from the partisan-structured politics of the nineteenth century to the politics of advertising, interest groups, and candidates that characterize the twentieth century." If anyone wants to know what led to subversion of the Founders' plan, there you have it! The countless "social services" once administered felicitously by the local charities of a free people have been transferred by the ladies to distant Washington, D.C.

Anderson trumpets such "transforming of the political system" much like a child bragging about pulling the lever that wrecked a train. If before all this happened "women were not personally ambitious," is it possible that women were less selfish then? Or not interested in the politics some men had devoted their lives to studying? Revealing the basic flaw involved, Anderson repeats the cliché that some men are "threatened" by "successful" women plying male trades, apparently oblivious to the central fact that men are not drawn to women in male roles because most men *are not drawn to men.*

* * *

While, because of his Progressive Party, Theodore Roosevelt is perhaps the most famous example of the movement, Woodrow Wilson's book, *Congressional Government* (1885) was probably the forerunner, according to Sidney A. Pearson, Jr., writing on "Herbert Croly and Liberal Democracy."[25] It is important to recognize that, for all its seductive power, "progressivism" (apparently endorsed by Ms. Anderson) amounted to an overt attempt to restructure our constitutional system. As Pearson puts it, "Croly certainly agreed with Wilson's view that the Founders' Constitution was inadequate to the tasks required by modern government."

> The social-political science of the Progressive Movement and Croly's place in it are best understood as a critique of the political science of the Founders. The Progressives were not simply "republicans with a new suit of clothes," but were rather a new type of democrat in the American regime. It was the conscious aim of Croly and the Progressive Movement to establish American government on fundamentally different principles than those of the original Founders.

This is a startling revelation, after a century of subversive views eating insidiously away at our national heritage. Granted, true individualism had played a huge role in our nation's success but it was always tempered by loyal acceptance of the Founders' (and God's) plan as the most practicable solution to republican government. It was not feminist "individualism" intent on more government control.

Pearson offers more revelations of what Progressivism stands for, all of which are strikingly similar to what Pernoud and Anderson favor: "a positive national ideal based on human welfare"; "more centralized national democracy"; "a new Constitutional Convention to draft a new document"; "to challenge the old system root and branch"; "satisfy changing social needs"; "from a fundamental undemocratic founding toward a more democratic future"; "greater emphasis on equality of social conditions"; "radical surgery"; "radically different conception of democratic community"; "public opinion (is) the bedrock of democracy"; "faith in democracy (that superseded) traditional religious faith"; "property regulated by the government for the common good of society as a whole"; "collective effort"; "politics reduced to public administration"; "authority will depend ... on its ability to apply scientific knowledge to the realization of social purposes". Pearson comments that, while the left has considered Croly's perspective "insufficiently egalitarian," the right has complained that it "neglects the right order of the soul." Pearson offers this conclusion:

> As the twentieth century wound on through two world wars and nihilistic revolutions in Russia and Germany, both deriving their appeals, in part, from ideas of "social justice," "science," and "community," faith in democracy as the cure for the ills of democracy has faded in some quarters... That he helped to design the liberal-progressive paradigm seems also beyond doubt,... Grasping its continuity through much of twentieth century politics, however, is integral to any systematic understanding of American politics, especially since the New Deal. What is important to remember is that its essential philosophical elements were in place long before it became a dominant political force. And it is the philosophical elements that are largely taken for granted by later generations who have forgotten the origins of ideas.

Pearson's essay alerts us to aspects of feminism that, along with the suffragette movement, are mere detritus of the "liberal-progressive paradigm." Croly's idea of administrative, consensual "leadership" is a far cry from the real leadership required in a healthy polity blessed with ordered freedoms; his model resembles both the Politburo's and the feminists'. In calling for competing factions and productive tension so basic to the idea of freedom, the founders realized this better than Croly with his middling preference for a "conformity with public opinion of the community" that tends toward either no leadership or gridlock.

*　*　*

In the same vein, in his books, *The New Science of Politics* and *Science, Politics and Gnosticism*, Eric Voegelin offers a scholarly analysis of the philosophy of politics from origins traced not to Croly but back through Heidigger, Hegel, Marx, Nietzsche, and beyond, to find in modern movements "variants of the Gnostic tradition of antiquity." Feminists will scoff at the idea that their ideology is adulterated gnosticism indulging in "a dialectic-material process of nature which in its course leads from the alienation resulting from private property and belief in God to the freedom of a fully human existence; or through the assumption of a will of nature which transforms man(woman) into superman(woman)."[26] (parenthesis added) In contrast to Pernoud's and Anderson's feminist platform, Voegelin writes of visions of order and the need for "a structure of reality," remarking on Hobbes' discovery that "public order was impossible without a civil theology beyond debate; it is the great and permanent achievement of the Leviathan to have clarified this point." But Hobbes erred (as do feminists) in denying "the existence of a tension between the truth of the soul and the truth of society; the content of Scripture, in his opinion, coincided with the truth of Hobbes."[27] Without both Scripture and the "truth of the soul," truths of society rapidly become lost.

Of course, as with Kristi Anderson and Pernoud (despite the latter's oblique reference to "cathedrals"), feminists never resort to Scripture, since their gnosticism is far removed from "right order" and rooted instead in the truth of their own women-centered desires. There, the truths of Scripture, society and the soul, in fact any abiding truth at all, are irrelevant. Any sort of "theology" is anathema unless it centers on women's concerns, such as those of Elizabeth Wurtzel, whose reviewer Margaret Schulman condones as "nonlinearly imaginative" much like "a guided tour through a moronic inferno," yet "a genuine education of the feelings" and a vehicle for "the expression of emotion" or "feminine self-expression."[28] Such are the ravages of postmodern thought and feminist deconstruction.

4. More Challenges to Society's "Male" Blueprint

Anderson and Pernoud's books are only two samples of the "herstory" genre festering in university "centers of learning" – as yet unchallenged by the unsuspecting media and their readers. In the July/August, 1998, issue of *Society*, the editor displays an ad for a periodical entitled "Gender Issues," dedicated to "publishing basic and applied research on the relationships between men and women; formerly feminist issues." It is an offering by "Transaction Periodicals Consortium, a division of Transaction Publishers, at Rutgers – the State University." Whether one detects a burgeoning nest of rodents or a Pandora's box, it's perhaps already familiar to the reader. On July 18, 1998, *The Fresno Bee*, a McClatchy newspaper, ran an item by Jodi Enda of Knight Ridder Newspapers headlined "Feminists mark key anniversary." It consists of about a thousand words on the increased "political power" of women, with the usual fanfaronade seen in Anderson's book, this time about the campaign of women's groups like the Center for the American Women in Politics at Rutgers University (Transaction Publishers' bailiwick!), the National Organization for Women, and Emily's List, all aligned essentially against the regnant system of government and the male of the species. "Women still seeing disparities," complains the headline, as if men and women were not by nature disparate. Supposedly unfair conditions in the "home, the workplace and the world of politics" overwhelm these ladies, as if women had been inferior all these years, incapable of enjoying the pursuit of happiness along with their menfolk.

Ms. Enda offers nothing of intelligence on the strange urge for political power of the fair sex. Again, if they are individually cut out for actual "power," why do they need so many *groups*? (See Wendy McElroy, below.) Or is it mere group action they enjoy, regardless of where the piper leads? Have they *individually* studied political philosophy or even read the U.S. Constitution? As an example, after a 1997 female G.O.P. "volunteer of the year" had argued for some moments in favor of a certain piece of civil rights legislation, offering the usual rubric in its behalf without really understanding what was involved, she ended up remarking that she had never read the Constitution. (Even worse than Mrs. Samuel Clemens, who at least knew the words.) Granted, too many 1990s men haven't either, but at least they do not get a hearing until they do.

Ironically, in her news item Enda lets the cat out of the bag when she claims credit for the ladies' helping to elect possibly the most laughable president in our history (and the twentieth century was not graced with a surfeit of wise leaders to begin with), mainly because he and his party catered to their Croly-like urge to reconstruct America according to their own fancies. Indeed, besides distracting males from their vocation, these entertaining, attractive creatures again and again prove questionable partners in politics, as shown in the National Organization of Women's (N.O.W.) tolerant position on Bill Clinton's alleged sexual harassment.

The occasion for Enda's item was an obscure anniversary of the Nineteenth Amendment, or perhaps the 1848 commencement of the Suffragette Movement; she is unclear. In any event, she unapologetically promotes the customary focus on "women's power" without concern for whether it has brought improvement. Undermining her own cause, she quotes conservative Phyllis Schlafly of Eagle Forum as saying on another occasion that "I think women have all the rights that men have," unaware that women have always possessed as many "rights" under the Bill of Rights or Equal Protection Clause as men do, perhaps even *more*. While the issue of "rights" has unfortunately been inflated by women (and "minorities"), the better focus would be anthropological, theological realities and the long-term, constitutional common good, i.e., how best to use the resources available to the human race.

* * *

An essay by Lawrence M. Mead, "The Politics of the Disadvantaged"[29], sheds light on the likes of Enda's ladies and their complaints about "disparity," which he tabs as "visions of oppression without reference to realities others can see." As professor of politics at New York University, he seems a liberal who has felt mugged by conditions in the university, since he believes in government regulation of "fairness" and believes, "Today, virtually everyone agrees that blacks or women are entitled to equal opportunity," which, of course, is political ritual but not really true. Liberal-pretentious words of "entitlement" breed confusions over race and sex that hog-tie the intellect.

Aside from this, Mead's essay deals splendidly with the likes of Pernoud, Anderson, Enda, et al, by discussing the newborn "politics of identity" and "politics of injury," (although his treatment suffers from lumping women and blacks together). Feminists have indulged to excess in "claim-making by complaint." Unable to find fault with the vast array of civil rights laws on the books (rendering us a bewildered egalitarian society) and bereft of any real causes, feminists ape other groups in "complaining that equal opportunity is imperfectly realized." Mead tells of fanciful and tireless claims of "discrimination" against women in various ways, and of the proverbial "glass ceiling," all alleged as "unfair under existing norms." Meanwhile, men resent these incessant claims that they are "secretly mistreating groups that public policy… favors."

Of course, those on the left don't see that there are good reasons for the shortfall of women's representation in this or that field. As noted by Professor Mead, women "are not, on average, as competitive for demanding careers as men… women *on average* tend to take time off from careers to raise children." "The politics of disadvantage provokes upset more by the facts that onlookers are asked to take on trust than by the substance of its policy claims." In the end, Mead rightly sees much that is wrong and makes a powerful statement, but one wishes he went all the way and recommended that government get out of the "anti-discrimination" business. "Rights" law creates a casuistic conundrum impossible to resolve, with complainers encouraged to resort to "public relations" instead of "organizing" because they have been led to "simply assume government should address their problems because they exist." A result is the political correctness ruling our once forthright nation. "The whole trajectory of claim-making is from the objective to the subjective – from public grievances discernible by anyone, to private injuries that are contestable, and finally to threatened feelings that arise from the inner depths of identity."

Feminists' Pyrrhic "political price is enormous, since the appeal to victimhood is based on guilt, not on the making of common cause. The value that today's claimants ultimately assert is not some version of the American creed but their own identity." The platform of self-indulgence and subjectivity – rule of woman over objectivity, prescription, and rule of law – is a clone of Croly's outright rejection of our constitutional system and should be expunged irrevocably from our political dialogue. "Their feelings provide the ultimate ground for most of what they assert about society and its problems. But like the contestable empirical claims of the left, feelings are not arguable. One cannot have an impartial discussion about them even with one's friends, let alone one's enemies. The cultural arena personalizes all issues."

In stark contrast to Kristi Anderson, Mead makes a strong point in favor of higher norms:

> Feminists say that "the personal is the political," as if politics refuses to hear claims coming out of private life, and it should. The opposite is more clearly true: politics too readily honors private claims, and it should not. Activist women have largely created the new politics of complaint. It is they who believe that the personal problems of themselves and other victim groups deserve automatic standing in the political arena simply because of who they are.... By speaking of disadvantage and not of justice, today's claimants neglect the serious work of politics, which is to make common cause with people different from themselves.

*   *   *

One suspects that loving fathers and husbands who stifle the serious work of politics by lauding "equal opportunity" for women have dulled their senses regarding the remarkable intricacies involved. Perhaps this explains the prevalent distaste for "polemics" – the demanding dialogue behind the Constitution. As Russell Kirk put it,

> There is small danger that the majority of Americans will embrace a radical ideology actively. But there is considerable danger that the majority of Americans may fail to oppose such

movements intelligently. It is not required that radical doctrines be accepted with enthusiasm; rather, such nostrums flourish upon the indifference and ignorance of the majority.[30]

An exception is former British Number-One-ranked player, Buster Mottram, who analyzes women and professional tennis as a matter of sex appeal: women players cannot match male athleticity so as to deserve equal prize money, but they're enjoyable because of their shapeliness, sexuality and, if we are fortunate, their femininity.[31] His candor could benefit all public arenas! Instead of "coming a long way, Baby!" the ladies are only enjoying the benefits of their sexuality as women have for ages.

5. *Toujours L'Amour*

For another visit with France, Diana Schaub reviews Mona Ozouf's *Women's Words: Essay on French Singularity*[32], both of the ladies indulging in what our laws forbid, namely, discriminating as to sex by finding something "singular" in women. Such taboos do not deter Schaub's discriminating mainly to promote her own predispositions in favor of women's excellence and so forth. The review appears in *The Public Interest*, a worthwhile quarterly whose editors, however, follow the questionable practice noted above of having women review other women's books, a practice in itself discriminatory in favor of women, yet also condescending, as though editors are too kind to subject women's thinking to full public analysis.

As another example (no matter how deftly crafted) of "women's studies," Schaub's essay ends up astraddle the issue, defending both female "choice" and female "submission" as women have done since Eve. To an American woman writing of French customs, the paradox that Frenchwomen are more feminine is possibly unsettling, so Schaub doesn't go deeper. She tries to play both roles and proves how dexterous and delightful women at their best can be, if only American women didn't persist with the rickety platform of "equality", or even "superiority", which Frenchwomen more skillfully avoid while enjoying more power than American feminists could dream of. The magnetism of gentle nuance, innuendo, inference and elision – unknown territory – are beyond the women's studies mindset. Schaub therefore misses the irony and mistakenly finds a French "feminism" that is not feminism at all, but merely femininity. (Schaub and Mona Ozouf share to some extent the same predilections, so for simplicity their words will be merged.)

More to specifics, both Schaub and Ozouf recognize that "French feminists, even academic feminists, lack the militant thrust that transforms female unhappiness into a badge of honor; they do not adopt an aggressive tone," yet a focus on "unhappiness" imbues Schaub-Ozouf's writing, along with "brutalization" talk. But it takes a lot of gall to categorize Frenchwomen as "feminist" even though "they do not oppose men, collectively guilty, to women, their collective victims…." Here is no sign of feminism, yet Schaub labels French ways arbitrarily a "unique path for feminism." Ozouf is French, yet her definition also is missing. Then, reflecting the confusion, Schaub reports that Ozouf "finds herself between two camps and in opposition to both"!

Generally, Ozouf seems to portray an accurate version of Frenchwomen's propensities, activities and charms, and even surprises Schaub and most of us by mentioning that Frenchwomen "were drawn to Rousseau's ideal of conjugal bliss in a union combining love and friendship". Since "Rousseau is today the most reviled of the dead, white… males" and abhorred by American feminists, Schaub judiciously passes it by, since it reveals the chasm separating Frenchwomen from the more ideological American female – with the more womanly tradition of the former contrasting to the more independent, unwomanly status of the latter.

While apparently Anglo-Saxon feminism has yet to paralyze schools in France, it is not totally absent there. Despite her futile attempts to clarify various forms of "equality" as well as of "feminism" in France, Schaub doesn't see that the French people simply enjoy different customs for the sexes, which allow "healthier relations", and that Frenchmen play as strong a role in the arrangement as the women whom Schaub and Ozouf adulate. Unlike American men, Frenchmen are allowed their own turf while respecting that of their women. Both sexes understand and appreciate their relationship better than Americans, although neither Schaub nor Ozouf knows what to make of it. Explaining the Frenchwoman's lack of "resentment," Schaub gets stuck on the equality tar baby and its civil rights rubric on "minorities," "race", and the link between "the women's movement" and "the black struggle," which we already know to be puffery.

Schaub-Ozouf's is another gynocentric exercise oblivious to the broader challenge of understanding the human dichotomy of men *and* women. Frenchwomen did not acquire the vote until 1945, which Schaub-Ozouf do not see as a sign of good sense and preservation of the very harmony they commend. Far from wanting our womenfolk to be "universalist" in Ozouf's scheme of things, we should encourage them to be "particularist" in the sense of remaining loyal to their womanly nature and attributes. Ozouf's "women's words" of a "shared consciousness" are a wistful reminder of women's incomprehension of the power of their attraction, or why they are loved by men and children.

*　*　*

There is a delightful British film classic entitled "A Girl In A Million," in which a lovely female houseguest who cannot speak (she is literally dumb) entrances three bachelor scientists with her feminine touch around the house. She falls in love with one and he with her, they marry, and, in a traumatic moment she regains her speech, which leads to her voice filling the house – endlessly, unremittingly – until she sees her friends drift away. So, she makes herself "dumb" again and recaptivates them. Never underestimate the power of a woman, who, even without talking, in fact, *especially* without talking, can hold families together by sheer, quiet femininity. The story is a parable of course, and parables are rare in real life, but the lesson is profound – one probably understood by Frenchwomen better than by modern Americans.

In the long run, women's words are mainly of value where they have primary impact – in intimate, one-on-one, personal relationships – family, friendships, children, interiorities – where they enjoy the advantage of distinctly feminine ways. Because, no matter how the Schaubs and Ozoufs envision the coming age, the fact will remain that, contrary to John Stuart Mill, both a woman's "singularity" and "universality" will be determined to a large extent by her physiology, which means that "women's words" cannot be heard other than through their *voices*; and, whether by God or by selectivity, these are designed for intimacy and caring, not supremacy or "universality."

6. FLIRTING WITH A FEMINIST PATTERN FOR SOCIETY'S MOSAIC

And so, despite their much publicized "transformation" of America, the fact is that feminists are only camp followers for Croly's and Theodore Roosevelt's Progressives. Unable to "achieve higher status" or male power on their own despite their gatherings, they resort to the heavy hand of authoritarian government. As Elizabeth Fox-

Genovese reminds us, "feminism is no innocent defense of truth and justice but a political ideology actively promoted by an economic and cultural elite that has reaped many benefits from it."[33]

We see another manifestation of the "eternal irony" – the essential paradox of women like Schlafly, Fox-Genovese, Camile Paglia, Thatcher, Rice – as Fox-Genovese reviews another woman's book, *Domestic Tranquility: A Brief Against Feminism*, by F. Caroline Graglia. Ms. Graglia pursued a career in law and ends up promoting womanhood, much as Fox-Genovese has pursued an academic career primarily in "women's studies" and ends up torn between domesticity and "intellectual and professional life." (We shall consider both Graglia's book and Fox-Genovese's review in more detail below.) In their bifurcated lives, all are geared to Lawrence Mead's "politics of disadvantage."

* * *

If anyone needs proof of the oxymoron of "women's liberation," one need only look at our 1990s President, shaped by the sex-lax sixties, molded by the "civil rights" era, nurtured in the permissive sentiments of the Age of Aquarius and Marijuana, and elected by Lear's angry daughters to the second most powerful office in the world. Now, thanks to the Nina Burleighs, Dolly Kyle Brownings, Monica Lewinskys and other modern goddesses, we have a front-row seat to the burlesque of "women's progress" and "equal opportunity." Despite the ladies' pretext of holding down male jobs and pursuing "intellectually stimulating careers," the zoo antics of Mr. Clinton and his coterie of sexually arousable females stand revealed in all their ridiculous raffishness. "Universalist" reporter Nina Burleigh throws off the covers of "political power" for women in an article in *Mirabella* magazine:

> When I got up and shook his hand at the end of the game, his eyes wandered over my bike-wrecked, naked legs. And slowly it dawned on me as I walked away: He found me attractive.... I

felt incandescent. It was riveting to know that the President had appreciated my legs, scarred as they were. If he had asked me to continue the game of hearts back in his room at the Holiday Inn, I would have been happy to go there and see what happened .... It took several hours and a few drinks in the steaming and somehow romantic Arkansas night to shake the intoxicated state in which I had been willing to let myself be ravished by the President, should he have but asked.[34]

As *The Weekly Standard*'s "Scrapbook" added, "Actually, Nina hasn't yet shaken that 'intoxicated state.' Just last week she told the *Washington Post* that she would be happy to "give the president (oral sex) just to thank him for keeping abortion legal."

Then there is *The Weekly Standard*'s account of "Dolly Kyle Browning, the Dallas real estate lawyer and high-school sweetheart of Bill Clinton who alleges a 30-year affair ending in 1992. Though Clinton denied their relationship under oath in the Paula Jones case, Dolly has detailed their respective sex addictions (she's in recovery, he's not) in her *roman clef*, *Purposes of the Heart*, for sale at www.deardolly.com in hardcover leatherette."[35] Now, one cannot be too careful before rendering judgment based on such talk. Bill Clinton has yet to be convicted of anything. However, discounting John F. Kennedy, such reports have never plagued either a sitting or a former president (not even Warren Harding, dead or alive).

The promiscuity and dissembling suggested by the accumulation of evidence on William Jefferson Clinton involving a quite ostensibly married man whose wife has been a principal part of his public image, suggests the old saw "where there's smoke, there must be fire." It seriously damaged both his ability to govern and the national ethos itself, already tarnished by the "pathetic infantilism" of the national capitol.[36] To unrestrained judicial, executive and legislative misfeasance, we must now add the horny record of publicized sexual conduct by the top executive. And, more important to our study, one traces all these low roads back to the *60s' sexual liberation*, *"equality and the rights of woman"*, and the hallowed Nineteenth Amendment itself. The hordes of squealing bobby-soxers enraptured by the Beatles are come of age.

7. More Women's Liberation

But to return to our exploration of various samples of "herstory."

The Times Literary Supplement (London) offers a weekly parade of authors in the fanciful world of herstory, mostly women writers with a sympathetic ear for feminism and its pretensions, but occasionally dabbling male writers. For instance, in the July 24, 1998, issue, we read again of Peter Stanford's misguided attempt to produce "what purports to be a search for the truth about Pope Joan, a legendary cross-dressing Englishwoman of the ninth century who got herself elected Pope, and was finally unmasked when she gave birth to a child (fathered by one of her cardinals) while astride a horse in a procession to the church of St. John Lateran in Rome." Peter Stanford is "a former Editor of *The Catholic Herald* (and) a lively journalist specializing in cheeky treatment of serious themes" and is reviewed by a more traditional objective male, Eamon Duffy (bless him!), who tells us that "The only absolutely certain fact about Pope Joan is that she never existed."

"The main legend," demolished "with the advent of critical historical methods at the Renaissance" and ultimately by David Blondel in the mid-seventeenth century, nevertheless "gave rise to a cluster of lesser lunacies," with which Mr. Duffy entertains us while eviscerating Stanford's "cheeky" resurrection of Pope Joan. By conveniently shelving "hopeless claims about the historicity of

Joan, and discuss(ing) instead the multiple variations of the story concocted by artists, writers and dramatists," Stanford brings her to (a fictional) life. What motivates the publishing industry of our times to give credence to such humbug should cause concern, especially for the intelligence of our fellow beings who purchase it. The only explanation seems to be that, since ordinary people cannot be that stupid, it must be another sign of feminist Elysium, in which intelligent creatures are enchanted with visions of euphoria to enjoy a world of "sensuous imagery" without truth. That men like Stanford cynically serve as courtesans to the feminist Flat Earth Society is hardly a cause for optimism.

* * *

In the same issue of *The Times Literary Supplement*, Mary Le Quesne reviews other examples of "women of spirit", who, thanks to current emphasis on such matters, have been rediscovered as "long silenced feminine voices within Christianity and other traditions." This is part of "the Visionary Women series", via which editor Monica Furlong aims "to meet the current 'hunger for women's knowledge and understanding' by publishing, or republishing accessibly, the writings of or relating to women with 'valuable things to say about religious meaning and about the life of the spirit'." One questions why we should consider as "long silenced" women who were previously published. Perhaps there is a newly discovered norm for "silencing" unburdened by Webster's Dictionary. It is not so much "true value" we are talking about here as it is the spectacle of female Humpty Dumpties choosing to give women's words whatever meaning they choose to give.

Le Quesne offers no examples of specific thought from these books, so perhaps I am being unfair to those being reincarnated. Florence Nightingale certainly needs no refurbishing, nor does Joan of Arc, but the editors of the four books being reviewed, and Le Quesne herself, follow the usual practice of assuming at the start that their subjects deserve elevation to super-status merely for having been wrongly "neglected," since there is no other way to judge from this review. Fortunate now are Christina of Markyate and the twenty-two-year-old Christian martyr, Perpetua, whose lives are recreated for 1990s readers, although neither was actually "neglected" in history. One could possibly do the same for countless forgotten (now "disadvantaged") writers from the past. The ways of literature and publishing were certainly never egalitarian but more often random, preferential, and rigorously objective. That is, until the feminists came along, so now one is never certain that a published book is other than a passing fad or more fuel for the cause.

It does seem relevant that these books are claimed to offer "valuable things" from these women, yet Le Quesne only tells of Joan's "intelligence, courage and integrity," which we already knew along with her being a God-fearing teenager. One hopes that Florence Nightingale had valuable theological insights other than a "less appreciated intellectual and spiritual breadth and depth, which encompassed mathematics, philosophy and religion" and "several religious experiences expressed in journals, jottings and letters, and very original theological thought, tested on friends and jotted down in *Suggestions for Thought to the Searchers after the Truth*." "Original theological thought" can cover a multitude of fantasies but we can do without more Mary Baker Eddys or Ron Hubbards. That these books are given a token review without any details in itself tells us much about the feminist salient, where details are pretty vaporous.

Another underlying premise of these incessant reviews is that women's writing warrants recovering *solely because they are women*. Female experts feel no responsibility to provide excerpts justifying admiration for a woman's whole body of work, but expect us merely to take their word for it. It never occurs to them that Nightingale, for instance, might have faded in acclaim for her literary pursuits because, for whatever reason, people lost interest in them. With some exceptions, there is no reason females, any more than males, should be immune from the rigors of passing years, while there are reasons why in time scholars and teachers resort to other author/artists as more – pertinent. It is a remarkable defense mechanism that drives women to concentrate unremittingly on bolstering historical women in the public's eye merely because the test of time dropped their chosen resurrectettes from the Great Books List. After a while, the complaint of women's being "long silenced" becomes a cry of "wolf!"

* * *

Moving along, in the July 31, 1998, issue of *The Times Literary Supplement*, we see an egregious example of herstory travel writing, which fortunately is reviewed by an objective woman, Nicola Walker (Bless her also!). It is especially interesting, since she also reviews a standard travel book – according to her, "male dominated" – which offers more helpful insights into its scenic sites. In contrast, the herstorical sample, wishfully entitled *Amazonian: The Penguin book of women's new travel writing*, "offers eleven lively accounts of distant countries such as Pakistan, Cambodia, Bangladesh, a well as of locations closer to home … "[37] According to Walker, the female editors believe none too surprisingly, that "it is time for a new style of travel-writing, one in which the writer's 'inner journey is the most important part…. and certainly the most interesting'". Walker is generous in praising the eleven women writers as "intelligent and resourceful" even though their pretensions to travel writing are mere exercises in solipsism, drawing on "the kind of personal detail and introspection that have traditionally belonged in autobiography and fiction." Exactly. But, she asks, "Isn't it just as important that readers learn about wherever it is that the writer has chosen to go?"

While Walker castigates the ladies by remarking that "there are huge differences between the descriptive, the investigative, and the lack of purpose that is sorely apparent in *Amazonian*," and wonders whether "the writer's 'unique relationship' with place is really extraordinary enough to become the focus of narrative", she nevertheless indulges the lady travel-writers, congratulating them "for encouraging women to see independent travel as unthreatening. This new breed of Amazonians will undoubtedly become a force to be reckoned with." So, women frolicking in sensuous (and quite fictional) imagery pretending to be travel writing nevertheless deserve begrudging acceptance and even *promotion* as forerunners of things to come despite their failings. Feminism has indeed sapped us of objectivity. There are no "Fs" (failing grades) for the ladies, only for males! But the pretense of "You've come a long way, Baby!" collapses when Walker casually acknowledges "woman's fear of travel." Gentlemen, of course, never criticize the ladies for this lovable feminine trait.

* * *

An even more revealing story is that of Barbara Leigh Smith Bodichon, a Victorian woman who painted pictures, founded schools, and married an "exotic eccentric" French doctor but never had children. Kate Chisholm, herself an herstorian, reviews a book about Bodichon by Pam Hirsch: *Barbara Leigh Smith Bodichon* in *The Sunday Telegraph*.[38] As usual, the general thesis is that, despite all her energies and talent, she was not allowed to pursue life as a man but managed to defy destiny anyway by having a husband who "cooked and cleaned" while she painted alligators, "campaigned for women's equal right to education and work," "refused to wear corsets and shortened her skirts by four inches," and posed as "Boadicea" (aka, Boudicca) for a female painter. "A formidable original," a "Victorian freethinker," a "truly original woman, who when they were setting up (her school) recommended that instead of putting iron bars on the windows for the protection of the female students, they should have a little dog run up and down the corridors." With such ideas, perhaps England was better off without her leadership, although she did enjoy "committee work and entertain(ing) friends at her Sussex home."

Chisholm feels that Bodichon's "variety has led to her neglect," but I suspect a different reason. While she was as exotic and eccentric as her husband, who presumably also has been "neglected" as most of us will be eventually unless a Shakespeare or Gibbon writes about us, or we conquer Rome or London and charm the media with our ghostwriters' rhetoric, her life had no lasting historical, artistic or literary significance. Hirsch apparently chose to lionize Bodichon merely for having a strong personality and odd tastes.

Barbara Bodichon was certainly a busy woman but even Chisholm notes that she seemed torn between being "an artist or a political activist; an English feminist or a dutiful wife in Algiers." Here again, the post-enlightenment irony of womanhood: Regardless of one's sex, inevitably such confusions as Bodichon's lead to forgettable lives – the fate of mankind. In the case of women like Bodichon, theirs might have been eased if they had chosen to be more like Mary – and true to themselves. Her children might have made her immortal in ways that Hirsch and Chisholm can never be except in feminist journals and women's studies classes. Instead of serving as the matriarch of a family dynasty, she got sidetracked into painting alligators.

* * *

Of relevance here, despite his enthusiasm for Rousseau, egalitarianism and what Claes G. Ryn calls "moral abstractionism"[39], Allan Bloom's controversial *Closing the American Mind*, offers incisive comments on the sexes in America. For instance, as if anticipating this lady's and Bodichon's torn aspirations, he noted, "Women are pleased by their successes, their new opportunities, their agenda, their moral superiority. But underneath everything lies the more or less conscious awareness that they are still dual beings by nature, capable of doing most things men do and also wanting to have children."[40] Steven Goldberg et al make this same point even more comprehensively.

Bloom echoes George Gilder and others in ascribing to women "moral superiority," but I suggest this is over-gallant. The larger male brain, and numerous male philosophers over the centuries, resulting probably from men having to deal with the greater complexities of exteriorities, do not suggest moral inferiority. What women do manifest is a proneness for *moralizing*, which has its place but needs much caution. (For a literary metaphor, one is reminded of John LeCarre's *The Spy That Came In from the Cold*, in which the heroine's moralizing eventually got both her and her lover unnecessarily slain. Or there is LeCarre's intelligence agent, George Smiley, who, after solving an intricate espionage case, asked his cuckolding wife whether she had loved her paramour, only to hear her chiding, "Gawge, life is such a puzzle to you." And who can forget Harriet Beecher Stowe, Lincoln's "little lady" whose moralizing helped "make this big war" that cost 600,000 lives.) As Darwinists must explain Chesterton's apes that still do not draw on cave walls, enthusiasts for female "moral superiority" must explain why there have been no female Aristotles, Aquinases, Augustines or Adam Smiths. Women's morality is more personal, dictatorial, and adapted to individuals and families – interiorities.[41]

Bloom's insights (like George Gilder's) cannot be overemphasized: "Female modesty extends sexual differentiation from the sexual act to the whole of life. It makes men and women always men and women.

> The consciousness of directedness toward one another, and its attractions and inhibitions, inform every common deed. As long as modesty operates, men and women together are never just lawyers or pilots together. They have something else, always potentially very important, in common – ultimate ends, or as they say, "life goals." Is winning this case or landing this plane what is most important, or is it love and family? As lawyers or pilots, men and women are the same, subservient to the one goal. As lovers or parents they are different, but inwardly related by sharing the naturally given end of continuing the species. Yet their working together immediately poses the questions of "roles" and, hence, "priorities," in a way that men working together or women working together does not. Modesty is a constant reminder of their peculiar relatedness and its outer forms and inner sentiments, which impede the self's free creation or capitalism's technical division of labor. It is a voice constantly repeating that a man and a woman have a work to do together that is far different from that found in the marketplace, and of a far greater importance.[42]

With the proviso drawn from experience that even "as lawyers or pilots, men and women" are *not* the same, Bloom's approach deserves central focus in our handling of matters related to the sexes: marriage, "equal opportunity" (an absurd chimera in this instance), "non-discrimination," and "rights." Yet it is virtually ignored. As if speaking of the Bodichons, Paglias, Lewinskys, and others, Bloom has this to say (see also Santayana, Note 41, above):

> But a woman may have a child, and in fact, as becomes ever clearer, may want to have a child. Sex can be an indifferent thing for men, but it really cannot be so for women. This is what might be called the female drama. Modernity promised that all human beings would be treated equally. Women took that promise seriously and rebelled against the old order. But as they have succeeded, men have also been liberated from their old constraints. And women, now liberated and with equal careers, nevertheless find they still desire to have children, but have no

basis for claiming that men should share their desire for children or assume a responsibility for them. So nature weighs more heavily on women. In the old order they were subordinated and dependent on men; in the new order they are isolated, needing men, but not able to count on them, and hampered in the free development of their individuality. The promise of modernity is not really fulfilled for women.[43]

Here I only regret Bloom's joining the crowd to disparage traditional women of the past as "subordinated and dependent on men." As noted before, this is merely a modernized (feminized) version of what were quite realistic and generally accepted arrangements in more perceptive times. Even though Adam's headship is fundamental, Eve was certainly not "subordinated or dependent," any more than Mary, Joan, Elizabeth, Victoria, Catherine or all the other women of long ago. As suggested, "headship" is a job, not a sinecure for subordination.

* * *

To diverge momentarily, reading the above feminist writers recalls our earlier reference to art and music as parameters or guides. Although the art of life should require no less, one is struck by the unawareness of feminists who probably consider themselves, as did Barbara Bodichon, artists and art lovers in every sense of the term, yet only apply their artistry to pretty pictures and play of words. As noted below, feminist thought is much like fascism, or more specifically, the Nazi propaganda machine, which, as Deal W. Hudson tells it, is now known to have deliberately invented the twelve-tone music pattern exemplified by Anton Webern and Arnold Schoenberg "as a means of relaying Nazi espionage about the atomic bomb."[44] Apparently, "the written notation of this ugly music was used to pass Nazi secrets in and out of the Manhattan Project at Los Alamos, New Mexico." Propaganda Chief Joseph Goebbels shrewdly knew that "whatever the Nazis condemned would be embraced by the intellectual classes," so the Reich condemned the atonal, twelve tone music, and Goebbels was proven right when the music experts reacted in an anti-Nazi protest by praising it. Ironically, the new music was perversely accepted in the repertoire despite its obvious unpleasantness. Now, the musical elite (personified by Pierre Boulet) scoffs at this revelation, claiming the atonal imposture has proven itself worthy, despite honest audience reaction.

Similarly, the imposture of feminism has been allowed into the public consciousness, despite its ahistorical, unnatural, antibiological discordances, and the political, literary, academic elites have again been duped. For all their pretensions, they have proven themselves extremely inartistic. In stark contrast, "Few have written more wisely on art and culture than Jacques Maritain. In *Art and Scholasticism*, written just after World War I, Maritain traced the deterioration in modern art to the artist's turn toward ideology." Deal Hudson goes on to draw on Maritain's wisdom:

> They have grown so accustomed to the political filters of their aesthetic and cultural judgments that the loss of melody and tonality failed to alarm them. They needed to look no further than these lines from *The Merchant of Venice* that foreshadowed the whole sad affair: "The man with no music in himself, nor is moved by concord of sweet sounds, is fit for treasons, stratagems, and spoils.... Let no such man be trusted."
>
> Maritain understood the spiritual roots of this malaise. He understood that by referring artistic creation to God, beauty was less likely to be reduced to an excuse for self-expression or ideology.

The now familiar tale of "single mothers," "career women," "girls playing soldier with the boys" (Betty Friedan's words), "women ruling over us," and drunken sports hooligans, with audiences slavering apishly over Schoenberg, reflects a society "with no music in itself" and "fit for treasons, strategems, and spoils".... let no such man or woman be trusted.

8. Believing More Impossible Things (the White Queen)

Traveling separate ways, Steven Goldberg, Nicholas Davidson and Michael Levin each went to great lengths to review all the feminist literature available in laying the groundwork for their books, truly a heroic task requiring much patience. Despite their incisive exposure of its weaknesses, now, over ten years later, the feminist literature thrives. Other men have also produced definitive scholarly research debunking feminist claims of "goddess" cultures, "priestesses," "matriarchies," and the like, as, for instance, William Oddie, Manfred Hauke, Aimé Georges Martimort, and Philip G. Davis. (I do not repeat these men's full enterprise, but offer only examples.) Invariably, the general drift of feminist work is, well – all the same: perfunctorily dismissive of countervailing evidence, while doggedly and indiscriminately clinging to revisionist womanhood.

For instance, there is Charlotte Moore's review of Anne and Bill Moir's *Why Men Don't Iron*.[45] She starts quite favorably: "This book offers scientific support for all you ever thought about the human race but were afraid to admit," yet by her own glibness proceeds to contradict herself. Like many sisters in print, she bounces words around wittily without producing a worthwhile result, which in this case would be analysis of the book's content itself. "Scientific support" should call for some appreciation of science on her part to allow intelligent discourse, which Moore never offers. Instead, she ridicules the authors for "bouncing their readers along like rubber balls," "silly scaremongering," being "reductive," "hard to take seriously," "aggravating and charmless," and so on, all while doing the same herself. She trips over her own tartness in criticizing the book as unable "to acknowledge its own limitations" while never acknowledging her own other than her ignorance of biology. She asks herself why she is "so reluctant to accept these 276 pages of confident assertion as *the* analysis of the human condition" yet never provides the answer, perhaps because its scientific evidence reveals feminism as a sham. She complains of its "self-referential mode of argument," while offering nothing but her own "self-referential" mode and revealing her own feminist colors with a subtle boost for "gender-neutral child-rearing" without elaborating.

All in all, Moore's review is a vehicle for faultfinding without showing the reader anything other than that one cannot expect rational discussion from a feminist. If her review is an example of the dialogue we must endure from feminists (and it appears to be), then things do not look rosy for the civilized world. Their canon has been so contaminated from years of women's studies without standards of truth and excellence that they end up ill equipped to argue except by ridicule, which is not argument at all but schoolgirl bluster. The scientific evidence amply reinforces the findings of Anne and Bill Moir, yet Moore simply shuts it out. (In other respects, their book does warrant criticism, which we shall discuss later.)

* * *

"Pushing people too hard is preferable to pushing them not at all. Man has achieved his greatest work through suffering, not placidity."[46] Thus, in their immunity from such criticism, these "progressive" ladies offer no great work. They seem unable to think "large." They are smart enough to know better and might welcome constructive criticism were their position not intrinsically so weak it couldn't stand up. Women like Midge Decter and Phyllis Schlafly have offered powerful criticism but it is simply rebuffed, usually on *ad hominem* grounds rather than substance. When men like columnist-historian Paul Johnson resort to criticism, the usual retort is "misogynist!" or "chauvinist," although such words have all the impact of empty shotguns: Have gun, cannot hit target. According to any standard dictionary, the former term requires "hatred of women," and the latter "an unreasoning, often fanatical pride in, support for, or attachment to one's own sex," none of which is involved in efforts to restore the two sexes to the common good. In fact, men who have spoken out against feminism through the years have usually been strongly heterosexual and loving toward women.

As an example, writerette Sue Gaisford recently wrote *The Spectator*, sarcastically chiding Johnson, "There are too many columnists in English-language journalism and some of them stoop, as he says, to personal abuse that is ignorant, nasty, queasy-making and brutal. His 18 July (1998) column is all those things and snarlingly misogynist as well. Isn't it time you sacked him?"[47] (Reminiscent of the Red Queen?) She is referring to a column in which Johnson lambastes several writerettes but also praises several others, spreading his gentle rain equitably one would think, even if one happened not to be in the favored group. Gaisford's wild-swinging putdown does nothing to disprove Johnson's point and, in fact, merely substantiates his judgment. After all, he speaks very favorably of his preferred writerettes, presumably on merit, so is hardly "misogynist," the use of which term pegs Gaisford as a shallow thinker. In other columns, he chastises males as well as females without mercy, and has even promoted greater use of women in industry, commerce, and the like[48], all of which seems to make him more of a critic than a woman-hater.

As for Gaisford, she distorts Johnson's ironic Hobbesian "abusive, ignorant, brutal, nasty but not, alas, short" into an aimless "ignorant, nasty, queasy-making and brutal." Not much fun, these writerettes.

* * *

The same issue of *The Spectator* offers a review of another biography of a "forgotten" woman, Suzanne Valadon, the French artist and Maurice Utrillo's mother. This book by author-rescuer June Rose is reviewed by Richard Shone, who offers a barely objective yet generous opinion of the book and Valadon's life, while paying her the respect due an early-century painter who lived in memorable times: "(I)t is not a thrilling read. There is too much upholstery about the Latin Quarter, 'artistic circles,' and stylistic movements. It is like a smooth tourist coach-trip through the admittedly spectacular landscape of French art. But glimpsed here and there is the tiny, indomitable figure of Valadon herself, by turns charming and caustic, seedy and posh, whose distinctive talent was nearly swallowed whole by the self-inflicted colourfulness of her way of life."[49]

"Valadon's misfortune was that, as her fame as an artist grew, she was outstripped by her son (father unknown). The large sums Utrillo's paintings fetched in the 1920s allowed Valadon freedom from material worries, but they were the cause of an appalling domestic situation." She had married another painter, twenty years her junior, who proved jealous and underhanded, while her son Utrillo was rarely sober. Her work deteriorated into "spatial muddle and factual brutality. There is a current fashion (exemplified in other reviews of this book) to denigrate Utrillo in order to aggrandise Valadon. It is true that Utrillo's was a restricted talent but his earlier works attained a perfection in their urban melancholy and expressive sureness of tone of which Valadon was incapable. Utrillo's popular fame and the many fakes of his paintings have clouded his posthumous reputation (he died in 1955, married, devout and sober) just as Valadon has suffered from being known as his mother *tout court*. Neither view will do, and if June Rose's biography helps rescue Valadon it is all to the good."

One suspects that Shone himself is an art critic and not a historian or philosopher, since Valadon's life leaves a lot to be desired for a woman. Like Bodichon and the others whose "self-inflicted" lives were torn between career and family with predictable dysfunction despite the "spectacular" experience, her atonal life is essentially quite forgettable and hardly a paradigm. In fact, the refrain is common to many modern women, some quite famous, who completely abdicate family ties to enjoy "full equality" in a world where there is little equality. One senses that June Rose didn't explore such risky passageways because they would embarrass the feminist predisposition to create out of Valadon another example of undeserved neglect. And, despite his courteous abstention, Shone himself allows at least a suspicion that feminism is at work with his casual mention of the "current fashion" of denigrating Utrillo in favor of his mother. Thus proceeds the effort to reshape the literary and artistic landscape in accordance with the epistemology of women's "studies".

* * *

Even women who scoff at feminism show its influence apparently without comprehending the deeper currents. For instance, while Independent Women's Forum Board Member Diana Furchgott-Roth offers a revealing survey of male and female occupations showing that men still predominate, her analysis is geared solely to a woman's *preference*, not from any higher perspective of either the common good or common sense.[50] Since 1920, our republic has increasingly preferred the dialectic of "choice" over *duty*. "Feminists are right," says Furchtgott-Roth. "Women are smart and successful. They belong in the House and in the Senate. So why the affirmative action programs?" There's that atonal theme again, from another "she who must be obeyed."

All this is not to say that all women's writing in the past has been worthless. Much of their writing has made it into the canon and deservedly so. Thanks to affirmative action, however, and the allure of academic feminism, many women are published these days whose writing offers no "there there." They write reasonably well when they're not readjusting the truth to suit their cause, but, as shown above, feminist writing is by nature untruthful. As, for instance, Philip G. Davis suggests in his *Goddess Unmasked*, archeological evidence of supposed long-ago "goddess societies" is lacking, "specialists have long since turned their backs to it," and "the tale of the Goddess is neither an established fact nor a credible hypothesis, but a myth, a normative story", yet the ladies persist in their untruthful, "nonlinearly" imaginative efforts (see also Elisabeth Schüssler Fiorenza, Chapter VII, Note 8, above):

> The line between scholarly theory and religious belief has clearly been crossed, for instance, when Riane Eisler describes the Paleolithic female figurines as "important psychic records" and goes on to claim that the identification of the earth with the Mother Goddess "was central to our lost psychic heritage," all in the first three pages of *The Chalice and the Blade*. This psychic historiography is what permits the leaps of imaginative speculation and the arguments from silence which permeate so much of the Goddess literature. Goddess writers themselves are fond of quoting French feminist Monique Wittig's advice: "Remember. Make an effort to remember. Or, failing that, invent." The full import of this guidance is now becoming apparent.[51]

The problem lies in the difference between objective and subjective writing, the former being defined as "free from personal feelings, prejudice, etc., unbiased"; and the latter, "personal." While a writer can have intense "personal feelings" and still adhere to the truth, feminism at its roots is biased and prone to distortion, making "truth" whatever they wish it to be. They are immune to the evidentiary rule that, if you disbelieve anything a witness says, you may reject his entire testimony. Many women write to impress, to shock, to appear to know when they don't, to seem on top of things, to be in with the latest gossip, etc., and thus are not easily believable.

To avoid total disdain from the reader, I must acknowledge the women writers who are well regarded by respected literary pundits, for instance, Flannery O'Connor, Simone Weill, Gertrude Himmelfarb, and Hannah Arendt. Lest I too be accused of "misogyny," neither do I read liberal male writers beyond a few opening sentimental howlers typical of the genre, or to the full extent necessary for a resounding rebuttal. Flannery O'Connor is often admired for her devout Catholicism and incisive writing, yet her novels can be biblically harsh, cruel, and almost inhuman. She was a bold, imaginative woman, yet still without the extra fatherly touch of a Faulkner or Joyce. Perhaps a woman has to be firm, like a hub, as her men turn the spokes and she rejects "saccharine substitutes." Ralph C. Wood writes approvingly of O'Connor, while noting her "hard thinking":

> As in so many other matters, Flannery O'Connor foresaw our reduction of transcendent faith to sentimental subjectivity…. She described our current generation as a brood of wingless chickens. This is what Nietzsche meant, she explained, when he declared God dead. It also means that nihilism is the atmosphere of our age, the gas that we all breathe, whether inside or outside the Church. The Church has made Christianity nearly indistinguishable from the coziness of a warm blanket and the kindliness of a golden heart. With typical starchiness, O'Connor added that "a golden heart would be a positive interference for a writer of fiction."[52]

One suspects that she would have benefited from a more Burkean "moral imagination, which the heart owns, and the understanding ratifies, as necessary to cover the defects of our naked, shivering nature, and to raise it to dignity in our own estimation."[53] Surely, such warm-blooded perspicacity would not necessarily be anti-Christian. No, women are not more moral than men, but more determined in their own interpretation of religion, morals and ethics. Their intuition is often allowed to override the transcendent.

No one is perfect, but it brings us back to the gender gap: there are no female Kierkegards, Webers, C.S. Lewises, von Miseses,

Russell Kirks, Heidiggers, Roepkes or Leichtensteins. The thing about reading female writers generally is that their minds operate more from the right side of the brain than the left side, and thus do not always assume that the square of the hypotenuse is equal to the sum of the squares of the two sides.

* * *

Another interesting example appears in Katherine Duncan-Jones's review of *The Collected Works of Mary Sidney Herbert, Countess of Pembroke*, edited by Margaret P. Hannay et al, appearing in *The Times Literary Supplement*.[54] "The traditional image" of Mary Sidney Herbert (Mary), who was the sister of Sir Philip Sydney, author of *Arcadia*, "has been remote and sombre… both secondary and severe… grimly pious… a snobbish and death-obsessed woman," from which Hannay and Duncan-Jones (D-J) try to rescue her. In passing, D-J says we can now see that Mary was "a brilliantly versatile writer, and one whose best writings are characterized by an intense delight in sensuous imagery and verbal play… her *Psalmes* 'have a lilt of joy'. She responds with 'exuberance' to images of music and dancing… Natural imagery, also, consistently excites her. She loves to amplify accounts of storms and shipping, and of vegetation." From this base, D-J attempts doggedly to find her influence on such notables as Shakespeare, Spenser, and Coverdale; whether true or not, we shall never know, for D-J seems afflicted with an herstorical urge to revise Mary's stereotype "as an inaccessible aristocrat" into something more fashionable, as though for some unexplained reason Mary's existing image is undesirable, or perhaps D-J knows that Mary would have preferred a new image. Or perhaps D-J is merely indulging in fiction.

From D-J's excerpts, one can say that Mary did indeed write charming poetry, although one suspects that many poets have been prone to "natural imagery" ("murmuring pines and the hemlocks"), "accounts of storms and shipwrecks," "exuberance," and "vegetation." (One also suspects that D-J would not write of Frost's or Tennyson's "loving to amplify," which must be a peculiarly female attribute). Mary's work deserves recognition but not if tainted by feminist advertisement.

* * *

A further bit of "herstory," although not specifically *about* women as much as it is *by* a woman, is Pauline Maier's *American Scripture*, a story about the Declaration of Independence and Maier's aversion to its elevated status in our culture. Here is a striking exercise in revisionism offering a rearranged history of the founding to suit the author's feminist intuition. I say "feminist" because she rejects the work of the Founders and other men who helped shape our history and prefers instead to attribute our political journey to American togetherness: "(T)he remaking of the Declaration of Independence no less than its original creation was not an individual but a collective act that drew on the words and thoughts of many people, dead and alive, who struggled with the same or closely related problems. The resonances of Jefferson's and Lincoln's texts depended in part on the resonances they captured, and their messages were convincing because the hearts of their audiences had been – to adopt the language of Lincoln's early New England ancestors, on which he drew so heavily in the dark years of the civil War – 'prepared' to receive it.'"[55] This seems more dreamy detritus from the "liberal-progressive paradigm" and Croly's oxymoronic idea of administrative, consensual "leadership" in "conformity with public opinion of the community."

Not only does Maier slight the historical roles of individual male figures but she casually dismisses her "formidable opponents" (Willmore Kendall, Melville Bradford and Garry Wills, not to overlook Russell Kirk, George W. Carey, Raoul Berger, and Stanton Evans, whom she does not mention, all of whom apply customary historical accuracy to their scholarship) merely by finding the "subject too complex for simple answers" and then proceeds to present her own simplified version, a considerably fictionalized story. While the Founders certainly drew on a storehouse of established wisdom to forge a new government, Maier reroutes the path of history through a beehive of activity informed by what Santayana called "intuition without method."

For Maier, history is a quilting party, needing no heroic, serious men or beautiful women but only a loose-gun "continuing act of national self-definition" by the American people who she apparently assumes care little for Santayana's warning that "those who cannot remember the past are condemned to repeat it."[56] Her story has no "there there" but only a facile plot to satisfy her vague idea of what history should be, a pleasant family union lying somewhere between the right and the wrong and far from Aristotle's optimum mean. That such imaginative women are teaching history instead of writing fiction is an ominous sign of the times highlighted by obsequious praise from male professors who should know better. However, at least one male pundit, Sebastian de Grazia, bucks the tide in a *Times Literary Supplement* review of Maier's book, even while offering token encouragement to her work ("Appendix C… is alone worth the price of the book."). Otherwise, his assessment agrees generally with mine:

> In a "collective act" in the spring of 1776, not God, not Jefferson nor any of the "superhuman men" of the time but, "as if by instinct," virtually all Americans "created" or "made" the Declaration. After some sluggish years, new generations with Lincoln as their ultimate spokesman wonderfully "remade" the document by casting aside "revolution" and uplifting "equality"….
>
> Maier goes on to outstrip her data…. Maier's unfamiliarity with the territory is clearest in the book's relatively small section on American scripture. Her testimony for American worship of the

Declaration comes mostly from Lincoln at Gettysburg, from Fourth of July high jinks and low oratory, and from the personal account of her quick field trip to the National Archives exhibit, seen from the perspective of "a Catholic girlhood".... Pauline Maier single-mindedly scratches a furrow from Runnymede to Massachusetts, skirting common law and the Levellers, seeking no guidelines. She declares little use of "academics" who have a "taste for the history of ideas and for the European origins of things American", and for the studies of the "political philosophy," "political ideology" and "European rhetorical theory" of the Declaration. "I dissent from any suggestion...," "I have chosen not to belabour my differences with people like (Kendall, Bradford and Wills)...," "I prefer to tell the story as I see it....," Maier bristles. The result; a worthwhile book unnecessarily over-extended and provincial.

There's a half-truth for you! Having found serious flaws far beyond the above brief excerpts, de Grazia still condescends in gentlemanly fashion to offer faint praise. "Why not *his*tory from a professor of history?" he asks, yet still considers it all "worthwhile," but perhaps his editor required such saving pittance.[57]

Why shouldn't a woman be able to write a good book and receive the recognition it deserves? Answer: There should be no reason. Years ago, this was the case with the Brontës, whose novels established them as major figures in English literature, although Emily's took longer than Charlotte's because of its starkness and paganness in an age of Victorian readers. Probably driven by the penury and domestic unhappiness of their solitary lives in which the only amusements were walking and reading, their natural Irish talents took to writing stories in a time when people appreciated good writing. Although the girls unsuccessfully published poetry under pseudonyms, Charlotte's *Jane Eyre* received instant success on its own, which suggests that their sex was not a handicap with a public familiar with Jane Austen. However, there was the natural expectation mere mortals have for men and women. Allan Bloom's recognition that "Modesty is a constant reminder of (the) peculiar relatedness and its outer forms and inner sentiments which impede the self's free creation" held true then as now.

More recently, along with the lavish attention accorded the ladies discussed herein, one sees daily advertisements of new books by women, on women, praised by women. For instance, another Transaction Publishers advertisement (Fall, 1998) shows a new book on *Women in Austria*, edited by Erika Thurner, on "achieving equality in all spheres of life… a long struggle that is still not complete… growing interest and vibrancy in women's studies… new research… an international audience." Another notice proclaims two books, *Letters to a Young Feminist* and *Women and Madness*, by "a leading feminist, Dr. Phyllis Chesler," the first proclaimed by Adrienne Rich to be an "intense, rapid, brilliant… a pioneer contribution to the feminization of psychiatric thinking and practice"; and the second by Gloria Steinem, "a warm personal, political, irresistible guide for young feminists, women and men. As a pioneering author and activist, Phyllis Chesler marks with flowers of wisdom the path she helped clear, and offers advice to those who will extend it into a future only they can know." And this just scratches the surface!

One might reasonably feel apprehension, not only for the settled harmony of our delicate sexual dichotomy but also for the survival of our society and the American Republic. An intelligent, healthy society would treat these masquerading ladies politely but reject their self-absorbed pretenses to scholarship.

The style in the Brontës' 1848 was simpler, more Puritan, less indulgent in self, perhaps more durable and less ostentatious. They respected the norms of those more rigorous times. Although thoroughly modern herself, Mary Ann Evans used the pseudonym "George Eliot" to neutralize any hesitancy based on her sex, and her work fitted in with Hawthorne, Scott and Thackeray in the public esteem, although there are marked differences between hers and at least the first two. (The female preacher in *Adam Bede* represents a poetic license that Samuel Johnson would certainly question.) But women writers were not ignored in those days because of any particular suppression or exclusion, but because people expected something more from them. As Bloom put it, there was "a voice constantly repeating that a man and a woman have a work to do together that is far different from that found in the marketplace, and of a far greater importance." So, while *Wuthering Heights* eventually achieved success along with *Jane Eyre*, their authors' underlying story is still of unrequited lives nurtured in moorland wildness, far from the comfortable arena of most modern male and female writing. And, though we appreciate the Flannery O'Connors, Eudora Weltys and their bona fide sisters enured to similar misfortune, their stories, for whatever high purpose, and even when bitingly humorous like Zora Neale Hurston's, are often cold and joyless; they *think differently*.

* * *

For the nonce, however, herstorical books and articles proliferate. In the October 23, 1998, *Times Literary Supplement*, Elisabeth Van Houts reviews George Duby's *Women of the Twelfth Century* by asserting her own version of events, recasting medieval women as a 1990s version of Jackie the Giant Killer.[58] Pointedly eschewing priestly, orderly exposition of past events, and choosing instead to find much sexual activity (not surprisingly, since that is the way the race perpetuates itself), Van Houts follows the now familiar script of correcting a male author's "bias" by finding medieval women to be possessed of "political, managerial, and communicative skills of a high order." Duby notes that such women were remembered through their contacts with monks and priests, which seems reasonable in view of the high position of the Church in those centuries. Houts, however, cannot stomach the presumed slight and finds that women were also remembered through "stories of their achievements... passed on in the female line, from mother to daughter, until they were recorded in writing by a member of the family (normally male).... " There's that defensive mindset again.

Although she mentions that this was Duby's last work and "his most personal and intimate testimony as a historian... (as well as) a direct and touching book," Houts's sexism takes over: "Many a medieval text written by a woman has reached us in a form packaged by a male author, whose priestly status gave it the ecclesiastical imprimatur it needed. Often enough, what the man added to give the text more weight was distracting rhetoric and grammatical sophistication. Duby is fortunate to have had female translators – Cynthia Postan in the 1970s and now Jean Birrell – who have done the opposite. Twentieth-century co-operation between the sexes has produced an eminently digestible introduction in the history of women in the twelfth century." One suspects that, with such a twist, Duby's work may not have ended up the way he intended. With what William Oddie calls a self-absorbed "nurture of feminist consciousness," such women never tire of complaining about their lot, as though male writers were inept and at every moment in history short-changing women. One doubts Houts's "legendary women" showed the lack of appreciation she does. After all, although they possessed "skills of the highest order," they probably understood the meaning of adult womanhood.

In the end, herstorians simply lack the credible intellectual stature of true historians. As Christopher Dawson, "the great Catholic historian of the last century" (Dermot Quinn's words), wrote,

> The historian himself is primarily engaged in the study of the past. He does not ask himself why the past is different from the pres-

ent or what is the meaning of history as a whole. What he wants to know is what actually happened at a particular time and place and what effect it had on the immediate future. The facts may be of little importance, but if they are true facts, they are important to him as a true historian. The historian studies the past for its own sake with a disinterested passion that is its own reward.[59]

In other words, the antithesis of herstory. Even here, the ladies can't claim originality, as they practice what Dawson calls "philosophical liberalism" – or the assessment of cause and effect to history according to ones personal bias. (Eric Voegelin's philosophical study of history sought higher truths, not utopian escape from reality.) The field was ripe for feminist revisionism in which "sociology" is carried to ridiculous extremes. In their hope to revolutionize society according to feminist patterns, they are indulging in the White Queen's "memory that works both ways," sometimes known as wishful thinking. Shorn of religious meaning and Dawson's "intuitive understanding and universal vision," herstory amounts to raw chauvinism.

VIII

"Non-Feminist" and a Few Other Feminist Women Writers

Women are not interested in morals. They aren't even interested in unmorals. The ladies of Jefferson don't care what she does. What they will never forgive is the way she looks. No: the way the Jefferson gentlemen look at her.

William Faulkner, *The Town*

I would like to say that I am not concerned with sexual morality, but with more basic political and economic facts.

Jean Elshtain[1]

The primary appeal of the women's movement, then, lay in the message that everything that troubled her was somebody else's fault. How could any thinking or spiritual discipline designed to help her carry the burden of freedom stand against the siren song of her victimization?

The result of that question is history. There is no need to expand upon what, most of all she herself, knows: a quarter of a century of agitation on her behalf has left her emotionally and intellectually worse off. Especially intellectually. All the demands for unneeded preference in admissions and hiring, all the absurd litigation, all the efforts at speech control, and most important, all the programs to manage and "improve" the behavior of the men in her life, whether husband, boss, roommate, or date, have left her more disaffected and more mentally self-indulgent than before.

Midge Decter[2]

1.

Midge Decter is probably the premier American female writer on feminism. Her law training and womanly common sense have combined to produce a perspective unexcelled on the subject from a woman's standpoint. Her 1973 book, *The New Chastity and Other Arguments Against Women's Liberation* came when most people had little idea of the enormity of feminism and it should have alerted the nation to feminism's nefarious pitfalls. Typically of our watered down culture with its increasingly effeminate, uninformed or irresponsible males, however, it did not do so. The Bill Clintons, George Bushes, admirals, generals and politicians choose the path of least resistance aiding and abetting a regime of bureaucratized sexual indoctrination. Ms. Decter's book is a brilliant treatise, without the trappings of a densely researched work but a straightforward intuitive exegesis.

Steven Goldberg came soon thereafter with his equally valuable professorial treatise on the inevitability of patriarchy, followed by George Gilder's and Nicholas Davidson's highly readable studies, and Michael Levin's all-encompassing scholarly treatise on "feminism and freedom." All in all, supplemented by several other scientifically argued books revealing the vacuity of feminism, as well as religious-oriented research by Oddie, Martimort, Hauke and Davis, the public has enough literature available to roll back the tide of "women's liberation" and return to healthy normalcy. Again, that it has not happened is a sign of male disinterest and ignorance, on both the left and the right.

Meanwhile, aside from a flood of beauty-parlor feminist literature, other ladies have begun to see the light and are finding the field open to sorties into the world of book publishing. They find docile sponsors in editors conditioned to the ideas of "sex equality" and "non-discrimination," and eager to capitalize on a market for women writers of any faith or party. It seems that women do read more, albeit mostly eclectic fiction and trendy new-age poetry rather than von Mises, Burke, Kirk, Chesterton, Irving Babbitt and that sort. (See Pia Nordlinger, below) In the burgeoning ranks of 1990s George Eliots and Jane Austens, there are a number who even profess to be "conservative," or "against feminism," although, like the veteran who has trouble doffing his old uniform, most of them remain encumbered with thirty years of indoctrination. While disdaining the multi-isms of "proto-", "paleo-", "gender-", "socialist", "radical", or "environmental" feminism, they now favor "equity", "pro-life," "individualist", or "pro-life" feminism, thus leaving feminism per se still enshrined. Lacking concern for the crucial human equation, such imaginative parlor games are valueless.

While some women sense the need for correction, they refrain from stirring men to resistance and attempt to fill the void themselves with books, committees, or forums, all designed to offer communal input but ultimately lacking the full potential of robust male leadership. One such example is F. Carolyn Graglia's *Domestic Tranquility: A Brief Against Feminism*, which in itself serves as an intriguing example of the imbalance. It is a loving account intended to reinforce the idea of women's natural role in marriage and can only help our cause but, at the same time, it reveals a lack of male incisiveness and objectivity, which perhaps is fitting for a book designed primarily as a message to women. She is motivated by childhood memories of Philip Wylie's negative caricature of mothers, as well as subsequent feminist distortions of the human comedy. However, since men are largely responsible for what has happened, it will take enlightened men to recover our sexual sanity. But every sensible voice will help and hers is certainly that.

An ad quotes Graglia as asking, "Where are the men? Why don't they oppose the feminists? Why is F. Carolyn Graglia the only person opposing them?" Not finding that passage in her book, I do find this one: "Until recently, society had led (the housewife) to expect that repelling vicious attacks upon her worth was more the responsibility of men than women. Except for a few brave souls, however, men have declined to defend the housewife – for many reasons. Some men have felt a quasi-chivalrous reluctance to counter an offensive waged by women."[3] She goes on to offer several examples of men's sorry passivity or even active support for feminists, in which I believe her assessment far too kind, though probably commensurate with her womanly treatise. A few men have indeed defended the housewife with a much broader stroke than Graglia's, and, in fact, she even mentions several, although without drawing on their wealth of convincing research. Graglia is too kind to say that the American male appears to be a modern version of the ancient hen-pecked Spartan.

Furthermore, one might question the intelligence or accuracy of both male and female reviewers of Graglia's book, who seem to view it as the much-awaited, definitive answer to feminism, when Decter and Goldberg have been around for twenty-five years and the other rebuttals for at least fifteen. Something else is needed to explain this remarkable docility or senseless refusal to inform ourselves. "God bless her for writing this book," raves one male reader, who rates Graglia's offering as "an unassailable case against feminism… she is unstinting in her condemnation of them. (tracing rightly much of today's societal breakdown to feminism)…. Deep down the real reason the feminists hate men, Graglia tells us, is because men do not love them enough to challenge them when they misbehave. That is a very unpopular thing to say, but Graglia has the moral fortitude to say it, and say it very well."[4] Again, although this may be true, I do not find it in the book. Certainly American males do need to find more gumption and recover better understanding, but of a sort that the "liberated" ladies might not agree with. One can't be sure what Henry Adams's dinner partner saw a century ago.[5] (The reactionary imperative is central to patriarchy, although thus far I don't see the female gratitude for this that Ms. Graglia does; it does seem exemplified by John Knox's women, below.)

William Kristol is quoted in the ad as considering Graglia's book "a stunningly bold and deep assault on the most powerful movement of our time," which may be another half-truth, if we recall at least Catholicism and communism, and the fact that while Graglia's book is purposeful, wide-ranging and from the heart, "a stunningly bold and deep assault" it is not. Kristol himself has dubious credentials, since he is presumably the "Bill Kristol" on the Executive Committee of the "Susan B. Anthony List", a political committee dedicated to "training pro-life women in the political arena," "convincing good woman candidates to run for office," and promoting "strong (female) leaders in the US House of Representatives."[6] Their pro-life cause is worthy, but it seems questionable to use the issue of abortion as a reason to resort to general female "leadership" when there are men available. Of course, "Emily's List" pursues the same goal for pro-abortion women and a counter-effort is needed but this is no justification for flooding the corridors of power with the fair sex merely for select causes. The cancer of feminism and liberated women is the cause for women's focus on self and "choice" to begin with; until it is entirely cured, abortion will remain a supposed "right." A paradigm of wise, male solons well instructed in responsible self-government is still the nation's only hope. We certainly do not need herstorians governing us.

But there is something about this subject that benumbs even the most intelligent males, as seems apparent in David Gelernter's review[7] in which he practically gushes over Graglia's book almost as if he had neither read it nor knew much about feminism. He refers to her having "practiced law," as though modern women were heiresses to the Madisons, Lincolns, Borks and Bergers, and not mandated adornments to the postmodern law office. He praises Graglia's "accusations (as) meticulously documented and footnoted," "honest, passionate, furious, and not for the faint-hearted" (finding apparently in this gentle housewife a clone of Robert the Bruce or William Wallace), the book "documents the family's 'startling deterioration' since feminism got a claw hold" (more effectively described elsewhere, along with the "surge in illegitimacy, divorce, and female-headed households"), "Graglia never beats around the bush or plays it safe" (Read Levin, Goldberg, Gilder, Davidson and Decter!), she "leaves the impression of fearlessness above all," and, "this is a revolutionary book." All of which leaves the impression that Mr. Gelernter, despite his usually intrepid writing, is being gallant. Neither he nor Graglia deserves rejection, but their implicit assumption that equality rules the human sexes deserves interment.

Another blurb adds, "Mrs. Graglia makes her points cannily. Her research includes sources who don't share her traditional views... so the book packs a double wallop... *it all adds up to the most stinging indictment of feminism ever written.*" (my emphasis) Considering the literature, this is pure bosh.

This reception of her book by conservatives who should know better, as well as certain aspects of the book itself deserve comment. Although, she makes ample use of her gift of words, questions abound, and one suspects her law practice did not involve arguing to juries. Her message is possibly intended for young women without experience in feminism but it is hardly "a stinging indictment." It is yet another example of gently nudging up against general ideas without any knockout punches – avoiding pithiness, as for instance when she writes innocently that feminists consider Gilder "misogynist" without offering a rebuttal.

Mrs. Graglia has a distinctly feminist perspective herself, approaching feminist ideas as if they were only half wrong. She strays when remarking that "traditional marriage is flawed by the fact that it is a particularly risky relationship for women" and that "she is fatally dependent on one man", which Graglia probably realizes works both ways. Is not this the whole point of traditional marriage? (See Gelernter, below.) Also, she doesn't consider the prospect that, if feminism is wrong, then women's "liberation," "equality of opportunity," laws mandating "non-discrimination as to sex," Titles VII and IX, the co-ed military (and V.M.I. and the Citadel), the assault on male clubs, etc., are also *all wrong.*

In the course of her dialogue, Mrs. Graglia tends to accept feminist pejoratives having little ties to reality, such as the "overvaluation of male roles." Actually, the importance of work for a man is well known – a craft, a profession, a trade, an art – it is all he has to offer, his only contribution. Without it, unlike a woman, he is nothing. How can one "over-value" such a stereotype for a young male expected to work for his family? For that matter, how "over-value" either the male or the female? In a way, her book offers a woman's interiority far more sedate but reminiscent of James Joyce's less respectable Mrs. Molly Bloom[8], as well as Pernoud's herstory, *Women in the Days of the Cathedrals*, doctored up with quoted asides lending the appearance of scholarship to a purely personal narrative.

As a result, Mrs. Graglia misses essential gravity in anecdotes such as the female letter-writers complaining about David Gelernter's article on "why mothers should stay at home." She merely quotes two of the writers and then answers with her personal opinion that "caring for (her own) children never seemed remotely boring, tedious, or lonely."[9] This was her response to the most self-centered, trivial complaining imaginable – such as whining that one "didn't want to stay home," "being financially dependent on a spouse is irksome and humiliating" (Amy Wax), and "how hard it is to take care of kids," to which Gelernter offered a compelling, eloquent response unmentioned by Graglia. I offer just a short excerpt here to show how it could have reinforced her presentation:

> There is a passage in Amy Wax's letter that captures, it seems to me, all the bitter sadness, the abject loneliness and failure of our feminist republic. For a woman to depend on her husband for financial support is, she writes, "irksome and humiliating." It must be humiliating also for a man to depend on his wife for a home and the care of his children. Or are those things too insignificant to engender humiliation? It must be humiliating for children to depend on their parents – surely children are capable of being humiliated; and for us parents who feel that what we get from our children is worth more than what we give, wouldn't that be a humiliating sensation also? I wonder whether she doesn't mean that love itself is humiliating.
>
> Lady feminists and gentlemen boors are united in their dislike of a world built on mutual dependence, and a world built on mutual independence has a tendency – look around you! – to fall apart. I have read many sad sentences in my time, but none sadder than Amy Wax's.[10]

In noting such omissions in Graglia's book, one senses she does not feel the need for virile exegesis, but only for feelings, aphorisms and conclusions.

There are good parts to her book, as in her closing pages (296-312); her commentary on Ruth Bader Ginsburg (which, along with the book itself, suggest why women should not be judges); her commentary on motherhood; on law practice; and isolated incisive remarks, but otherwise there are too many non-sequiturs. Public discourse should involve more than a mother and wife's outpouring of feelings cloaked as argument, devoid of great abiding principles, a grasp of "providential social forces" or history and human nature. Caroline Graglia's raconteuse style addressed to women seems an effort divorced from higher authority, the Bible, the Church, or even the nature of man.[11] Sociologists at least engage that last category.

There is a noticeable increase in forthright articles by men like Gelernter: for instance, Matt Labash, Charley Reese, Hilton Kramer, James Bowman, Norman Podhoretz, William J. Corliss, Steve Sailer, Stephen Seiler, Brian Mitchell, Walter A. McDougall, and others all write convincingly on the subject. As noted above, a few men have been addressing the problem of feminism for decades, and a single subjective book by a woman hardly amounts to a "backlash." Will it take an equivalent of *The Feminine Mystique*? Regrettably, one doubts that *Domestic Tranquility* will fill the bill.

2.

Reminding us of the formidable task remaining, as well as 2000s editors and politicians' deference to women on matters of sex, the eminent Catholic magazine, *Crisis*, chose to review F. Caroline Graglia's book a woman who herself has been a leading feminist and promoter of women's studies, Elizabeth Fox-Genovese.[12] Fox-Genovese, whom we have met above, is a classic example of the thoroughly modern woman, immersed to the eyeballs in feminism, yet professing womanliness and mothering. Oblivious to paradox, she appears to want it both ways. One senses in her writings the urge for power that inherently defies feminists – the Regans and Gonerils in our society, longing for public authority and vindication for past "exclusion" – while also enjoying the customary respect for themselves as lovable female creatures.

Indeed, in her book Graglia writes similarly about Fox-Genovese, noting the latter's recognition that "many women attach great importance to child-rearing" while agreeing with Betty Friedan that "domesticity was not a satisfactory story of an intelligent woman's life"[13], an assertion that encapsulates the feminist creed. It opens up whole areas for inquiry yet remains unchallenged by males thinking, "What's for dinner?" Graglia tells of Fox-Genovese's bragging, "Observing that her husband 'has lost a good deal in the way of service since the early days of our marriage,' she states that he is more likely to do the cooking than she and has 'especially lost the right to be the one who is busier, who faces the greater demands from the outside world.' But mastering a man in this way seems, to some women, an adolescent thrill."[14]

Such an inflated self-image reveals much about feminist families: Women's studies "busy-ness" enhances neither scholarship nor the common good, and indulgence of a wife's ego at public expense along with tolerance for unnatural role reversal seems inordinately eccentric. How can husbands be so hebetudinous? One would like to exercise customary courtesy and respect for privacy but when wives publicly parade their family matters so blatantly, the ordinary niceties are submerged. If Friedan's and Fox-Genovese's perception of an "intelligent women's life" amounts to this sort of pretense, they only emphasize the need to rethink women's suffrage.

Surprisingly, despite their distinct disagreements, and aside from some womanly fence straddling, Fox-Genovese offers a generally friendly and supportive review of Graglia's book. She notes Graglia's fierce determination" and "impressively sharp lawyer's mind" (the same mind which I find too gentle, womanly and rambling), and suggests that these conflict with Graglia's "brief for the softer, gentler female persona" and "traditional womanly qualities that she celebrates." Thus the inevitable irony of women in argument: Fox-Genovese trying to make the point that Graglia cannot possibly argue "fiercely" and still be "womanly" (at least without being a harridan!). Yet Fox-Genovese lives this same irony herself, forever weakening feminist pretensions to public "power" and prestige, and undermining their claims to "the right to be the one who is busier, who faces the greater demands from the outside world." It is all a masquerade, with Fox-Genovese essentially a Wizardess of Oz trying to be other than her true self.

In her review, Fox-Genovese reverts to form in referring to "oppression suffered by the women of the 50s"; "intimidating, if not necessarily insurmountable obstacles"; "some women who do everything right will be raped"; "the treatment women have received throughout history and the obstacles that continue to thwart many women throughout the world today"; "several constraints, including outright violence, that have hedged women in"; "the tide of economic revolution that has carried both feminism and sexual liberation to victory." Much of this is the usual stuff, oblivious to the facts, for instance, that rape has been a crime for millennia, and that truly intelligent women either avoid or minimize putting themselves at risk while using effective defense measures.

Perversely, some women resent having to think of self-defense, claiming it would make the world their prison (see Jennie Bristow, Note 53); they prefer to reform the public square to their liking, which, unfortunately for them, may take a while. The eternal irony needs due care: If one is not to covet the neighbor's wife, it would help if she not invite it. Flaunting her attractiveness, baring much of her body, and strutting the avenue are not anti-rape measures. Although the paradox of womanhood forever adds piquancy to life's pageant, one need not be a Puritan to see that, divorced from a marian context it can distract from worthwhile patterns. The industrious market place soon becomes a model's walkway – or a situation comedy informed by talk-show palaver and the ubiquitous adornment of crossed bare legs. Ultimately, Fox-Genovese's (as well as numerous others') ideas are over-reaching, much as if the *Titanic* women were to complain of "doing everything right yet having to disembark from a ship in the middle of the ocean." She should focus instead on raising gentlemanly males for service "in the gates," and realign her own priorities.

As if not used to resistance, however, Fox-Genovese enters untenable areas, as, for instance, when she disparages Graglia's minimizing "obstacles to (women's) intellectual and professional ambitions" because "it is hard not to believe that some things broke her way." Aside from being petty, this remark is as applicable to Fox-Genovese's as it is to Graglia's or practically any other acclaimed woman's career in academe or the public arena today. More than for men, "intellectual and professional" contributions by women amount more to convenient role-playing (avocations), income, vanity, and presumed power than lasting value for the republic.

Like Buster Mottram's insight on women's tennis, A.N. Wilson's anecdote in *The Spectator* adds a relevant touch:

> When John Wain was retiring as Professor of Poetry at Oxford, he urged Philip Larkin to stand as his successor. Larkin asked why Wain would suppose that he would want to put himself through the hell of giving public lectures for almost no money. "It's the chicks, Philip," explained Wain. "The way they cluster around you after you've finished speaking."[15]

Missing such humor, Fox-Genovese wrongly assumes workplace fungibility of men and women in remarking on Graglia's "uncharacteristic lapse from analytic rigor in her facile discussion of traditional marriage and family, ignoring the significance of historical change." Such unawareness of the history of the 1964 legislation is jejune. She also shows naiveté in claiming that Graglia "manifests no understanding or compassion for women who wish to sustain some aspect of their intellectual or professional lives, even on a minimal basis, while their children are growing up." This condescendingly assumes that home mothers are helpless compared to her own pretentious "intellectual or professional life" and cannot enjoy reading or intellectual pursuits on their own during the rigors of child-rearing. Although Graglia does not go into this, one of the authors she cites, Helen Lopata, shows Fox-Genovese's error. (E.g., see George Gilder.)

An old codger recently wrote to *The National Masters News*, complaining of a track meet's affirmative action in awarding women disproportionately higher prize money than the much faster, stronger and more numerous male competitors. Co-ed activities apparently are not as uniformly salubrious as Ms. Fox-Genovese assumes.

All of which, Fox-Genovese's presumptions notwithstanding, suggests that brave new access by women into the general workforce is neither felicitous nor preordained. Since it's not a standard for the highest and best use of female attributes, that Fox-Genovese and the sisterhood cling to the idea hardly lends substance to their cause. Graglia's more natural option serves as a far better standard for a healthy society, while Fox-Genovese's is woman-centered through and through. Until Fox-Genovese resolves the tension in her life between the feminist facade and the human realities, her "intellectual" endeavors will continue to provide grist for diligent analysis.

3.

Another example of women's "conservatism" is Wendy McElroy's idea of "individualist feminism."[16] One would think that libertarians would sense a problem with any sort of "ism," "equality" talk, or "injustice toward women," all such terms suggesting some need for government intrusion. As customary in libertarian circles, however, McElroy is allowed to present her theories without question. Since man historically has taken vigorous action against "injustice toward women", as with criminal laws against rape, battery, and prostitution, it seems superficial now to claim the problem of historical injustice as a "feminist" issue. More accurately, feminists only use it as a sort of Chinese dragon to lend credibility to their otherwise weak position. They stretch the basic concepts of "justice" or protection from violence into distorted designs of welfarism, redistribution, egalitarianism, social or economic determinism, or general leveling down, rather than the realities of a free society. Liberty and feminism, whether "individualist" or any other sort, are oxymoronic.

Revealing her hand at the outset, McElroy starts out with the premise that "women are, and should be treated as, the equal of men." The reader will recall my running endeavor to rebut this idea, whether in art, religion, nature, politics, economics, or elsewhere, so I shall only remind the reader that women are in some ways *more than* "*equals*" of men, and vice versa, enough certainly to render the whole idea fanciful. In sharing the general American confusion over "equality", McElroy hasn't grasped this yet. She tries unsuccessfully to distance her thought from feminism by resort to various qualifying adjectives, urging readers to accept their own, preferred versions of "feminism" or "equality" per se, but, as usual, getting bogged down in contrived semantics: equality of privilege, equality under existing laws, under more "just" laws, of socio-economics, from affirmative action, of culture, of respect, or merely equality in legal status. The brier patch inevitably snares those who ignore biology, psychology, religion, custom, nature, males, females, mothers, fathers, art, children, crime, drugs, schools, doggedly to grope after "equality and the rights of woman".

McElroy seeks legitimacy for feminism by coloring it beguilingly as "libertarian" or "individualist", as though God or nature had no jurisdiction. Disdaining the "socio-economic" and claiming a "natural law" approach, she reverts to talk of "laws that protect the person and property and men and women identically." In thus individualizing man and woman not under *natural* law – or even common law – but according to a very contrived *positive* law, her approach inevitably corrupts the whole idea of a loving marriage as well as of a common-sense division of labor according to our natures. (See, for instance, Anne Moir's and David Jessel's *Brain Sex* on this very topic. Also, the Church thinkers.) "Every adult had the right to choose any lifestyle that did not involve aggression against another," she naively asserts for her utopian image of struggling forebears. This libertarian principle often seems extreme even for men, and much in need of refinement, but for women it defies reality. For instance, who defines "aggression"? What about behavior, dress or exposure that *invites* aggression? And, if women are more vulnerable to "injustice", "violence" or "brutalization", does it make sense that such a principle would encourage them to risk behaving like men? The libertarian law is itself far too shallow a formulation for application to women, ignoring as it does the facets of our sexual dimorphism.

As for other herstorians, history and anthropology become putty in McElroy's hands to show that women have been short-changed throughout history. Practical needs of former epochs, arrangements benefiting both male and female welfare, lack of dissent and, in fact, outright approval by women in the past (our great grandmothers, etc.) all are ignored as McElroy contrives her feminist vision in terms of "right to choose"; "an adequate living"; "equality, justice, class"; "voluntariness"; "discrimination against women" (tellingly, never of "discrimination *in favor* of women"!); "women manacled"; "self-ownership"; "the franchise a sacred right"; and so on. McElroy even dabbles in the discredited notion that women were analogous to slaves. She then choreographs her invention of "individualist feminism," as a "comprehensive, integrated system of beliefs concerning women's relationship to society. It has a deep, rich history that significantly influenced the status of women in the nineteenth century. It embraces a large body of literature – novels, political tracts, poetry, diaries, speeches – and it involves a distinctive historical interpretation of events such as the Industrial Revolution, which it views as being overwhelmingly beneficial to women." Must we now assume that the Bible, Shakespeare and the Greek dramatists were all either "feminist" or gyno-centered?

McElroy extrapolates noticeably, "the richness of this tradition is not surprising when you realize that the very roots of American feminism *were* profoundly individualistic." In reality, however, it has been mostly a joint enterprise rather than individual female accomplishment, since women are famously *group-oriented*. As Robert H.

Knight suggests, "the sexual revolution was far from being a spontaneous, organic movement of individuals without collective efforts. From Margaret Sanger's Planned Parenthood to Alfred Kinsey's sex studies to the successful efforts by the *Playboy*-funded American Civil Liberties Union and its allies to gut laws against pornography and indecency, to the feminist homosexual rights movements,.. there was and is a conspiracy against sexual mores, the family and religion – the final target."[17]

If McElroy's "individualist feminists" were truly "individualistic," they would need no movement. They would be – traditional women. Abstract concepts like Moses Harman's "self-ownership in marriage and other sexual arrangements", which McElroy wistfully promotes, are an ephemeral dream unrelated to customary marriage vows, "to have and to hold one's partner until this day forth." Like it or not, woman is "formed for attentions not hard labor" and her truest happiness is not destined to be self-autonomy.

No one should ever suggest that a woman's "interior" lines are easy ones! Perhaps, as Barbara Albrecht saw, "in a woman's graced femininity," her "primary function is therefore receptiveness to the Spirit as exemplified by Mary," which it would be hard to believe does not also require receptiveness to her husband. In contrast, McElroy's treatment seems extremely wooden and incomplete. Edmund Burke knew what the feminists do not: "The cause of civil liberty and civil government gains as little as that of religion by this confusion of duties."[18]

* * *

It would be interesting to explore the implications for political discourse from a 1998 study finding that "motherhood makes women smarter" mainly by subjecting pregnant women to mental demands not previously experienced.[19] As further evidence of distinct brain functioning, highly suggestive of a woman's more specialized interests involving children and families more than public issues, this offers much food for thought. How much better it would be to return to the time before feminist complaining when we relied on good men and women to persevere together in life's pageant.

Mark Steyn comments on the ineptness of sex non-discrimination law, singling out Marcia Clark, "the disastrous lead prosecutor in the OJ (Simpson) trial and herself a fine tribute to the pitfalls of identity politics. She was chosen by the DA (District Attorney) not on grounds of merit but because, as a woman prosecuting another woman's murder, her gender was supposed to trump OJ's race."[20] Another example (mentioned above) was Bill Clinton's un-Ulyssesian Secretary of State, the modern Boudicca, Madeleine Albright, who gestured and frumped her way through international intrigue, while her Nerovian boss romped in Elysian randiness. (Whether, like Thatcher, Golda, Bhuto, or Madeleine they test themselves shedding young men's blood in battle, skepticism increases as to women as leaders of men.) As Richard John Neuhaus commented on Albright's womanly sense of morality – a formulation perhaps better suited to family, but better known in foreign-affairs circles as a marshmallowy "moral equivalency" –

> "Moral equivalency" was a phrase much used during the Cold War to describe a mindset determined to fudge the difference between the evil empire and other empires that are far from perfect. Thus: "Yes, it is true the Soviets put political dissidents into lunatic asylums and persecuted Christians and other believers, but there is still racism in America and look what we're doing to the ozone layer." Moral equivalence is the right term for a recent speech by Secretary of State Madeleine Albright opposing the Wolf-Specter bill, which would provide mild penalties for countries engaged in religious persecution. "Even the most patriotic among us," she said, "must admit that neither morality no religious freedom nor respect for human rights were invented here – nor are they perfectly practiced here…. If we are to be effective in defending the values we cherish, we must also take into account the perspectives and values of others." The "per-

spectives and values" of the Chinese regime mandate the arrest, torture and forced labor of Christians who belong to churches that refuse to submit to government control, the Saudis permit no open Christian worship at all, the Sudan enslaves Christian children, and in Pakistan Muslims who convert to Christianity are punished by death. That countries have such odious "perspectives and values" must indeed be taken into account, but Ms. Albright's point seems to be that they should be *sympathetically* taken into account, as in don't criticize them.[21]

Neuhaus goes on to remind us that, despite Albright's downgrading the country she served (and no nation has ever been perfect), our heritage ranks pretty high in institutionalized respect for human dignity, a fact Albright, for all her new-found power as a woman, does not seem to comprehend. It is true, of course, as some will remind us, that men can be equally wishy-washy, but women in power were supposed to bring improvement. Instead, moral ambivalence seems to have blossomed since women's suffrage. After all, women's distinctly feminine moral sense is rooted in caring and relationships, not rules and principles of behavior.

Albright's tolerant attitude towards China raises other questions, such as, considering China's well-known practices of female genital mutilation, killing of newborn female babies, abortion, and generally degrading treatment of women, why should feminism acquiesce? How has McElroy's, Fox-Genovese's, N.O.W.'s, or even Graglia's subrosa feminism helped resist such Chinese practices in ways comparable to Christianity, conservatism, or even classical liberalism? Should not feminism take a bold, effective stand against accommodation with that nation on general grounds of humaneness toward women? Apparently not. Feminism, it turns out, lacks the substance to deal with true inhumanity when the chips are down but seeks instead to strut its stuff only where it can get away with it, that is, in wealthy, liberal societies where women have the time, money and egos to indulge in their rodomontade.

As Russell Kirk commented on the risks in ignoring religion,

> Another consequence would be an increased danger from virulent ideology of one sort or another, for ideology rushes in to fill the vacuum left by the decay of religion....[22]

Here is where protections against rape are rooted, yet do McElroy's feminists join the effort to preserve our right to worship and pray, or teach the young to do so? If not, they have no leg to stand on, and, of course, they do not. As with feminism, "The liberal concern was not if we made the right choices," writes Wayne Allen, "but whether the state could relieve us of their consequences."[23] If one substitutes "sex" for "race," Allen's judgment of the effect of a lack of a "moral coherence" on the 1960s civil rights laws is equally applicable here:

> Nowhere is this more evident than with the so-called civil rights movement, when the left transformed political equality into economic parity, which was forcibly ensured by the coercive state. Indeed, affirmative action is nothing more than economic redistribution by way of (sexual) quotas, transforming right from a claim to act into a claim to have revealed liberalism's complete descent into materialism." (parenthesis supplied)

Algis Valuinas's essay on "Learning From the Greeks" offers a manly contrast to feminist thinking on morality, lifting us to a higher plane. He compares the Greek heritage with the Bible, each providing strong lessons in wise living and patient suffering. Regarding Job's demand for an accounting, to ease his "incomprehension,.. knowing that his fate is not, in fact, just":

> Job is reduced to a state in which his most urgent need is to know more than a man can ever hope to know: why life should be as it is, rather than what he thought it to be.
>
> .... The wisdom he needs, paradoxically, is that he cannot know everything. It is the Lord's majestic apparition – and, for maj-

esty, there is again nothing equal it in Greek literature – that settles Job's troubled mind and allows him to go on living in the world without demanding to know things that belong to the mind of God alone.[24]

As Athena admonished at the end of Aeschylus's *Oresteia*, "The fear of the Lord is the instruction of wisdom; and before honor is humility." Since the old ways were unencumbered with questions of "equality" of humility, Tocquevillian men and women still knew this; twentieth-century women do not. Without fear of God, there is no wisdom, as Valuinas explains Greek tragedy and the Bible:

> Solomon, however, avers that without fear there *is* no wisdom: one's soul must tremble naked before the Lord. And then he adds a parallel point about honor: it is not something to be seized brazenly by men sure of their own greatness, in battle or in any other pursuit, but rather to be earned in good time by men humble before God and their fellows.

One learns that feminists, whether "individualist" or otherwise, scorn both humility and fear of God. It is no longer considered civil to expect American women to be publicly humble. They have been taught to "assert themselves."

"Thinking she as been 'excluded' from his art, the ballerina now wants to play both the lovely female and the strong male."

4.

There are numerous other "conservative" female writers claiming to abjure feminism while offering ingenious alternate versions appealing more to their own tastes. But a rose by any other name is still a rose. Christina Hoff Summers offers her own word game by distinguishing between "old" feminism (good) and "new" feminism (bad) and then separating out "equity" feminism (old, good) from "victim" or "gender" feminism (new, both bad). Then, she tries to distance herself from this egregious nonsense but remains tied to "equity" feminism. To the alert reader, this leaves her in the same predicament as Wendy McElroy and Elizabeth Fox-Genovese, caught in a brier patch of redundancy deemed respectable only for its loyalty to "equality and the rights of women."

If, as she avers, Sommers doesn't "believe American women are oppressed or that someone is waging war against them," why need any kind of "feminism" at all? Are the criminal or tort laws on rape in need of "equity" feminism? What sort of "equity" is she envisioning, and by whose standards – the Chancellor's? Natural law? Or will her rules of "equity" decree that men must care for domestic duties equally with women? How does she think that liberalism, the Church, conservatism, and her menfolk have not served women in accordance with the law of equity for centuries so as now suddenly to need a new brand of "equity"? For that matter, how is she trying to make things better for her menfolk? What higher authority; common moral understanding; beneficial, natural standard of human behavior, is guiding her? If none other then "sex equality," then she is on thin ice.

Her primary concern seems to be none of these but merely the scraggly straw man of "oppression." Absent this, where does she set the appropriate boundaries of sex roles? Does she accept the fact that no one has proven Steven Goldberg wrong and that, like it or not, we probably are *patriarchal* with all this entails? If not, and she resists the idea, and her idea of "equity" amounts to government engineered sex equality, then she is indeed one of the "gender" feminists she scorns. As Michael Levin too has convincingly shown, feminism's trail has led from the suffragettes to greater curtailment of our ordered freedoms and a distortion of society. This is hardly "equity." If Sommers and her "individualist" friends endorse this trend, their cause is neither just nor beneficial.

Ironically, Ms. Sommers gave a recent talk on her theories at an *Accuracy in Academia* Conference on "Diversity or Conformity."[25] One cannot be certain which pattern she prefers but it should be clear that her idea of "equity" feminism certainly has little to do with true diversity, since it implies an enforced conformity to feminism's socialism, not individual responsibility and proven folk ways (the common law).

The idea that "feminism" itself is somehow benignly necessary despite its divisive manifestations seems to carry weight among even the most careful scholars and writers. For example the estimable Harold O.J. Brown writes that "There are aspects of the feminist movement that even the most orthodox Christians must praise, but if their praise is insufficiently critical, they may suddenly discover themselves far down a road on which there is no turning back."[26] Like the Church, Dr. Brown may be ceding too much, since there is a fine line between "critical praise" and outright endorsement. First, we should ascertain just what the "praiseworthy aspects" are that outweigh the risks (as the ancient Trojans forgot to do). Only Dr. Brown can explain what aspects require "feminism" instead of "masculinism" or "civil society" to resolve "problems". If the premise is that men have ignored women's "problems" for millennia and now need "feminism" to remind them, it will take more proof than we have seen thus far.

To suggest that Shakespeare, for example, did not see life's intricacies from a woman's point of view as well as a man's, or that Bizet or Puccini had it all wrong in their operas, or that Jane Austen or George Eliot knew nothing of men and women without input from modern feminism, seems preposterous. If doctors and scientists have short-changed women in their practice and research, it is not evident. If Western leaders or law enforcers have ignored women or encouraged rape and assault, where is this apparent? On the other hand, if women's suffrage is claimed as a trophy for feminism, this is questionable for at least two reasons: First, it would have occurred more felicitously, guided by fitting social parameters – a wine in its time- without the compulsion of self-centered, militant feminists. Women were not without influence previously and, according to James Bryce for one, most women were not that eager for the vote to begin with. Secondly, one has yet to prove that women's suffrage has been a blessing, which should be the paramount consideration. So, Dr. Brown's deferential acceptance of "a number of feminist demands… (as) not merely harmless but actually desirable" seems questionable, especially when he follows this with the warning that, if given free rein, feminism could even "overthrow Christianity."

Women's managing their own money, after wealth became more prevalent thanks to industrious males and enterprise, was a natural development needing no suffragette activism, or "moderate" feminism. Even Wendy McElroy seems to acknowledge this. In considering the subject of "equity" for women throughout history, examples of *un*complaining women are legion. The Mormon women didn't complain on their trek across the plains and mountains of the American West, as their men drove their wagons and, on one tortuous crossing, even pushed carts filled with their belongings! (One of Brigham Young's ideas that he later acknowledged as impractical.) Mary Sidney didn't complain as she wrote poetry with her brother Algernon. Jane Austen didn't complain as her family persevered in Georgian England, nor did the Brontës in their time. Austen rejected a suitor, choosing instead spinsterhood, writing, and the interior life of "daughter, sister, and aunt," as she shared her talented family's "tastes, prejudices, interests, and…. sense of humor."[27] Group-focus on women inevitably causes an imbalance in the delicate biological system of the sexes no less nefarious than homosexuality. Perhaps it is much like a noxious weed sprung from a seemingly harmless seed, or a vile tumor expanding from merely an inconvenient blemish. The seed of feminism serves no benign purpose that cannot be dealt with otherwise and more felicitously. It deserves not obsequious praise but eradication.

* * *

It is probably obvious by now that my seriatim engagement of myriad feminist obstacles along our path results in repetition of various arguments pertinent to each sally. Lest this be too tedious for the reader, let him think of John Bunyon's pilgrim and, "take heed of misinterpreting; for that, instead of doing good, will but thyself abuse, by misinterpreting evil issues."

> Take heed, also, that thou be not extreme,
> In playing with the outside of my dream.
> Nor let my figure, or similitude,
> Put thee into a laughter or a feud;
> Leave this for boys and fools; but, as for thee,
> Do thou the substance of my matter see.
> Put by the curtains; look within my veil;
> Turn up my metaphors and do not fail.
> There, if thou seekest them, such things to find,
> As will be helpful to an honest mind.[28]

As Dr. Brown reminds us, conservative Christians insist "that life was created for a purpose, and that it is up to us to fulfill that purpose in accordance with certain divine laws." Just so.

* * *

Undivine fence-straddling on feminism, however, is quite the norm. For example, in 1988, another example appeared in *National Review* (September 2, October 14, and November 25). Nancy Cross started it off with a review of Edith Stein's *Essays on Women* in which she quoted Stein's remark on the sexes, a "brutal relationship of master and slave." (Apparently, Stein also had trouble with Saint Paul's teachings on men and women and indulged in strained promotions of female leadership in the Church, instead of accepting marian roles in faith and service.) In singling out "modern woman's dilemma," Cross demonstrates again the ravages of thirty-five years of feminist teachings on "women's issues." She tries to distance herself from "feminist dogma or fundamentalism," while, like Dr. Brown, inviting a "creative response to the questions that the women's movement has legitimately raised." Yet she too doesn't say what these "legitimate questions" are.

In the October 14 issue, Nicholas Davidson took Cross to task for her "ill-considered words" on "the woman's movement" of Gloria Steinem and Rosemary Radford Ruether, suggesting instead that any such "movement" would more accurately be Beverly LaHaye's Concerned Women for America or Phyllis Schlafly's Eagle Forum. He goes on to question, as I have done, Cross's confused positions on women's roles and biblical teachings, suggesting that her patent acceptance of women's Ruetherian roles "still rests on a quest for dominance," a lurking beast in feminist thought.

Finally, in the November 25 issue, Nancy Cross shows the essential opacity of her feminism when she abjures its very thought by declaring her "irritation with which I approach almost everything in print these days about women," including the same Steinem and Ruether she had quoted approvingly, yet adheres to the "women's movement's legitimate questions." Apparently, she is "irritated" but not *that* irritated. The "legitimate questions" apparently include her complaint that "the role of woman has been grossly misunderstood and devalued in a world that grasps for power and prestige." Ironically, this is true but not as she supposes. Actually, it has resulted from agnostic-liberal assaults on Church traditions and from feminism itself, so her argument is circuitous. Feminism's "sex equality" has thrown women into the arena where they are judged as men, while men in turn are downgraded to androgynous standards. Surely, the "legitimate question" must be, "How can the women's movement boast of such dysfunction?"

How is the "stirring in woman's consciousness" any different now than that stirring in Eve's, with her narrow and self-involved focus? Ms. Cross blames our ills on patriarchy per se, while conveniently ignoring that in their own crucial roles women are not blameless (the inevitable trade-off). Instead of answering such questions, she takes refuge in Biblical talk and debunking materialism, all of which demonstrates once again: With few exceptions, our most objective discourse on exterior matters comes more often from men than from women.

A problem with multi-named feminisms lies in the omission to distinguish Western from third-world societies, since disparities are considerable. For instance, it is pointless to deal with our Judeo-Christian traditions as if they were synonymous with world practices. It is not for us to tell New Guinea, India, or Zambia how to treat marriage, nor for the United Nations to tell us how to deal with abortion. Much of the rhetoric on "brutalization of women" is muddied because its spokeswomen possibly are thinking of the Third World. For instance, Nancy Cross may be thinking primarily of Libya or Afghanistan in her edicts on women; at least one hopes so, since a picture of American or British men and women as "masters and slaves" is laughable. In any event, our scope here is limited to the Western world, where rhetoric on "exclusion" or "genuine problems of women" seems overdrawn.

* * *

Again, while it is time to discard such misconceptions, it will be up to men to do so. Repeating Patricia Lança's quote of Dale O'Leary (Chapter III), "it will take calculated rudeness. The feminists have relied on the politeness of men. They have demanded that dangerous and utter stupidity be treated with respect," as if she is hoping against hope that men will again become manly. Alas, it will take some doing, if we recall the spectacle of an American president or consider his British counterpart's words on manhood:

> Tony Blair says Britain is no longer "about living in the world of a hundred years ago, when guys wore bowler hats and umbrellas, all marching down Whitehall." He told *Newsweek* yesterday that films like *The Full Monty* about unemployed Britons trying hard to make money as male strippers reflected the new mood. "Not merely in a sense that it's a highly successful film, and that says something about the state of the British film industry now. There's a great sense of confidence and adventure and greater sense of comfort with ourselves." The country was discovering an "exciting" view of its future which was "look, what we're actually good at is being inventive, creative, dynamic and outward-looking." (*Daily Telegraph*)[29]

Tony Blair would probably be quite chagrined to realize that, if the voters had not perceived him and Mr. Clinton as creditable equivalents of those men "wearing bowler hats and umbrellas," he and Clinton would never have been elected.

* * *

It will not be easy to enlighten the distaff bloc. In the same issue of *The Salisbury Review* as Lança's piece, another female book reviewer strays into sentimentalism – fancies that are "in the air." Ann Glyn-Jones reviews Arthur Herman's *The Idea of Decline in Western History* and leaves the reader with a confused picture featuring mainly Glyn-Jones's dislike for the book.[30] The book's message itself deserves a more reasoned treatment than a sketchy summary of Glyn-Jones's bias in favor of familiar liberal fads: "global warming"; "ecological disasters"; "world-wide pesticide poisoning"; the "perils of scientific hubris which so alarm the Greens"; the infallibility of "organic husbandry"; and the rest of her litany. Herman apparently omits to catalogue all these to her satisfaction while he tackles underlying socio-cultural problems. In all this, unfortunately, one suspects that Glyn-Jones's solution to life's problems will only mean more power for the state.

For some reason, Glyn-Jones is stirred by Herman's book simply to condemn both him and Western society, which leaves one questioning her objectivity. For instance, one might probe deeper to find the substance and causes of her assumed hazards instead of giving vent to beatnik puritanism. Far better for Glyn-Jones to approach her task from the perspective of the common good, or from a higher plane such as Job sought in his travail. Then, she might better cope with our "most urgent need... to know more than a man can ever hope to know: why life should be as it is, rather than what he thought it to be."[31]

Also, like Jürgen Habermas, she will have to wrestle with more profound questions than merely her personal fears. Whether one agrees with Habermas or not, for instance, he at least reflects on the common good and, as David M. Rasmussen puts it, "makes a definite accommodation to the classical republican attempt to anchor the claims of law and politics in a social, and not purely individual, context" – a "context" preferred by Glyn-Jones as well as most feminists. Habermas's thesis at least "meets the criticism concerning the liberal disassociation between rights and responsibilities" indulged in by the ladies, all of which, considering that among Americans aged 25 to 29, more women now have college degrees than men, does not leave one optimistic about either college educations or the level of political thought these days.[32]

As a passing example of where this leads, the estimable conservative *National Review* itself grazes occasionally in the ladies' pasture of political emotivism – the squishy ground of secular revisionism promoting female political leaders. Despite the publication's often incisive candor on the gender gap, it then suggests even more of the same. Judging from similar promotions by other men, the regnant generation of males seem not fully to comprehend distinct, age-old sex roles.

For instance, in the August 17, 1998, issue of *National Review*, one reads of a little 60-year-old wife's qualifications for political leadership. "Maryland's Thatcher, Ellen Sauerbrey," remarks the usually more astute writer. Here, he subjects us to governance by sweet little ladies "looking out of place," "well-coiffed," whose hearts are being broken, usually "a little stocky," often with "wide mouths and toothy smiles," and, of course, always with "pleasing mannerisms" and planning to "establish commissions" on difficult issues. We are offered not one word on *constitutional government* but only a nice lady's version of politics as usual – how to take care of people, cut taxes, cite figures – female sophisters and calculators who have learned how to play male roles.

Recalling Genesis, Ephesians, Isaiah, St. Paul, C.S. Lewis, Chesterton, and all the others regarding our Judeo-Christian heritage requiring husbands to accept the family responsibility of leadership and representation in the outside world, why suddenly assume that wives and daughters are equipped to do the job? Or that they *should*? As Mickey Hargitay remarked about his hysterical wife Jayne Mansfield after their boat had capsized, "She's just being a woman," which perhaps explains her later remark that "One of the things being in politics has taught me is that men are not a reasoned or reasonable sex"[33], hardly reflective of the "deep thought and a combining mind" required to build workable political coalitions.

5.

Reading through the growing body of writings by "conservative" women commenting on feminism, one is struck by the absence of objective male monitoring. Like a herd of young mares suddenly let loose to pasture, they cavort with their versions of goings-on and we are asked to consider it sound commentary even when it smacks of tea-party talk. Wendy Shalit, who does better than most, confronts the tyranny of a feminist enclave celebrating the 20th anniversary of Catherine MacKinnon's *Sexual Harassment of Working Women: A Case of Sex Discrimination* (1978) and finds herself "considerably marginalized."[34] The ladies she observes at a Yale Law School symposium are so far gone in their envy of males that they shut out any reasoned discussion of traditional social mores. But then reversing herself, even Ms. Shalit criticizes her fellow conservatives for "taking advantage of women."

Shalit feels that "conservatives long ago surrendered the notion that a woman could be taken advantage of" – a rather bloated barb, since, whether or not she, MacKinnon or the rest realize it, a woman is still "formed for attentions" and they should show more savvy about it. (Besides, the notion has been mostly marginalized by feminist pretensions of all-powerful women to begin with, which Shalit conveniently ignores.) Implying that conservatives do not think women can be raped is absurd.

In her puzzlement about a "certain private unhappiness among women" and the fact that "women still feel continually offended by men and pine to be treated more courteously by them," Ms. Shalit misses a grand opportunity to probe more deeply. She fails to focus on her most important suggestion, the possibility of a *"non-legal understanding of how the sexes should relate to each other,"* which one suspects her great-grandmother understood *a century ago*. After mentioning some of the old movies that taught us about ladies and gentlemen, she only repeats a sister panelist's comment that "men were more civilized then". (Yes, back before the 60s and women's liberation!) Her piece should be another wake-up call to men (especially editors!) to resume responsibility for the subject.

Ingrid Merikoski puts it succinctly in a review of Arthur Herman's book on the eighteenth-century Scottish Enlightenment,

> .... Adam Smith and Andrew Ferguson warned, in an overly specialized modern society, "the minds of men are contracted and rendered incapable of evaluation." What would always be needed – in Scottish society, in questions of character, and in the world-views of individual people – are order, self-discipline, and balance. Herman suggests that the Enlightenment's main message for the Scots – and for all of us as the Scots' philosophical heirs – is that "true liberty requires a sense of personal obligation as well as individual rights"; that modern life must be spiritually as well as materially fulfilling; that advancements in science are enhanced by arts and culture; that private affluence should foster civic responsibility; and that, following a Burkean impulse, "a confidence in the future depends on a reverence for the past."[35]

The intricate balance of sexual power ("carnival of sexuality," as C.S. Lewis put it) deserves far more thought, including respect for the idea of ladies and gentlemen, which, for all the Victorian transgressions, still allowed the best balance ever. Central to our study, one hopes that Merikoski and Herman appreciate the crucial sequitur that "the feminized minds of women also are contracted and incapable of evaluation."

In missing this, Wendy Shalit lacks the instinct to go for a knockout, which would require putting much of the onus on her sex to shape up to a Pauline standard and return to separate roles for men and women. Like several others we discuss, her essay exemplifies our problem: It takes two to tango. Women cannot complain about men's "former civility" while they themselves behave "uncivilly" in a holistic social sense. Nor can men complain about women's – well, "ways". As Hagar the Horrible should not belittle his wife's housework, nor should she belittle his peculiar form of work. Gentlemen did not "harass" in more "civil" times but neither did ladies *invite* harassment through greater exposure, accessibility and ubiquity. Familiarity breeds contempt even for women, another truism better understood by great-great-grandmothers. Modern women have supposedly been "liberated" but complain about men's uninvited attentions to the point where they obviously haven't been "liberated" at all. Long-proven customs need renovating to the point where both sexes are allowed to operate in their own spheres, with maximum benefit from each, and minimum risk to women. Until civil women accept this, they should cease complaining about men not being "civil."

* * *

Examples are rife. Young men used to seek adventure and experience before settling down. It was part of the over-all plan of maturation, while young women learned their skills in schools and hospitals, parlors and families. The latter were presented at the Court of St. James in their mid-teens, while boys had to earn their spurs to become worthwhile men. Such was the felicitous practice, yet now girls seek adventure and fame in far-flung areas where they do not belong. As a recent item in *The Sunday Telegraph* reads, "A British aid worker found dead in a remote jungle in Beliz was murdered, it was confirmed yesterday."[36] The twenty-seven-year-old victim had been stabbed and "her body was found in bushes near a dirt track… after she failed to return from a trip to a village near the Raleigh International volunteer project where she was helping to build classrooms." Her father, a Cornwall lawyer, said the family had just received a letter saying how much she was enjoying herself…. "She wanted one big adventure before she got a serious partner and settled down." Thus the wages of "sex equality and the rights of woman."

The same occurs too often, as with Amy Biehl, the twenty-six-year-old Fullbright Scholar and Stanford student who was researching women's rights and helping to register voters when she was brutally murdered in 1993 by a group of black South Africans solely because she was white, as if to demonstrate how women can be truly victimized. Strangely, however, her parents chose publicly to support the release of their daughters' killers and even embraced the murderers' families, saying they understood why South African blacks want to kill white people.[37] "'We're not angry, just empty,' says her father. Sadly, that's so – in more ways than one," writes Gene Healy of the case. Apparently, only Anglo-American males are guilty of sexual harassment and brutalization of women. There seems a plaintive, almost incredibly naive helplessness infecting liberalism and its fantasies, which one might have expected a university education to help cure. Yet such womanly-marshmallowy fads are the ruling sentiment in our great republic! When a society shows no more comprehension of basic distinctions between men and women; when the need to have fun and, like Mrs. Jellyby, to do good in strange, murderous lands supersedes civilized norms and common sense, it surely must be a dying breed. (Of course, Ms. Jellyby had the sense to run her far-flung project from the safety of her London flat.)

Instead of sending young women off to Africa, a more workable standard for marriage and womanhood might be found in the marital bliss of Richard and Isabel Burton, he the intrepid "anthropologist, prolific writer, fluent linguist" and explorer of Africa, and she the "independent-minded, fiercely loyal woman who married him despite his notorious reputation" and wrote:

> I want to live.... I want a wild, roving, vagabond life.... I wish I were a man. If I were I would be Richard Burton: but, being only a woman, I would be Richard Burton's wife.

Such ingredients are the stuff that real lives are made of and are apparently well documented in Mary Lovell's biography of the couple, unadorned with herstorical embellishments probably because of Burton's irrepressible manliness.[38] One would not expect Burton to allow a wife or daughter to be murdered in a foreign land and merely "feel empty" when the murderers were released unpunished; yet, with "the ability to become totally absorbed into another culture," he was far from a chauvinist. Come to think of it, Isabel Burton represents the epitome of womanhood, hungry for life yet wondrously met with a man to fit her plan, to complement her urges in ways Amy Biehl, Valadon, Bodichon and "individualist" feminists will never realize.

While it is true that young men often met the same fate in the old scheme of things, Western society saw the risk as part of the passage to manhood, which is not the case for the female of the species. We are not an overpopulated China where women are inhumanly downgraded. Besides, as I have tried to show, there is something much more vulnerable and more precious in the female of the species than there is in the male – something that old customs and Western ways appreciated but current habits do not. From their narrow, "individualist" perspective, feminists miss the big picture. It is simply foolhardy for girls to "earn their spurs" before acceptance in society, and it is both selfish and stupid of them to vie with young men undergoing the rite of passage. In the end, one must ask, "Would the slain woman have been a better mother from her jungle experience?" With a greater store of unconditional love? One sees little of Pauline motherhood in "building classrooms in Beliz." All this is not to ignore that such an end is tragic but rather to suggest that the Victorians would have sent Burton, Stanley or Livingstone to do the job and preserved her life for a "serious partner".

*   *   *

This might be the time to remark on the inanity of blathering about "sexual harassment" as if it were a new discovery, while also mingling boys and girls in play. In children's soccer leagues, mothers are involved to an extreme which would have been deemed incongruous sixty years ago and, from some reports, none too beneficially. For instance, probably inspired by the feminine mystique, the Massachusetts Youth Soccer Association now promotes "non-results-oriented competition in youth tournaments. Nobody keeps score and no players receive trophies unless all do."[39] An example of the oreo-morality of matriarchy? Family females on the sidelines do little to foster male virtues in eight-year-old sons and, more strangely, it is accepted procedure now to have little girls playing soccer with boys! A male coach eases our fears, "They're only eight years old!"

Of course, this is mild compared to schools that allow ten-year-old *boys and girls to wrestle one another.* "It's coming down the pike," one benighted wrestling coach proudly boasts, which presumably also means co-ed boxing, with current female boxers paving the way. T.V. notable Mike Wallace, who has skewered countless hapless targets of investigation, was recently "intimidated" by a 23-year-old female baseball pitcher who had become "the first woman to win a game in a men's league professional game."[40] It seems the young woman's "intense pre-game stare sent the veteran reporter into retreat." Yet, in fact, as she explains, "If you knew my personality, I'm quiet and I like to keep to myself. (The sudden media attention) has been the tough part." Who encouraged this shy young woman to enter the male arena so naively? Perhaps one may be excused if one senses an Alice-in-Wonderland aura in our doings, with baseball, football and all the rest now being oddly transformed into a brave new world of sexless integers: Female jockeys, racecar drivers, pro-golfers, girl PFCs, and the others all vie with the boys.

Now, one might ask the ladies, after condoning such inane practices, how can they complain five years or fifteen years later when the same "little boy" who played soccer or wrestled with their precious daughter happens to make a pass at her or whatever they must do to "harass"? (Remember, Dear Reader, rape is a crime, so presumably we are not talking about that.) Or, how can a wife complain, when her pro-football husband who once wrestled with girls chooses to knock her around the room? Have not we laid the groundwork for such "uncivil" behavior by carelessly mixing sexes on the playing fields of Eton?

* * *

Another intelligent woman who could use more support from her menfolk is Minette Marrin, writing of British women's present difficulties in "finding a husband."[41] It is reminiscent of World War II days when women had similar difficulties, so perhaps we are coming full circle (one can hope). It also seems a comic irony that an attractive woman in these days of "women's liberation" and "more power" can still be complaining about a woman's not finding men! Considering the trouble that women have gone to make themselves unlovable and more manly in conduct and attitude (while still undecided whether to wear pants or gowns, thus revealing the poignant duplicity of the fair sex), it should not be surprising that young men are shying away. Marrin suggests casually the possibility that some such men have simply chosen homosexuality but doesn't bother to pass judgment on the misguided souls, when severe judgment is what they and "society" sorely need.

Despite such glancing parries, however, Marrin hits the nail on the head as to basic causes. After candidly noting the generation of "Superfluous Women, condemned to a single and childless life by a mistaken idea of emancipation," she observes,

> But it doesn't seem to have occurred to them that in a market – and however romantic one might prefer it to be, marriage is and always has been something of a market – everyone has to have something to bargain with.
>
> This lack of realism has been one of the central errors of feminism. In feminist thought women were encouraged to look at the world much too much through their own perspective, to the exclusion of men's. This was not only unreasonable, and unjust to men; it has also turned out to be very much against women's own interests. It has prevented them, until recently, from making any serious effort to understand men, as distinct from ordering them to change. On the contrary, women were encouraged to concentrate on establishing careers, and putting off having babies for as long as physically possible, often until middle age, so that you now often see women with grey hair suckling babies.
>
> At this latish point in their lifeplan, women were prepared to accept men into their routine, to share bills, housework and childcare; however, unconsulted about this, and unattracted by it, a great many men have made other plans.

This is exceptionally well said (it being basic to the present book). For one thing, Marrin's writing brings home the paradox that a woman's greatest value is when she writes, conducts herself or thinks most like a woman, which means that "career" women may be living in a make-believe world where their best attributes are wasted. At the same time, it follows that the more they remain true to their womanhood, the less they belong in a "career" where the resulting tension is beyond the breaking point. Minette Marrin's perspective should be understood by all, because it destroys continuing misconceptions that mislead British-American politicians, voters and society ever more negatively. We either do away with the regnant "lack of realism" or our social dysfunction continues to fester and women will continue down their primrose path of dalliance.[42] It bears repeating that, in the guise of almighty "earning power," women are being encouraged to play twisted roles that serve both them and society ill. It is touching that this young woman can offer such deep wisdom disproving the whole feminist case in one fell swoop, shattering the pretensions of all-knowing males who call for more women in power, and do it so casually, so delicately.

*　*　*

As a striking counterpoint, Anthony Fletcher reviews Stevie Davies's *Unbridled Spirit*, a book on "Women of the English Revolution" apparently much like Régine Pernoud's "women in the days of cathedrals," i.e., a revisionist attempt to recreate women in an image alien to womanhood.[43] In the 1660s, Ms. Davies is quoted, "As a woman you glimpsed a world where you had a say," as though she has no say now (it were better for right order if she didn't) nor did women in the ages of Mesopotamia, Greece, Rome and all the other eras of suppression. Here is the same inferiority complex that inherently disproves its own claim to new power. Mr. Fletcher takes the bait in applauding "a fascinating parade of extraordinary women" – newly discovering the worth of women and transmogrifying it into an all-powerful late-20th-century renaissance. But the paradox remains: If, as he summarizes, women then were "lacking the secular individualism of the modern age," why contaminate their memory now by suggesting their inferiority to the diseased modern rootstock?

Despite attempting to distance themselves from "modern feminism", both Davies and Fletcher show preoccupation with "equality", leading to talk of "spiritual equality between men and women" – to repeat, an obscure construct of only recent vintage. Joan of Arc or Catherine of Siena, for instance, thought naught of "spiritual equality with men," nor probably did the women whom Davies writes about. The human pageant has always included "radical women" along with radical men, yet only now is there an aberrant focus on the women rather than the actual shakers and movers. (Nicholas Davidson brought this out in his book fifteen years ago.)

Women's studies inspire a flood of such "research with a mission." The mere fact, however, that a woman like Margaret Fell was "formidable indeed, a militant controversialist into her eighties, whose stamina did not fail," cannot persuade us that such attributes were either lovable or ignored in 1600. In fact (to the candid eye), as successors to Madam Fell, 2000s women elevated to high posts seem generally out of character (unless emulating Xanthippe), as quite probably Fell was herself. Otherwise, we would have seen many more such women throughout history. That her behavior is an exception rather than the rule tells us much. Similarly, other examples from Davies's book call for a caution that Fletcher lacks.

It is self-defeating to adulate "the many unbridled women that this book seeks to celebrate," calling to mind other famous "unbridled women" like Eve, Jezebel, Lady MacBeth, Goneril, or Lizzie Borden, hardly subjects for celebration. (The term, "unbridled," infers a demotion of traditional "bridled" women, and in itself should alert us to the mischief.) What value to an average housewife, a talented teenager, troubled divorcée, or lonely widow to know that "prophetess" Elizabeth Pool gained an audience with The Army Council; or "the perplexity" of "visionary" Anna Trapnel's "audiences, who could not decide whether to treat her as a witch, a vagrant or a woman possessed by God"; or that Ralph Josselin and Nehemiah Wallington both loved their wives, with the former viewing "the union as an almost, but not quite, equal partnership" and the latter respecting his wife's "impassioned discipline"; or that Lucy Hutchinson's writings reveal a woman of "great drive, aware of the loss of the self that has died with (her husband)"?

All this is a woman's effort to bolster her image of women (the need for which only she can explain), endeavoring to paint a woman's life in an adventurous, glamorous or activist pattern far from Minette Marrin's reality. According to Fletcher, Davies even labors to trace from the efforts of a 1660 Quaker lady (Fell) "the breakdown of Calvinist predestinarianism, with its exacting cerebral demands," a dubious accomplishment deserving in itself much more cerebrum. Despite Fletcher's inference to the contrary, both he and Davies reveal dubious secular motivations in celebrating Margaret Fell's Quaker manifesto's kinship with the Reformation:

> Through sectarianism, seeking and finally Quakerism, many men and women had been set free to find their own spiritual paths. The reaction, well sketched by Davies early in the book in an account of the conservative pamphleteer Thomas Edwards, was fierce. But there is a legacy, Davies is convinced, which echoes to the present. By posing the notion of spiritual equality between men and women, the Reformation had prised open minds. Changing conceptions of gender limited the opportunity for spiritual prophecy to be taken seriously after 1660. Women's claims contracted before they expanded on a broader front.

These closing words by Fletcher reveal conflicts. For one thing, the emergence of "changing conceptions of gender" suggests that human nature had regained the upper hand and thus quashed any grand visions of "radical women". At the same time, Davies is allowed to pretend that women have the inside track with God, even to the point of greater proneness to "spiritual prophecy". If this be true, it is a great secret. Finally, any eagerness to downgrade Christianity and let men and women engineer "their own spiritual paths" leaves one uncomfortable. While each person is distinct before God, one doubts that each can invent his own religion. All in all, the book is another revisionist feminist publication; and his review, a puzzle.

* * *

A further example of the genre appears in the February 7, 1998, issue of *The Spectator* in the form of a review by feminist Claudia Fitzherbert of *The New Feminism*, by Natasha Walter.[44] The resulting brew of conflicting opinions and delusions is hardly edifying other than to remind us again of the inanity of letting "these delicate creatures" act as our leaders or advisors.[45] "Natasha Walter is an old-fashioned equality feminist," announces Fitzherbert, as if this were other than a pretentious label. First, the reviewer describes Walter's position as "wary of perceived differences between male and female ambition, and refreshingly dismissive of claims of sex superiority. And while she makes a forceful case for women never having had it so good, she believes that feminism remains central for the simple reason that women remain poorer, and less visible than men." All of this is untenable for several reasons. Since women outlive men and thus control most of the West's wealth, one can hardly judge them as "poorer". That they may be "less visible than men" is only natural in view of their greater propensity for interiorities than men, who are out in the world producing, hunting, gathering and so forth. That "equality feminists" are unhappy with this suggests a severe case of illusions.

> As if to alert us, we are told that Walter's
>
> ...solution lies in a revolution of the organization of work. Patchwork careers are the answer, for men as well as for women. Women can have it all but not at the same time. The acceptance of career breaks might be the most important single change that could release men and women into a more equal working world.
>
> It might indeed, but how to forge the new ideal? Walter doesn't say. Her method is to establish the absolute truth of an uncontentious point, and then to rest her case.

"Uncontentious," to suggest radical market restructuring from her armchair? From both of these women, one senses ominous clouds on the horizon, what with Walter's obvious bent towards socialism or dictatorial tyranny to gain her ends and Fitzherbert's hint that Walter doesn't go far enough to "reorganize work." After all, in a free society, "achievement of material equality" would require an inartistic surrender of their womanhood in order to compete on an equal basis with men; besides, the ladies' conversation always returns to their true destiny which is to settle down with a good husband and have babies. So, the eternal irony rears its head again in a confused dialectic, complaining about men while suggesting all sorts of utopian arrangements for the "betterment" of women.

Natasha Walter's book was also reviewed in *The Times Literary Supplement* (March 20, 1998), by Mary Margaret McCabe, and Walter responded in the March 27 issue, strengthening her image as a reform authoritarian, adhering to feminism and its "transformation of public life." She wants the socialistic minimum wage, parental leave for pregnancies, sex equality, all supposedly without affirmative action. Her gynocentricism would stiffen laws against rape but ignore unwritten laws and customs that formerly served to kept women out of harm's way. The "frustration of women with a legal system that serves them so badly" blinds her to the impossibility of either "equality" or a docile, neutered humanity. Again, such exchanges between women on "making the world safe for women" need more specifics, e.g., in which country?

* * *

In contrast, the wisest male thinkers (e.g., early Catholics or Enlightenment Scots) tend to talk of an "Order of Being" or higher truths, such as Catholic lawyer and Professor Heinrich A. Rommen's discussion of natural law,

> Heraclitus of Ephesus (*cir.* 536-470 B.C.) is famous for his thesis

that "all things flow; nothing abides". But this ceaseless changing of things led him directly to the idea of an eternal norm and harmony, which exists unchangeable amid the continual variation of phenomena. A fundamental law, a divine common *logos*, a universal reason holds sway; not chance, lawlessness, or irrational change. Natural occurrences are ruled by a reason that establishes order. Man's nature as well as his ethical goal consists, then, in the subordination or conformity of individual and social life to the general law of the universe. This is the primordial norm of moral being and conduct. "Wisdom is the foremost virtue, and wisdom consists in speaking the truth, and in lending an ear to nature and acting according to her. Wisdom is common to all.... They who would speak with intelligence must hold fast to the (wisdom that is) common to all, as a city holds fast to its law, and even more strongly. For all human laws are fed by divine law."[46]

Instead of conforming to the general law or even redefining it sensibly as change occurs, feminists ignore it entirely or claim "male tyranny." However, no system of law can allow the license feminists dream of.

Also in contrast, here is Russell Hittinger's depiction of Heinrich Rommen's motivation to resist radical efforts to transform settled law:

> Every generation, it is said, finds a new reason for the study of natural law. For Rommen and many others of his generation, totalitarianism provided that occasion. As he put it in his book on the state, "When one of the relativist theories is made the basis of a totalitarian state, man is stirred to free himself from the pessimistic resignation that characterizes these relativist theories and to return to his principles." Rommen's writings were prompted by the spectacle of German legal professionals, who, while trained in the technicalities of positive law, were at a loss in responding to what he called "*Adolf Légalité.*"[47]

Since feminism is avowedly a "revolution,"[48] we are in the position of 1930s Germans. While our task should be much easier, we first must retrieve the fundamental structure of natural society as it involves the two sexes. (Those who dismiss this as alarmist might read the thought of two esteemed former congresspersons, Pat Schroeder and Susan Molinari.[49])

* * *

As another reminder, *The Weekly Standard* offers a chatty essay by Pia Nordlinger presumably to challenge our reading habits. In the July 27, 1998, "Casual" feature ("and the Ladies of the Clubs"), Ms. Nordlinger shows off her reading inspired by two book clubs, peopled mostly by women.[50] The gist of her revelations is that women prefer books by women – gynocentric books – not about "male thoughts and male calculations" or "a man's perspective" (possibly building, inventing and producing). In fact, women, she says, have "an unintended aversion to maleness in fiction." Hmm, considering that the world's great thinkers are male, is this aversion a sign of women's superior wisdom? Perhaps the main shortcoming is her limited perception of literature, which facetiously assumes that men's books are "full of professional soccer and guys who sit around making lists of the Top Five Best Movies" or that a man's perspective is "presumably loaded with profanity, sex, and sports." Here, she misses the irony that, since the Nineteenth Amendment, women have intruded into so many areas where men once persevered that the latter no longer emulate their educated great-great-grandfathers.

While all this may be trying for some, if we can get through the slough of despair, perhaps the way ahead will improve. Meanwhile, in her gauzy article, Nordlinger mentions not a single piece of serious non-fiction. Her examples – all novels – are noteworthy more for their diversionary or imaginary qualities than Faulknerian or Shakepearean universalities: Capote, Toni Morrison, *Valley of the Dolls*, *100 Years of Solitude*, and others. What matters is whether they are about men or about women, "marvelously funny," or "sappy gynobibliophilia." For her, "conservative" is a spy book by W.F. Buckley, Jr., and "masculine" is "a gung-ho military tract, *The Hunt for Red October*," or "Ernest Hemingway at his most misogynist." "Red-meat conservative" means working for the middling Heritage Foundation, all of which reveals Nordlinger's rather slippery grasp of things. She magnanimously tries to "level the playing field by championing" (Nick Hornby's) "marvelously funny book," *About a Boy*, under whose charm she has fallen, which suggests that Ms. Nordlinger, with her trendy conformity to ladies' book clubs, might not "champion" anything of real adult value.

Secular humanism, public co-education and feminism have all taken their toll of the national intellect, as evident in Nordlinger's pegging herself as an "anti-gender-feminism, anti-identity-politics Hillary-basher" who "still tends to read books by or about women." The former is intended to earn conservative credentials, while the latter reveals her essential femininity. "Books by or about women" nowadays, of which there is no shortage, are either fictional or revisionist fodder for "women's studies". Only female European refugees in this century seem to have come closest to reasoned exegesis on deeper topics.

The nearest Nordlinger's article comes to seriousness is her quote of Francine Prose's asseveration on "the best writing" as having not as much "to do with gender as it does with nationality or with the circumscriptions of time…. There is no male or female language, only the truthful or fake, the precise or vague, the inspired or the pedestrian." Even with these pedestrian half-truths, the ladies reveal how "gender" has indeed influenced "the best" as well as the not-so-good writing. "Uncircumscribed by time," the best writing tends to be *timeless*, and, due to different brain structures, sex is quite determinative of the "best," as Nordlinger's writing itself demonstrates.

6.

As Don Quixote braved his way across Spain, he encountered a succession of foes scorning his dedicated knighthood. It is not for us to belittle his travail as we meet our own seemingly endless parade of ladies speaking their piece. Comes now Elizabeth Powers to offer an anti-feminist slant.[51] One might think her an ally, yet as so often the case except for Midge Decter (and now perhaps Minette Marrin), we meet a lady who adopts a traditionalist mask while thinking gynocentrically. She and the next windmill we encounter spin their accounts in terms of personal experience rather than the combined efforts of men and women that we older knights were accustomed to.

Mind you, Ms. Powers has almost all the right ideas, since she knows the words, but her tune is one-dimensional and ultimately atonal as she labors to make it all – interesting, probably to women. She starts with her "childhood eating habits" (in the fifties), her "idea of cooking," the salad ingredients resorted to by her working mother (who was an office secretary), her parents' "prepackaged foods combined with genteel table manners," their difficult financial straits due implicitly to her "father's sporadic employment," and other aspects, for all of which she now feels naturally nostalgic and somewhat apologetic. For her, it conjures up memories of their "propriety" (for which we should feel wistful), yet she is not quite old enough to realize that "those habits of graciousness, decorum, and civility that her mother and father unwittingly impressed" on her were not "unwitting" at all. Which makes it ever more clear that she is very much a "thoroughly modern woman" somewhat embarrassed by the ways of her grandmother (although she would probably deny this) and quite imbued with the chimera of modern woman's supposedly elevated status.

Powers then launches into a display of intellectuality – an educated female savoring the sisterhood's "lucrative professions, particularly in the law", the "higher spheres," "areas of intellectual life from which women had traditionally been excluded," "a great deal of freedom," and so on. College has indeed made its mark on Elizabeth Powers, especially one suspects in the canon of women's studies. Actually, her essay does not reflect much intellect, as much as a trendy snobbishness oblivious to the fact that women lawyers haven't improved the Bar, the Bench, nor, for that matter, the law. Aside from a few exceptions, women are still not drawn to serious thought. All in all, Powers's are a breezy liberated woman's credentials. She condescended to a change of pace when she "did meet a man who decided he wanted to marry me" just as she was considering "a position at a major university," which more "unwittingly" than her parents reveals mainly a very inflated American female ego!

Nevertheless, all this aside, we should give her credit for remarking the "coarsening of American manners," although one might expect a college graduate to see the irony that women no longer "excluded from intellectual life" are missing where it matters most and thus a primary cause of our children's "coarsening". While Powers exhibits a lot of words, she never reaches the point of forgoing self-centered "literary and academic pursuits" to acquire the education young women used to seek with the aim of being good parents like her mother. Perhaps, as a new woman, she cannot go so far and opts for tainted pearls on Francis Bacon and feminist misconceptions about marriage. Hers is a woman's concentric, mostly personal view, lacking the depth it could acquire in a shared parental wisdom.

* * *

In her turn, Judith Rich Harris's latest book on child-rearing, *The Nurture Assumption: Why Children Turn Out the Way They Do* switches from her earlier advice on how parents can shape their children to the other extreme of urging that they cannot. Now, she discovers that "parents don't matter, it's all in the genes."[52] While my understanding of her work is based solely on Steve Sailer's review in *National Review*, the signs suggest another exercise in virtual unreality. As Sailer points out, lending weight to Elizabeth Powers's views, there is too much evidence showing not only the importance of good parenting but also the negative impact of bad parenting – too much so, in fact, to justify Harris's claim that parenting does not matter. Strangely, Harris is a grandmother and should know better.

A further paradox is that too many men have dropped out and need savvy women to lure them back in line. Linda Bowles, for instance, could remind us that Ms. Harris is wrong to ignore the wisdom of Proverbs 22:6, that if we "train up a child in the way he should go; and when he is old, he will not depart from it."[53] Of course, while her grasp of fundamentals and the need for a conscientious, educated citizenry allows Ms. Bowles to dispense sound ideas in her columns, one is never certain whether she realizes we still need to rear up male leaders, with all that implies. As with Midge Decter and Minette Marrin, no matter how well they diagnose our problem, they never quite go as far as Henry Adams's dinner partner to suggest the need for *sapient manhood*. When, however, Bowles writes of a "man's values," "untrustworthy leaders," needing "to rescue our children from the state," and "what leaders will we choose?" the underlying premise seems to be, *wiser males*.

* * *

Here is where women like the London *Sunday Telegraph*'s Alison Eadie flounder beyond their depth frivolously writing of "putting women on top."[54] Juggling ambiguous statistics, she notes that women still lack top executive jobs but do well in personnel management. Further, since men are less qualified and educated, she assumes "it must be only a matter of time before human resources directors are elevated to the top job. Then the future will truly be female." This is too definitive to be humorous, so Eadie apparently is another Charlotte spinning her web.

* * *

Next, while on the subject of children, we might look at Patricia Hersch's *A Tribe Apart: A Journey into the Heart of American Adolescence*, another commendable effort but lacking a man's robust reinforcement.[55] Like Ms. Powers's treatise on children and manners without noticeable reference to men, Ms. Hersch also writes of her experience with children, ages 11 to 17, without the help of male authority, as if to show the inevitable conundrum of single-sex parenting. Men learn much in the army, at work, and in organized efforts that a woman learns only in marriage. One wishes that Ms. Hersch's "journey" had discovered this truism and how to capitalize on it.

Were it not for the fact that the ladies would then be less womanly, one wishes they offered such thought as we saw in Robert P. Hunt's review of George Wiegel's *A Century of Catholic Social Thought*, discussing John Courtney Murray. It is worth repeating here, in part:

> What concerned Murray in 1960 – and what has since become an even graver problem – was that Americans no longer affirmed the moral and political truths that bound us together as *civitas*: a community united by a common purpose that transcended material subsistence or narrow self-interest. Murray argued that the only way to recover a truly public philosophy was for the nation to reaffirm the higher truths on which the nation had been founded....[56]

Do 2000s women *ever* offer such higher thoughts of community other than, "it takes a village," or to gather for questionable solutions to problems like drunk driving, "our kids," "choice," crime, and, of course, "great strides for women"? Have the suffragettes or the libbers *ever* done so? Indeed, the "revolution" might begin right here, which would require repeal of much of the 1960s legislation and its progeny. Here again is the irony: true community would require more traditional roles – taking us back to duties – where we belong.

David Klinghoffer reviews Hersch's book, offering his own commendable reflections on the subject. Mainly, he emphasizes the need for male adulthood, which both Hersch and Powers avoid, and rightly calls for "renunciation" of "the demands for immediate comfort, pleasure and excitement," as well as "accepting responsibility for the lives of others," which means for a man usually either getting married or military service. Unfortunately, he fails to explore why the idea of manhood has declined. The ladies also miss this aspect. After over eighty years of "sex quality and the rights of woman", we have managed to botch this facet of our heritage. Powers and Hersch must learn that "it takes two to tango." And, if David Klinghoffer really wants a "revolution", or if he truly thinks we should not "beat around the bush", let him consider this: While, as Pat Moynihan, Charles Murray, and others have warned, the welfare laws have done great damage,[57] these do not approach the harm done by laws decreeing that we *cannot discriminate as to sex*.

In order to bring about the "revolution" Klinghoffer calls for, it will take repeal of such laws and a return to a free citizenry informed by the biblical heritage of God's creation, the tradition of ladies and gentlemen, and our inherently patriarchal society. Then, the female of the species would be better off and responsible men would approach their full potential. In 1920 and 1964, (to use Edmund Burke's words) we treated "the humbler part of the community with the greatest contempt" in complaining of "inadequate representation", when in fact, "in justice to that old-fashioned constitution, under which we have long prospered,... our representation has been found perfectly adequate to all the purposes for which representation of the people can be desired or devised."[58]

Klinghoffer's revolution will obviously require changes no less dramatic than the demise of the Berlin Wall, or tearing down the judicial "wall of separation" having no legitimate connection with our Constitution. The shackling of our natural religious impulse and reverence for God's order of being has played no small role in blurring traditional sexual roles.

* * *

At this point, for further evidence of the feminist malaise, let us look at a recent exchange in *Commentary*, where "Letters from Readers" are always educational, exhibiting both the depths of misguided American intellectualism and the frequently brilliant responses of the magazine's formidable contributors. This skirmish involves an article by one of the latter in the June 1998 issue, with letters and his rebuttal appearing in the August issue. Gabriel Schoenfeld, who is senior editor, wrote the original piece, entitled "Auschwitz and the Professors," dealing rather whimsically with Harvard's dilemma finding someone to fill the vacant Holocaust chair, and commenting generally on "the way in which courses on the Nazi slaughter of Europe's Jews – 'Holocaust 101,' in Elie Wiesel's alarmed and alarming phrase – are now routinely exploited as commercial bragging points in the self-promotion of American institutions of higher learning." He goes on to tell of the "tastelessness" of campus "Holocaustology" and the "careerism of Holocaustologians" who discuss "the murder of six million Jews" little differently than "agricultural macroeconomics or the sociology of chimpanzees – which is to say that even at its best, it is often full of the most egregious professional jargon." Needless to say, feminists have joined in this unfortunate new canon and it is their responses we shall concentrate on.

While Schoenfeld pays respect where it is due, he also tells it like it is, so the "women's voices" and "gender studies" injecting sex into the Holocaust tragedy come in for their share of candor, which the perpetrators do not take kindly to. In fact, the feminist sisterhood boasts of their efforts as "cutting-edge scholarship in an emerging field." However, Schoenfeld suggests that, in this instance, Harvard might have backed into a wise decision by "suspending indefinitely the search for a Holocaust chairman.... (I)f scholars who still study and teach about the Holocaust in a serious way were to speak up against those bent on transforming the murdered Jews of Hitler's Europe into so many 'variables', 'case studies', and 'gendered' objects, we might see a slow rotation of the wheel toward human decency." All of which seems sensible and encouraging, at least until we see the responses.

The "Holocaustologians" resented Schoenfeld's "distortions" and defended their "serious scholarship" (although other letter writers reinforced his position). But here is how he responded to the feminist platoon, first, regarding one woman's claim to "seriousness and commitment":

> Indeed, her own serious commitment to feminism is the most important fact about her. To judge by her footnotes, apart from what she draws from the standard English-language literature (she cites no European-language sources), many of her ideas appear to come from tracts like *Feminist Revolution* (1975), *Radical Feminism* (1973), *Subject Women* (1981), *Discovering Reality: Feminist Perspectives in Epistemology, Metaphysics, Methodology, and Philosophy of Science* (1983), in addition to *Ms.* magazine.
>
> Drinking deeply from this particular gourd, (she) proceeds to graft onto the Holocaust every modish cliché imaginable about male and female behavior, and then to "theorize" about what it all means for feminism. Nowhere is this exercise pursued more avidly than in "Women and the Holocaust: A Reconsideration of Research"....

This woman had written, "To imply that 'I assign co-responsibility for the catastrophe (of the Holocaust)' to Jewish men and Nazis is a claim so vile as not to warrant a reply. No one who has conscientiously read my work or heard me speak could arrive at such an outrageous conclusion," in response to which, Schoenfeld quotes from her own essay:

> It has been difficult to confront the fact that Jewish women were victims as *Jewish women* (her emphasis), not only because some Jewish men exploited Jewish women, but also because Jewish men could not protect women and children from the Nazis. In other words, it has been too difficult to contemplate the extent to which gender counted in the exploitation and murder of Jewish women, and the extent to which the sexism of Nazi ideology and the sexism of the Jewish community met in a tragic and involuntary alliance. Men could and did oppress women sexually, and women were aware of that possibility.[59]

To interpret this as "assigning co-responsibility for the catastrophe to Jewish men" seems a quite reasonable inference and, for the lady to consider it "vile and outrageous," shows either a poor memory or confused judgment. It is just one example of several in this exchange that demonstrate the essential vacuity of feminist academics who make careers out of such gibberish.

Schoenfeld quotes another sample from this lady's thought, which suggests the ridiculous more than the sublime:

> While women's consciousness, "herstory," culture, and so on became the standard by which to understand and judge the world, there was confusion about whether the quintessential woman – the most typical or representative woman – was to be a woman of the past or a new woman of the future. The confusion resolved itself in a psychoanalytic mode: the past is the future. Then struggles arose about which woman of the past would serve as a model. The result was that we did not emerge with a consciousness, let alone a politics, that produced genuine solidarity with all women, although we did advance different claims to superiority.
>
> The valorization of oppression damages not only our politics but our research.... The archeological perspective that we have

on women's culture must be reexamined. Why do we take this point of view? How do we want to use it? Against what are we fighting? What new world are we making? Does our work sustain or even reinforce oppression? Are we articulating ways to understand and combat oppression? How does our work further the liberation of women? And if it does not, in what sense is it feminist?

As Schoenfeld comments, "And so on, and so forth, and so forth," as if to ask, is this what higher learning is all about? A male teacher considers hers a "very important contribution," as with many men taken in by feminology. Her rhetoric is akin to the mindless student posturing of the 1960s when adolescent thought masqueraded in senseless jargon. As Schoenfeld tolerantly puts it, "Beneath the babble, there is actually a clear statement of an agenda here. That agenda is *not* the historical understanding of the Holocaust. It is, rather, the 'liberation of women' as Joan Ringelheim conceives it."

In response to another male's praise (a Mr. Berenbaum) of a certain Holocaustic book for allowing "all viewpoints" not only of "ardent feminists" but also of those who disagree with them, Schoenfeld asks, "But are we dealing here with scholarship or with a Democratic-party caucus? My criticisms of the Ofer-Wetzman book revolved not around the question of its representativeness but around the way it distorts and obscures understanding of the Holocaust, and I cite specific instances to show what I meant. It is wholly typical of the way "true professionals" conduct discussions these days that Mr. Berenbaum resolutely declines to enter into a discussion of those specifics, confining himself instead to generalities."

Schoenfeld cites two female writers' "lengthy and basically unexceptional lecture (which) makes not the slightest effort to… address a single one of my objections to their book. A pattern of evasion is becoming evident here." Crediting another lady for "genuine and original contribution" in her two books, he nevertheless condemns "the tasteless boasting and narcissism of the handouts she has written for her center (at Clark University), and her own ready descent into the cant of gender studies." One detects also a pattern of groupthink in these circles, a pattern that does little justice to the age-old search for truth.

Several other examples of Schoenfeld's forthright handling of the opposition are worth a look:

> Like Debórah Dwork, Nechama Tec, too, is a scholar of standing; indeed, she is fully aware of the twaddle being written and taught by others. In a letter early this summer to the *Wall Street Journal*, she spoke out against "feminist zealots" and those "propelled by extreme feminist views" to interject "political agendas" into Holocaust studies. In the light of these invigorating words, it is all the more incomprehensible to me that she should now decline to utter a word of criticism beyond the modest admission that "both the academic research and teaching of the Holocaust are not consistently of the highest quality." This sentence deserves a Pulitzer Prize for understatement.

(Here is the familiar trait of womanly middleness, as Ms. Tec defends Dwork, Ofer and Weitzman, even while claiming an aversion to their feminist views.)

> A gallant but bemused Robert Jan van Pelt charges that I have written a "misogynist rant," reducing women scholars to the "benighted emanations of a witches' sabbath." Sidney Bolkosky, more reasonably, claims that, although he worries "interminably about…. travesties" and about the "blatantly offensive and ridiculous examples of academic and nonacademic tripe," my own effort is vitiated by my "annoying" and "selective" use of evidence. Aside from the fact that I do in fact mention some of the scholars whom Mr. Bolkovsky accuses me of ignoring, and that I single out for praise Saul Friedlander, whom I stand charged with maligning, my purpose – again – was not to smell the flowers but to call attention to the weeds. Like all my critics, Mr. van Pelt does

not wish to get mixed up in an actual discussion of these weeds. I have already indicated why I think this may be so.

While Mr. Schoenfeld's original article questions the need for a college Holocaust center at all thanks to corruptive trends in such endeavors, he quite clearly supports continued scholarly research in the field, a distinction his opposition seems to have ignored. One senses in too many of these responses from academe a trace of closed-mindedness, such that ordinary English seems not to sink in, out of fear perhaps of loss of status. Or is it that their bailiwick is being threatened? In either case, the responses are not a sign of robust intellect and, despite dogged defense of their "scholarship," the ladies are inordinately involved in the misdirection. As Schoenfeld perceives the problem, "the style of argumentation employed by (the opposition to his views) – hortatory, self-righteous, vacant – is, alas, yet another signpost showing just where things stand." So much for feminist Holocaustology.

Next we shall visit with a more traditionalist women's group whose members at least assay to offer "an intellectual antidote" to feminism.

7.

The Independent Women's Forum (IWF) was founded in 1992 essentially to counter the obloquy issuing from the feminist camp during and after the Supreme Court confirmation hearings for Clarence Thomas. The aim was commendable, appropriate, and obviously timely, although one wonders why Phyllis Schlafly's Eagle Forum (EF) or Beverly La Haye's Concerned Women of America (CWA) could not have done the job. Perhaps these new ladies, who include "businesswomen, economists, lawyers, truck drivers, and mothers," were not as traditional as the latter two groups but still felt repelled by Anita Hill's bushwhacking of Thomas and decided to join forces. If they had other reasons, it is difficult to tell from their literature. Whatever the case, as with most women's organizations over the past one hundred and fifty years, ever since fridges, canned goods, washers, driers, cars and microwaves freed the ladies from household chores, their impact presents a fascinating challenge.

La Haye's (CWA) focus is primarily on the family and Schlafly's (EF) also "pro-family," along with whatever conservative cause they deem appropriate. "Independent Women", in turn, promote "individual responsibility, strong families, limited government, and opportunity." Of course, all such causes are standard campaign fare these days, but that old friend "opportunity" will prove elusive unless the ladies mean "ordered freedom," a far better term. Of course, we may agree that whatever laws we pass should not tend to erode the family institution, but, by frequent resort to terms like "gender equity", their literature reflects less of restraint and more of a yen for new worlds to conquer.

One wishes the American (and British) people in the twentieth century had given more thought to their campaign rhetoric. The words can have so many different meanings, not all of which are necessarily desirable or appropriate. For instance, an ordinary dictionary defines "opportunity" as "[1] A fit or convenient time, [2] Favorable circumstance, [3] A chance for advancement in business." It is impossible to know what IWF members (and likewise, politicians) intend. It is time to find out.

Anglo-Americans would do well to revitalize their political thought not by contriving new ways of government meddling but by returning to their ordered freedoms. Whether the Nineteenth Amendment will allow this is questionable. Besides Kirk, Burke, and others, one can learn from Gerhart Niemeyer, an Episcopalian turned Catholic who died in 1997, leaving behind "a vast body of writing." In his magnum opus, *Between Nothingness and Paradise*, he wrote, "the great confrontation with political irrationality in our time has not the character of a debate or even discussion." It was "the work of his life" to re-engage, as mentioned, the "common universe of reason" demolished by ideologies like feminism, and it should also be ours.[60]

Instead, one must endure lofty words on the Fourteenth Amendment, the Gettysburg Address, Civil Rights laws, the horrors of slavery and Jim Crow, Selma, Martin Luther King, Jr.'s euphoric throng on the Capitol Mall, and so on. "Women's oppression," "exclusion," "sex equality and the rights of woman" fit right in with this paraphernalia. But where in the United States Constitution does all this, or the word "opportunity", appear? When do women's groups engage in political philosophy or scholarly dialogue? Perhaps such terms are passé.

One hopes that IWF will fill the void. While they claim to have "changed the terms of the debate (on "sexual harassment") because of the depth and analytical approach we bring to these topics,"[61] this is not yet apparent in their literature. Reflecting the decline, CBS's Ed Bradley highlights the IWF as "an increasingly high-profile group that says the time has come to put a new face on feminism"[62], as if he knew what "feminism" amounted to or what "new face" might be propitious. His comment is about as consequential as a 300 A.D. Roman courier's announcing a "new face" for Roman women as the hordes descend upon the capitol.

Similarly, the *Boston Globe* enthuses, "The IWF has a profile almost unheard of for a group that is the new kid on the block. In the market place of ideas, from the national news media all the way down to local radio, the IWF has shown its real strength…. (The) IWF is well on its way to becoming the foremost media nemesis of the feminist movement."⁶³ IWF's literary offering is *The Women's Quarterly*, the Summer, 1997, issue of which carries a rear-cover blurb explaining IWF's "success" as the result of its members' being not "radical ideologues" but mainly interested in promoting (the above-mentioned) "policies that will help all Americans," a grand vision indeed. They suggest that by joining their ranks you will "add another voice of reason – yours – to the cultural and political debates of our time," which apparently has columnist Mona Charen convinced, as she praises *The Women's Quarterly*, "My type of women's magazine! With humor and sarcasm but also with warmth and passion, these women offer an intelligent refutation of the leading feminist nonsense that is swallowed so uncritically by the mainstream press."

Just what are these ladies offering in the way of "political debate"? A reading of their sample literature suggests Charen's appraisal comes close, as they chitchat against the extremism of Gloria Steinem, Patricia Ireland, and N.O.W., regarding co-ed combat and sleeping arrangements, the growing miasma of "sexual harassment", the confusions of "discrimination", and the like, but actually reveal little in the way of alternative thinking. The dialectic is reminiscent of F. Carolyn Graglia's motherly comfort zone, no doubt pleasant for those in the loop but of little help in solving the puzzle, as it leans toward gynocentrism rather than the common good.

Ways to approach abortion, levels of female involvement in the military, discrimination, "sexual harassment", jovial ambivalence on patriarchy; whatever the issue, the general tenor is engaging but not confrontational on ultimate solutions. There is no focus on religion or God's order of being, or the Constitution, or the profound significance of marriage with its sacrifices along with its joys, so presumably the hope is to contrive a new way mostly out of wholecloth. Life for these ladies is mainly an *individual project*, needing only "how to" kits for getting along, protected of course by "sex equality" laws. Focus on our culture or heritage would amount to "radical ideology."

IWF's former president, Ricky Silberman, is very much a case in point. While she disapproves of the careless passage of the laws that gave birth to Titles VII and IX, and the ridiculous "sexual harassment" law, she nevertheless seems to condone them as a sign of women's progress. Much taken with her own public career (commissioner of the Equal Employment Opportunities Commission, 1985-1994, itself an imperial encroachment on a citizen's mundane duties), she takes for granted that women can serve three masters, Caesar, career and family. Ignoring that the cure for our many ills lies in revival of our culture, including our sexual constitution, she accepts the unnatural sex roles now plaguing us. For her, the twentieth-century "hallmark was not the awful wars and revolutions, or the rise and fall of totalitarian ideologies; rather, (historians) will say that the enduring change the twentieth century made is the fundamental reshaping of the status of women in society."[64] In other words, for all IWF's "resistance to feminism," its president is resigned to the feminist cancer.

While Ms. Silberman suggests that all this "raises questions," apparently she is not ready herself to answer them, or to promote IWF's announced goals of "families, limited government, individual responsibility," which would answer the "questions" quite forcibly. Instead, for her it is merely "a yeasty time, a time for experiment, a time of opportunity and the excitement of real choice," never mind Burke's partnership between the dead, the living and the yet unborn, which Midge Decter echoes in a recent lecture peroration: When we accept the reality of marriage, ".... we may be through debating and redefining the term 'family' and begin to relearn the very, very old lesson that life has limits and that only by escaping Self and becoming part of the onrushing tide of generations can we ordinary humans give our lives their intended full meaning. We have been endowed by our Creator not only with unalienable rights but with the knowledge that is etched into our very bones."[65]

Invitingly, IWF's July, 1998, newsletter *ex femina* includes an item by the Center for Military Readiness's Elaine Donnelly, which tells of the follies of military co-ed policies and calls for corrective measures. Immediate repeal of the misguided legislation decreeing "sex equality" in the military is called for. Is IWF pursuing this goal?

Our "liberated" society in this "time of experiment" is at a loss to deal with basic sexual instincts and acceptable behavior. For IWF, "family" is an abstraction devoid of the peculiar ingredient known as the human male from whence mundane matters of love and support once sprung. To deal with many of IWF's concerns will need a functioning man and woman, an arrangement once centered so distinctively on the power of a traditional woman. Will these women return to this reality?

Also reflective of current confusions, Judge Richard Posner can only remark on the sexual-harassment brier patch, "this is a particularly hard area of law, through no ones fault, just because of the nature of it."[66] Yet non-discrimination statutes on sex are definitely our fault and need repealing! Then comes John Stossel of ABC News, "taking a hard look at Title IX's effects on men's sports," drawing on "legal scholars" who tell him that the reason for the law "is years of sex discrimination." Despite the awesome imprimatur of T.V., however, without honest scholarship such people flounder helplessly in the labyrinth of "sex discrimination." Stossel and several others engage in artificial rubric: "things haven't been equal"; "donations given fairly" (between sexes); "getting equality on the athletic fields"; "that's not (the taxpayer's) choice. The law says they have to do this, and that means they have to do it." (this, from a female attorney, not a very encouraging sign); "a court ruling that a horse swinging a bat was not gender equal"; "lawyers are so interested in equality"; and so forth.

These comments arose in ABC's program, 20/20 (May 1998), which closed with John Stossel's rightly remarking that "we could have had improvement without (Title IX)". But then he bowed to the egalitarians, "We had terrible sexism, but now we're aware of it." Balderdash! As we now know, "sex" was only a last-ditch "poison pill" intended to sabotage the 1964 bill, but did not.[67] Nor was there evidence of "horrible sexism" in 1972.

Then, after Stossel's well-considered *reductio ad absurdum* that "once you accept this logic that since men and women are equal, any inequality must be discrimination, then the suits go on and on," his co-hostess Barbara Walters shows her own befuddlement in responding, "But, on the other hand, if you didn't have Title IX, you would not have women's sports. It was so unbalanced." Ah, the White Queen again. In this simple comment, we see the problem confronting the American people: Walters is considered a credible T.V. pundit whom people rely on, and yet here she offers for public consumption an absurd bit of puffery, oblivious to truth: It was never shown to be "unbalanced", and women's sports didn't need Title IX for sustenance; her careless comment is utterly misleading – a woman's prerogative to speak inaccurately, while the perennial Adam (Stossel) cedes a crucial point.

If IWF truly wants to "change the terms of the debate because of its shallow depth and analytical approach," they might start here. Like Carolyn Graglia's book, however, the involvement of women seems to stifle robustness and offer a warm, cozy, often clever and cute, and always entertaining display of words without really grappling with the nuts and bolts of serious public policy. The dialectic becomes a vehicle for pointless self-expression, as, for instance, when the Hotchkiss School's female Dean of Faculty reports rosily on teachers meeting in the hallways to discuss "whether Frye's literary structures are sexually biased.... or whether normative values exist" while the male faculty makes no protest.[68] Thus the wages of "women's advances."

A woman's ways are different from a man's and it should never be forgotten that his perceptions are important too. Unlike their great-great-grandmothers, women now are generally at a loss over sexual harassment, as shown innocently by Ricky Silberman, "(W)ith women entering the workforce in greater and greater numbers, the time had come to draw appropriate legal distinctions between sexual conduct and sexual harassment. Since not all sexual conduct is harassment, the crucial dividing line is the *asserted*, unwelcomed nature of the conduct."[69] She might reread St. Paul.

Femaleness is so powerful that as soon as women venture into male arenas the winds of sexual "advances" immediately bestir storm-tossed squalls of interplay of one kind or another that require urgent "policy" formulation. Because women are flocking to the workplace, age-old protections of distance, separation, habit and habiliment are no more, and we contrive new laws of behavior to protect them from ever more types of "mistreatment." As if we had not learned from debtors' prison, Corn Laws, witchcraft bans, and all the rest, our approach is still clumsy. We are told not to discriminate as to sex (even though we always will!) and to hire women equally with men (like toying with unstable dynamite) and when women's sexuality causes "tilt!" we return to discriminating again, except it now must be orchestrated by women's groups and commissions. And some wonder about our virtue or ability to sustain civil society!

Anne Northrup, for her part, contends that "Most women want to believe that they are going to be judged by their hard work and their talents, not by whether they are coy or dress seductively," all while she stands garbed quite attractively. Sorry, Ms. Northrup, you can't fool Mother Nature. Ms. Northrup's thought, so naively oblivious to a woman's sexuality and its effect on the predatory male, reveals again the grand canyon separating the sexes. It will obviously take men to negotiate this area, not nice ladies lecturing without an inkling of their God-given power. For an adult woman to contend that she doesn't think primarily, or at least far more than men do, of herself, how she looks, her attractiveness, her femininity, or how men look at her, shows that women's gifts are not full objectivity but keeping people happy. Their milieus are not objective analysis, honesty, law-making, non-family work product, or the corridors of power. Her "talent" is far from Ms. Northrup's own job as congressperson (her benighted constituents notwithstanding).

* * *

A serviceable analogy may be found in education, where single-sex schools are gradually making a comeback. As Christine B. Whelan writes in *National Review*, "Scores of studies worldwide have shown that girls in single-sex high schools demonstrate a significantly higher rate of improvement on reading-achievement and science-aptitude tests between sophomore and senior years than their co-educated peers. And boys who attend single-sex high school have higher self-confidence, are more involved in extracurricular activities, and take more foreign languages and English classes than their counterparts in co-ed schools."[70]

In passing, even Ms. Whelan's excellent essay shows signs of a distinctly feminine sense of concepts, not always very incisive. While reporting on the feminist double standard in supporting such schools for girls but not for boys (also seen in New York City's school system), she accepts too readily the Supreme Court's legislation in this area in which the justices stretch to apply an unrealistic "equality" to men and women despite our very unequal natures. More appropriately, such rulings on sex should simply be removed from their jurisdiction.

Besides others reporting the advantages of single-sex schools, noted scholar and teacher David Riesman testified to that effect in the 1996 case of *United States v. Virginia* involving the V.M.I. and the Citadel, in which the Bader-Ginsburg opinion ran rough-shod over our natures and traditions.[71] Ms. Whelan, who is a college senior, fudges on this ruling ending the all-male tradition at the Virginia Military Institute, a case that will live in infamy. Even while supporting single-sex schools, she distingushes the V.M.I. case by reluctantly accepting the court's rationale that "no justification for V.M.I.'s all-male status.... outweighed" the fact that "no comparable school could be created for women," as much to say that, because men cannot have babies, we should outlaw childbirth. In other words, we are now to assume that women have an equal right to attend military school and presumably fight and die on foreign battlefields, by which rationale there can be no hope of recovering our social norms. That the court and a slumbering people have accepted this strange reasoning under the aegis of the equal protection laws reflects great stupidity. Again, the 1964 Civil Rights Act and 1972 Education Bill are the chief culprits.

But more to the point, once we accept the concept of single-sex schools as beneficial to education, it must follow that single-sex work-place environments must also have intrinsic value, at least enough to allow employers to decide for themselves. There are myriad reasons for the better performances by both sexes in single-sex schools, reasons that we may never know to the fullest, nor need to know. Boys and girls learn best to be men and women undistracted by each other. Separate rooms at home, separate studies at school. But current law forbidding such "discrimination" deadens our ability to learn and profit from such understanding.

8.

The approach of the Suffragettes as well as of many women pursuing "equal opportunity" is somewhat similar to Mary Kenny's, as she writes about tailor-made news columns – "classic columns to order" – in *The Spectator*.[72] Objective criteria do not motivate her writing as much as the need to be readable or interesting, that she might rearrange history to bolster her appeal, perhaps as heiress to William Randolph Hearst's yellow journalism. Actually finding answers to social problems seems not her milieu. "Some (writers) are there to entertain, some to annoy…. and some to uphold consistent values in a bewildering world. Some are there because they know a lot about their subjects and you can trust their knowledge." It's all the same to her. "You have the Rebel Girl, the Femme Fatale, the Scornful Feminist, the Bluestocking, the common-sense Aunty, the Wise Mother, the Mad Old Trout. Archetypes may be as tiresome as stereotypes but in the popular press I think it can be useful to consider category." Useful for what purpose? To write drivel about writing drivel? Her resort to deconstructionist Michael Foucault might offer a clue to her own lack of solid grounding, explaining, for instance, her queries,

"What am I for? What is my function – to entertain, to reveal, to interpret, to comfort, to outrage, to be a polemicist?"

While the main purpose of the traditional Fourth Estate was to convey information, knowledge, and ideas, such as, for instance, the instruction considered by the American Founders for the enlightenment of a virtuous people enjoying "freedom of the press," Mary Kenny looks on it more as a job of "having something to say and developing it." It thus becomes a school assignment to "write a theme", or a contrived space filler, rather than a source of great thought or eternal truths, which probably are a year or two ahead of her. "You have either to have had a riveting personal experience – Jill Tweedie was wonderful because so much had happened to her – which fires up the opinion, or extra knowledge which illuminates it. Even prejudices should be substantiated." Well, one would hope so; otherwise, what value your writing? We see here the familiar tendency to assign value according to personal experience rather than intelligence, knowledge and *probity*. The high project of communicating wisdom becomes for Kenny merely "writing a column" – "cobbling together a piece, picking an expert's brains, reading through the cuttings", but preferably always done "with a feeling for the subject, from the inside."

While she does manage to pay lip service to integrity and substance by noting the importance of "specialized knowledge and conceptual thinking – that is, ideas," Kenny reverts to form in recommending that a writer have a role to play, e.g., "a feminist, a Catholic, a homosexual, defender of marriage, be an egoist but also be humble ("have a consistent philosophy"!), because this makes you reflect on the construction of society and the meaning of life, but temper this occasionally with humor (or anger). Go places and meet people. travel. read." *It is all a role to play – a masquerade.*

Kenny's rather flippant approach contrasts with James Fenimore Cooper's view of the American press in 1838:

> In America, while the contest was for great principles, the press aided in elevating the common character, in improving the common mind, and in maintaining the common interests; but, since the contest has ceased, and the struggle has become one of purely selfish interests, it is employed, as a whole, in fast undermining its own work, and in preparing the nation for some terrible reverses, if not in calling down upon it, a just judgment of God.[73]

One also finds apropos the following quotation from Arthur M. Schlesinger, Jr.'s 1949 book, *The Vital Center*:

> The defining characteristic of the progressive.... is the sentimentality of his approach to politics and culture. He must be distinguished, on the one hand, from the Communist; for the progressive is soft, not hard; he believes himself genuinely concerned with the welfare of individuals.... He has rejected the pragmatic tradition of the men who, from the Jacksonians to the New Dealers, learned the facts of life through the exercise of power under conditions of accountability. He has rejected the pessimistic tradition of those who, from Hawthorne to Reinhold Niebuhr, warned that power, unless checked by accountability, would corrupt its possessor.[74]

Here, although Schlesinger had other things in mind, we can again compare the late-20th-century gender gap to the earlier "progressives", or sentimentalist "soft" liberals who shaped our self-government in terms of "a vaguely utopian version of the welfare state combined with the imperatives of 1990s-style political correctness."

In contrast also, we should consider Michael Levin's reasoning: Because sex differences in performance are evidently genetic in origin, and hence not due to male misdeeds or unfair determinism, we have no compensatory or biological obligation to alter the performance gap, and in fact lack the ability to do so. As virtually all arguments for affirmative action, sex equality, or non-sex-discrimination are compensatory, equitable, economic or egalitarian in origin, these arguments are uniformly undercut by biological, psychological, sociological and anthropological facts. Using such manly logic, it is up to us to decide which policy would best serve our long-term common good.[75]

The play of healthy tension is ever crucial to our right order. The progressive's naiveté from lack of accountability should be offset by conservative respect for accountability and responsibility, and the ensuing tension between the two will "sharpen their wits, give acuteness to their perceptions and consecutiveness and clearness to their reasoning powers."[76] As apparent from many of the above encounters, we are now experiencing an imbalance toward the female side of the fulcrum.

*   *   *

A parallel to Kenny et al's writing is the "surge of interest" in Elizabeth I, on whom Alison Weir has written a book and been allowed an encomium in the pages of *The Spectator*, mostly consisting of the familiar herstorical reinvention of women as either heroic angels or manlike adventurers, all indulged by loving menfolk.[77] Weir's effort to apotheosize Elizabeth I is a sweetly worded flimflam. Everything good that can be said about Elizabeth she says, and much, much more; while almost everything historical she ignores. In a golden age of achievements, manned by "some of the most able (male) politicians ever to serve an English monarch" (not to mention, soldiers, sailors, treaty-makers, grand schemes, great inventions, discoveries, bloody wars, laws, constitutions), we are now to assume it was mostly Elizabeth's doing. With our present dearth of Western male leaders, Great Britain seems under the spell of female charms, forgetful of the fact that women are sugar and spice and we pay a price, while men are frogs and snails and more like nails – more roughhewn and potentially substantial.

In the same issue of *The Spectator*, there is a more believable guide in David Hughes's review of a book about sculptress Elisabeth (Lis) Frink; no less than Elizabeth I, a lovable Adam's Rib – endearing, piquant, talented, but incomplete in her femaleness uncomplemented by a male:

> "I need men for my work," she said, Falling in love with them was always a "blue flash," and (the author) is at his simple best when conveying happiness, the hardest thing prose can do. For, like Lis, he is no analyst: he works on quick response.[78]

Frink serves as a rebuttal to arguments for even the most disciplined women political leaders, who lose their womanly charm and end up displaced float queens. Even the most skilled practitioner can never hide her attractive incompleteness. She is always open to a solid male destined to serve her interests or, in a less ordered society, to do her harm.

The innate sex differences should limn the boundaries of appropriate interaction between men and women. The married couple is not a paradigm for commercial, military, courtroom, or fire and police functions; nor is manly endeavor a paradigm for nursery or kindergarten. The challenge is not to merge the distinct traits but to cooperate with respect to each other's. When, for instance, Midge Decter writes as follows, she is not asking us to conflate male and female but to benefit from the two:

> What is it Mother Nature knows that so many of us no longer do? It is that marriage and family are not a choice like, say, deciding where to go and whom to befriend and how to make a living. Together, marriage and parenthood are the rock on which human existence stands.... In societies, whether primitive or advanced, that have no doubt about how to define the word "family," every child is born to two people, one of his own sex and one of the other, to whom his life is as important as their own and who undertake to instruct him in the ways of the world around him. (she repeats the above in italics) Can you name the social reformer who could dream of a better arrangement than that?[79]

While Ms. Decter acknowledges "stresses and strains" in such an arrangement, she nevertheless reminds us that, while "the rock of the family can sometimes have a pretty scratchy surface.... it keeps you out of swamps." While her focus is primarily on the importance of family to children, we can apply her views to non-family arenas as well. If a hive of bees decided to judge their queen solely on her "work ethic and talent," it would be the end of the bee species. Or, for that matter, imagine the arachnid male judging the female on her work ethic: What would he know about her "talent" other than its tendency to kill the male?

When conditions are ripe, as in materialistic countries, women cultivate impressive power emblems without male leadership, but they are never sure what to do next, except to have conferences and make speeches. Ms. Decter touches on the difference between the father's exteriority and the mother's interiority when, after remarking on a couple's relative unawareness at their wedding of the drastic engagement with others they will realize with the birth of their first child – an "instinctual and lifelong engagement in the fate of others" – she then writes, "I think this may be truer of women than of men. A woman holding her first-born in her arms, for instance, is someone who for the first time can truly understand her own mother and the meaning of the fact that she herself had been given life." Decter does note with commendable honesty that she "cannot speak for the inner life of (the) husband", whose "experience is bound to be a different one". Here again is the change that marriage and childbirth effect in a woman – a change that is not so pronounced for a man, who has not been reared quite so centeredly. (See Chap. VIII, Notes, on the effects of motherhood on women.)

Mona Charen misses all this in her otherwise persuasive case against female congresspersons[80] noting that, contrary to great expectations of an improved world with females in control, women's voting pattern is indistinguishable from run-of-the-mill liberal males; thus, the republic hasn't improved, and, if anything, brutality has increased. Yet, despite the shortfall of female rule, she persists in equating male and female: "For better or worse, women are just as cautious, ideologically driven and hypocritical in politics as men," an oversimplification that misses the dire implications of the gender gap. Actually, men and women are so different in distinctive qualities each suited to its own sphere, that even "hypocrisy" applies differently, as also does "politics". Charen is crudely comparing apples to golf carts, surprisingly unaware of the full implications as well as the ample literature on men and women.

Reflecting further the corruption of feminism, Charen then blends the mix, "Both sexes have the capacity for greatness (Margaret Thatcher and Ronald Reagan leap to mind), as well as for cowardice and cupidity. If women seek power – and I'm not at all sure they are so hot for it – let them do so as qualified individuals, not as the voice of humanity." (With such loose thought – in itself somewhat hypocritical, the homage that fancy pays to conservatism – this is not her best piece of work! For one thing, comparing Thatcher to Reagan is like comparing Dido to Aeneas, or Portia to Antonio. In other words, what is her point? To transform a lioness into a lion? *It is impossible; her dream will not work.*) As with Wendy McElroy, what does she have in mind for women "as qualified individuals"? That, like Cincinnatus they beat their fridges into swords and take on the emperor? Or vanquish the barbarians, while their men languish at home with the children? Fortunately, lovable women like Frick and Burton prefer a different pattern, without which in Charen's limited world, we would soon be rootless, wandering savages. Garbled "qualifications" for women only relegate them to male roles.

* * *

In contrast, Cal Thomas offers a more sensible male perspective as he discusses *Vanity Fair*'s November, 1998, story, "America's Most Influential Women: 200 Legends, Leaders, and Trailblazers," in itself an Orwellian grotesquerie.[81] The main point again is that it defies reason and nature to insist on talking about females as "leaders" when they customarily tend to network instead of lead. Despite their efforts to appear manly, female "leaders" are anomalous. Although civil harmony removes the need for knights to do battle in an untamed world, the computer age hasn't gone so far as to license females to be male. Why mislabel mothers and wives as "leaders", "queens" or "trailblazers", when "mothers" and "wives" rank much higher? Carers, nurturers, teachers of the young, inspirers, and sustainers are as crucial as leaders and politicians.

Cal Thomas quotes Dr. Laura Schlessinger's perception of "'the pursuit of happiness through acquisition, constant stimulation and immediate gratification (which) always fails to deliver' as the motivation behind so many women abandoning their immediate family." He traces it to the feminist decree "that the only women who matter are those employed and working outside the home," and concludes as follows:

> In the *Vanity Fair* article, women who represent "the strongest voices for some of the nation's most pressing issues" are all socially liberal: the American Civil Liberties Union's Nadine Strossen, National Organization of Women's Patricia Ireland, National Abortion and Reproductive Rights League's Kate Michelman, Planned Parenthood's Gloria Feldt and so on. There isn't a conservative, "traditional" woman in the bunch. The stay-at-home moms probably won't notice. They're too busy being influential. They don't have time to read about their sisters who only think they are.

Is *Vanity Fair* indulging in a papier-mâché creation here – a wonderland of Red Queens costumed as creatures from another planet? When C.P. Snow wrote forty years ago of science and "two cultures", he had little idea that the world of men and women would suffer the same fate, only more glaringly.

9.

To close out this chapter of semi-feminist samplings, let us look at another adventure in semi-serious frothiness, ostensibly an effort to shed light on the discovery that men and women are different, but disappointingly diminished by its schizophrenic message; at times offering definitive input, other times a light-headed, if not profane caprice. The title is *Brain Sex* (1989), authored by Anne Moir and David Jessel, the former a doctor in genetics with experience as a producer with the BBC and the latter a journalist and presenter of T.V. programs. One can only guess which is responsible for the serious and which the profane.

The book itself offers a passable treatment of male-female differences per se but too often presents a gyno-sided view of the human species. It seems intended mainly to placate feminists by dealing with past discrimination, "women's inferiority", "male success", "womanhood an occupied territory", "subordination", "sexism", "macho ethos", "careers sabotaged by motherhood", "female emancipation", and so on. (But how justify thinking in terms of "emancipation", unless one includes "male emancipation"?)

Rooted primarily in genetics and not sociology, anthropology, and theology, the result lacks depth. Perhaps it is an example of inadequacy of joint intellectual effort, with Moir's gender-gapitis neutering the project. "Success" is a materialistic term in the savage competitive world of the male, who like the worker bees, plies his task perpetually. The worker bees are highly visible in the orchard but never the queen bee that motivates the whole hive. Nurturing is not designed for profit making or "conventional success" because it would not then be nurturing. Perhaps, in its finest manifestation, it is sublime. Moir and Jessel seem adrift in the stream – somewhat on the defensive – intrigued by human sex differences but, like a beginning artist, not sure how to deal with them.

Of my authorities, the authors cite Steven Goldberg and Glenn Wilson but not the others. Despite its reasonableness, they consider Michael Levin's observation "acerbic" that men get paid more because they "try harder more often."[82] As Midge Decter might agree, rather than expecting to change the habits of one's partners, perhaps one should accept them as they are, on which Moir and Jessel seem to waffle by suggesting that female "communicating is better than washing the car." Not if it needs washing!

Of importance to our study, they conclude, "the sexes are born with brains wired in different ways. They think in different ways, have different strengths, value things in a different way, and use different strategies in their approach to life.... A woman is more sensitive than a man in her very being. She sees more, and remembers, in detail, more of what she sees." (One should qualify this: She remembers more in some ways, pragmatically, but not always what does not interest her!) "The bias of her brain leads her to attach much more importance to the personal, and interpersonal aspects of her life.... She smiles more often than men when she is not happy, and is nice, more often than men, to people she may not like – possibly a defense mechanism to compensate for her comparative physical weakness." While much of this is true, there are probably other reasons for her behavior as well, such as her centeredness and proneness to "interplay, complement, and association".

An important aspect discussed by the authors is marriage's "biggest bugbear.... the inequality of the emotional contract."[85] Women want more emotion in their men, while men would rather not display it and even tell their partners not to express it. "Women may be more extreme in the manifestation of their feelings." It is all a result of the different wiring of the brain, with the female being programmed for caring for people and the male for action. They go on to report various results of this disparity, suggesting several negative behaviors by the male and several corrective measures by the female but are not convincing in this area. It is always the male that needs correcting! And one must disagree with their female-oriented metaphor of the wife as "navigator and rudder" with the husband as "engine". Many types of marriage exist but generally speaking the reverse may be truer, as it definitely is in the area of public policy. "Women as the hub" is a better metaphor.

Much of what the authors claim for women is not so much due to their being superior in "predicting and understanding human behavior", "sensing motives behind speech and behavior", "knowing where the rocks are", etc., as it is to their *thinking* they are. A woman notoriously thinks and argues *ad hominem* but this doesn't guarantee an accurate appraisal of individuals nor alert her to hidden shoals. It is certainly true that women possess "natural social skills", and can "manage a relationship much better than a man" but this only complements his skills at building bridges, inventing machines and forging self-government. After all, hers are her main social asset, distinct from a man's abstract thought, etc. While the authors do offer a sage observation, "Marriages go wrong when men and women fail to acknowledge, or begin to resent, each other's complementary differences," one just wishes the authors would practice what they preach.

They next take up Midge Decter's subject, parenthood, albeit in their ritual ironic voice. Here, they wade into treacherous waters, suggesting that fathers should learn to "cuddle", never mind his natural tendency not to do so, as though their preference wins out over nature and contradicts their own advice to benefit from differences. (Moir must be the source of this repeated call for more emotion and cuddling. The ladies need a lot of help putting this whole thing in perspective.) It is questionable whether fathers who "cuddle" and even kiss their baby sons are laying the groundwork for misplaced sexual orientation. Again, unlike Decter's treatment, most of their discussion seems to assume that the male needs to change in order to serve as a desired father (to Moir's tastes probably), a matter they have not explored deeply enough, although they do realize that "Fathers come into their own when the child begins to grow up," which is more of a time-worn truism than a new-found discovery. Here again, the authors wax defensive, as they quite rightly discuss the mother's crucial role of continuous contact with young children, thus setting them directly at odds with "women's liberation".

Then, we enter the world of employment, the Shangri-La for modern young women – where the almighty dollar beckons. While the authors note disparities in interest and ability, they are far from understanding the many aspects involved. For them, it is too much a matter of "status", "power", individual preference, "changing the very definition of conventional success", "inequality of achievement", either becoming more like men or changing the market place, and the like – all very jejune (and familiar to the reader). Again, the drift of their treatise is generally to recognize sex differences and then to ignore them! Or to suggest ways to adopt a gynocentric bias, as though centuries of organic gradualism haven't done the job. The assumption is that women's "self-esteem" is the answer, regardless of higher authority or genetic differences. All must focus on engineering a work environment favorable for women.

They seem unaware, therefore, that the power structure requires manly conditioning: if women do not build, fight, invent, lead, share, or endure the obedience-and-command process, how expect them to advance to positions of authority over men like school prom queens? If "men don't iron" (the title of Moir's new book), how ignore the other side of the coin, "women don't rule"? She and Jessel echo my own message in remarking that a woman's genius needs male support for fruition, and her scientific work, while "more precise than that of men, (is) perhaps a little lacking in breadth and initiative"[84], which again stirs concern for western civilization's destiny under the reign of "sex equality."

In the end, despite glimpsing the scientific facets of their subject, the authors roam ingenuously through the jungle of "women's liberation" and undermine their original good intentions. They close with a vista of new worlds: "As our understanding of the brain expands, a whole new agenda unfurls. We can only hope that our brains – male and female together – are capable of addressing it successfully." What Moir and Jessel miss is the value of Western humanity's former sexual order (as in Tocqueville's time) as well as the continued need to benefit from both a woman's touch in relationships and nurturing, *and* a man's adherence to proven ways and truth while producing for his family. All in all, if this combined effort is an example of what to expect from "male and female brains together," prospects are not encouraging. We need less cute whimsy and more seriousness.

IX

How Sundry Noted Men Have Dealt With Our Subject

I should like to see any kind of man, distinguishable from a gorilla, that some good and even pretty woman could not shape a husband out of.

Oliver Wendell Holmes[1]

The nobility of England and Scotland are inferior to brute beasts, for they do that to women which no male among the common sort of beasts can be prove to do to their females: that is, they reverence them, and quake at their presence; they obey their commandments, and that against God.

John Knox[2]

(S)o that we may only remember Knox as one who was very long-suffering with women, kind to them in his own way — and that not the worst way, if it was not the best — and once at least, if not twice, moved to his heart by a woman, and giving expression to the yearning he had for her society in words that none of us need to be ashamed to borrow.

Robert Louis Stevenson[3]

1. The Bible vs. the Romantic Age: John Knox and Robert Louis Stevenson

The battle of the sexes involves not only a contest between sexes (inter-sex), but also within each sex (intra-sex), with men vying for the right to claim expertise on women, and women on the all-around follies of men. It is all part of nature's oppositional tensions making for life's eternal balance. An example of how men differ on the subject (as well as an indication of how many men will greet the present essay) may be found in Robert Louis Stevenson's essays on "John Knox and His Relations With Women."[4] Why Stevenson (RLS) chose to dissect Knox's experience with women is not clear. Knox lived three hundred years earlier in a time when church conflict was rampant and spiritual values were being challenged. Elizabeth ascended the throne in England and Mary was persecuted in Scotland. Calvin and Knox both opposed Catholicism but Knox was the stronger reformer in civil matters, thereby drawing both detractors and fans through his vigorous Sunday sermons and tireless pastoral efforts, all of which apparently came to fruition after he was forty years of age. For his part, RLS's life was Victorian, "deeply religious" (his editor George Scott-Moncrieff notes) but noticeably romantic, progressive, idealistic, non-clerical and rationalistic. (In another essay ["Talks and Talkers," pp. 66-70], RLS reveals a condescension towards women that conflicts with his criticism of Knox, thus tending to bolster the latter's views.)

What challenged RLS was Knox's bold dissertation, *The First Blast of the Trumpet Against the Monstrous Regiment of Women*, in which Knox found said regiment "repugnant to nature, contumely to God, and a subversion to nature." This offended RLS's tender solicitousness for his own ideas on women, which he never really communicates other than at times to agree with Knox but generally to heap scorn on his views. Since he offers no rebuttal to Knox's position on the merits, RLS seems more interested in outward appearances than discussing what is best for women, men, or the common good.

There are aspects of RLS's treatment that are not entirely fair, since Knox lived in a time of great reverence for God, spoke with lofty, powerful, God-fearing grandiloquence (as did many people in those times and even after the times of our Founders), and took positive, controversial stands in the public arena, whereas RLS wrote mostly from a bed and specialized in children's stories – good ones, to be sure, but nevertheless not particularly tied to religion or to women. (If I complain that Knox cannot respond to RLS, the reader might suggest, nor can RLS respond to me, but in any event my argument will be in Knox's behalf.)

RLS's rebuttal is mostly ad hominem, with only cursory comment on Knox's view that the growing visibility of women in public activities – "the regiment of women" – is simply anti-Christian and should be resisted, which is not surprising coming from a sixteenth century cleric familiar with biblical admonitions against women's rule and such. RLS's sense of humor seems scant as he dismisses Knox's treatise as a "dull performance," with a "grim reliance on himself," "communicating his discovery to the world" (much like writers do), "parading his argument" (like RLS, and I), "bitter and hasty" (like RLS), a "blast blown out of season," and so forth. RLS regards Knox's book as "shocking dogma", "wrong", "error and imperfection", yet offers no compelling evidence to the contrary other than his own cynicism. In view of subsequent developments with the gender gap and the growing research on sex differences, events seem to have borne out Knox's convictions more than RLS's, which unfortunately are typical of many males in our time.

As for Knox's somewhat sketchy authority (Genesis, Paul's epistles, Tertullian, Augustine, Ambrose, Basil, Chrysostom, and the Pandects), RLS considers it merely "the phantom of an argument" and not entirely successful, although RLS's own resort to "Deborah and Huldah, and…. the prophecy of Isaiah that queens should be nursing mothers of the Church" is entirely valueless. (As Aimé Georges Martimort indicates in his seminal research, Deborah and Huldah [like Miriam and Anne] were prophetesses to whom special charisma was given but not leadership. They were neither ordained ministers nor deacons with pastoral functions, but only recipients of the Holy Spirit along with men. Christian women were never accorded leadership or pastoral roles and served mainly to instruct women and children, anoint with oil, and provide hospitality and assistance.[5]) "Nursing mothers of the Church" can hardly amount to a standard for female authority over males.

The Knox-RLS conflict reflects a general human insouciance with the question of a right order for the sexes ("sexual constitution"), a dichotomy which singular males like John Knox speak out on while most males like RLS remain spectators, a failing that noticeably accompanies historical lapses of various sorts. In his soul, RLS even agrees with Knox, as when he writes, after lauding John Aylmer (afterwards Bishop of London) for defending women's rule as mere custom and conditioning, "For all that, his (Aylmer's) advocacy is weak. If women's rule is not unnatural in a sense preclusive of its very existence, it is neither so convenient nor so profitable as the government of men."[6] RLS opposes Knox *because of his style*. Aylmer's "courtly spirit contrasts singularly with the rude, bracing republicanism of Knox," writes RLS, apparently willing to overlook Aylmer's overt obsequiousness. But where will a robust defense of the common good begin if not with men like Knox? Even John Calvin, Knox's "great master" according to RLS, agreed with Knox in theory on the question of women "and owned that the governance of women was a deviation from the original and proper order of nature, to be ranked, no less than slavery, among the punishments consequent upon the fall of man. But in practice, their two roads separated."[7]

Calvin shied from "the original and proper order of nature" because, since custom and public consent provided that "realms and principalities should descend to females by hereditary right," the subject should be left alone. RLS sees in this approach "that passive obedience, that tolerance of injustice and absurdity, that holding back of the hand from political affairs as from something unclean…; a spirit necessarily fatal in the long run to the existence of any sect that may profess it; a suicidal doctrine that survives among us to this day in narrow views of personal duty, and the low political morality of many virtuous men."[8] Why then was RLS so disturbed by Knox's abjuring such "passive obedience"?

Stevenson writes of Aylmer's opposition to Knox, "it was rather to the old order of things (hereditary rule) than any generous belief in the capacity of women, that raised up this clerical champion." (Aylmer) Apparently, Aylmer gets carried away in "the remembrance of Elizabeth's virtues" to the point that "he has to hark back again to find the scent of his argument" until at the end he "can indulge himself to his heart's content in indiscriminate laudation of his royal mistress," including even "the simplicity of her attire and marvelous meekness of her stomach," a humorous irony noted by RLS in adding that "years after, in no very meek terms, she threatened him for a sermon against female vanity in dress, which she held as a reflection on herself."[9]

For the Scottish Stevenson, rather than "thinking meanly of women," Knox's main sin is in favoring England's Elizabeth over Mary Queen of Scots on religious grounds.[10] Knox and Elizabeth are Protestant and poor Mary is Catholic. Stevenson undoubtedly was influenced by trends in the air, not the least of which was Romanticism and its emphasis on emotion, love and a growing preoccupation with the female.[11] This led him to downplay Knox's sixteenth-century devoutness and superimpose his own Romantic pliancy, regardless of any thought for right order.

In fact, it is not as if Knox's views were all that radical, since, besides RLS, Calvin, and even Aylmer, RLS mentions "the bold book of Knox's colleague, Goodman – a book dear to Milton – where female rule was briefly characterized as a 'monster in nature and disorder among men.'" Yet RLS viciously persists in denigrating "poor Knox" whose "position was the saddest of all," indicting him for lacking "respect for women generally," speaking "with a snarl," "humiliated" for his "intemperate publication," his "sense of unspeakable masculine superiority," and, despite Knox's continued defense of his position, RLS even distorts his own blast in claiming Knox "found himself wrong."

In short, RLS seems to be substituting his own version of the facts in defense of his Queen Mary. Knox moderated his stance in regards to Elizabeth not because, as RLS alleges, "the regiment of women was one of those imperfections of society which must be borne with because they cannot be remedied" (which, like Aylmer's subservience and that of many men today, is docile fatalism), but because Knox was human, wanted to return to England during Elizabeth's reign, and was willing to compromise so that he might keep waging the main battle.

Stevenson seems puzzled by Knox, and makes the all too common mistake of judging him according to the predilections of his own time rather than Knox's. Considering that Knox's life didn't gain momentum until he was forty but in his pastoral function involved considerable association with women, while RLS died three weeks after reaching only forty-four, one is inclined to give more weight to Knox's insights than to RLS's. However, we should not ignore Stevenson's views, since they provide a good example of the bemused gallantry of many men approaching the subject nowadays. Actually, RLS himself doesn't offer much insight on the subject.

In his more biographical "Private Life," RLS acknowledges Knox's "language of compassion", "vehemence in affection", self-confidence, "disciplined emotions", and "good heart", even while generally disliking the man. But, again, RLS does not come off very well in these passages, disclaiming any attempt "to make fun of the whole affair" while doing just that, and finding Knox "shifty" while he himself indulges in shiftiness, namely, switching from positive to negative or vice versa in his judgment of Knox. RLS is simply pricked by his own Victorian stiletto, convinced that Knox is wrong in his sixteenth-century assessment that women are "weak, frail, impatient, feeble, and foolish", and determined unhumorously to defend women at all costs even as he sees that Knox had a way with the ladies, who seemed to appreciate his manly honesty. After all, they are physically weaker (at least upper-body), and the other traits, though arguable, are usually their most endearing. A century after RLS, we've suffered a further loss of humor, as we now forbid ourselves the delightful custom of naming hurricanes after females, surely the most servile surrender imaginable to Lear's stupid daughters. Although Knox's life could serve as an antidote, RLS prefers otherwise.

Stevenson does offer a commendable, though hazy notion of his own pleasant world of the sexes – generally of "tenderness for a woman that is not far short of passionate" conjoined with "disinterestedness and beautiful gratuity" – and suggests this requires either a man of "quite womanly perception" or (like Knox),

> .... a strong and positive spirit robustly virtuous, who has chosen a better part coarsely, and holds to it steadfastly, with all its consequences of pain to himself and others; as one who should go straight before him on a journey, never tempted by wayside flowers nor very scrupulous of small lives under foot. It was in virtue of this latter disposition that Knox was capable of those intimacies with women that embellished his life; and we find him preserved for us in old letters as a man of many women friends; a man of some expansion toward the opposite sex; a man ever ready to comfort weeping women, and to weep along with them.[12]

Frankly, like most modern men, Stevenson seems not to have given much thought to men and women in society, as when he carelessly ascribes "real brutality" to such remarks by Knox as "the garments of women do declare their weakness and inability to execute the office of man," which actually might be considered a truism, especially in his day. Skirts were not designed for authority but for attractiveness, allure, convenience, charm, aptness; and bodices, capes, shawls, bustles, ornate hats, were also designed for other purposes than oratory or leadership.

What man could stand up under such scrutiny as his? RLS supplies much supposition to bolster his case: "We may suppose", "I believe", "I can fancy", "I imagine", "you would have thought", "she may have been", "he might have", or "I daresay", all of which suggests that with his great imagination, as with some female writers, RLS should have stuck to writing fiction rather that to batter this long-dead reformer. There is a degree of civil discretion needed in biographers, out of respect for those who lived in different times, faced different challenges, and marched to different drummers.[13]

In the end, for all RLS's attacks, Knox emerges from these essays with a manlier, stronger image than RLS. However, in all fairness to both of them, here is how RLS closes out his depiction of John Knox:

It is only with a few rare natures that friendship is added to friendship, love to love, and the man keeps growing richer in affection – richer, I mean, as a bank may be said to grow richer, both giving and receiving more – after his head is white and his back is weary, and he prepares to go down into the dust of death."[14]

John Knox died in 1572 in his sixty-seventh year. His story is important to our quest, since his incisive views, very much politically incorrect but never proven false, have a direct bearing on this present essay. Despite his faults as Stevenson saw them, the fact that so many men continue to agree with Knox seems to call for a better response than Stevensonian sarcasm.

* * *

Nineteen years old at the time of Stevenson's death, G.K. Chesterton became an admirer of his stories and in 1927 wrote several essays on him, his life and his work. He felt that Stevenson possessed a certain genius and "made a great contribution" toward the solution of "larger problems which are beginning to press once more upon the mind of man," and even went so far as to suggest in true Chestertonian paradox, "…. his relation to the huge half-truth that he carried was in its very simplicity a mark of truthfulness. For he had the splendid and ringing sincerity to testify, in a voice like a trumpet, to a truth that he did not understand." (I trust the reader will see the irony here, regarding RLS's aversion to Knox's "trumpet blast." We have already read Chesterton's own blast, likening suffragettes to a "witches' sabbath," but this issue doesn't arise in his essays on RLS.) Although he believed that RLS "had a natural gift of lively and flexible comment" and of "touching nothing that he did not animate," for our purposes the following passages are pertinent to RLS's style and his essays on Knox:

> The truest adverse criticism of Stevenson was written by Stevenson. It was also very Stevensonian; for it took the form of saying, about his own fictitious characters, that his temptation was always "to cut the flesh off the bones". Even here we may

note his peculiar cutting or hacking accent; it sounds like some horrid crime of Barbecue or Billy Bones. Indeed that word is sufficiently symbolic of Stevenson.... It was ... because of a certain bony structure in his whole taste and turn of mind; something that was angular though slender like his own slim and brittle frame and long Quixotic face. Nevertheless the words were uttered as a condemnation; and they were a just condemnation.

The real defect of Stevenson as a writer, so far from being a sort of silken trifling and superfluous embroidery, was that he simplified so much that he lost some of the comfortable complexity of real life.[15]

* * *

Whether Stevenson or Knox was right is yet to be determined. For those willing to understand, American newspapers – often unwitting vehicles – are offering the answer. For instance, on September 25, 1998, *The Fresno Bee* displayed an article entitled, "Feminist leaders support Clinton", with a photograph of a platoon of grim-faced ladies dolled up as usual for attraction yet geared for "serious" talk – a "clarion call" – to women across the nation. It seems that the President's philandering and duplicity does not trouble these women, since, as if to warn us of what to expect under female rule so clearly seen by John Knox but not by Stevenson, these gentle ladies would rather have a president who kowtowed to them than a more upright man who did not. For them, "self-government" means government for the self, and concerns for the common good must bow to concerns for "women's issues", which, for the unaware, is shorthand for gynocentric flapdoodle, women's studies, abortion rights, goddess religion, state-enforced neuterdom, weak men and disorderly women. The "women's issues" that for centuries were civilization's main concern, that is, how to protect women from the zoo-predations of men like Bill Clinton, in these ladies hands becomes mere license, a fast track to more artificial power, regardless of our natures, our freedoms, or higher authority. Even Stevenson might recoil at the "monstrous regiment of women" in President Clinton's administration. We shall consider their contribution to culture – the abortion anomie – as we visit with Adam Smith, next.

2. Right Order Patterned on Adam Smith's Theory of Moral Sentiments

Adam Smith's first book was *The Theory of Moral Sentiments* (1759). Like Knox, Burke and Stevenson, he also was a native of Scotland (1723-1790). "Few people knew that Adam Smith's thinking stretched far beyond his classic economic primer *The Wealth of Nations* – that Smith was, in fact, a moral philosopher concerned not only with how people prosper, but also with how they should live."[16] Indeed, his book, *The Theory of Moral Sentiments*, offers a wealth of thought to inform our cause. That a man so conscientiously probed the complexities of such a daunting subject is truly inspiring. While he studied theology and is primarily known as an economist, in this book "he assigned himself a difficult and dangerous task: to establish for educated men in an increasingly revolutionary age the reasonableness of morality and the necessity of the fruits of virtue – illustrated by the wisdom of the classical authors of antiquity. This book… is, then, proof to skeptics of the importance of morality; and an antidote to those who think that free-market economics can be divorced from moral society."[17] Although Smith does not deal with feminism per se (which was only a wild seed in his day), one can add for our own purposes, "or that feminism can be divorced from either."

Smith covers relevant parameters of "propriety", "sympathy", "passions", "the effects of prosperity", "the sense of duty", "utility", "custom and fashion", "notions of beauty and deformity", "prudence", "benevolence", and others, with soundings in Aristotle,

Plato, Cicero, Grotius and more recent thinkers, none of which happen to be female. Although I shall not offer a full treatment, I shall delve into a number of his ideas related to right order – art, nature, the need to uphold existing morals, the natural division of labor, and generally how to judge it all.

"In every part of the universe we observe means adjusted with the nicest artifice to the ends which they are intended to produce; and in the mechanism of a plant, or animal body, admire how every thing is contrived for advancing the two great purposes of nature, the support of the individual, and the propagation of the species."[18] Life functions in all its parts according to an over-all design, over which we assume no control. We are very apt "to imagine (natural principles) to be the wisdom of man, which in reality (are) the wisdom of God." Since "the orderly and flourishing state of society" is preferable to "its disorder and confusion", society needs laws of justice to hinder its destruction." In fact, "man… has a natural love for society, and desires that the union of mankind should be preserved for its own sake… his own interest is connected with the prosperity of society…."[19]

As if aware of present-day elevation of "women's issues" over "the union of mankind," Smith entitles one chapter, "of the utility of this constitution of nature," much like George Gilder's "sexual constitution": "All the members of human society stand in need of each other's assistance, and are likewise exposed to mutual injuries. Where the necessary assistance is reciprocally afforded from love, from gratitude, from friendship, and esteem, the society flourishes and is happy. All the different members of it are bound together by the agreeable bands of love and affection, and are, as it were, drawn to one common centre of mutual good offices."[20] Present-day excesses of immigration (with focus on race) and diminished standards of public education have upset Smith's ideal, but his example suggests what still might be. He is talking about the common good, by which the American Founders were guided and in which liberated women have shown little interest.

Smith recognizes that "all constitutions of government, however, are valued only in proportion as they tend to promote the happiness of those who live under them" (his book was published in 1759), thus the question arises of where to draw the line on "happiness" for the dissatisfied. He goes on to explain that, rather than talk of individual advantages, "You will be more likely to persuade, if you explain the connexions and dependencies of its several parts, their mutual subordination to one another, and their general subserviency to the happiness of society... (so that)all the several wheels of the machine of government be made to move with more harmony and smoothness, without grating upon one another, or mutually retarding one another's motions...."[21] Ahem, post-1960s America.

While we grope in the tangle of "sexual harassment," life was more basic in 1759. Smith considered "breaches of moral duty" to fall within three categories: first, "breaches of the rules of justice... deserving punishment from both God and man." Second, "breaches of the rule of chastity," and, third, "breaches of the rules of veracity." As for the breach pertinent to our study, "sexual harassment," he writes as follows:

> (T)hese, in all grosser instances, are real breaches of the rules of justice, and no person can be guilty of them, without doing the most unpardonable injury to some other. In smaller instances, when they amount only to a violation of these exact decorums which ought to be observed in the conservation of the two sexes, they cannot, indeed, justly be considered as violations of the rules of justice. They are generally, however, violations of a pretty plain rule, and at least in one of the sexes, tend to bring ignominy upon the person who has been guilty of them, and

consequently to be attended in the scrupulous with some degree of shame and contrition of mind.²²

One senses in these words a bias not against women but in favor of them, which we probably knew all along, even as many bow to feminist claims to the contrary. One also detects the common sense of those more reverent, orderly times when people could discuss such matters openly, although thoughtfully, without pretense, posturing, hypocrisy or feminist rant.

*   *   *

Perhaps a brief contrast here will help make the point that more such thinking is called for, rather than the narrow, ad hominem ventures of female writers such as Rebecca West. For all the lively, incisive *personality* of her coverage of the Nuremberg trials, Carl Rollyson writes that "West had a fabled knack for taking her subject's measure, for using biography to suggest social, psychological, and historical significance."²³ In other words, one might say, getting personal in going for the jugular. Rollyson has written a book on West and obviously loves his subject, but an objective reader might wonder whether she deserves his exalted vision of her career as "a saga of the century" (vying apparently with Gertrude Kelly and the other rediscovered ladies), writing "about the shaping of contemporary consciousness," with her "very personal and yet historical voice," "not afraid to speak for herself and for history. Few writers would approach Yugoslavia, Nuremberg – or any other subject for that matter – daring to assume such authority." "West had a gift for bringing history home, for showing how it functions in our daily lives"; and she writes of our part insanity, and doubt of pleasure, with constant conflict in our personal lives; about "humanity's self-destructiveness," as she "explains how it is that a Goering could triumph." If one wants sheer, numbing personal criticism, one will be happy with West; if one prefers a pattern of order and harmony for all times, men like Adam Smith are the answer.

As if to underscore the enigma of women writers as well as women in power, so gifted with word strokes, Margaret Thatcher once said that "If you want anything said, ask a man. If you want anything done, ask a woman"[24], thus showing the British people the essentially girlish nature of their masterful Prime Minister. (Imagine a male PM saying that about women!) If she believes her remark, she is fooling herself, especially since females are the proverbial talkers; if she doesn't, she is dissembling and, either way, she misses the point: if men say things better, it is because they understand more seriously and more responsibly; and, in the long run, this makes them better doers. Women don't say things like Aristotle, Augustine, Aquinas, Burke, Mill, or Smith, and Western civilization needs such things said.

* * *

Returning to Adam Smith, whose moral sentiments are antidotes to modern excesses, we should reconsider the impact of statutes against "discrimination," "hate," or "bigotry," which Smith would call mere "casuistry," he writes, "The great pleasure of conversation and society… arises from a certain correspondence of sentiments and opinions, from a certain harmony of minds, which so many musical instruments, coincide and keep time with another. But this most delightful harmony cannot be obtained, unless there is a free communication of sentiments and opinions."[25]

Regarding the natural "desire to penetrate into each other's bosoms, and to observe the sentiments and affections which really exist there," he adds,

> This passion to discover the real sentiments of others is naturally so strong, that it often degenerates into a troublesome and

impertinent curiosity to pry into those secrets of our neighbors which they have very justifiable reasons for concealing; and, upon many occasions, it requires prudence and a strong sense of propriety to govern this, as well as all the other passions of human nature, and to reduce it to that pitch which an impartial spectator can approve of.[26]

Regrettably, our legislators exercise no such restraint in passing non-discrimination laws or laws against "hate". Instead, they and the courts who followed their example, like the casuists Smith criticizes,

> …. attempted, to no purpose, to direct, by precise rules, what it belongs to feeling and sentiment only to judge of. How is it possible to ascertain by rules the exact point at which, in every case, a delicate sense of justice begins to run into a frivolous and weak scrupulosity of conscience? When it is that secrecy and reserve begin to grow into dissimulation? How far an agreeable irony may be carried, and at what precise point it begins to degenerate into a detestable lie? What is the highest pitch of freedom and ease of behavior which can be regarded as graceful and becoming, when it is that it first begins to run into a negligent and thoughtless licentiousness? With regard to all such matters, what would hold good in any one case would scarce do so exactly in any other, and what constitutes the propriety and happiness of behavior varies in every case with the smallest variety of situation. Books of casuistry, therefore, are generally as useless as they are commonly tiresome.[27]

In transferring to the state the power to govern employment and education of the fair sex, Titles VII and IX especially wreaked havoc by smothering the people's own responsibility to exercise discretion in deciding "the highest pitch of freedom and ease of behavior which can be regarded as graceful and becoming" between the sexes. The complexities of human sexual arrangements, built up over centuries of civilized, well-crafted custom, were scornfully discarded in one careless moment of political gimcrackery. With such denaturing of civil society, dimming in us "what is generous and noble,.. gentle and humane," there is now a tendency to regard the fair sex with "negligent and thoughtless licentiousness." If one wants to understand where our craven "political correctness" originated, one can read Smith's words regarding "the style of these writings":

> None of them tend to animate us to what is generous and noble. None of them tend to soften us to what is gentle and humane. Many of them, on the contrary, tend rather to teach us to chicane with our own consciences, and, by their vain subtleties, serve to authorize numerous evasive refinements with regard to the most essential articles of duty. That frivolous accuracy which they attempted to introduce into subjects which do not admit of it, almost necessarily betrayed them into those dangerous errours, and at the same time rendered their works dry and disagreeable, abounding in abstruse and metaphysical distinctions, but incapable of exciting in the heart any of those emotions which it is the principal use of books of morality to excite.[28]

How could Smith have so accurately foreseen the extent to which race-sex tinkering would erode our common practices of brotherhood, tolerance, sexual restraint, chastity and decorum? Instead of ladies and gentlemen, we now have puppets controlled ineptly by a non-judicious judicial oligarchy. A woman's greatest power stems from her "graceful and becoming freedom and ease of behavior," now merged with a more physical, competitive male standard, so that for an all-too-typical mother today, a college education for her daughter means participation in Division I softball. As Smith writes of such positive law, "In no country do the decisions of positive law coincide exactly, in every case, with the rules which the natural sense of justice would dictate. Systems of positive law, therefore, though they deserve the greatest authority, as the records of the sentiments of mankind in different ages and nations, yet can never be regarded as accurate systems of the rules of natural justice."[29] When a thoughtful citizenry see that its positive laws do not conform to "rules of natural justice," it is time to repeal them.

Smith sees that "fashion...will sometimes give reputation to a certain degree of disorder," such as that resulting from over thirty-five years under the civil rights acts. To prevent this, self-government rightly becomes an exercise in deciding what is to be ordered by "reason and nature" and "habit or prejudice," such that we arrive at "that character, sentiment, or passion which ought to predominate" with a minimum of casuistic laws, dishonesty, and disorder.

To this end, art will play an important part, and Smith writes in depth about this parameter as it relates to our judgment of custom and moral sentiments.

> Connected variety, in which each new appearance seems to be introduced by what went before it, and in which all the adjoining parts seem to have some natural relation to one another, is more agreeable than a disjointed and disorderly assemblage of unconnected objects. But though I cannot admit that custom is the sole principle of beauty, yet I can so far allow the truth of this ingenious system, as to grant, that there is scarce any one external form so beautiful as to please, if quite contrary to custom....[30]

In a general sense, mankind carries the responsibility for its own welfare to arrange its affairs so that customs will generate heart-felt civility, with the beauty of social interaction at its maximum. Skillful and artistic composition of the primary pigments, the sexes, is a prerequisite to orderly living. Is it balanced, for instance, to see, in one arena, a barely clothed beauty displaying her enduring young charms and, in another, a small female chirping out commands to adult males? Or for a smiling, pleasing female analyzing harsh truths to a jury; no matter how accurately she sees the facts, are her words as weighty, convincing, fit, or even as understandable? Isn't she trying to be manly?

Generally speaking, pre-World-War-I citizens were at least closer to having "been educated in what is really good company, not in what is commonly called such, who have been accustomed to see nothing in the persons whom they esteemed and lived with, but justice, modesty, humanity, and good order, (and thus) are more shocked with whatever seems to be inconsistent with the rules which those virtues prescribe."[31] "Those, on the contrary, who have had the misfortune to be brought up amidst violence, licentiousness, falsehood, and injustice, lose, though not all sense of the impropriety of such conduct, yet all sense of its dreadful enormity, or of the vengeance and punishment for it. They have been familiarized with it from their infancy, custom has rendered it habitual with them, and they are very apt to regard it as, what is called, the way of the world, something which either may, or must be practised, to hinder us from being the dupes of our own integrity."[32]

Thus, can one sympathize with the post-WWII Baby Boomers, Generation Xers, and their offspring: despite the havoc of the 60s, it is on them that any recovery will depend as well as to the remaining grandparents who allowed it to happen (the Tony-Bennett;Bing-Crosby;Frank-Sinatra generation, from whom the Beatles fans took over).

By analogy, we can consider Smith's "eminent artist" as the leader who "will bring about a considerable change in established modes" of the arts including the art of government. Such were the American founders, who established with their wisdom a constitutional republic dependent on a virtuous people to sustain their civil way of life. That we have not sustained their art is no longer in doubt. Our political "artists" have changed fashions for the worse, lacking "a certain practice and experience in contemplating" the task of sustaining self-government and an orderly society. They forget that, "The same principle, the same love of system, the same regard to the beauty of order, of art and contrivance, frequently serves to recommend those institutions which tend to promote the public welfare."[33]

A lovely lady on television's nightly news pleasantly announces "a million-dollar federal grant to help fight "domestic crime," oblivious to the fact that "domestic crime" is a sign of dysfunctional families and a dysfunctional society largely caused by "federal grants." The reason children shoot and kill schoolmates and teachers is because fathers did not do their job, and that is because *mothers did not do theirs*. To blame instead the weapons and lack of federal moneys is idiocy. A generation reared on television's excesses of females playing tiny-fisted, karate-chopping bimbos; shapely marines with ample breasts and squeaky voices; tough-talking, sucker-punching females with baby faces; or virago-faced, man-talking female bosses, judges and media pundits, is bound to have been "familiarized from infancy" to "licentiousness and falsehood." We have seen the experiment and it does not work; now, let us get back to reality. Musicians like Maurice Ravel compose piano pieces for female pianists; so, let politicians and entertainment moguls discriminate likewise.

With regard to the priesthood, a certain male seriousness is expected from the vocation that we do not find in women, at least without inordinate distortion of their personalities. As Smith describes the expectations for priests,

> We cannot expect the same sensibility to the gay pleasures and amusements of life in a clergyman, which we lay our account with in an officer. The man whose peculiar occupation is to keep the world in mind of that awful futurity which awaits them, who is to announce what may be the fatal consequences of every deviation from the rules of duty, and who is himself to set the example of the most exact conformity, seems to be the messenger of tidings, which cannot, in propriety, be delivered either with levity or indifference. His mind is supposed to be continually occupied with what is too grand and solemn, to leave any room for

the impressions of those frivolous objects, which fill up the attention of the dissipated and the gay. We readily feel, therefore, that, independent of custom, there is a propriety in the manners which custom has allotted to this profession, and that nothing can be more suitable to the character of a clergyman, than that grave, that austere and abstracted severity, which we are habituated to expect in his behaviour. These reflections are so very obvious, that there is scarce any man so inconsiderate, as not to have accounted to himself in this manner, for his approbation of the usual character of this order.[34]

With regard to the military profession, in which Smith acknowledges traits of "gayety, levity, and sprightly freedom, as well as of some degree of dissipation," he nevertheless believes that, if "we were to consider what mood or tone of temper would be most suitable to this situation, we should be apt to determine perhaps that the most serious and thoughtful turn of mind would best become those, whose lives are continually exposed to uncommon danger, and who should, therefore, be more constantly occupied with the thoughts of death, and its consequences, than other men."[35]

In fact, as if to squelch forever the fitness of females for military ranks other than in support roles, and to explain the inevitable "sexual harassment" awaiting female warrioresses, Smith continues with a less than matronly scenario:

> A camp is not the element of a thoughtful or a melancholy man: persons of that cast, indeed, are capable, by a great effort, of going on, with inflexible resolution, to the most unavoidable death. But to be exposed to continual, though less imminent danger, to be obliged to exert, for a long time, a degree of this effort, exhausts and depresses the mind, and renders it incapable of all happiness and enjoyment.[36]

Smith writes of the natural tenderness we feel towards children, "In the eye of nature, it would seem, a child is a more important object than an old man, and excites a much more lively, as well as a much more universal sympathy. It ought to do so.

Everything may be expected, or at least hoped, from the child. In ordinary cases, very little can be either expected or hoped from the old man. The weakness of childhood interests the affections of the most brutal and hard-hearted."[37]

This leads to the abortion syndrome – the "culture of death" of our own times. As to infanticide, Smith offers some of his most cogent passages. (One cannot help but notice that, throughout his treatise, he is addressing men more than women, as though he still recognized an over-all male responsibility.) He discusses the difficult conflict between custom and "the natural propriety of action." Custom, he says, can be so misguided as to be "destructive of good morals, and it is capable of establishing, as lawful and blameless, particular actions, which can shock the plainest principles of right and wrong."[38]

While Smith allows for some leeway in savage societies, he makes no bones about rejecting the practice of infanticide in civil societies, which must include abortion:

> Can there be greater barbarity, for example, than to hurt an infant? Its helplessness, its innocence, call forth the compassion, even of an enemy, and not to spare that tender age is regarded as the most furious effort of an enraged and cruel conqueror. What then should we imagine must be the heart of a parent, who could injure that weakness which even a furious enemy is afraid to violate? Yet the exposition, that is, the murder of new born infants, was a practice allowed in almost all the states of Greece, even among the polite and civilized Athenians; and whenever the circumstances of the parent rendered it inconvenient to bring up the child, to abandon it to hunger, or to wild beasts, was regarded without blame or censure. This practice had, probably, begun in times of the most savage barbarity.[39]

As if addressing modern feminists, the National Organization of Women, and misguided Anglo-American fathers and politicians who speciously defend infanticide with enthymems on a woman's control of her body, Smith finishes his indictment as follows:

> When custom can give sanction to so dreadful a violation of hu-

manity, we may well imagine that there is scarce any particular practice so gross which it cannot authorize. Such a thing, we hear men every day saying, is commonly done, and they seem to think this is sufficient apology for what, in itself, is the most unjust and unreasonable conduct.

.... There never can be any such custom. No society could subsist a moment, in which the usual strain of men's conduct and behaviour was of a piece with the horrible practice I have just now mentioned.[40]

The "culture of death" insidiously festering in the United States is, without a doubt, a feminist culture. Unless ancient Adam's male progeny takes a stand, we become less civilized. Without wisdom, the communication media will continue to control the public conscience, sap our common understanding, and diminish our "moral sentiments".

People in the new Russia must relearn a free-market culture – a system of laws and ordered freedoms that societies acquire only in time. We are in the process of forgetting what they are relearning. With our trend toward female leadership, we are at the threshold of socialism, while they are at the exit.

Adam Smith would be a good teacher for the Russians too, with his careful disquisition on desirable traits for civil society, which as he frequently reminds us are grounded in nature. Here too, human discretion is required, since "The rules which she (nature) follows are fit for her, those which he follows for him: but both are calculated to promote the same great end, the order of the world, and the perfection and happiness of human nature."[41]

* * *

As for "the order of the world," Albert Einstein might help, with his discovery that the physical world has multiple frames of reference. That is, the speed of light never varies relative to moving objects, while the speed of everything else does.[42] In a way, the human sexes also have a dual-frame of reference that should be carefully accommodated in our sexual arrangements. Males are more generalist, credible, and useful in multi-purpose roles, whether ditch digging, tree pruning, news reporting, or legislation. Females are specialists along interior lines.

For each sex to appreciate the theory of $E = mc^2$ relating the mass of an object and its energy as it might apply to the human sexes would be a significant advance at the millennium. The unwavering speed of light might be likened to the feminine mystique permeating life irrepressibly, while the form and substance appear in the bearded male. Light floods the surface, and the topography reveals its shape, as von Balthasar wrote of his dialogue with Karl Barth, "we know of form only through an encounter with a substance *in concreto*."[43] The human male and female were cast in different modes for a purpose, to accommodate and articulate discrete aspects of human existence for optimal realization. To each is revealed different spheres and "the mysterious formal principle" that regulates, "explains and arranges the order and nature of our respective material dogmatics."[44] Without a higher authority or formal principle marriage becomes a fumbling human gesture.

For instance, we can imagine how it would calm the complaints of one Carole Siemens, letting off steam in *The American Spectator* on the faults of that magazine.[45] Her approach is all *personal*, ad hominem, in criticizing humorist Benjamin J. Stein for not *thinking more like young women* or about their problems. Granted, Stein's style is insubstantial but she isn't forced to read him; surely there is more to criticism than a woman's barbs. $E = mc^2$ shows that the two sexes think differently, see differently, act differently, and have different expectations. Other than that, they are perfectly compatible. Instead of listening to angry claims like Carole Siemens's, or playing havoc with human nature, we should be reconciling the two sexes in a unified field theory for the common good, learning more about male quarks and female quirks, leptons and lectures, super strings and superwomen, male substance *in concreto* – all discrete aspects of the human species. It's high time we did.

* * *

Finally, Smith elaborates on the wages of "merit and demerit":

> Man was made for action, and to promote by the exertion of his facilities such changes in the external circumstances both of himself and others, as may seem most favorable to the happiness of himself and others, as may seem most favourable to the happiness of all. He must not be satisfied with indolent benevolence, nor fancy himself the friend of mankind, because in his heart he wishes well to the prosperity of the world. That he may call forth the whole vigour of his soul, and strain every nerve, in order to produce those ends which it is the purpose of his being to advance, Nature has taught him, that neither himself nor mankind can be fully satisfied with his conduct, nor bestow upon it the full measure of applause, unless he has actually produced them. He is made to know, that the praise of good intentions, without the merit of good offices, will be of little avail to excite either the loudest acclamations of the world, or even the highest degree of self-applause.[46]

Thus was the stable regime of the former limited franchise – a rigorous duty long since dissipated since expansion of the electorate a mile wide and an inch deep. Now we "strain every nerve" in "our good offices" to urge all to "get out the vote" – men, women and teenagers who have little idea what to vote for or what is at stake – diluting the franchise even more. If we prefer to shield women from criticisms typical of public service, we should cease talk of "sex equality." (Who says A must say B.) The original manliness even with all its carousing and drunkenness produced the needed restraint and vigor of thought to sustain the engine of self-government. It should be allowed to continue to do so.

Seldom do we see politicians with the wisdom to promote Smith's idea that the "rich" "are led by an invisible hand to make nearly the same distribution of the necessaries of life, which would have been made, had the earth been divided into equal portions among all inhabitants; and thus, without intending it, without knowing it, advance the interest of the society, and afford means to the multiplication of the species."[47] No need here for endless legislation, endless meddling. "The smallest active duty," will also involve the welfare of their own families and neighbors, and inevitably how best to maintain an appropriate balance of the sexes. The "invisible hand" should have been allowed to work for the sexes also, uncontaminated by "non-discrimination" law. As Phyllis McGinley remarked, "Women are not men's equals in anything except responsibility. We are not their inferiors, either, or even their superiors. We are quite simply different."[48] Arbitrary statutes cannot cope with this. Thoughtful women understand blunt realities, but they need good men like Smith to put it all together.

3. THE FEMINIST GODDESS MOVEMENT

As Canadian Professor Philip G. Davis writes, "we live in paradoxical times" – a time when his wife's grandmother could comment that man "progressed from Kitty Hawk to moon landings within her lifetime," and "more people have access to education and the ownership of property than ever before," yet "a time of widespread personal alienation and social dislocation… violence, drug abuse and family breakdown" despite widespread "wealth and leisure." In exploring the larger question of how this happened, Davis has studied the development of several aspects of feminism since the enlightenment, and published his findings in a book entitled *Goddess Unmasked:*

The Rise of Neopagan Spirituality. In the process, with scholarly care and devastating exegesis, he furnishes another link in the chain that will restrain the feminist Prometheus by revealing the thoroughly contaminated family tree of both the Goddess movement and modern witchcraft (Wicca).[49]

The contrast between the thought of eighteenth-century men like Adam Smith and that of twentieth-century women is probably related to such revolutionary ideas circulating in Europe in the nineteenth century. It seems that, perhaps because of political upheavals, some men saw no limits to human inventiveness for the sexes and a number of famous men went to great lengths to elevate strong, emancipated women, around whom new societies would flourish, in all of which, of course, in their fertile male fancy, free love abounded. It should moderate the enthusiasms of feminists to realize that much of their movement was engineered by the excesses of libidinous males. Instead of a manifestation of female power and intellect, the driving impetus has come from randy males indulging in visions of free love and susceptible females. As Jules Michelet expressed his own passion, "Woman is a religion."[50]

Davis carefully traces the various veins of post-enlightenment ideology leading from France, Germany, England, and North America. The first modern witch was an opportunistic, imaginative male charlatan, Gerald B. Gardner.[51] The resulting "studies" in which feminism is grounded are almost entirely sham, with the key players mostly eccentrics, misfits, lost souls, iconoclasts, quacks, liars and sexually loose guns. Any sincerity that might have guided various original participants was submerged in the rush of creative egos to come. Pre-enlightenment thinkers who believed in a natural order ordained by God were displaced by those believing "there was a natural order... that could be discovered and grasped by the vigorous application of human intelligence."[52] Tradition would surrender to innovation, inspiring Santayana's aphorism condemning innovators to relive history. The emphasis on individuality gave birth to the "modern movement for women's rights," without any tie whatsoever to "natural order."

Here also was born the fallacy of treating women as mere entities warranting the same "rights" as men, signalled by Mary Wollstonecraft's *Vindication of the Rights of Women*[53], another female who wrote a great deal but not much on target. Edmund Burke's rebuttal of her support for the French Revolution will endure for ages, while her thought is only known for its feminism and opposition to social convention – a flatulence resulting from "fancies in the air" in those hell-bent times of uprising. Although deserving burial long ago, it still fosters current fancies and has been singled out by Christina Hoff Sommers as the origin of a supposedly historical "equity feminism".

The fatal flaw in such theories, as noted, is that without inclusion of masculinism in the human formula, singling out of any kind of "feminism" renders it an unsolvable riddle – a destructive conceit. As a concept, "the rights of man" included those of women, while Wollstonecraft's singling out women was much like dealing with one side of a right-angled triangle without thought for the hypotenuse. Applying the term "equity" to natural, non-criminal relations between the sexes is about as helpful as a Rocky Mountain ewe's seeking "equity" during rutting season. ("Civility" is more apt.) It was not so much that "age-old restrictions" were "man-made" and "antiquated" as it was that the innovators *wanted us to believe they were*. Bereft of a frame of reference, they decided to fake it. Although slower than bovid rams, however, people are beginning to catch on.

Inevitably, (as in 1790s France) enlightenment revisionism led to excesses and, as Davis reports, a reaction set in, inspired not by reclaimed catholicism or church spirituality but by a secular humanism driven by emotionalism, "claims of the heart, soil and blood," idealism, utopianism, romanticism, and of course Marxism. Feminists were inspired to greater extremes such as idealizing women to the point of gynocentric worship and orgiastic solipsism. Quoting Johann Jakob Bachofen, "Herein lies the magic power of the female figure, which disarms the wildest passions and parts battle lines, which makes woman the sacrosanct prophetess and judge, and in all things gives her the prestige of supreme law."[54] "Female physiology is the essential, irreducible manifestation of the Goddess"[55], and, despite its untruth, feminists urge that the Goddess idea be used for "models for contemporary social reform…. '(I)t is necessary for all of us to conceive that this female-oriented creative-collectivism existed'."[56]

Davis's scholarly research provides a valuable and comprehensive treatment of "goddesses" and Wicca from which one can draw one's own conclusions. Although his interpretations are more specific to his specialty (religious studies) and may not always agree with ours, the research speaks for itself to those willing to listen. The fact that many men like Bachofen were more preoccupied with erotic female charms than the social realities that informed men like Smith, Burke, Knox, James Fitzjames Stephen and even Rousseau suggests a remarkable triviality in certain areas of post-enlightenment history. While some men are able to maintain their objectivity as to the fair sex, others are not.

Davis reinforces our insights into the general disarray that follows feminist ideas, such as the craven performance of the universities in fostering a sham "canon"; erosion of the family, of academic freedom, and of "standards of objective, verifiable evidence"; "the emphasis on subjective perspectives associated with distinctive biological and social groups, (instead of) objective truth"; feminism's own biased, unrealistic criteria for criminality of assault and "sexual harassment"; the transformation of "scholarly investigation and debate… from a quest for knowledge into a quest for power"; and other manifestations of which the list is growing quite long. It is a brave new world indeed.

An occasional sensible vein appears. Although Goethe and Schiller contributed imaginative material for the Romantics, and later for the occultists and female-centered enthusiasts, they also retained a classical dimension. As Davis puts it, "Drawing on the examples of ancient Greek and Roman literature, they upheld a vision of formal perfection, clarity and harmony which was far removed from the rampaging emotions of the Romantics."[57] In the present book, we pay respect to "Classicism," using it as a pillar along with Biblical, biological, customary, and organic parameters for the rebirth of sanity. Although Davis doesn't fully convey feminism's complicity in our social anomie, he has shed light on a distinct aspect of feminist history and provided a helpful guidepost for our pilgrimage.

X

From Classicism To Postmodernism – Aristotle Through Bryce and Stephen – To Egalitarian Rights and Devolution

The questions in dispute mainly are: when, where, and how the interference shall take place; and under what conditions and to what extent? The general view is that, in matters relating to labour, the line shall be drawn at adult males; that legislation for the protection of women and children is justifiable, and quite within the sphere of legitimate and positive law; but that interference with the rights and liberties of grown men is an impertinence and a danger which ought to be resented and resisted.
George Howell[1]

Can diversity management survive the collapse of ethnic and gender preferences? Sociologist Linda Gottfredson has formulated reasonable diversity management principles compatible with a framework free of group preferences. Above all, she calls for policy emphasis on individuals, not groups: develop individuals, not groups; tailor treatment to individuals, not groups; recognize within-group variations; treat more obvious group differences as important but not special; reexamine but maintain high standards; test assumptions and support claims in situations where ethnicity or gender qualifications are assumed to be an asset; and, above all, "find the common ground."
Frederick R. Lynch[2]

1. Aristotle on Men and Women

At this point, to show how we have weathered the centuries, we shall take another look at "Classicism" through the eyes of Aristotle and certain nineteenth-century commentators, closing out with postmodern attempts to deal with "sex" (of which the above excerpt by Frederick R. Lynch is an example). Much of the earlier wisdom has never been discredited despite postmodern "progress." Although Aristotle's views of men and women need revision to some extent to reflect subsequent scientific knowledge, they nevertheless offer a remarkably detailed scheme of human characteristics that still holds true today. He saw men and women as different and did his best to explain the implications, while people in our times neglect the differences despite the evidence.

For instance, we have come to appreciate the characteristics of the human female which serve to endear and enhance her nurturing skills, recognizing Aristotle's gauges of "strength" vs. "weakness," "superiority" vs. "inferiority" as inappropriate unless geared to obvious specialties of each sex. The larger male is physically stronger, while the female is possibly physiologically more durable, but even that might be stretching a point. Other areas, such as emotions, shape, texture, chemistry, facial appearance, mentality, and so forth, all reveal differences that only superficially could be rated as "good," "bad," "better," or "worse," yet some persist in doing so. Often, such comparisons are irrelevant, like trying to prove whether the color red or green is "stronger" or "better."

Of course, some will complain that, as a pagan, Aristotle was as misguided as Davis's neopagan Goddess adherents, but careful discrimination suggests that, because Aristotle was at least guided by natural law, his thought was not far removed from ours today, imbued with Christian teaching on men, women and marriage, as well as the thought of Tocqueville, J.F. Stephen, C.S. Lewis, Steven Goldberg and others. Thomas Aquinas rendered Aristotle quite respectable for our purposes, as have Eric Voegelin, Christopher Dawson and others, and the Pope's thought itself reflects Aristotle's understanding of women to some extent. There are truths that cannot be shaken, as revealed in the "distinctive, objective, focused, logical" thought of responsible male thinkers through the ages, despite recent fancies of less honest feminist ideologues ("Remember. Make and effort to remember. Or, failing that, invent." – Monique Wittig)

The differences of the two human sexes serve nature's or God's purpose to provide a functional dyad. Aristotle saw this as he attempted to formulate patterns, intrigued as he was by the inherent irony even to the extent of musing whether man and woman were of the same species.[3] Even so, (and one hopes he was not overly sanguine) he believed that,

> Between man and wife friendship seems to exist by nature; for man is naturally inclined to form couples – even more than to form cities, inasmuch as the household is earlier and more necessary, than the city, and reproduction is more common to man than to the animals. With the other animals the union extends only to this point, but human beings live together not only for the sake of reproduction but also for the various purposes of life; for from the start the functions are divided, and those of man and woman are different; so they can help each other by throwing their peculiar gifts into the common stock. It is for these reasons that both utility and pleasure seem to be found in this particular kind of friendship. But this friendship may be based on excellence, if the parties are good; for each has its own excellence and they will delight in this fact. And children seem to be a bond of union (which is the reason why childless people part more easily); for children are a good common to both and what is common holds them together.[4]

The usual note of caution is needed to remind us that the matrimonial "bond of union" is a far cry from a similar arrangement in *public life*, where a woman's special attributes are not as compatible, unless exercised in areas such as, for instance, Mother Teresa's, Clara Barton's or Florence Nightingale's. Show business offers no credible example to the contrary.

Of course, Aristotle doesn't stop there and, in a later section, on economics, explores the human pair bond as to its more practical aspects. He goes so far as to say that political science functions in order to constitute a city and that a city is made up of families or "households". "We should have, therefore, to organize properly the association of husband and wife; and this involves providing what sort of woman she ought to be."[5] Here, we can agree to more postmodern wording, such as, "what sort of man and woman they ought to be," without becoming involved in an argument as to which comes first. (It is unsettling to recognize the contrast between Aristotle's approach and the current fashion.) There is a solid order in his thought that cannot arbitrarily be refuted. Since we still tend to see women as the hub of the family, the quality of the female would seem of paramount importance to a particular family. To have it otherwise would be to diminish the value of women, and it is entirely possible that valuing young boys and girls primarily as independent variables as we tend to do in modern America and Britain, rather than as potential family co-partners, will continue to weaken the social value of men, women, and the family. Human beings are far from perfect, so natural stereotypes help.

In Aristotle's time, custom required what we now consider outmoded arrangements involving property yet they sustained his world and need no justification now. In fact, had we retained such customs, they might have allowed greater benefits than we realize. Here again he is poignantly forthright:

> As regards the human part of the household, the first care is concerning the wife; for a common life is above all things natural

to the female and to the male. For we have elsewhere laid down the principle that nature aims at producing many such forms of association.... But it is impossible for the female to accomplish this without the male or the male without the female, so that their common life has necessarily arisen.... the male and the female cooperate to ensure not merely existence but a good life. ... At the same time also nature thus periodically provides for the perpetuation of mankind as a species, since she cannot do so individually. Thus the nature both of the man and of the woman has been preordained by the will of heaven to live a common life.[6]

Surely, the Pope could not disagree with such homey exposition, nor should the feminists. It perfectly adapts man and woman to their earthly roles, to ignore which would lead surely to oblivion. Much that the Catholic Church adheres to in this area is grounded in such natural sentiments.

The plot thickens, however, as Aristotle continues, still offering obvious truths that will raise the eyebrows of more fastidious moderns. He suggests that the commonality of man and woman lies ingeniously in those same complementary differences that are obvious to all but the blind:

> For they are distinguished in that the powers which they possess are not applicable to purposes in all cases identical, but in some respects their functions are opposed to one another though they all tend to the same end. For nature has made the one sex stronger, the other weaker, that the latter through fear may be the more cautious, while the former by its courage is better able to ward off attacks; and that the one may acquire possessions outside the house, the other preserve those within.... and in relation to offspring she has made both share in the procreation of children, but each render its peculiar service towards them, the woman by nurturing, the man by educating them.[7]

Again, such plain truth sparkles. Material wealth has brought changes in our habits and needs, to the point of weakening Aristotle's male and granting more freedom to his female, but his basic parameters remain. One still reads of "the female fear" ("strength gives men intimidating edge"[8]), the traditional division of labor, and husband-wife responsibilities, at least enough to show Aristotle's continuing relevance. C.S. Lewis's idea of the husband's potential for family "foreign affairs" and Catholic thought in general on a woman's nurturing and "interiority" remains firm. Our mistake has been to trade such broader perspectives for a more self-centered approach, as for instance, encouraged by the Enlightenment, Romanticism, science and now "technology," so that males are free to drift aimlessly and egotistically and females to flit through life at random and often unfulfilled. As Linda Bowles, Phyllis Schlafly and others might agree, public co-education has nudged the human species away from Aristotle's distinctly dimorphic sexes.

It is not that he doesn't appreciate the delicate realities involved:

> The saying of Hesiod is a good one: "A man should marry a maiden, that habits discreet he may teach her." For dissimilarity of habits tends more than anything to destroy affection.[9]

Again, does one sense that men were manlier in Aristotle's day? And women less like Lady MacBeth or Gloria Steinem?

This fine attunement of qualities had waned by the time Henry Adams's dinner partner spoke out, which serves to remind us of what we are missing. Strident, complaining, dissatisfied, dishonest and essentially disorderly women are a far cry from the Greek ladies of Aristotle's time, otherwise he would not have written as he did of the Spartan women during the Theban invasion, who, "unlike the women in other cities,… were utterly useless and caused more confusion than the enemy." His explanation of this comedy is that legislators wanting to "make the whole state hardy" made the mistake of neglecting the women, who "live in every sort of intemperance and luxury." "When "wealth is too highly valued,… after the manner of most warlike races,... the citizens fall under the dominion of their wives,"[10] which tends to dispel the siren innuendo that women have not always enjoyed "equity."

Once the distinctions between the sexes are acknowledged, a workable protocol seems appropriate and Aristotle doesn't shy from defining it. Without condoning all the practices of his early times (slaves, abortion, and the like), we can consider aspects that are still relevant:

> Of household management we have seen that there are three parts – (one, regarding slaves is irrelevant here) another of a father, and the third of a husband. A husband and father, we saw, rules over wife and children, both free, but the rule differs, the rule over his children being a royal, over his wife a constitutional rule. For although there may be exceptions to the order of nature, the male is by nature fitter for command than the female, just as the elder and full-grown is superior to the younger and immature. But in most constitutional states the citizens rule and are ruled by turns, for the idea of a constitutional state implies that the nature of the citizens are equal, and do not differ at all.... The relation of the male to the female is always of this kind. The rule of a father over his children is royal, for he rules by virtue both of love and the respect due to age, exercising a kind of royal power.[11] (parenthesis added)

Here is immense value, reflecting inescapable truths that also govern in St. Paul's day, in old Rome, in medieval times, in our colonial period, the Victorian Age, and even today: A husband's unavoidable "headship". With his postmodern sensitivity to Lear's angry daughters, Gilbert Meilaender might consider Aristotle's approach as "wooden", yet the underlying truth remains. Similarly, the Pope and the Bishops, campaigning politicians, college students under the heel of the thought police, dutiful Republicans posturing for female votes, and, above all, the large number of men and women who think we are actually changing into a gender-less society ruled by "sex equality and the rights of woman" – all shy at Aristotle's truisms.

The fact remains, however, that most women expect manliness from men – usually, in a civilized mode. Things are little different between the sexes now than they were in 300 B.C. Despite claims to the contrary, an effective father's authority is ultimate, and if he doesn't measure up to Aristotlean standards, both the family and society suffer when the children grow into savages, uneducated in the rules of civilized society, unlawful and disrespectful; and the wife either a bewildered, lost soul or a harridan. There has been no proof to the contrary. Ask the hapless wife found guilty of murdering her philandering husband. Aristotle appears mainly to be addressing men not because he is "excluding" women but because males *need to be instructed more than women* and ironically it must be either by other men or by experience.

> Clearly, then, excellence of character belongs to all of them; but the temperance of a man and of a woman, or the courage and justice of a man and of a woman, are not, as Socrates maintained, the same; the courage of a man is shown in commanding, of a woman in obeying…. All classes must be deemed to have their special attributes; as the poet says of women, "Silence is a woman's glory," but this is not equally the glory of man.[12]

Although Aristotle's prescriptions are strong medicine, with common sense they remain relevant. To ignore them entirely only belies human nature. Teaching young men the skills and disciplines of "command" in its various guises is a demanding practice, with deep roots in lore and psychology, reliance on the human heart, self-discipline, and untold reward for both individual and society. When it comes to female soldiers, the post-1990s American military establishment, for instance, is shockingly oblivious to natural human traits so well known to Aristotle and his modern counterparts. The same confusions enervating the ethos of Athens, Sparta and old Rome are evident in modern America. Our co-ed public school "system" has shown itself no less inept at "educating" the young, disdaining the search for truth and age-old standards of learning and scholarship.

* * *

While women now enjoy a much greater share in property rights, they are no more suited to leadership or command than women in 350 B.C. If any further proof is needed of Aristotle's wisdom, the effect of the Nineteenth Amendment's gender gap reminiscent of the Spartan women and their obstruction of the natural order should suffice. As a result of "every sort of intemperance and luxury," many liberated Western women (e.g., the National Council of Women's Organizations led by Martha Burk) are causing "more confusion than an enemy".

"For it remains true," as Jeffrey Wallin urges, writing of George Washington's contribution, "though it is seldom recognized to be true, that nothing is more astounding than the actual working out of self-government, the deepest meaning of which is self-restraint, both individual and writ large, something possible only among people of good will: among friends."[13] That it took men of the noblest stature, highest ability, and demanding experience to carve out our heritage using tools from ages past never seems to occur to modern male politicians preoccupied with garnering female votes as they and their lady friends forget the "deepest meaning of self-restraint." As Wallin interprets the meaning of George Washington in Patrick Garrity and Matthew Spalding's *A Sacred Union of Citizens; George Washington's Farewell Address and the American Character*,

> The key to national self-sufficiency was "to create the political grounds – a public and private character – that would successfully reconcile, or comprehend, justice with utility, duty with interest, the general good with particular advantage."[14]

Where have we seen such thought from feminists? No matter how artfully women ape high oratory (in girlish voices), it is more effective coming from its natural source – from men – not actresses' lips. Others are noticing the effect, as for instance (although he doesn't mention the ladies), Morgan N. Knull, reviewing Robert

Allen Rutland's *James Madison: The Founding Father:*

> The more perceptive or honest among us cannot help noticing that the real "devolution" occurring in Congress is expressed not so much in a resurgence of state sovereignty... as the near absence of statesmen. This vacuum of leadership is one more respect in which the present has become disjointed from the past. The regime of civic republicanism that Madison trusted would fortify and sustain the United States seems distant from the avarice and hubris of our contemporary leaders.[15]

2. Irving Babbitt

Another deserving voice is that of Irving Babbitt, whose work offers strong reinforcement for any recovery of sound male leadership. In his *Democracy and Leadership*, he writes, somewhat similarly to Russell Kirk (as well as A.V. Dicey whom we discuss below),

> The notion.... that a substitute for leadership may be found in numerical majorities that are supposed to reflect the "general will" is only a pernicious conceit. In the long run democracy will be judged, no less than other forms of government, by the qualities of its leaders, a quality that will depend in turn on the quality of their vision.[16]

He takes care to distinguish the "man of vision" from the "mere visionary" whom we see in the ranks of feminist ideologists pursuing their selfish interests: "A still graver symptom... was the appearance of leaders who were more and more ruthless in the pursuit of either of their personal advantage or that of some class or faction."[17] As if to alert us to "individualist feminists", he continues,

> It can scarcely be maintained of the Romans who thus precipitated the decadence that they exercised to any serious degree their... will to refrain. The right opponents of these anarchial individualists, one may venture to affirm, were not the mere traditionalists, but the individualists who had qualified for true leadership by setting bounds to their expansive lusts, especially the lust for domination... Persons who postpone everything else to "comfort" and to commercial prosperity are probably more

numerous in America today than they were in ancient Rome. Disturbing as this symptom may be, it is less so than the increasing role played in our national life by "blocs" with highly unethical leaders – leaders who seek to advance the material interests of some special group at the expense of the whole community.[18]

As this was written in 1924 and makes no mention of feminism (nor do Babbitt's other major works, *Literature and the American College* and *Rousseau and Romanticism*), presumably he was not yet informed on the subject or merely chose to forbear. In any case, his words certainly encompass the feminist bloc's strident demands regardless of the "whole community."

3. NINETEENTH-CENTURY THOUGHT ON MEN AND WOMEN

To confirm that men still thought with Aristotlean vigor well into the nineteenth century, we need only read the words of Tocqueville, James Bryce, Herbert Spencer, and others. In his *Democracy in America* (1832), Chapter XII, Book 3, Volume II, on "How Americans Understand Equality of the Sexes," Alexis de Tocqueville presents a well-crafted, discerning essay on a concept of "sex equality" that doesn't require "equality" per se as much as customarily courteous, realistic relations between the two sexes. Since this is more familiar to the reader, we shall not elaborate on it here, but proceed directly to James Bryce. The "decadence of manhood" took hold later in the century under the sway of the Suffragettes, especially noticeable in the Progressives, but men in general were not immune. The trend continues today.

James Bryce offers considerable food for thought in his monumental study, *The American Commonwealth*, in which he explores almost every facet of our nation around 1900, but we shall focus only on that part dealing with the status of American women.

More lengthy excerpts are included in Notes below. During his sojourns in America commencing in 1870 and continuing at least until 1913, when he retired as British Ambassador after having served since 1906, Bryce came to realize, "In no country are women, and especially young women, so much made of." "Overbearing husbands… are more condemned by the opinion of the neighborhood than in England. There are exacting wives in England, but their husbands are more pitied than would be the case in America." Such peace and harmony would seem to belie wild claims by women's studies matriarchs that American women have been excluded for centuries, especially when Bryce adds that the balance of power in America "inclines as much in favour of the wife as it does in England in favor of the husband."[19]

Bryce himself shows the influence of America when he fluctuates between, on the one hand, lavish praise for American women and their "equality", and, on the other, incisive comments to the contrary. He does not anticipate, for instance, an erosive gender gap, even though he sees that women tended to vote more on emotional issues like "whisky prohibition" and "charity", while showing less interest in the mundane matters of self-government that virtuous republicanism involves. "The nation as a whole owes to the active benevolence of its women, and their zeal in promoting social reforms, benefits which the customs of continental Europe would scarcely have permitted women to confer."[20] Little does he foresee the loss of freedom, responsibility and eventual welfare state this would bring. In fact, it seems likely that most leftist thought from Marx through Whitman, Dewey, Roosevelt, Richard Rorty, even Hitler and Stalin, and onward, tends to be more feminine than masculine, as reflected in its culmination in centralized "compassion", or tax-funded, state-enforced welfare rather than ordered freedoms. In addition, his affection for

America seems to blind him to the pitfalls of "progressivism" and the late-century urge for "reform", which eventually would erode the founding principles of the nation itself.

Even so, Bryce can still address various aspects of "sex equality and the rights of woman" that make for a comprehensive debate. On co-education, he is open-ended, in that he rather likes the idea, even as he notes, "Each sex is said to improve the other: the men become more refined, the women more manly."[21] One cannot be certain that Bryce fully understands the implications, since his views go against much serious thought on the subject as well as experience, yet he later suggests that women are *not* made manlier by increased participation in public affairs. (In the event, many remain feminine while adventuring into male pursuits, while others do turn "manlier" in one way or another.) He mentions the fear that "social enjoyments" by women students might "exceed their devotion to study," yet ignores the even more serious possibility of a similar tendency among male students, tending to dumb down the whole process of learning and scholarship. He also writes that some youths preferred single-sex classes so as to avoid in co-ed classes what amounted to popularity contests for the girls' favor. All in all, this area is not his strongest forte, as he displays an optimistic spirit more than critical perspicacity.

Elsewhere, he notes that American women seem to be developing more independence, which strikes an ominous note, especially when he mentions that the idea of equality might tend to upset the delicate sexual balance and cause "a growing detachment of the wife from a husband's life and interests, so that she is more disposed to absent herself for long periods from him; and some observers maintain that the American system, since it does not require the wife habitually to forego her own wishes, tends, if not to make her self-indulgent and capricious, yet slightly to impair the more delicate charms of character; as it is written, 'It is more blessed to give than to receive'."[22] In other words, to ease wifely duties, we would improve her lot by relieving her of wifely affections.

Bryce praises the American handling of the woman question, yet strongly abjures the idea of egalitarianism per se: "The fact is, that the Americans have ignored in all their legislative as in many of their administrative arrangements, the differences of capacity between man and man. They underrate the difficulties of government and overrate the capacities of the man of common sense. Great are the blessings of equality; but what follies are committed in its name!"[23] But he slights the "differences of capacity" between man and woman, even though mentioning some, such as the hostility of many women to the suffrage[24]; that some felt "evils might attach to it"[25]; that politics "are more likely to soil women than women to purify politics"[26]; while the polls are no purer, they're quieter[27]; and, perhaps most importantly, "It is sometimes said that the privilege yielded to American women have disposed them to claim as a right what was only a courtesy, and have told unfavorably upon their manners"[28]; or "the respectful deference with which they are treated was remarked... as in fact tending to affect inauspiciously the grace of female manners."[29] One notes that certain items represent no improvement at all, since, to be effective, vigorous "politics" requires robust debate, which is not noted for "quietness." Here we see a concern more for form than substance, which again marks the drawbacks of female participation in self-government, seen clearly by Bryce despite his rosy vision.

Fearing that the greater capacity of some men will be submerged in the egalitarian crowd, how can Bryce justify the addition of the female vote that would not only submerge it but also subvert it to emotional ends? The Eighteenth Amendment (Prohibition of whisky) was passed by a male legislature influenced no doubt by the raised voices of the as-yet non-voting ladies, yet was repealed after fifteen years of disruptive experience. Male objectivity should have avoided this experience. The delicate balance needs constant care to minimize such deviations. For his part, Bryce still thinks that in pushing for prohibition women were on the right side of such questions, which tends to temper full reliance on his judgment.

Bryce does offer a clear insight into possibly the most serious risk of women's suffrage, namely its doubling the constituency of an elected representative, thereby compounding the difficulty of reaching wise decisions.[30] [This is related to a companion problem, namely, that of proportional representation, to which America has already succumbed and which Great Britain now contemplates despite compelling arguments against it. Bryce's contemporary, A.V. Dicey, targeted this problem, as will be discussed below.] Its tendency is to divert a legislator's attention from the common good to pleasing myriad constituents most of whom care mainly for their own selfish interests. This is not to say that men are not also susceptible to selfish interests but that the introduction of the female element upset the balance toward the left and away from virtuous, far-sighted republicanism. The women's vote was bound to have such an effect and the emergence of the gender gap proves it.

Bryce reminds us that there are many functions in which women excel and are able to offer their services. Even in his time, they were free to attend college and join the professions, although it was left up to particular schools and states how many could be accommodated rather than to the national government. Now, the former federal, constitutional procedure has been stunted in favor of authoritarian, national control. In Bryce's day, as if to rebut Titles VII and IX, while there were women lawyers, they tended more toward attorneys' office work rather than the courtroom, still reflecting natural human preferences and abilities. Women were good at charity and philanthropic work and the "persuasive assiduity" of the female sex rendered women effective lobbyists. They had the right to vote for church officials, although they didn't serve as deacons, ministers and so forth.[31] "Sometimes a distinct set of women's societies is created, whose action on and through women is all the more powerful because the deference shown to the so-called weaker sex enables them to do what would be resented in men."[32] Here are definite signs of potential weakness in the over-all decision-making process, and of encouraging less lovable characteristics in women.

All in all, Bryce paints a rosy picture of American women, with only passing mention of future problems and discordances. Perhaps his Scotch-Englishness and ambassadorship protected him from deeper concerns for the common good and distracted him from more classical thought. For him, as for many, late-Nineteenth-Century America was an exciting place in an exciting time when manifest destiny ruled. No doubt, the ladies charmed him, for as yet they were still comfortable with the old order of things – the Tocquevillian order of the sexes, in which each knew his or her role and made no complaints – and society in general prospered.

Since aggressive female assertiveness was still rare, Bryce as yet understood little of our sexual constitution, assuming probably that it would all work out for the good. Although he doesn't mention it, he was probably conditioned to the traditional sexual protocol of Saint Paul and Aristotle, in which physical strength is still relevant – might makes right – and in fact, somewhat more than Tocqueville, his comments are condescending, since he never reaches the point of acknowledging real "sex equality." British soldiers were dying for the British Empire in quite manly fashion around the globe to disprove the idea. Bryce never gets to the point so pertinent today of considering the propriety of women commanding men, or of female headship over males. Their "persuasive assiduity" he would probably not take that far.

* * *

One of the men Bryce dedicates his work to is Albert Venn Dicey, a jurist who was born three years earlier in 1835, and died the same year as Bryce, 1922. In 1885, "A.V. Dicey" published his very important *Introduction to the Study of the Law of the Constitution*, which "put forward doctrines of constitutional law which (became) not merely classic but which remain alive today as standards".[33] His analysis of the unwritten constitution of Great Britain is applicable to our own in many "essential and fundamental" respects. His perspective is valuable because, more than Bryce, he was concerned with the "ought" more than merely the "is," and offers a good counterbalance to Bryce's more sanguine progressivism's embracing a "need for change." Dicey serves as an example of how conservative Englishmen thought around 1900 with regards to matters like women's suffrage, although Dicey's discussion of women, while incisive, is only incidental to his main subject and therefore limited. It appears in his Introduction as a criticism of "woman suffrage" and "proportional representation."

As for "the idea that the possession of a vote is a personal right," he concludes that a "fair-minded man" who is prepared "to go a little further into the nature of things… will ultimately say that… (this) is a delusion. It is in truth the obligation to discharge a public duty, and whether this miscalled right should be conferred upon or withheld from Englishwomen can be decided only by determining whether their possession of the parliamentary vote will conduce to the welfare of England."[34] As for the idea that women should vote by reason of "sex equality" – "the absolute political equality of the two sexes" – Dicey categorically is in the Aristotlean-Pauline-C.S. Lewis-Steven Goldberg camp[35]:

> It treats as insignificant for most purposes that difference of sex which, after all, disguise the matter as you will, is one of the most fundamental and far-reaching differences which can distinguish one body of human beings from another. It is idle to repeat again and again reasoning which, for the last thirty years and more, has been pressed upon the attention of every English reader and elector. One thing is certain: the real strength (and it is great) of the whole conservative argument against the demand of votes for women lies in the fact that this line of reasoning, on the face thereof, conforms to the nature of things. The anti-suffragists can re-echo the words of Burke whilst adapting them to a controversy unknown to him and practically unknown to his age:

> The principles that guide us, in public and in private, as they are not of our devising, but molded into the nature and the essence of things, will endure with the sun and the moon – long, very long after Whig and Tory, Stuart and Brunswick (suffragist, suffragette, and anti-suffragist), and all such miserable bubbles and playthings of the hour, are vanished from existence and memory.

As for the idea of proportional representation supposedly to "exactly reflect the will of the electors", or "with precision or accuracy the state of opinion, e.g., as to woman suffrage," Dicey is equally opposed: Essentially, he doubts the desirability that "any opinion existing among any large body of electors should be represented in the House of Commons as nearly as possible in the same proportion in which it exists among such electors."[36] Here his thinking parallels Bryce's in regards to doubling the confusion of government by adding the votes of women, whose interests were already amply considered without an actual franchise. "The more complicated any system of popular election is made, the more power is thrown into the hands of election agents or wire-pullers. This of itself increases the power and lowers the character of the party machine…. The House of Commons is no mere debating society. It is an assembly entrusted with great though indirect executive authority…."[37] Even though every influential opinion might deserve a hearing, it only needs one man to ensure it whenever he spoke in favor of it. "The argument for woman suffrage was never stated with more force in Parliament than when John Stuart Mill represented Westminster. The reasons in its favour would not, as far as argument went, have commanded more attention if a hundred members had been present who shared Mill's opinions but were not endowed with his logical power and his lucidity of expression."[38]

Dicey goes on to show how unnecessary, and even ridiculous, it would be to include representatives of every opinion, good or bad, in every decision, sometimes reaching the outlandish result of a government that could not function at all. Here is a compelling defense of the need for *quality* in self-government rather than our current disposition for *quantity*. Some will cry, "Elitism!" yet the issue is *wise leadership*, which requires truth, excellence, knowledge, intelligence, character and experience, not dumbing down to tumbrils, mobs, and demagoguery.

Dicey's thinking serves to remind us of what we have lost pursuing egalitarian aims, diffusing and weakening our former clarity of thought, succumbing to "progressive" changes that have eroded the original strengths of our own constitutional system, and bowing to the "lucidity" of men like J.S. Mill whose principles are prone to ambiguity. As with all such liberals, their carelessness has led to weaknesses that they themselves would probably censure today. With regards to current law-school teaching characterizing our Constitution as a "living document", fostered by irresponsibly un-Diceyan American juridicial inventiveness, a conservative 1990s thinker, Wilfred M. McClay, warns,

> If everything is open to change, then nothing finally matters but the narcissistic self, the one still point left in a turning world.... But this is a recipe for disaster. It produces lives stunted by the false excitement of a provisionality that is, at best, nothing more than an extended existence.... The experiment of America, like

all experiments, means nothing unless it is undertaken for the sake of what is not experimental, and for the sake of those convictions, beliefs, and fundamental commitments embodied in the term "ordered liberty."[39]

This is not women's primary area of interest, but one in which we should expect more from American males unencumbered with prevailing fancies.

4. A Plea for Liberty

Mill's reform-liberal siren song *still is the regnant power today*, thanks to an uncritical people captivated by material wealth. Since they tend to favor socialistic solutions, women are generally on the side of Mill. As Thomas Mackay wrote in 1891, "The latter third of the nineteenth century in England was a period of advancing government intervention… (serving) to circumscribe the rights of contract and property," while extension of the franchise was transferring "effective control of the Parliament from aristocratic hands into those of the middle and working classes…(which) could not be stimulated to express… opposition to interventionist proposals…"[40] In *A Plea For Liberty*, Mackay's collection of essays offered by various authors to stimulate such opposition, Edward Stanley Robertson writes on the "Impracticability of Socialism," contesting Socialist Albert Schäffle's odd claim that "the employment of women's labour, *now no longer needed in the family*, would find its fitting place without effort." (emphasis Robertson's):

> This appears to me to be the strangest of all the strange utterances of Socialism. No longer needed in the family! If for "family" we read "factory," there would be some sense in it, and perhaps, after all, the words may have been accidentally transposed. For my part, I confess myself incapable of conceiving a state of things in which women would not be absolutely essential to the "family" as wife, mother, nurse, housekeeper, to say nothing of any other function. I can easily enough conceive the existence of factories

without women workers; but that women should be set free from the family in order that they may enter the factory strikes me as being a complete inversion of the order of nature.[41]

Here is our old friend "order of nature" again, in a context which might make even feminists wonder whether they have brought "improvement."

In his turn, George Howell's essay, which we have previously mentioned, offers a century-old opinion as to what should have been expected from Title VII of the Civil Rights Act, enacted seventy-three years later. He understands far better than Christina Hoff Sommers and her followers that their seductive artifice, "equity feminism", is a mere ploy to mislead the unwary. For Sommers, "equity" means a bigger slice of the pie regardless of the "order of nature" or the interests of men, children and society. It seems that the United States is not gaining in wisdom, and each passing year signals "an epoch of dependence, the sure precursor of decay in men and nations":

> The multiplication of laws is perilous; each new Act, almost of necessity, creates the need for further legislation; it propagates itself, until fewer circumstances arise to render it obsolete or useless. We have too much law, and too little justice. Additional law will scarcely tend to augment equity, in the true sense of the term. Therefore, instead of increasing the bulk of statute law, or extending it in newer directions, of bringing it to bear upon labour, in the manner proposed by recent advocates, the object rather should be to curtail it, to simplify it; to codify that which is useful and approved; to repeal what is bad and mischievous, and to give a fuller freedom to the faculties of man in all that is noble and good. The demand for more law indicates a decadence of manhood, an absence of self-reliant, self-sustaining power. It marks an epoch of dependence, the sure precursor of decay in men and in nations.[42]

* * *

To remind ourselves that men like Howell are not yet consigned to the dustbin, we might consider a recent whimsical item by columnist Charley Reese, in which he remarks that "the brilliant and learned soldier-scholar, Sir John Glubb (1897-1986), wrote in a monograph that one of the characteristics of the impending fall of a nation or empire is the rise of feminism."[43] (For instance, women had become more active and visible in old Rome about the time the empire began to show signs of weakness – around 200 to 300 A.D.) Reese's 1998 comments are relevant: "Well, guys, it's all over. A lady friend of mine remarked casually that since they put wheels on suitcases, a woman doesn't need a husband anymore. First, it was central heat and air, so they didn't need us to chop wood and start the fire. Then came the automobile with an automatic starter, so they didn't need us to saddle horses, hitch up the buggy or crank the car. Then they went to work, so they didn't need us to bring home a paycheck…."

Regarding his wife, and women's greater "pragmatism" or sense of "reality" mainly centered on themselves and their families,

> Alas, she had not the least bit of interest in freedom for Scotland or the Battle of Trafalgar, the fall of the Alamo, pirates, Indians or the winning of the West. None of that concerned her or the house or the children, so it was nonsense…. So nations fall when women rise to prominence simply because affairs of state strike them as nonsense. You can see that in Washington, where feminists think of the military as nothing more than a job opportunity for women. Recently defeated New York senatorial candidate Geraldine Ferraro, when she was in the House of Representatives, once came to the floor during a debate about Turkey and thought they were discussing some agricultural subject…. Clearly the Washington feminists think that it is more important for naval aviators to behave like choirboys than to fly their high-tech fighters to hell and back…. But Clinton, who is a male chauvinist pig if ever there was one, gets a free pass from the feminist harpies. I guess that proves they are more leftist than feminist and Clinton surely is a leftist chauvinist pig…. Still, I don't mind if wheels on suitcases have made me obsolete. To tell the truth, I never was very fond of loading and unloading six suitcases and three carry-ons every time we took an overnight trip.

And Reese is being kind to the ladies, taking care to ascribe the foibles to "Washington feminists" when indeed all Anglo-American women share them, and by his not mentioning that males invented the numerous conveniences. He knows full well the depth of female self-centeredness, previously committed benignly to family sustenance and nurturing but now expanded to national prerogatives that threaten the ultimate "fall of a nation." As he mentions in a later article, "Feminist ideology, which has strayed so far from reality it's hardly worth a comment, is a variation of extreme individualism. This philosophy holds that the primary No. 1 goal of each individual must be his personal happiness and fulfillment. And it equates motherhood with slavery."[44] Yet, threatened with the Damoclean female franchise, politicians tremble and cower rather than speak the truth.

5. Liberty, Equality, Fraternity

One of the strongest nineteenth-century statements against "sex equality" was that of lawyer-journalist James Fitzjames Stephen's *Liberty, Equality, Fraternity*, first appearing in periodical form in 1872, and representing an "enduring contribution to intellectual affairs," according to Stuart D. Warner, editor of the Liberty Classic edition. "Fitzjames Stephen's attack on Mill's *On Liberty* proved to be one of the most significant exchanges in Victorian intellectual history, marking the point at which so-called 'hard-headed' and 'sentimental' liberalism decisively divided."[45] One only wishes that the division had been more pronounced and that twenty-first-century pundits might learn something from this exchange in which, in the present writer's view, Mill was so convincingly routed. To the core, Stephen is an unwavering Aristotlean on the subject and provides a strong anchor for recent research.

The "law of the strongest" remains the paramount consideration in this arena.

John Stuart Mill's thought on women is bizarre. Because society is more fluid and allows more freedom for individuals to do certain things they couldn't do before, he jumps to the conclusion that, therefore, we ought not "ordain that to be born a girl instead of a boy... shall decide the person's position all through life."[46] But no human being "ordains" any such thing! Here Mill shows little knowledge of a woman's nature or what determines her "position all through life," a life which she usually enjoys no less than men enjoy theirs and possibly more. Instead, he arbitrarily dismisses this reality and condescends to judge her distinct and crucial role as one of "subjection", thereby revealing his reductive bias against women. As Stephen puts it in rejecting Mill's whole argument, "There is something – I hardly know what to call it; indecent is too strong a word, but I may say unpleasant in the direction of indecorum – in prolonged and minute discussions about the relations between men and women, and the characteristics of women as such. I will therefore pass over what Mr. Mill says on this subject with a mere general expression of dissent from nearly every word he says."[47] Mill's thought represents the ultimate open-ended, unchecked license that rationalizes away ordered freedoms in the cause of one's personal preference. His first mistake is to assume that men and women were being treated as "unequal," when reflection always shows that it is merely sexual dimorphism at work, unless we can convince ourselves that, say, lions and lionesses are "unequal."

In his turn, Stephen sees the impossibility of "sex equality" mainly for the reason that men are physically stronger. This may be a valid point regarding the criterion of "strength" now ignored by our benighted American political/military establishment; but it has less relevance for general biological, gerontological criteria. However, he makes good sense in applying his criterion of strength also to marriage, where the male protective strength serves as the man's contribution to the union, although one cannot ignore her "strength" in childbearing and nurturing. But he does see the lurking problem that, if a man and a wife are treated as "equals," "it is impossible to avoid the inference that marriage, like other partnerships, may be dissolved at pleasure. The advocates of women's rights are exceedingly shy of stating this plainly."[48] In the event, "no fault" divorce law has borne out this pratfall.

Like Aristotle, Stephen believes that "Strength, in all its forms, is life and manhood,"[49] whereas John Stuart Mill believes, "What is now called the nature of women is an eminently artificial thing – the result of forced repression in some directions, unnatural stimulation in another.... (N)o class of dependents have had their character so entirely distorted from its natural proportions by the relations with their masters."[50] If this low opinion of women is a basis for feminism, women have indeed been duped! Stephen offers this counterbalance:

> To sum the matter up, it appears to me that all the moral laws and rules by which the relation between the sexes is regulated should proceed upon the principle that their object is to provide for the common good of the two great divisions of mankind who are connected together by the closest and most durable of all bonds, and can no more have really conflicting interests than the different members of the same body, but who are not and can never be equals in any of the different forms of strength.[51]

Stephen's 1872 view of the charming human-pair-bond conforms to present-day knowledge of human biology, chemistry, psychology and brain structure and reinforces the present writer's views. More lengthy excerpts from his book appear in "Notes". As for Mill, his position is unrewarding essentially because his wife and he were more iconoclastic than interested in over-arching truth. (They consulted often. As with Moir and Jessel, one suspects Mill compromised his message at her will, as did Anthony Trollope's Barchester Bishop Proudie for his wife.) His views of present conditions would be interesting, since they disprove his theories of facile reform, with "everything open to change" and nothing left but "the narcissistic self."[52]

6. POSTMODERN CONFUSIONS

For a brief look at Mill's reform-liberal influence, let us visit a 1997 book by Frederick R. Lynch aptly entitled *The Diversity Machine*, reflecting present misconceptions on "sex equality." Despite his aversion to "gender identity politics" arising from the Civil Rights Acts, Lynch endorses concepts like the 1996 California Civil Right Initiative that repeated the 1964 mistakes. Like a climber on El Capitan who tumbles when his gear dislodges yet keeps returning to the same flawed crevice, proponents of such measures never get to the top. A sample of the confusion appears in one of this chapter's epigraphs.

Although Lynch writes of "the deeper question of whether the diversity machine can break free of collectivist ideological roots in race and gender identity politics and the 'justice' of proportional representation"[53], he neither "breaks free" himself nor sees what we need to break free of – non-discrimination law. With its Orwellian dialectic, his exposition serves only to shock the sensibilities. We are being asked to cure addiction by joining the orgies.

As a reading of Adam Smith should make clear, such egalitarian laws are bound to sow confusion and casuistry; positivist bans against "discrimination" lead only to an addlepated citizenry. Compared to Dicey, Smith, Aristotle, and the others, the resulting rhetoric waxes convoluted and trivial, mainly because of a lack of ethical rhetoric. Reminiscent of the Spartan women's intransigence while the city tottered, modern women's "reappraising full-time work and careers and rebalancing work and family commitments"[54] and the effects of mortgage rates on women's "careers"[55] are now more important than "refining and enlarging the public views."

Until we repeal "non-discrimination" mandates, instead of the lucid, logical dialogue of Smith, Stephen, Spencer or Sorokin, and others, we shall continue to see such prose as this:

> If the past is a guide to the future, high government and corporate officials will likely flee the specter of sharpening ethnic-gender polarization by avoiding debate or reform of policies that would further trigger ethnic-gender divisions: abortion, affirmative action, diversity management, and immigration.[56]

> In a multiethnic society, discrimination by ethnicity and gender is such a volatile matter that the principle of nondiscrimination must be enshrined legally in terms as absolute as possible. On a matter of such great importance, the symbolic aspect of the law is crucial.... While it is likely that newspapers and police departments will continue to use ethnicity as a factor in making work assignments, strong laws against non-discrimination (sic?) will ensure that they do so with the greatest of care and as little as possible. The law should ensure that no one *loses* an educational or occupational opportunity because of race, color, creed, national origin, or gender. This goal may not be far off. By court decree and ballot initiative, experiments in doing without race and gender preferences are already beginning.[57] (parenthesis supplied)

This is an alarming statement of autocracy. Typical of the confusion, Lynch's editor in one passage mistook "discrimination" for "non-discrimination" and the courts judging such matters have done no better. The "discrimination" he abjures is in reality *bigotry* – a far cry from "discrimination" per se, a natural human requirement for survival. Lynch decries "identity politics," while forgetting that one cannot pass laws banning "discrimination" without causing "identity politics." (An odd result of this mindset was his allies' protest when a Houston-Texas initiative supposedly ending affirmative action was defeated because its language actually mentioned "affirmative action"! This was considered a "devious tactic," as though succinctness is now passé. All such peculiar initiatives deserve interment.)

Stultifying political correctness arises from "formulating principles of diversity management," an exercise much like combing Medusa's hair. "Diversity" is defined as "unlikeness, difference, variety"; and the word "manage" as "direct, control, arrange, contrive"; therefore, presuming to manage variety is oxymoronic.

A final example of the "civil-rights" mentality should suffice:

> Although temptations to adjust employment and promotion exam results ethnically will persist, some employers are beginning to reconcile the use of standardized employment tests with reduced fears about "disparate impact" on minority groups by more carefully identifying the skills needed for specific jobs, using tests designed to check for those skills, and using supplemental criteria.[58]

Lynch deserves credit for narrating an alarming tale but his is a voice crying from the maelstrom, sucked up in the vortex and barely audible.

Lynch is a social scientist grounded in the present, and his more statistical, postmodern approach (state-engineered individual rights of all sorts) weaves a tangled web. David Gress has written a timely and challenging book, *From Plato to NATO: The Idea of the West and Its Opponents*, in which he discounts the idea that our history justifies a politically correct (non-discriminating) "liberal, secular, relativistic society," as Roger Kimball describes it, instead of a dynamic order of competing ideas and powers.[59] Echoing a familiar theme reminiscent, among others, of George Santayana and Russell Kirk, Gress warns, "the West will not long survive if it forgets its history or the dynamic that produced its particular voice and contribution to the chorus of humanity." The current generation of scholars like Lynch would do well to heed such advice as they seek to reinvent America along undiscriminating egalitarian lines.

7. The Education of Henry Adams and Richard M. Weaver

To return to more traditional thought, we shall consider two other links to the past, already mentioned above – Henry Adams and Richard M. Weaver – whose extensive writings include commentary on the increasing ravages of sexual "progress," mainly as to the supposed rewards of greater "freedom" for women since about 1840. Their testimony remains relevant until rebutted by credible evidence.

Henry Adams felt deeply about women, which Leon Wieseltier in his Introduction to The Library of America's *The Education of Henry Adams* interprets broadly as an "adoration of the Virgin" and a "worship of women". Whether one agrees with this or with Wieseltier's rather cynical view of the book as "one of the earliest expressions of modern nervousness," he is right to call it "mysterious", as it is indeed an intriguing, subjective tale of the essence of life in Adams's changing times. He seems continually at a crossroads, tormented by a fondness for old ways yet unsure how to slow their loss – or how to avoid the "inertiae" of various trends. Men had succumbed to science, their machines, and conquest, and women to their new freedoms; leaving something sadly missing – something crucial and (Adams is worth his salt here) worth discovering. Since his criticism never extends to causes, perhaps it was too soon for his generation to know them fully, but he at least tried to express a sincere view of the symptoms – always in his elevated, enigmatic-epic style.

Adams's thoughts on the "force" of women and the "power" of the Virgin show traces of either the Goddess movement or Catholic Mariology. One might also conclude that he simply liked women and was merely seeking to maintain a proper balance in the onrush of progressive trespasses. "Inertia of sex could not be overcome without extinguishing the race, yet an immense force, doubling every few years, was working irresistibly to overcome it."[60] Like George Gilder, Adams emphasizes the importance of a woman's sexuality, not in the manner of Freudian or Goddess theory, but appreciative, and never pretending full knowledge. His prose was more poetic than polemical.

* * *

In contrast, preventing a sorely needed rehabilitation of honesty and a vigorous analysis, the facile flow of words in 2000s politics is ever apparent. Richard M. Weaver analyzes the problem in *The Ethics of Rhetoric*. In his *Visions of Order*, he explains the subject:

> (W)hen Aristotle opens his discussion of rhetoric in the celebrated treatise of that name, he asserts that it is a counterpart of dialectic. The two are distinguished by the fact that dialectic always tries to discover the real syllogism in the argument whereas rhetoric tries to discover the real means of persuasion. From this emerges a difference of procedure, in which dialectic makes use of inductions and syllogisms, whereas rhetoric makes use of examples and enthymemes.[61]

Weaver explains that the "enthymeme" is a syllogism with one of the propositions missing or, according to Webster's, "a rhetorical syllogism which is probable and persuasive but may not be valid." Despite the more reliable logic of dialectic, "a society cannot live without rhetoric" – "the most humanistic of all disciplines" – yet he realizes that the decline in support for our "Western culture is closely associated with the decline of rhetoric." Here he is thinking of a rhetoric eroded by "scientific attack" demanding "facts" and leading to "denatured speech", yet his words would apply as well to a denatured *rhetoric* of phony, emotivist enthymemes, like "a woman's choice," "color blindness," "equal opportunity," "sex equality," or disguising government intrusion as "protecting the children," so as to sway a gullible crowd. Weaver had yet to see the further decay caused by women's groups who, with the female gift of words without anchors, resort to flimflam.

Another example is the witchhunt against "discrimination," "hate," and "prejudice". The bugaboo against racial "prejudice" is now even extended to "sexual prejudice" ("sexism"), as if we can no longer discriminate as to the opposite sex, a stunning dictate having untold effect on our youth. Adam Smith warned against such trends, and yet the public rhetoric wallows in enthymemes and casuistry ignoring that not all prejudice is bad or bigoted. As Weaver explains,

> When democracy is taken from its proper place and is allowed to fill the entire horizon, it produces an envious hatred not only of all distinction but even of all difference.... It is of course the essence of fanaticism to seize upon some fragment of truth or value and to regard it as the exclusive object of man's striving. So democracy, a valuable but limited concept, has been elevated by some into a creed as comprehensive as a religion or a philosophy, already at the cost of widespread subversion.[62]

Such subversion also occurs when professors carve careers subverting natural inequalities, as reported recently in an Associated Press article on a "study" being conducted under the guise of "scholarship" by two professors intent on proving that "prejudice may be engrained at a deep, subconscious level," as though (1) this were not a truism, and (2) that it matters to any but post-1964 brainwashed Anglo-Americans. The "research" is based on tests involving "word-pairing tasks intended to measure implicit or automatic association to social groups."[63] Reasonable observers might suggest that, if people did not show "implicit or automatic" discrimination as to "social groups", or as to the different sexes, with varying degrees of reactive behavior (usually probably healthy), they would probably be blind or stupid. (See also "employment bias" case, Chapter VIII, Note 54.) As Weaver, like Burke, reminds us, "On the whole it is best that most men have a prejudice on behalf of their culture which is not easily overturned. It means settlement in their lives, confidence in their way of doing things, and consciousness of status. These things comprise the tradition of a culture, and although tradition is not the sufficient reason for a culture, it is a necessary condition."[64] The goal should be to teach the Commandments and brotherly-sisterly love to the young, not to desensitize them to basic distinctions.

Weaver was born in 1910 and died in 1963, having taught English at the University of Chicago and written for various journals. He wrote with professorial style and thought, sometimes similar to Adams with his lyrical quality, offering a considerable wealth of profound insight reinforced with a sense of art, ethics, history and form: "Awareness of the past is an antidote to both egotism and shallow optimism. It restrains optimism because it teaches us to be cautious about man's perfectibility and to put a sober estimate on schemes to renovate the species."[65] His broadmindedness did not extend to "sex equality":

> I put forward here an instance which not only is typical of contempt for natural order but which also is of transcendent importance. This is the foolish and destructive notion of the "equality" of the sexes. What but a profound blacking-out of our conception of nature and purpose could have borne this fantasy? Here is a distinction of so basic a character that one might suppose the most frenetic modern would regard it as part of the to be respected. What God hath made distinct, let not man confuse! But no, profound differences of this kind seem only a challenge to the busy renovators of nature. The rage for equality has so blinded the last hundred years that every effort has been made to obliterate the divergence in role, in conduct, and in dress. It has been assumed, clearly out of this same impiety, that because the mission of woman is biological in a broader way, it is less to be admired. Therefore the attempt has been to masculinize women. (Has anyone heard arguments that the male should

strive to imitate the female in anything?) A social subversion of the most spectacular kind has resulted. Today, in addition to lost generations, we have a self-pitying, lost sex."[66]

He would be disappointed to see the emergence of males intent on "enshrining the principle of non-sex-discrimination in terms legally as absolute as possible." Like most reflective men since Aristotle, Weaver holds firmly to inalienable truths about women, which men in all ages had best affirm lest their womenfolk find form lacking and strength misplaced. There seems little question that, whatever fault one finds in postmodern female adventures, the ultimate fault lies not in our women but in men. Echoing Dembski (see below), Carrel, and others, Weaver writes, "There is a social history to this. At the source of the disorder there lies, I must repeat, an impiety toward nature, but we have seen how, when a perverse decision has been made, material factors begin to exert a disproportionate effect."[67] Both Adams and Weaver reflect the turmoil of a society in sexual free-fall, as they sought answers to the human enigma of an "irreducible complexity" being deliberately "reduced".

Weaver saw that "it is only those who are capable of discrimination and of feelings *against* things who can be custodians of culture. Accordingly, I am satisfied that T.S. Eliot made a true appraisal of our times in asserting that 'our own period, is one of decline; that the standards of culture are lower than they were fifty years ago; and that the evidences of this decline are visible in every department of human activity.'"[68] Weaver died before the 1964 Civil Rights Act was enacted surrendering our right to discriminate as to sex, but we can imagine how he would have viewed its eventual stranglehold on the wellspring of our culture. He foresaw the weakness in our current public dialogue on matters of the most crucial import, amounting to a basic inadequacy of speech: "Another way of understanding this conflict of opinion is to recognize that the 'optimists' have the current rhetoric on their side even while the 'pessimists' have the proof."[69]

We "pessimists" are still not getting our message across thanks largely to the disinterest of the Fourth Estate, who have lost sight of foundational truths. "They have the rhetorician's advantage of a language in circulation and a set of 'prejudices' in the mind of the majority."[70] We deal instead in comfort-seeking, crowd-pleasing platitudes, half-truths and deceitful enthymemes masquerading as political debate. Weaver further refines his idea of rhetoric with a plan of attack:

> It is the object of this writing to bring a rhetoric along with the proof to show that the present course of our culture is not occasion for complacency but for criticism and possible reconstruction. This requires meeting a rhetoric derived from circumstances with one based more on definition and causal analysis."[71]

Indeed, cleaning up our own political rhetoric would allow real debate on "civil rights acts", "right to vote", "sex equality", and the common good. This last item includes preserving our culture and its sexual order as a "means of uniting society by making provision for differences. Differences do not create resentment unless the seed of resentment has been otherwise planted."[72]

* * *

We need remind ourselves that the main source of such resentment is probably women's studies (not to overlook various ethnic studies). As Barbara Amiel wrote in 1989 with regards to the "fascist tinge" characteristic of the "women's movement," "One look at catalogues from Harvard to U.C.L.A reveals a women's industry that will not give up without a tremendous battle. After all, what can a woman do with a degree in women's studies but get up every morning and go into the personnel department to raise employees' consciousness, or take a look at Isaac Newton and women's problems in cosmology?"[73] Michael Ledeen writes of "obscure authors being elevated to 'first rank' status simply because they are women... rather than because they wrote masterpieces."[74] Jane Larkin Crain reviews a book by Professors Susan Gubar, Sandra M. Gilbert and Elaine Showalter, in which they follow the pattern of focusing on women's "private psychiatric distresses" and "need of their own literary tradition," describing "women as reactive victims" and "infantilizing the sex they purport to champion."[75] Carol Iannone writes that in "pouncing on every conceivable reference to gender," these same "bogus scholars make a bogus case."[76] Jeffrey Hart, in turn, refers to "the feminist bowdlerists" as "the new Stalinists in the Academy. They certainly believe that there are commanding grudges, which are more important than truth, fairness, intelligence, and good writing."[77] Indeed, from such samplings it is evident where the seeds of resentment have been planted.

Despite the doubts of Betty Friedan and others, "The devaluing of the family and the domestic arena (partly the root cause of modern feminism and also later accelerated by it) and the irruption into the public arena of a large number of intelligent and educated women have created a dynamic which is far from exhausted, and which is no longer satisfied with the old goals. There is, in the words of the sociologist, Brigitte Berger, 'a new imperialism':

> It is clear that this new imperialism has been reflected in the life of the Church, too... And though the Church is often resistant to change, this property does not always act to protect its life from undesirable encroachments.... One thing seems certain: the more powerful the Christian feminist movement becomes, the more abundant will be the Church's bitter harvest of division, anger, suspicion and all uncharitableness.[78]

* * *

To combat such inroads, Weaver saw the need for form or structure in a culture that needs constant tending to remain ethical and valid.

As if to testify in behalf of the present treatise, he believes that we are "created for a design to be fulfilled" which does not "preclude healthful tension and that changing equilibrium which are necessary to...life and history". Man is equipped to fulfill this design – this exercise in self-government – by his "cognitive, aesthetic, ethical, and religious faculties or means of apprehension," which should remind us to put these same faculties to use:

> The first is the inquiring faculty, which gives him knowledge; the second, which is essentially contemplative, enables him to enjoy beauty; the third enables him to determine the order of goods and to judge between the right and wrong; and the fourth, which is essentially intuitive, gives him glimpses of his transcendental nature and his destiny.[79]

Our television-Hollywood culture slights all these functions. Weaver essentially tells us, however, that in deciding matters of policy and order we must be allowed to "maintain some rights of office among these various faculties." By allowing "non-discrimination" law to take away our "rights of office" to an ordering of our sexual ethos according to our natures and ethical conscience, we invite not "visions of order" but a regime of disorder.

8. Irreducible Simplicity

If the word "analogy" means that different dichotomies showing some similarities might show others, perhaps, with a bit of stretching we can find an analogy (or at least a metaphor) between the human sexes and certain biological systems (as we have suggested with Einstein's physics). Can we compare our macroscopic sexual order – the human pair bond (sexual dimorphism) – with microscopic systems of what Michael Behe calls "irreducible complexity" explicable only by a higher design? Especially with the advent of quantum mechanics, scientists are realizing that there is a design beckoning beyond the frontiers of "mere science," which can be explained only by metaphysics. William A. Dembski explains Michael Behe's concept in reference to a system of "several interrelated parts" from which the removal of one would "completely destroy its function," which shows that it could not have happened through "natural selection" as much as by higher design.[80] Assuming our two-part sexual "system" might remotely qualify, one can certainly agree that the removal of either man or woman would destroy the great love affair, and thus we have a system that must have been *designed* by other than human will and J.S. Mill's liberal progressivism. If this be the case, the nuances of the design are certainly worth study.

This is not to say that human beings are mere machines guided only by nature and the environment. Since our "free" choices are restricted by limits of conscience, intelligence, and natural law, the two sexes remain guided by defining criteria of conduct. One might have expected Dembski to scoff at such a notion beyond the realm of multiple-component biochemical knowledge, but he doesn't. If God can design a complex biology, surely he had designs for the human species, although the latter was a risky venture with the likes of Eve, Jezebel, Cain, Judas and the National Organization for Women. Once one acknowledges design, however, one invites Pauline instruction on its precepts, as men have perceived for ages. As Dembski explains,

> Design encourages scientists to look for function where evolution discourages it…. Moreover, design raises a whole new set of research questions. Once we know that something is designed, we will want to know how it was produced, to what extent the design is optimal, and what is its purpose. Note that we can detect design without knowing what something was designed for….
>
> Design also implies constraints. An object that is designed functions within certain constraints. Transgress those constraints

and the object functions poorly or breaks. Moreover, we can discover those constraints empirically by seeing what does and does not work. This simple insight has tremendous implications not just for science but also for ethics. If humans are in fact designed, then we can expect psychosocial constraints to be hardwired into us. Transgress those constraints, and we as well as our society will suffer. There is plenty of empirical evidence to suggest that many of the attitudes and behaviors our society promotes undermine human flourishing. Design promises to reinvigorate that ethical stream running from Aristotle through Aquinas known as natural law.

Henry Adams, Weaver, Stephen, and Saint Paul are among the many who have tried for millennia to rationalize the design – the most beneficial balance, or order, of the sexes – while more recent sociological studies have found a scientific basis for individual behavior (distinct for each sex) conducive to perpetuate the pair bond in a natural and healthy way. Although George Gilder argued convincingly for a "sexual constitution," distracted by their daily bread and individual tastes few wish to be bothered. However, the suspicion persists that our sexual constitution arises naturally by design in an "irreducible simplicity" such that its health depends upon our understanding of the respective natural functions involved.

9. More Contrasting Examples

We shall close out this chapter with a few examples threatening the orderly world of James Fitzjames Stephen and Richard Weaver. College professors now disagree as to the relative importance of scholarship, character and discipline. For instance, a hundred years ago, "mental discipline" was the top-rated purpose of their institutions; by 1938 it had become "good manners," while now there appears to be no consensus[81] and students are allowed to get drunk at football games. Another interesting example from our own times appears in an interview by Tom Bethell of an ex-gay who tells of his nonviable relationship with his father.[82] A direct masculine presence would probably have negated the stronger pull toward his mother and the feminine habits he acquired instead of natural masculine traits. It is a tune with hundreds of variations, yet always striking the familiar chord of children needing natural stereotypes conducive to a healthy society. Yet dysfunctional aberrancies like television homosexuals deserving benign censure are actually celebrated.

A woman reporter's cozy item depicts a father who believes "men's values really have changed" and wrote a book about it.[83] "Today's fathers want to have a different relationship with their kids than they did with their fathers," he claims. Speaking for all fathers, he "loves" consulting and advising other men to follow his bent yet only succeeds in exemplifying the dearth of manly leaders. Western Civilization was not carved out by men staying at home enjoying themselves with their families. Before things got so plush that Blondie could take up catering, the Dagwood Bumsteads had to earn a living, and either their vocations or the role of family breadwinner *made them better men*, while setting good examples for their children. Now, men who prefer being with their families are only indulging their urge to take over the mother's job and avoid working for a boss.

The item's headline at least shows the irony, "Men want it all, too", sending a message for our times of a great burst of *self*, probably explaining the seventeen-year-old gymnast's suing her parents for freedom to pursue the dollar as an individual.[84] Honoring her father and mother with a lawsuit shorn of daughterly gratitude will prepare her well for a life of marital bliss with a "new man" similarly oriented toward America's dollars.

On the national level, pundits like former Secretary of the Navy John Lehman are prime examples of "new males" catering to women regardless of the common good, which they apparently lost sight of around 1920. They think nothing of urging supposed "reform" based on combining males and females in uniform. In probably the least inspiring legerdemain of the year, Lehman has this to say:

> With respect to social engineering, the solution is simple: no double standards. Women should be allowed into every specialty in which they can compete and win that rating or win that job against all comers. Certainly there are women who have the talent and desire to be attack bombardiers or commandos skilled in hand-to-hand combat. But they should not be artificially pushed into quotas or allowed lower standards of physical capacity and training than men. They must meet standards appropriate to their profession and specialty.
>
> We must also come to grips with the double standard in the draft. Every 18-year-old male has to register for the draft today, but no woman has to. Although it is highly unlikely that we will ever need more troops than the all-volunteer force can provide, this disparity is an intellectual and a moral fissure running right through this ideology of gender equality in the services. Congressmen should either require the drafting of their constituents' daughters into the infantry or drop the registration of males.[85]

(If, *mirabile dictu*, he meant this as *reductio ad absurdum*, bless him.) If anyone wants to know the source of our present confusions, here it is – circumlocution from an ex-government official ignoring the basic differences between men and women, their respective values and functions in society, the crucial and delicate order of the sexes in any organization, and the age-old division of labor. Lehman's ideas stem more from bureaucratic "wordspeak" than deep reflection – all too typical of the "new man" devoted to technology. Small wonder the Pentagon now assumes the inane motto, "An Army of One!" makes any sense.

Another paradox appears in talk about "rebuilding the family," as in James Q. Wilson's Francis Boyer Lecture at the American

Enterprise Institute, in which he argues that, with regards to the urban underclass, "We have tried almost everything except for the one thing that matters most – rebuilding the family. However difficult, it is what there is left to try."[86] As Richard John Neuhaus comments, "He also argued that rebuilding the family cannot be done without a religious revival. 'Religion shapes lives in every culture that has ever existed, and does so more powerfully than the mass media or government programs.'"

How true! Yet neither Neuhaus nor Wilson sees fit to suggest that such a revival and rebuilding would require a dynamic return to the traditional division of labor for the sexes. There seems no way that one can "rebuild the family" or "revive religion" without returning to Pauline doctrine on family headship and mutual but distinct responsibilities of parents, requiring outright rejection of feminist ideology. The solution is obvious: repeal the Glass Ceiling Act. While Wilson and Neuhaus are half-right, we need to generate what Edmund Burke envisioned in his own time of strife – when a scheming faction was eroding the foundations of freedom – we need believe "that nothing but a firm combination of public men against this body,… supported by the hearty concurrence of the people at large, can possibly get the better of it. The people will see the necessity of restoring public men to an attention of the public opinion, and of restoring the constitution to its original principles."[87]

Meanwhile, "public women" are more the rage. In the same issue of *First Things* as Dembski's article, reminding us of our irreducible design's need for discreet females as well as males, a young woman writer's essay publicizes her "virginity" as though it were a topic of interest for high intellectual pursuit. One questions the benefits of women's liberation and women's words that we now trumpet a maiden's virginal siren song in a national journal, "I sincerely hope that virginity will not be a lifetime project for me....I haven't met the man yet.... " Again, however, while a return to marriage is needed, lonely hearts ads by young women will accomplish far less than repeal of sex-non-discrimination law.

It is not that men like Editor Neuhaus do not recognize the gender gap but that their tax-free status requires they abstain from confronting it. In the same issue of *First Things*, although he would not target womanly thought *per se*, Father Neuhaus makes several deft parries of misguided lady-thought, as when he writes of Ursuline Sister Pascal Conforti's drawing an analogy between Jesus Christ and 1990s people with AIDS,

> .... her locution reflects the curious ways in which, in some circles, AIDS has been sacralized, with its innocent "victims" depicted as Christ-figures bearing the sins of a homophobic society.... Jesus – who "let himself (as the Sister suggested) become unprotected for our sake" – is the ultimate AIDS victim. Such perverse manipulation of Christian symbols is no longer a surprise in the general media.... (parenthesis supplied)

One might forgive the sister's odd thought as merely a momentary slip, were it not that Father Neuhaus also reports of a "bishops conference's unfortunate statement on homosexuality," showing that bishops too are not immune from granting soft-hearted license to asocial, unnatural, unhealthy, and sinful ways.

In the same pages, Father Neuhaus goes on to tell of an amusing exchange triggered by an op-ed piece in the *New York Times* recommending a more "Thucydidean" recognition of "the tragic nature of our existence rather than turning to the illusory promises of psychotherapy." In a responding "stiff letter to the editor," Professor of Psychiatry Susan and her husband, Professor of Classics Victor Bers, proffered the notion that "Thucydides's discussion of the horrific plague that afflicted Athens indicated that he wrote in the hope that research would bring better diagnosis and treatment of the disease." Neuhaus comments: "Ah, so that's what Thucydides was getting at. What I hope was Mr. Bers' embarrassment in signing the letter was, perhaps, a small price to pay for keeping peace in the Bers household." As Rumpole of the Bailey would agree, she who must be obeyed can be quite inventive.

And then Neuhaus offers an insight into our abortion culture, or the culture that waxes eloquent on so many human problems and disappointments yet ignores the most nefarious of all – the taking of innocent, unborn human life. In response to two women's anthology on the joys and challenge of parenthood[88], he comments, "Yet one cannot help but marvel at the queer disjunction in the minds of those who are awed by the mystery of life that is wanted while, at the same time, they are indifferent to the wholesale slaughter of lives that are not. The reality, I fear, is that they are less in awe of life than their own wanting." Again, this is not to say that men do not write disjunctively, but to remind us that women often do. After all, adding their vote and leadership was supposed to improve our cultural values (i.e., the common good; or else it should never have been considered), not level them down to uniform disjunctiveness.[89]

Finally, Father Neuhaus nabs a lady Keystone Karegiver in another act of disjunction when he tells of Susan Chira's book, *A Mother's Place: Taking the Debate About Working Mothers Beyond Guilt and Blame*. The reader should by now recognize the self-centeredness reflected in the title and be prepared for the familiar focus on "women's issues" *per se*. It all boils down to a mother's gaining satisfaction finding excuses to get out of the home, presumably to assert "sex equality and the rights of woman" in flight from adult womanhood. As we shall see, this lady does not understand the value of women in their roles as the most naturally adapted purveyors of civil ways and knowledge to the very young. For her, as with all women's studies grads, life is merely an exercise in men's having it all and women's trying to seize their share. Despite her illusions, however, the "second-class citizenship" she scorns is not for the mother who reads worthwhile literature and inspires her children to greater achievement. Neuhaus pulls few punches here:

> Innumerable mothers who work outside the home feel guilty about not being with their children. Now Susan Chira has written a book that answers their problem, *A Mother's Place: Taking the Debate About Working Mothers Beyond Guilt and Blame* (Harper Collins). Her answer to mothers who feel guilty: Don't. The *Times* put it out for review to Marily Nissenson, who has written a book giving the same helpful advice. "Studies indicate," writes Nissenson, "that mothers who work outside the home take great satisfaction in their jobs. Work provides income, and it is important that children understand that." Who would have thought that there are studies indicating that (some) mothers who work outside the home take great satisfaction in their jobs? Not to mention that work provides income.
>
> It appears that women actually get paid for these jobs: Okay, kids, so you don't see Mommy very often, but we need the money, and it's important you understand that. Nissenson continues: "Women who choose the so-called 'mommy track' may find out too late that such a decision has led to permanent career compromise and, for many, a kind of second-class citizenship within their marriages. Because they earn less than their husbands, they have less leverage in the relationship." Marriage is a power thing; you wouldn't understand. The authors have stumbled across other studies that suggest a general principle: "Children seem to thrive most when their mothers are where they want to be." Memo to five-year-old Susan: So what if you haven't seen your mother for years. She is where she wants to be, which is not with you. Stop whining and thrive, kid.

Thus, another perspective on women bombardiers and executives. One wishes Father Neuhaus and his Catholic readers would extend their insight *specifically* to women police captains, judges, lawyers, congresspersons, and starship commanders.

* * *

In contrast to past ages, politicians and judges now do not speak in terms of the republic, the common good, the Federalist Papers, or rhetoric of first principles, constitutional rudiments and realities. Instead, they resort to catchwords and enthymemes – fads and inventions appealing to liberal fancies. The main reason for trivialization of campaign rhetoric is that we trivialized the franchise. (Liberals assumed teenagers were politically astute, so extended the franchise to eighteen-year-olds, yet when a twenty-year-old enlists with a Taliban enemy, they claim he is too young to understand.) We have learned to square the hypotenuse, surf the Internet, and scan the skies, but have forgotten to make sense of our own lives. As John Paul Russo cogently reminds us,

> From Isocrates, Cicero, and Quintilian, to Guarino da Verona, Montaigne, and Matthew Arnold, the humanities have always helped frame certain choices: what kind of student are we producing, what type of mind, what configuration of ideals, what practical skills, what standard of conduct? In short, by whom in the future does society wish to be represented? The goal was to educate a person who knows not only many things, but how to rank them; who has the spark of wisdom to know where to look again for wisdom…. (Matthew Arnold) urged humanists to carry on "the disinterested pursuit of perfection"; to construct a global culture founded on the best that has been thought and said throughout history; to evaluate the results of science on the basis of their benefit to human needs and freedom; and to nourish the sense of beauty.

It is now time to recover our heritage with regards to right order, sense of beauty, and the pursuit of perfection as to the human sexes, which should never become "disinterested" as much as passionate and determined, since the very existence of humanity depends on it. Those who bequeathed us the best that has been thought and said on the subject could wish for no less, for the desirable end is true wisdom.

Conclusion

The way of making truth known is not always the same, and as the Philosopher has very well said, "it belongs to an educated man to seek certitude in each thing as the nature of the thing allows."
                                                                                Thomas Aquinas[1]

Confucius is less concerned with the other world than with the art of living to the best advantage in this. To live to the best advantage in this world is, he holds, to live proportionately and moderately; so that the Confucian tradition of the Far East has much in common with the Aristotlean tradition of the Occident. In one important respect, however, Confucius recalls not Aristotle but Christ. Though his kingdom is very much of this world, he puts emphasis not merely on the law of measure, but also on the law of humility.... A man who looks up to the great traditional models and imitates them, becomes worthy of imitation in his turn.
                                                                                Irving Babbitt[2]

Reciprocity is the principle par excellence of interaction among rational beings, agents who adjust their relations to one another with objectivity.... Legal duties apply to external acts, which are subject to the external constraints of legislation; the duties commanded by virtue apply to the maxims behind the ac-

tions, to the internal intentions which are directed toward some end that ought to be a duty but that cannot be constrained from without.

Pierre Hassner, on Immanuel Kant[3]

Labor performed exclusively for compensation, Cicero believed, was never suitable for a gentleman. Nonetheless, he also believed that, although there might be careers more noble than one's own career, one should choose a vocation (genus vitae) in consideration of one's natural talents or capacities, and of the needs of one's civitas or community.

Brad Lowell Stone[4]

Again (à la James Burnham), who says A must say B. Once one realizes that men and women are different, one must seek a suitable equation for a felicitous working arrangement. As with most equations, "equality" means a balance of the whole, not of individual variables. Men and women need a healthy complementarity of human harmony, according to a higher mathematics – a salubrious balance of articulated interests, rights, and desires – with the ultimate equality the common good. I have hoped to convey its essence, touching all the bases despite the winds of fancy. Remember, we are dealing with the human sexes here, with Mary as the new female variable, not Eve; and an illusive sexual freedom not the goal.

The run of Western males seem deaf to feminism's discordant song. If more don't become aware, we lose the ballgame. The evidence is homespun, in the raw – ready for a free, learned and conscientious public *to see*.

As Thomas Aquinas reminds us, "to be able to see something of the loftiest realities, however thin and weak the sight may be, is, as our previous remarks indicate, a cause of the greatest joy."[5] He goes on to urge, "So that the human mind... might be freed from... presumption and come to a humble inquiry after truth, it was necessary that some things should be proposed to man by God that would completely surpass his intellect."[6] Ah, the cynic will respond, "Whose truth is right? How know which is God's truth?" But if Confucius and Aristotle teach things so close to Christian teachings, this should resolve itself. "For many things are shown to thee above the understanding of men."[7]

And too, theologians, scholars, scientists, and even lawyers must go a step further, recovering hidden truths – an exacting burden. Art reveals here its great power, although needing time to work its charm and wisdom. With her timeless image, Venus de Milo conveys better than ten thousand words why women are not soldiers, judges or statesmen. Perhaps even the purblind will see that the T.V. female Colonel puts the lie forever to gender equity on the day producers bare her "languorous look and lavish limb." Shrilling in a high, child's voice, "No problem! Sir! I'm a marine! Sir!" There are fewer ideal wives now: women are princes, knights, kings and whores in the public arena to be judged on "merit" and "performance," not on womanliness. A man's voice is like sailing the briny deep with a keel; a woman's, with a centerboard. A "tool woman" telling us how to form wood, join parts, and sand mahogany? Pretty rare, Al. There won't be a "Heidi the tool woman" show any time soon.

Accepted custom is to speak only deferentially or half-truthfully about women, ignoring Ben Franklin's witty advice to young suitors, "Before marriage, keep your eyes wide open; afterwards half shut." With their eyes half shut all the time, Americans are beguiled by the mask of feminism. While many criticize feminism of one type or another, it's time we realize that feminism in general disrupts the old Tocquevillian harmony. For instance, there is the widespread notion that someday we should have a woman president, despite all the evidence against it. Far from an advance for women, men, society, or the republic, such an occurrence would only be a sign of decay.[8]

It should be apparent that my aim is not to criticize all women but only those out of place in male roles. Our search has shown that not only feminism is at fault but also the whole trend of liberal society over the past one hundred and fifty years. Most of the shame belongs to men, as they continue to allow it to happen. Along with J.S. Mill and others, Rousseau's destructive influence remains considerable. As Roger Scruton contends, "He sought out real authority in order to dismiss it as a sham." Ironically, in so doing, while never a fan of "women's liberation", he paved the way for it:

> Whatever institution he viewed as corrupting is likely to be the source of knowledge, and whatever he recommended in its place will be fraught with paradox. Rousseau's attack on society in the name of "nature" exemplifies what to me is the root error of liberalism in all its forms, namely, the inability to accept or even to perceive, the inherited forms of social knowledge. By social knowledge, I mean the kind of knowledge embodied in the common law, in parliamentary procedures, in manners, costume, social convention, and, also, in morality. Such knowledge arises "by an invisible hand" from the open-ended business of society, from problems that have been confronted and solved, from agreements that have been perpetuated by custom, from conventions that coordinate our otherwise conflicting passions, from the unending process of negotiation and compromise whereby we quieten the dogs of war."[9]

All of this, we in America have ignored for over a century, but especially since the progressive-liberal inroads of TR, FDR and LBJ, the First World War, the reform mania of the early century and the enshrinement of civil rights after 1964. Instead of quiet, resolute diplomacy and the invisible hand we resorted to meddlesome statutes. Thus, rather than moderating the impulse, the Nineteenth Amendment (the gender gap, if you will) has accelerated it, threatening to transform the vaunted *novus ordo seclorum* into *ultima Thule*. Behind their facade, feminists are being allowed to dismantle Western civilization: *Ubi solitudinem faciunt pacem appellant* (where they create a desert [desolation], they call it peace.)[10]

At this point, Edmund Burke would remind us, "laws made against an whole nation were not the most effectual methods for securing its obedience."[11] And (adapting his words to our task with regards to the 1964 congressional dalliance with sex), "no partial, narrow, contracted, pinched, occasional system will be at all suitable for such an object (in his case, governing a mere two million Americans).... It will prove that some degree of care and caution is required in the handling of such an object; it will show that you ought not, in reason, trifle with so large a mass of the interests and feelings of the human race. You could at no time do so without guilt; and be assured you will not be able to do it long with impunity."[12] (parenthesis supplied)

The time for decision is at hand: "The question now, on all this accumulated matter, is – Whether you will choose to abide by a profitable experience or a mischievous theory? whether you choose to build on imagination or fact? whether you prefer enjoyment or hope? satisfaction in your subjects, or discontent? If these propositions are accepted, everything which has been made to enforce a contrary system must... fall along with it...." With regards to the mischievous and nefarious theories of feminism and sex equality, I wish, Sir, to repeal the Civil Rights Act, because (independently of the dangerous precedent of suspending the rights of the people to discriminate or exercise preference as to sex during the courts' pleasure) it was passed, as I apprehend, with less regularity, and on partial principles, than it ought. The college presidents, the generals, the employers, the editors, the churches, the sociologists, the historians, the political philosophers, the economists, the biologists and medical doctors were not allowed to testify in full before such natural selection was condemned. Ideas of prudence and accommodation to circumstances should have prevented the Congress from usurping the power to take such drastic and unwise action.[13]

Instead, the acts remain in place and women are establishing new systems of "gender-bias" circumlocution reminiscent of Dickens's Office of Circumlocution in *Little Dorrit*, presided over by the Barnacle clan. After Martha Burk's senseless bullying of Augusta National Golf Club, she must have felt that the Circumlocution Office had achieved its functions. That what the feminists had to do, was "to stick on to the national ship as long as they could. That to trim the ship, lighten the ship, clean the ship, would be to knock them off; that they could but be knocked off once; and that if the ship went down with them yet sticking to it, that was the ship's look out, and not theirs."[14]

Aside from Steven Goldberg, sociologists have yet to join our inquiry in force, perhaps because womanhood defies facile categorization. Married women vs single women provide a contrast, and indeed surveys have shown a disparity in voting habits, but this only proves that women think differently, and more for the family principle or the self than the long-term public good. And thank goodness for their input! But the franchise should be more of a solemn vocation than a perquisite. As for the usual purrs, "It was inevitable," let them think of Burke's good man who resisted the "the triumph of evil," or Solzhenitsyn, Bolivar or Washington.

Roger Scruton's essay on Rousseau and liberalism serves again as a fitting vehicle: "The modern world gives proof at every point that it is far easier to destroy institutions than to create them."[15] Rousseau, like the later Progressives, thought nothing of such destruction. In fact, they preferred it, to allow society to start from scratch. "Liberalism is an intellectual tradition formed from the interplay of two political ideals: liberty and equality." To heighten the paradox, liberals decry authority even while resorting to its enforcement of their projects. "(Civil rights laws) lead to an abstract and a priori code, established not by the attempt to rectify injustices as they one by one arise, but by the supreme act of a legislator, being not God but (Senator Fogbottom); it is destined to fail." (parenthesis supplied)

More specifically, despite his readiness to experiment with established ways, even Rousseau adhered to traditional norms regarding the fair sex (as we discovered when discussing Mona Ozouf's *Women's Words* in Chapter X). As Scruton tells us,

> *Emile* is a fascinating work, and by no means to be dismissed. The best parts are those that elicit the least sympathy from the book's normal admirers – the parts dealing with sex education and the virtue of chastity. Here Rousseau was forced to admit that the method of experiment could not produce the desired result. Chastity comes about only when pleasures are forbidden, when the other sex is shrouded in mystery, and when an elaborate story is told, embellished and believed, concerning the beauty and remoteness of sexual union. Modern sex education is conceived as a "liberation" from fear, doubt, and disease – a "how to" manual for children, which is also a form of vicarious pedophilia for their teachers. But sex was the one matter in which Rousseau was prepared to acknowledge that the artificial, not the natural, is the source of moral knowledge, and that custom must win against choice.

* * *

When a hiker branches out from a proven mountain trail and gets lost in the clouds, his best course is to find his way back to the point of departure and proceed from there. Of course, he must first realize his predicament. It may be only a matter of time before the people awake. Some will complain of a critic's "not offering solutions", when the solutions are apparent from the predicament – in this case, locate the trail preferably by backtracking, returning to what was successful – what led safely up the mountain – and going on from there, avoiding at all costs the mistaken path. Trying the wrong idea again will only bring known hazards, or more progressive, emotivist, constructivist contrivances that neither the heart nor reason should ratify. Otherwise, prepare to perish on a mountain cliff.[16]

* * *

The Fresno Bee ran an article on country singer Pam Tillis, with a charming photograph, revealing a modern Mona Lisa with faint smile and lovely face, subdued-enlivened eyes in quiet, assured repose far from modern thoughts of victimization or exclusion. Such is the face that fleets sailed for, generals dreamed of and admirals longed for. "Formed for attraction, not hard labor", an eternal child's visage in a woman's body. Of course, show business is mere entertainment and not always an uplifting experience or instructive, but perhaps that's the point: women are good at show business, in appropriate roles with their charms at a premium, sometimes grotesquely aware and displaying it for their own benefit, while other times enjoying the gift like a child with a cozy secret, enticing without trying – the eternal irony of womanhood.[17]

Besides the differences in performance of the sexes due to genetic differences, we recognize the over-riding function of a woman's attractiveness. "There's nothing like a dame." For feminists to label this "sexism" is morally and intellectually spurious. Pam Tillis's photo, like many, portrays the woman's power amply. While in the appropriate milieu she is in her element, to see faces like hers on campaign ads for Senate, Mayor, and the like is discordant.[18]

*   *   *

I believe we would be better off without the Nineteenth Amendment. Removing it would be like dynamiting the key obstruction of a logjam. While women would not be giving up that much and would regain much more, we could also reestablish a healthy balance of power that would see stronger, manlier, responsible males. Since responsible, married women tend now to vote with their husbands, their votes would not be lost. The less knowledgeable, less interested women would lose little and the republic would gain in the long run. It would be more in accord with the founders' original intentions, the lasting wisdom of which remains paramount.

Given the unlikelihood of such a radical corrective measure at this stage, the next option is equally important and would require a repeal of Title VII of the Civil Rights Act, Title IX of the Education Act, and their progeny, which have essentially cloaked us in the temporary awkward paraphernalia of a misplaced matriarchy, with dire implications for future generations. The masquerade ball is over; it's time to unmask. The best solution would be to return to the founders' plan and allow nature, civility and the market place ("the invisible hand") take its course. The most salutary effect of such a correction would be a new birth of freedom – the easing of tensions so a people could regain their sanity and throw off the iron mask of subservience in a slumbering age. They would be free again to live according to the hearts and reason not of authoritarian-reform-liberalism but in keeping with "the constitution of our country with our dearest domestic ties; adopting our fundamental laws into the bosom of our family affections; keeping inseparable, and cherishing with the warmth of all their combined and mutually reflected charities, our state, our hearths, our sepulchres, and our altars."[19]

With the guidance of a successful Western heritage, and unshackled with artificial schemes of "sex equality", we should be able to accomplish this with minimal disruption. We should know by now that inequalities will always be with us. If women want to compete with men, they are free to do so unarmed with the sword of imperious statutes. It would be according to customs of society and the judgment of free citizens. If an employer, admiral, general or school dean prefers to segregate the sexes or choose one over the other and even exclude one, that's his or her choice. There must be some vestige of common sense in our people to convince them of the advantages of a civilized culture so that, instead of surrendering to an unproductive standard for the female of the species, they opted for a healthy balance of male and female roles and fortified themselves with determination to stay the course this time.

THE END

Notes

FOREWORD

[1] *Josef Pieper: An Anthology*, p. 66, "'The Common Good' and What It Means" (Ignatius).

[2] Id, p. 110, "Useless and Indispensable."

[3] Saint Augustine, *Confessions*, p. 278 (Oxford, 1991).

[4] Claire Fulenwider, *Feminism in American Politics* (New York: Praeger, 1980), p. 56; as quoted in *Feminism and Freedom*, by Michael Levin (Transaction Publishers, 1987), p. 23.

[5] See *Coolidge: An American Enigma*, by Robert Sobel, p. 304.

[6] *Conservative Chronicle*, October 1, 2003.

[7] Gratias Harold O. J. Brown.

[8] Gratias Ralph Ralph E. Ancil, *The Wilhelm Roepke Review*, Winter/Spring 1998.

[9] Id.

[10] *First Things*, Nov. 1998.

[11] See Paul Adam Blanchard's "Insert the Word 'Sex' – How Segregationists Handed Feminists a 1964 'Civil Rights' Victory Against the Family," in the Howard Center's *The Family in America*, March 1998.

[12] See "Science and Design," by William Dembski, *First Things*, Oct. 1998, on Michael Behe's *Darwin's Black Box*.

Introduction (pages 1–12)

[1] A 2003s example is a "book brief" by Steve Lenzner on Michael Kochlin's *Gender and Rhetoric in Plato's Political Thought*, confusing "gender" for "sex" and lauding "the triumph of woman's equality." (*The Weekly Standard*, Dec. 30/Jan. 6, 2003) Despite "men and women hav(ing) distinctive occurrent aspirations and desires," the reviewer asserts, "the natural standard for excellence is the same for both sexes." Such is the obsequious doctrine of androgyny. (There will be other examples.) The brief offers no specifics about the book apparently out of fear of being labeled "proto-feminist," "sexist," or possibly "misogynist" or "chauvinist." Thanks to feminist abuse of such semantic pratfalls, we no longer see forthright treatment of the sexes, as men surrender to wives, girlfriends, and the likes of Martha Burk, whose attempt to bully Augusta National Golf Club into accepting female members is reminiscent of the Red Queen. Chic talk of "justice for women" without thought for age-old intricacies of right order suggests moral lethargy. Instead of evasion and subservience (like Adam), one wishes men would finally "just say No!" and repeal sex non-discrimination law. It was hardly a "triumph."

[2] *Order and History*, Vol. II, p. 2, by Eric Voegelin. See also, *Eric Voegelin*, by Michael P. Federici, pp. 90-91, 76.

As Federici puts it, "It is important to note that that while differentiation is a multifaceted process, experience with transcendent reality is its engendering substance. The insights that are gained and articulated into language are the consequences of experiences that Voegelin calls 'leaps in being.' The leap in being 'gains a new truth about order' but it is neither 'all of the truth,' nor does establish 'an ultimate order of mankind.' Rather, 'the struggle for the truth of order continues on the new historical level.'" (p. 76)

[3] *Christianity and Culture*, by T.S. Eliot, p. 14.

[4] Id, p. 17.

[5] Id, p. 50. See also Christopher Dawson: "For a community to conduct its affairs without reference to these (transcendent) powers, seems as irrational as for a community to cultivate the earth without paying any attention to the courses of the seasons." (*Religion and Culture*, p. 49) As John J. Mulloy comments, "The maintenance of a society involves

both a community of belief – certain agreed upon values, whether explicit or implicit – and a continuous and conscious social discipline. To secure these objectives, there must be some factor in culture which can command the allegiance of the society's members against the temptations of an anti-social individualism." (Afterword to Dawson's *Dynamics of World History*, p, 455.)

[6] *Christianity and Culture*, by T.S. Eliot, p. 77.

[7] Id, p. 79.

[8] Id, p. 93.

[9] Id, p. 170.

[10] *Deaconesses*, by Aimé Georges Martimort, p. 11.

[11] *Gods or Goddesses?* by Manfred Hauke, p. 87.

[12] *Written on the Heart: The Case for Natural Law*, by J. Budziszewski, p. 27.

[13] *Modern Age*, Winter, 1998, p.3.

[14] *Crisis*, A review of George Wiegel's *A Century of Catholic Social Thought*, Robert P. Hunt.

[15] *The Social Crisis of Our Times*, by Wilhelm Roepke, p. 49.

[16] *The Moral Foundations of Civil Society*, by Wilhelm Roepke, p. 43.

[17] *Christianity and Culture*, ibid, pp. 199-200. See also "A Grammar of the Self," by John E. Coons, *First Things*, January 2003, for an excellent, challenging essay on a vision of "God as Preceptor."

[18] "*Morality, Spirituality, and Democracy*," by Robert Wuthnow, *Society*, March/April 1998.

[19] A review by Ian Garrick Mason of *The Future of the European Past*, by Hilton Kramer and Roger Kimball, *Crisis*, Feb. 1998.

[20] "Still Small Voice," by Peggy Noonan, *Crisis*, Feb. 1998.

[21] A review by Dean M. Carignan of Mary Midgeley's *Can We Make Moral Judgments? Crisis*, Dec. 1992.

[22] "Was There a Big Bang?" by David Berlinski, *Commentary*, Feb. & May 1998.

[23] Id.

[24] "Political Cod Liver Oil," by Barbara Alby, *California Political Review*,

March/April 1999; followed up in May/June "Correspondence."

[25] *Vindicating the Founders*, by Thomas G. West.

[26] Id, p. 97.

[27] Id, p. 162.

[28] Id, p. 163

[29] Id, p. 161.

[30] Id, p. 165.

[31] *The Virtue of Civility*, by Edward Shils, p. 4.

[32] Id, pp. 4-5.

Chapter I (pages 13–27)

[1] *The Basic Symbols of the American Political Tradition*, by Willmoore Kendall and George W. Carey, p. 152.

[2] *Memoirs of a Superfluous Man*, by Albert Jay Nock, p. 232.

[3] "Farewell to the Gilded Age: The Critic and Society," by Morris Dickstein, *Partisan Review*, Summer 1992, Vol. 3.

[4] *Why Men Rule*, by Steven Goldberg, p. 1.

[5] "When Everything is Permitted," by Wolfhart Pannenberg, *First Things*, Feb. 1998.

[6] *Why Men Rule*, ibid, p.2.

[7] Id, p. 229. I question Prof. Goldberg's lending credence to a "true feminist movement," any such separatist concept being anthropologically unrealistic and unproductively divisive.

[8] *The Failure of Feminism*, by Nicholas Davidson.

[9] *Men and Marriage*, by George Gilder.

[10] Roger Kimball, "Reflections on a cultural revolution," *The New Criterion*, Feb. 1998 and previous issues.

[11] Wolfhart Pannenberg, ibid, p. 27.

[12] "Asian Values and the Asian Crisis," by Francis Fukuyama, *Commentary*, Feb. 1998.

[13] *Commentary*, June 1998

[14] "Feminizing Jewish Studies," by Hillel Halkin, *Commentary*, Feb. 1998.

[15] Peter Augustine Lawler, reviewing Thomas G. West's *Vindicating the Founders*, in *Crisis*, May 1998.

[16] *Vindicating the Founders*, by Thomas G. West, p. 82.

[17] Id, p. 91. Reinforcing my view of Thomas West's mistaken incorporation of "equality" into the founding tradition is George W. Carey's analysis, reflected in his review of *Vindicating the Founders* ("The Declaration as Political Creed," The University Bookman, Summer 1998:

> West's account) excludes, for example, a rich, vast, and growing literature that deals with the beliefs, institutions, and practices of colonial America; a literature that provides an overview and appreciation of the context in which the Declaration and its language is to be understood. …. Certainly a wider and more historically oriented view of the tradition would reveal that the Declaration was not understood by its signers or by the people they represented as embodying the American creed from which commitments could be derived. Indeed, the heart of the document, the charges against King George III, can only be understood in light of the British constitutional tradition and the common law. West's tradition is, to put this another way, contrived, retroactively imposed, and largely ahistorical. It asks us to focus our attention on a small section of the Declaration and to give the words of that section, primarily the "all men are created equal" clause, a meaning divorced from the purpose of the document, the circumstances of the time, and our prior experiences.

[18] Id, p. 103, quoting from *Democracy in America*, by Alexis de Tocqueville.

[19] *Men and Marriage*, by George Gilder, p. 173.

[20] Wade C. Mackey: "Demographic Implications of the Declining Role of the Father in Western Society," *The Journal of Social, Political, and Economic Studies*, Fall, 1999.

CHAPTER II (PAGES 29–43)

[1] "Aesthetics and God," by Father Chad Ripperger, F.S.S.P., *The Latin Mass*, Fall 2002; "Christian Art and Culture," *The Latin Mass*, Spring 2002.

² *Edmund Burke: A Genius Reconsidered*, by Russell Kirk, p. 28; from "The Character of (Mrs. Edmund Burke)," in *Somerset, Notebook*, op. cit., pp. 52-54.

³ *Gilbert K. Chesterton*, by Maisie Ward, pp. 152-3.

⁴ *Return to Chesterton*, by Maisie Ward, pp. 152-3; quoted in *Wisdom and Innocence*, by Joseph Pearce, p. 38.

⁵ Martin Gayford, *The Spectator*, Feb. 1998.

⁶ *Writings*, Thomas Jefferson, "Travel Journals: Memorandums on a Tour from Paris to Amsterdam," Strasburg, and back to Paris. (1788); Library of America. Jefferson put it more strongly in his journal of May 15, 1787, regarding the women working on the canal of Languedoc: "The encroachments by the men, on the offices proper for the women, is a great derangement in the order of things.... Ladies who employ men in the offices which should be reserved for their sex, are they not bawds in effect? For every man whom they thus employ, some girl, whose place he has thus taken, is driven to whoredom." *The Life and Selected Writings of Thomas Jefferson*, edited by Adrienne Koch and William Peden (Random House), p. 135.

⁷ *National Observer*, 1970s, date unknown.

⁸ *The Art Spirit*, by Robert Henri, Forward by the Author, p. 4i.

⁹ Id, p. 1. See also Christopher Dawson: "To understand the art of a society is to understand the vital activity of that society in its most intimate and creative moments ... Hence an appreciation of art is of the first importance to the historian and the sociologist, and it is only by viewing social life itself as an artistic activity that we can understand its full meaning.... social activity is of its very nature artistic." ("Art and Society," *Dynamics of World History*, pp. 72-73.)

¹⁰ Id, p. 57.

¹¹ Id, p. 61.

¹² Id., p. 100.

¹³ Id, p. 63.

¹⁴ Lord Byron, *Hebrew Melodies*.

¹⁵ *Heretics*, by G. K. Chesterton, "On Mr. Rudyard Kipling and Making the World Small."

[16] *A Portrait of the Artist as a Young Man*, by James Joyce, p. 223.

[17] Percy Bysshe Shelley, "A Defense of Poetry," The Harvard Classics, Vol. 27, Editor Charles W. Eliot, N.Y., P.F. Collier & Son, 1930, pp. 329-359.

[18] *Matthew Arnold Prose and Poetry*, editor Archibald L. Bouton, New York: Charles Scribner's and Sons, 1927.

[19] "Poetry or Religion? Text, Tact and Tactic in Matthew Arnold's Critical Method," by John S, Reist, Jr., *The Intercollegiate Review*, Spring 1998.

[20] Geoffrey H. Hartman, *Beyond Formalism*, Yale University Press, 1970.

[21] *What is Art?* by Leo Tolstoy, The Library of Liberal Arts, 1960, pp. 189-190.

[22] Id. p. 54.

[23] *Tragedy Under Grace: Reinhold Schneider and the Experience of the West*, by Hans Urs von Balthasar, Ignatius 1997, p. 42.

[24] Id, p. 45.

[25] Id, p. 46, quoting from *Las Casas vor Karl V. Szenen aus der Konquistadorenzeit*, Insel, 1938, by Reinhold Schneider, cf. 155.

[26] *What Is Art?* ibid, p. 185.

[27] "Imaginative Origins of Modernity: Life as Daydream and Nightmare," by Claes G. Ryn, *Humanitas*, Vol. X, No. 2, 1997.

[28] Plato's *Republic*, trans. by Benjamin Jowett, Modern Library paperback, Book V, pp. 167-68.

[29] Jeffrey Hart, *Conservative Chronicle*, April 29, 1998.

[30] Llewellyn H. Rockwell, Jr., *The Free Market*, Ludwig von Mises Institute, quoting from von Mises's *Socialism*, June 1998.

[31] *The Republic*, ibid., Book III, p. 106.

[32] Id, pp. 104-105. The dialogue with Glaucon also includes the following excerpts relevant to our subject, suggesting how society acquires a sense of right order even as it might relate to the sexes:

> But there is no difficulty in seeing that grace or the absence of grace is an effect of good or bad rhythm. ... And also that good and bad rhythm naturally assimilate to a good and bad style; and

that harmony and discord in like manner follow style; for our principle is that rhythm and harmony are regulated by the words, and not the words by them. ... he who has received this true education (in music) of the inner being will most shrewdly perceive omissions or faults in art and nature, and with a true taste, while he praises and rejoices over and receives into his soul the good, and becomes noble and good, he will justly blame and hate the bad ... even before he is able to know the reason why....

[33] Edmund Burke: "Letter to the Sheriffs of Bristol, April 3, 1777. From *Edmund Burke: A Genius Reconsidered*, by Russell Kirk, pp. 72-73.

[34] Roger Kimball, *The Spectator*, March 7, 1998.

[35] *Democracy and Leadership*, by Irving Babbitt, p. 31.

[36] John Paul Russo, "The Humanities in a Technological Society," *Humanitas*, Vol. XI, No. 1, 1998.

[37] *Summa Contra Gentiles*, Book One, by Saint Thomas Aquinas (Univ. of Notre Dame).

[38] *Democracy and Leadership*, ibid, pp. 36-37.

[39] "Uproar over author's controversial theory about women drivers," *The Sunday Telegraph*, Oct. 25, 1998, on Allan Pease's book, *Why Men Don't Listen and Women Can't Read Maps*. Apparently, women have trouble parking in reverse, while men are more reckless. See also "Why Women Can't Read Maps," by Rod Little, *The Spectator*, November 23, 2002, on the "basic mental differences between the sexes."

[40] Widget Finn, "Women on course for top posts in management," *The Sunday Telegraph*, Oct. 25, 1998 "Appointments."

CHAPTER III (PAGES 45–60)

[1] *Rudyard Kipling: Gunga Din and Other Favorite Poems*, Dover Thrift Edition, Dover Publishing, Inc., p. 70.

[2] *Feminism and Freedom*, by Michael Levin, p. 70.

[3] Id, p. 70.

[4] Clipping from 1970s *National Observer*, exact date unknown.

[5] *Platitudes Undone*, by Holbrook Jackson with responses by G.K.

Chesterton, Ignatius, p. 70.

[6] *Why Men Rule* (formerly, *The Inevitability of Patriarchy*), by Steven Goldberg, p. 92.

[7] Id, pp. 92-93.

[8] *Men and Marriage*, by George Gilder, p. 169.

[9] "Big Girls Don't Cry," by Barbara Rhoades-Ellis, *Heterodoxy*, October 1998.

[10] *Surprised By Joy*, by C.S. Lewis, pp. 8-9.

[11] *Ben Franklin's Wit and Wisdom*, p. 34. Excerpts from *Poor Richard's Almanac*.

[12] *Reflections on the Revolution in France*, by Edmund Burke, p. 94.

[13] Michael Weiss, *Academic Questions*, Summer 1992.

[14] Susan Arpad, *Contact*, California State University, Fresno, Winter 1989.

[15] *Written on the Heart: The Case For Natural Law*, by J. Budziszewski, p. 195.

[16] *The Moral Foundations of Civil Society*, by Wilhelm Roepke, p. 117.

[17] Id, Introduction to Transaction edition, by William F. Campbell, p. xix.

[18] Id. p. 134.

[19] *The Degradation of Academic Dogma*, by Brooks Adams, p. 119, quoted in *The Conservative Mind*, by Russell Kirk.

[20] "Mr. Emerson's Tombstone," by Wilfred M. McClay, *First Things*, May 1998.

[21] Id, p. 157.

[22] David M. Rasmussen, a review of Jürgen Habermas's *Between Facts and Norms*, in *First Things*, April 1998.

[23] *The Gender Agenda: Redefining Equality*, by Dale O'Leary, review by Patricia Lança, *Salisbury Review*, Spring 1998.

[24] Ellen Goodman, *The Fresno Bee*, April 21, 1998.

[25] Chester E. Finn, Jr., reviewing Lani Guinier's *Lift Every Voice: Turning*

a Civil Rights Setback Into a New Vision of Justice, in *Commentary*, April 1998.

[26] *Federalist* No. 51, James Madison.

[27] "God and Gender in Judaism," by Matthew Berke, *First Things*, June/July 1998.

[28] John Leo, *Conservative Chronicle*, May 13, 1998.

[29] Florence King, "The Misanthrope's Corner," *National Review*, May 18, 1998.

[30] Jeffrey Hart, *Conservative Chronicle*, April 29, 1998.

[31] Mona Charen, *The Fresno Bee*, May 19, 1998.

[32] "Closed Books," by David S. Bernstein, *National Review*, May 18, 1998.

[33] *A Man's Second Disobedience*, by Roger Scruton (1998).

[34] Roger Kimball, *The New Criterion*, 1998.

Chapter IV (pages 61–78)

[1] *What Women Say About Men*, © 1993 Armand Eisen, Andrews & McMeel, Kansas City.

[2] *Men and Marriage*, by George Gilder, pp. 39-40.

[3] "Human Remedies for Social Disorders," by James Q. Wilson, *The Public Interest*, Spring 1998.

[4] *The Pluralist Game*, by Francis Canavan, p. 103.

[5] Id, p. 102.

[6] *The Closing of the American Mind*, by Allan Bloom, p. 126.

[7] *Thus Spake Zarathustra*, by Friedrich Nietzsche, p. 207.

[8] James Dobson, "Spouses Must Row Madly To Avoid Drifting Apart," *The Fresno Bee*, April 18, 1998.

[9] *Women In Love*, by D.H. Lawrence, pp. 189-90.

[10] Id, pp. 191-92.

[11] *What's Wrong With the World*, "The Higher Anarchy," by G.K.

Chesterton, p. 143 (Ignatius, collected works).

[12] "God and Gender in Judaism," by Matthew Berke, *First Things*, June/July 1996. (David Blankenhorn's book, *Fatherless America*, elaborates on this aspect. See also Wade C. Mackey, Note 20, Chapter I.)

[13] See *The Naked Ape*, by Desmond Morris; *On Aggression*, by Konrad Lorenz.

[14] *The Closing of the American Mind*, ibid, p. 126.

[15] *Platitudes Undone* (Ignatius), by Holbrook Jackson and G.K. Chesterton.

[16] *The Education of Henry Adams*, by Henry Adams, p. 410.

[17] *What Women Say About Men*, ibid.

[18] James Q. Wilson, ibid.

[19] *Edmund Burke: A Genius Reconsidered*, by Russell Kirk, p. 75.

[20] *From Freedom To Bondage*, by Herbert Spencer; Introduction to *A Plea For Liberty*, edited by Thomas Mackay, Liberty Classic.

[21] "Table Manners and Morals," by Elizabeth Powers, *Commentary*, May 1998. Liberal-progressivism has changed this assessment somewhat as to younger males. They now often show the influence of feminism in their sex-egalitarian views of marriage, as, e.g., in an exchange between Damon Linker and readers in *First Things* (Nov. 2002, and Feb. 2003). Whether his "new man" will prove the norm one cannot predict but, in view of human nature, it seems doubtful. Trends in homosexualism, children without fathers, feminization of the national dialogue, lower education levels, etc., certainly do not recommend his "new family."

[22] "Preparing For Marriage," by George Sim Johnson, *Crisis*, May 1998.

[23] Id.

[24] *Mere Christianity*, by C.S. Lewis.

[25] *What Will Happen To God?* by William Oddie, pp. 63-64, quoting from the *Book of Isaiah*.

[26] Gilbert Meilaender, *First Things*, June/July 1992.

[27] *Fatherless America*, by David Blankenthorn, p. 122.

[28] *The Pluralist Game*, ibid, p. 105.

[29] *What Will Happen To God?* ibid, pp. 55-56.

[30] See, e.g., *Feminism and Freedom, The Failure of Feminism*, et al., ibid.

[31] Robert W. Hefner, "Cultural Possibility of a Modern Ideal, *Society*, March/April 1998.

[32] *The Church and Women: A Compendium*, Ignatius, 1988.

[33] See comprehensive account in *The Family in America* (Howard Center), March 1998, by Paul Adam Blanchard: "Insert the Word 'Sex' – How Segregationists Handed Feminists a 1964 'Civil Rights' Victory Against the Family."

CHAPTER V (PAGES 79–99)

[1] "Essay in Aid of a Grammar of Dissent," by John Henry Newman; from *The Heart of Newman*, edited by Erich Przywara, pp. 425-26.

[2] *Discourse to Mixed Congregations*, by John Henry Newman, p. 51 (Ignatius).

[3] "Mr. Emerson's Tombstone," by Wilfred McClay, *First Things*, May 1998.

[4] "Hume? A Czech? Or an Undry Martini?" by Andrew Brown, *The Spectator*, April 25, 1998.

[5] "A Bit of Jiggery-Popery," *The Spectator*, May 9, 1998.

[6] "Martha's Vineyard," by Ralph McInerny, a review of Martha Nussbaum's *Cultivating Humanity*, in *Crisis*, May 1998.

[7] "True Christian Feminism," by Richard John Neuhaus, *National Review*, Nov. 25, 1988.

[8] Apostolic "Letter *Mulieris Dignitatem* of the Supreme Pontiff John Paul II on the Dignity and Vocation of Women on the Occasion of the Marian Year." (1987-8)

[9] Id, p. 100.

[10] Id, p. 69.

[11] Id, pp. 64-65.

[12] *The Church and Women*, rear cover, Ignatius.

[13] *The Failure of Feminism*, by Nicholas Davidson, p. 309.

[14] Florence King, reviewing *Other Powers: The Age Of Suffrage, Spiritualism, and the Scandalous Victoria Woodhull*, by Barbara Goldsmith, *National Review*, May 24, 1998.

[15] *The Church and Women*, ibid, Barbara Albrecht, pp. 44 -45.

[16] Id, pp. 43-44.

[17] *Mulieris Dignitatem*, ibid, p. 104.

[18] Ibid, p. 97.

[19] *God or Goddesses?* by Manfred Hauke, p. 236.

[20] Nancy M. Cross, reviewing *Essays on Women* by Edith Stein, *National Review*, Sept. 2, 1998.

[21] *What Will Happen To God?* by William Oddie, pp. 6-7.

[22] *God or Goddesses?* ibid, p. 260.

[23] "Farewell to the Woman Question," by Midge Decter, *First Things*, June/July 1991.

[24] "The Reverend's Feast of Flesh," on Rev. John Pelling, *The Sunday Telegraph*, March 1, 1998.

[25] "Cherie is no First Lady," by Germaine Greer, *The Sunday Telegraph*, Dec. 15, 2002.

CHAPTER VI (PAGES 101–153)

[1] *What Will Happen to God?* (*WWHtG?*), by William Oddie (1989); Rev. Oddie's writing on the Episcopal Church of the United States' decision to ordain female priests.

[2] *God or Goddesses?* (*GoG?*), by Manfred Hauke, p. 256. Leon J. Podles argues the same case in his 1999 book, *The Church Impotent: The Feminization of Christianity* (Spence Publishing).

[3] *WWHtG?* Ibid, p. xii.

[4] *GoG?* Ibid, p. 196

[5] Id, pp. 56-57

[6] Id, p. 214.

[7] E.g., id, pp. 73 and 104.

[8] Id, p. 93.

[9] *WWHtG?* ibid, p. 9; quoting from *Womanspirit Rising: A Feminist Reader in Religion*, by Carol P. Christ and Judith Plaskow.

[10] *What's Wrong With the World*, by G.K. Chesterton, "The Queen and the Suffragettes." See also "On Female Suffrage" in same volume.

[11] Michael Weiss, *Academic Questions*, Summer 1992.

[12] "The Project of Rejuvenilization," by Roger Kimball, *The New Criterion*, May 1998.

[13] *GoG?* Ibid, pp. 113-114.

[14] Id, p. 247.

[15] Id, p. 249.

[16] "Christians Set for Chosen Women Revival," *Fresno Bee*, "Local News," May 24, 1998.

[17] *GoG?* Ibid, p. 251

[18] *Politics*, Book II, p. 2015, "On the Spartan Constitution," by Aristotle.

[19] *The Church and Women: A Compendium* (*TCaW*), "The Place of Women as a Problem in Theological Anthropology." (Ignatius)

[20] Id, pp. 27-28.

[21] Id, p. 33.

[22] Id, p.35, "Is There an Objective Type Woman?" by Barbara Albrecht.

[23] *TCaW*, id, p. 46.

[24] Id. p. 71; "On the Position of Mariology and Marian Spirituality Within the Totality of Faith and Theology," by Joseph Cardinal Ratzinger.

[25] Id, pp. 76-77.

[26] Id, p. 79.

27 Id, p. 94, "Mary as a Model of Catholic Faith," by Leo Scheffczyk.

28 Id, p. 100.

29 Id, p. 103, "Woman's Dignity and Function," by Jutta Burggraf.

30 *United States Military Academy Report on Women at West Point*, prepared for the Department of the Army Committee on Women in the Armed Forces, February, 1992.

31 "Why Women Can't Read Maps," by Rod Liddle, *The Spectator*, November 23, 2002.

32 *TCaW*, ibid, "Observations on Women to the Diaconate," by Manfred Hauke, p. 139.

33 Id., p. 141, "Regarding the History of Deaconesses," by Bruno Kleinheyer.

34 Id, p. 153, "How Weighty is the Argument from 'Uninterrupted Tradition' to Justify the Male Priesthood?" by Hans Urs von Balthasar.

35 Id, p. 161, "Faithful to Her Lord's Example – On the Meaning of the Male Priesthood," by Helmut Moll.

36 Id, p. 177, "Admittance of Women to Service at the Altar as Acolytes and Lectors," by Joseph D. Fessio, S.J.

37 *The Theology of Karl Barth* (*TToKB*), by Hans Urs von Balthasar, p. 5.

38 *WWHtG?* Ibid, pp. 83-84.

39 *TCaW*, ibid, p. 185, "On Women Priests," by Barbara Albrecht.

40 *WWHtG?* Ibid, p. 97.

41 Id, pp. 95-96.

42 Id, p. 96.

43 *TCaW*, ibid, "Women Priests: Why Not?" by Bishop Desmond Connell.

44 *TCaW*, ibid, p. 259, "Feminist Theology – A Challenge," by Helmut Moll.

45 "Sexgate, the Sisterhood and Mr. Bumble," by Norman Podhoretz, *Commentary*, June 1998.

46 *TToKB*, ibid, pp. 10-11.

⁴⁷ *Deaconesses: An Historical Study*, by Aimé Georges Martimort, p. 11.

⁴⁸ Id, p. 241.

⁴⁹ Id, p. 247.

⁵⁰ Id, p. 250.

⁵¹ *Strengthening the Bonds of Peace: A Pastoral Reflection on Women in the Church and Society* (1994). Developed by the Committee on Women in Society and in the Church." National Council of Catholic Bishops/United States Catholic Conference (NCCB/USCC).

⁵² *The Spectator*, June 27, 1998.

⁵³ *One In Christ Jesus: Toward a Pastoral Response to the Concerns of Women in the Church and Society*. Ad Hoc Committee for a Pastoral Response to Women's Concerns (1992); NCCB/USCC.

⁵⁴ *CMR Notes*, The Center for Military Readiness, Elaine Donnelly, June 1998. "DACOWITS" is an acronym for the Department of the Army Committee on Women in the Service.

⁵⁵ "The Angry Professors," by Edward E. Ericson, Jr., reviewing *Poisoning the Ivy: The Seven Deadly Sins and Other Vices of Higher Education in America*, by Michael Lewis, *The University Bookman*, Spring 1998.

⁵⁶ Id.

⁵⁷ Matthew Parris, *The Spectator*, Oct. 10, 1998, "I believe Mr. Blair means it. The trouble is: means what?"

⁵⁸ *Through the Looking Glass*, by Lewis Carroll, p. 169.

⁵⁹ Id, p. 157.

⁶⁰ Id, p. 188.

⁶¹ *The Fresno Bee*, July 1, 1998, Associated Press.

⁶² *WWHtG?* ibid.

⁶³ Id, p. 10.

⁶⁴ Id, p. 11.

⁶⁵ Paul Johnson, *The Spectator*, June 27, 1998.

⁶⁶ Paul Johnson, *The Spectator*, June 1998.

⁶⁷ *WWHtG?* Ibid, p. 27.

[68] Id, p. 33.

[69] Id, p. 35.

[70] Id, p. 49.

[71] Id, p. 51.

[72] Id, pp. 51-52.

[73] Id, p. 52.

[74] Id, pp. 57-59.

[75] Id, pp. 64-70. "The question inevitably poses itself: are there in human beings any consistent tendencies and capacities which we can describe as 'masculine' and 'feminine,' and which correspond to this division? Despite the sustained (and sometimes unscrupulous) feminist attempt to argue that there are not, there exists in fact a considerable body of evidence, which has emerged in a wide range of disciplines, indicating that this question must be answered clearly in the affirmative."

[76] Id, pp. 137-138, quoting from *The Female Woman*, by Arianna Stassinopoulos Huffington.

[77] Id, p. 140.

[78] Id, p. 153.

[79] "The Big Black Book," by Philip Vander Elst, a review of *Le Livre Noir du Communisme: Crimes, terreur, repression*, by Stephanie Courtois, et al. *The Salisbury Review*, Summer 1998.

CHAPTER VII (PAGES 155–206)

[1] *History on Trial: Culture Wars and the Teaching of the Past*, by Gary B. Nash, Charlotte G. Crabtree and Ross E. Dunn; as quoted by Keith Windschuttle, *The New Criterion*, June 1998.

[2] "The problem of democratic history," by Keith Windschuttle, *The New Criterion*, June 1998.

[3] *The Burden of Vision*, by George Panichas, p. 117, quoting from "Three Masters: The Quest for Religion in Nineteenth-Century Literature," by Father Florovsky, pp. 158-159.

[4] Id, p. 15.

[5] *The American Commonwealth*, Vol. II, p. 1232, by James Bryce.

[6] Borrowing from Harold O.J. Brown's *Religion and Society Report*, August 1998.

[7] *What Will Happen to God?* by William Oddie, p. 141.

[8] Id, p. 142, quoting from Elisabeth Schüssler Fiorenza's *In Memory of Her: A Feminist Theological Reconstruction of Christian Origins* (1983), hailed by the *New York Times* as "feminist theology coming of age."

[9] Id, p. 145.

[10] *Feminism and Freedom*, by Michael Levin.

[11] *Women in the Days of the Cathedrals* (*WDC*), by Régine Pernoud, p. 250.

[12] Susan Arpad, Director of Women's Studies, Cal. State Univ. Fresno, Public Information newsletter, *Contact*, Winter 1989.

[13] *WDC*, ibid, p. 7.

[14] Id, p. 8.

[15] *Commentary*, July 1998, David Gelernter's response to letters from readers on the death penalty.

[16] Pernoud, ibid, p. 246.

[17] Ibid, p. 249.

[18] *WDC*, ibid, p. 8.

[19] *Reflections on the Revolution in France*, by Edmund Burke, p. 299.

[20] *After Suffrage: Women in Partisan and Electoral Politics Before the New Deal* (*AS*), by Kristi Anderson, p.1.

[21] *AS*, ibid, p. 169.

[22] *AS*, ibid, p. 169, quoting Pendleton Herrington.

[23] Id, p. 168, quoting Job E. Hedges.

[24] Id, p. 170.

[25] "Herbert Croly and Liberal Democracy," by Sidney A. Pearson, *Society*, July/August 1998.

[26] *Science, Politics and Gnosticism*, by Eric Voegelin, p. 11.

[27] *The New Science of Politics*, by Eric Voegelin, p. 159.

[28] Margaret Schulman, reviewing Elizabeth Wurtzel's *Bitch: In Praise of Difficult Women*, in *Commentary*, July 1998.

[29] *Society*, July/August 1998.

[30] *The American Cause*, by Russell Kirk, p. 4 (ISI; first edition, 1957, Regnery).

[31] Buster Mottram, *The Spectator*, July 11, 1998. Some women seem to understand the sexual verities better than others, as for instance, actress Marilyn Monroe, who was quoted in *The Fresno Bee* as remarking, "I don't mind living in a man's world as long as I can be a woman in it." She would probably have been amazed at harridan T.V. "Voyager" captains, linebacker "Warrior Queens," demure and cuddly Buffy the Vampire Slayer, virago office managers, and so forth, although more nubile lawyers like Ally Mcbeal might have captivated her, as long as the "man's world" is foolish enough to indulge in such fancies. It is odd, however, that television creators and the viewing public have such short memories: In "Star Trek the Next Generation ," there was a humorous episode in which the hero, Captain Picard, had been transformed into a boy and forced to issue commands in a squeaky high voice, which was rather comical indeed. Then, in the new-age Star Trek Voyager series, the matronly female captain issues her commands in a comparable squeaky voice, yet no one sees the humor.

[32] "French Salons/American Saloons," by Diana Schaub, reviewing Mona Ozouf's *Women's Words: Essay on French Singularity*, in *The Public Interest*, Fall 1998.

On a related point, Barbara Boxer's ultimate victory in the 1998 California Senate race is a shocking sign of our rhetorical languor. Her opponent Matthew Fong never really challenged her, perhaps out of gentlemanly restraint, or perhaps from a lack of combative juices, rendering him merely a liberal copy in a different package. Or perhaps he had been too long in bureaucratic state government. In late summer, 1998, California State Senator Ray Haynes offered an alternative approach which might have bested Boxer, more like the political dialectic of old before we adapted to the ladies: "That revenue drives spending is not subject to debate. …. (The Republicans') muddled message of fear is, 'We are not as bad as the Democrats.' It has been our cry for the last eight or nine years. Until we articulate a compelling, believable message of smaller government, less bureaucracy, and lower taxes, we will lose elections. More important, until we collectively articulate that message, we deserve to lose elections." (*California Political Review*, Sept./Oct. 1998, correspondence")

This will take more study of history and constitutional (political) philosophy – serious thought on long-term policy – rather than how to cater to current voting blocs, especially to women, as politicians are prone to do. We need men to grapple with issues like romanticism, idealism, secular humanism, utilitarianism, progressivism, and *egalitarianism*, who learn how to sway a preoccupied citizenry with what is best for all – the common good – how to refine and enlarge the public views, probably the most difficult part of which being to show *why we are not a pure democracy*. Mere expertise in the *technique and mechanics* of the parliamentary process is only a means, not the end. Because Matt Fong engaged Boxer on her own terms without offering a *higher, more knowledgeable* alternative, the campaign was diminished in every way – mired in womanly fears, sentiments, and misconceptions rather than uplifted with manly probity, rigorous argument, and deep wisdom. Typical of present trends, the 1998 election was a sterile campaign to match our faltering culture. Fong's anemic posturing was a legacy of the Nineteenth Amendment.

Boxer's own anemic thought amounted to empty quackery "focusing on her differences with Fong on environmental protection, abortion rights, health-care reform, and gun control," providing "a clear picture between the two of" them. In other words, she promotes the conflicting reform-liberal, socialist emotivist clichés that shackle our once virtuous, free republic because she assumes they will again sway the crowd that elected her the first time around. Her womanly approach to self-government is to devise ever more things the government can do at taxpayer's expense, while ignoring that, in its perfervid 1990s role "environmental protection" is like a runaway train, "abortion rights" means a license to kill the children Boxer pretends to be protecting, "health care reform" is merely Clintonese socialism already proven a bust in Great Britain, and "sensible gun control" is slyly cloaked to give Boxer carte blanche to dismantle the Second Amendment – all social suicide. This is not the place for full-blown political argument but suffice it to say that, while every sensible person wants to protect the environment, it should not be by cluttering up the law books or stifling enterprise with evermore regulations. Americans have for too long allowed such a dialectic to control our political process, losing sight of more important priorities like the Constitution, freedom and virtue, self-defense, while empowering demagogues gradually to implement tyranny in a sheep's clothing of emotional false alarms (demagoguery!).

Like Jennie Bristow, the belly-aching British woman loath to protect herself (see Note 53, Chapter VIII), with her anti-child gun locks Barbara Boxer would make guns inaccessible in an emergency, much like making the world safe for children by putting locks on Daniel Boone's rifle. It is similar to the largely female-inspired ban on alcohol that proved a flop in the 1920s, representing, as Irving Babbitt saw them, the "kind of enthusiasms most feared ... the mass enthusiasms mobilized by the state to enforce morality through Prohibition, or to make the world safe for democracy through world war." (James Seaton, "On the Future of the Humanist Tradition in Literary Criticism," quoting Irving Babbitt, *Humanitas*, Vol. XI, No. 1, 1998)

[33] Elizabeth Fox-Genovese in *Crisis*, reviewing F. Caroline Graglia's *Domestic Tranquility: A Brief Against Feminism*, July/August 1998.

[34] As quoted in *The Weekly Standard* (7/20/98), "Scrapbook": "Margaret Carlson's Competition."

[35] "Drinks With Doc and Dolly," by Matt Labash, *The Weekly Standard*, July 20, 1998.

[36] Mark Steyn, writing on Ted Kennedy's "Hate Crime" law, *The Spectator*, July 25, 1998.

[37] Review by Nicola Walker of travel books, *Amazonian* and *The Granta Book of Travel*, edited by Dea Birkett and Sara Wheeler, *The Times Literary Supplement*, July 31, 1998.

[38] Review by Kate Chisholm of Pam Hirsch's *Barbara Leigh Hunt Bodichon, 1827-1891: Feminist, Artist and Rebel*, *The Sunday Telegraph*, August 2, 1998.

[39] *The New Jacobinism: Can Democracy Survive?* by Claes G. Ryn, p. 71.

[40] *The Closing of the American Mind* (*TCAM*), by Allan Bloom, p. 131.

[41] The thought of some, less discerning women, as sampled in the pres-

ent book, reminds one of : a passage in Roger Kimball's essay on Walter Bagehot: Bagehot possessed abundantly a gift he discerned in Shakespeare: an "experiencing nature." He delighted in what he called "the grand *shine on the surface of life.*" A central word for him is "enjoyment." Keenly moral, he abominated moralism: "Nothing is more unpleasant," he wrote, "than a virtuous person with a mean mind." ("Walter Bagehot," by Roger Kimball, *The New Criterion*, October, 1998.) Smiley and his wife remind one of George Santayana's observation in *The Life of Reason* (1905-1906), Vol. II:

> The human race, in its intellectual life, is organized like the bees: the masculine soul is the worker, sexually atrophied, and essentially dedicated to impersonal and universal arts; the feminine is a queen, infinitely fertile, omnipresent in its brooding industry, but passive and abounding in its intuitions without method and passions without justice.

[42] *TCAM*, ibid, p. 102.

[43] Id, p. 114.

[44] *Crisis*, July/August 1998, "Sed Contra: Maritain Vindicated Again," by Deal W. Hudson.

[45] Charlotte Moore, reviewing *Why Men Don't Iron*, by Anne and Bill Moir, *The Spectator*, July, 25, 1998.

[46] *The Spectator*, July 25, 1998, editorial.

[47] *The Spectator* , July 25, 1998, "Letters."

[48] Paul Johnson, *The Spectator*, Feb. 7, 1998.

[49] Id, "Model Artist and Mother," by Richard Shone, reviewing June Rose's *Mistress of Montmartre: A Life of Suzanne Valadon*.

[50] Diane Furchgott-Roth, "Sex and Affirmative Action," *Heterodoxy*, October, 1998.

[51] *Goddess Unmasked: The Rise of Neopagan Feminist Spirituality*, by Philip G. Davis, pp. 84-85, quoting from Monique Wittig's *Les Guerillières*, as quoted in "Why Women Need the Goddess," *Womanspirit Rising*, p. 277.

[52] Ralph C. Wood, "In Defense of Disbelief," *First Things*, October, 1998.

[53] *Reflections on the Revolution in France*, by Edmund Burke, p.171.

[54] "The Lilt of Joy," a review by Katherine Duncan Jones of *The Collected Works of Mary Sidney Herbert, Countess of Pembroke*, Vol. II, edited by Margaret P. Hannay, et al, *The Times Literary Supplement*, July 31, 1998.

[55] *American Scripture: Making the Declaration of Independence*, by Pauline Maier, p. xx.

[56] *The Life of Reason*, by George Santayana.

[57] Sebastian de Grazia, reviewing Pauline Maier's book, ibid, in *The Times Literary Supplement* circa Sept. 1998. Another example of revisionist feminist history may be found in *Redeeming American Political Thought*, by Judith Shklar. This book amounts to a woman's liberated (unrestrained) approach to political thought from a distinctly democratic, egalitarian angle, with all the pitfalls that such thought entails. She, like Régine Pernoud, Kristi Anderson, Pauline Maier et al, adheres to perfect Rousseauvian human harmony while daintily dismissing male wisdom of the past. If women like these are considered the norm for society, or the true intelligentsia, the Founders' knowhow, vision and hope for a virtuous citizenry will have been all for naught.

[58] Elisabeth Van Houts, "Reflections in a castle pond, " reviewing Georges Duby's *Women in the Twelfth Century*, Oct. 23, 1998.

[59] *Dynamics of World History*, by Christopher Dawson, p. 303. (ISI)

CHAPTER VIII (PAGES 207–285)

[1] Jean Elshtain, *Partisan Review*, Vol. LIX, No. 3, Symposium on "Education Beyond Politics" (1992).

[2] "Farewell to the Woman Question," by Midge Decter, *First Things*, June/July 1991, "Opinion."

[3] *Domestic Tranquility: A Brief Against Feminism*, by F. Caroline Graglia, p. 96.

[4] Conservative Book Club monthly listing, March 27, 1998.

[5] *The Education of Henry Adams*, by Henry Adams, p. 410.

6 Fund-raiser letter, March 9, 1998, "Susan B. Anthony List."

7 *National Review*, September 1, 1998.

8 *Ulysses*, by James Joyce.

9 *DT*, ibid, pp. 363-364.

10 "Why Mothers Should Stay at Home," by David Gelernter, *Commentary*, February; leading to "Letters," June, 1998.

11 Unfortunately, after a century of being buffaloed by suffragettes, men are not doing their job very well and it is time to acknowledge that fact. American lawyers must accept much of the blame. In its dismantling of our religious heritage starting with the 1947 case of *Everson v. Board of Education*, the United States Supreme Court has displayed an appalling unawareness of fundamental law. By erecting a fictional "wall of separation between church and state," the lawyers impetuously ordained our downfall. For their part, the people acquiesced with a numbing docility more subservient than the German populace's acceptance of Adolf Hitler. After all, in the United States, we are supposed to be a *self-governing* people. As Matthew Spalding tells us, "Jefferson's famous letter to the Danbury Baptists – with its claim of 'a wall of separation between church and state' – doesn't offer unmitigated support for modern secularism." ("Present at the Creation," by Matthew Spalding, *The Weekly Standard*, August 3, 1998, on "America's Founders and Religion," regarding the Library of Congress exhibition (through August 3, 1998). In fact, it should not offer any support at all. Jefferson himself was a churchgoer and, as James H. Hutson informs us, Jefferson allowed church services in various government buildings, to the extent that "it is no exaggeration to say that on Sundays in Washington during Jefferson's presidency, the state became the church." Spalding provides this cogent passage:

> "Whatever may be conceded to the influence of refined education on minds of peculiar structure," Washington once noted, "reason and experience both forbid us to expect that national morality can prevail in exclusion of religious principle." The real separation of church and state – the one the founders actually intended – must allow and encourage a certain mixing of religion and politics on the level of political action. While individuals can worship freely according to the dictates of their consciences, there must be a common understanding of morality

underlying their religious differences. It is this consensus that needs to be revived, and government – based on the consent of self-governing citizens – cannot remain neutral.

[12] "Domestic, But Tranquil?" by Elizabeth Fox-Genovese, reviewing F. Caroline Graglia's *Domestic Tranquility*, in *Crisis*, July/Aug. 1998.

[13] *DT*, ibid, p. 143.

[14] Id, p. 144.

[15] A.N. Wilson, *The Spectator*, Nov. 12, 1994.

[16] "Individualist Feminism: The Lost Tradition," by Wendy McElroy, *The Freeman*, Aug. 1998.

[17] *The Age of Consent: The Rise of Relativism and the Corruption of Popular Culture*, by Robert H. Knight, p. 35.

[18] *Reflections on the Revolution in France*, by Edmund Burke, p. 94.

[19] "Motherhood Makes Women Smarter," by Robert Lee Hotz, *The Fresno Bee*, Nov. 11, 1998, (*L.A. Times* by-line).

[20] "Identity Parade," by Mark Steyn, *The Spectator*, July 25, 1998.

[21] *First Things*, Aug./Sep. 1998, "The Naked Public Square" (Richard John Neuhaus).

[22] Russell Kirk, "Edmund Burke and the Future of American Politics," *The University Bookman*, Winter, 1997, pp. 41-42.

[23] "The Principles of Right," by Wayne Allen, *Modern Age*, Summer 1998.

[24] "Learning from the Greeks," by Algis Valuinas, *Commentary*, Aug. 1998.

[25] "AIA Conference Explores Pitfalls of Diversity," by Trevor Whetstone, *Campus Report*, the newspaper of Accuracy in Academia (Reed Irvine).

[26] *The Religion & Society Report*, March 1998, Harold O.J. Brown, editor.

[27] *Jane Austen: A Life*, by Claire Tomalin, reviewed by Brooke Allen, *The New* Criterion, Feb. 1998.

[28] *The Pilgrim's Progress*, by John Bunyon, Part I, "The Conclusion," p.

149 (Signet Classics).

[29] "Sophist's Corner," *The Salisbury Review*, Spring 1998.

[30] "The Anti-Historians," by Ann Glyn-Jones, reviewing Arthur Herman's *The Idea of Decline in Western History*, in *The Salisbury Review*, Spring 1998.

[31] "Learning from the Greeks," ibid.

[32] *National Review*, "For the Record," August 17, 1998.

[33] *What Women Say About Men*, by Armand Eisen, p. 65.

[34] "Feminism Lives," by Wendy Shalit, *National Review*, April 6, 1998.

[35] "A Scottish State of Mind," by Ingrid Merikoski, a review of Arthur Herman's *How the Scots Invented the Modern World*, in *The University Bookman*, Vol. 42, No. 3, 2002.

[36] "Murdered Aid Worker on Her Last Adventure," *The Sunday Telegraph*, Aug. 30, 1998.

[37] Gene Healy, "Cultural Revolutions," *Chronicles*, Oct., 1998.

[38] "The Fierce Couple: Richard and Isabel Burton," by Christopher Ondaatje, reviewing Mary S. Lovell's *A Rage to Live*, in *The Spectator*, October 10, 1998.

[39] *National Review*, "For the Record," Aug. 17, 1998.

[40] "Female Pitcher Intimidates Wallace," *The Fresno Bee*, Aug. 21, 1998.

[41] "It's their fault if they can't get a husband," by Minette Marrin, *The Sunday Telegraph*, Mar. 16, 1998.

[42] *Hamlet*, I, iii, 47, by William Shakespeare.

[43] "The first radical women," *The Times Literary Supplement*, August 28, 1998.

[44] "All mouth and no teeth," by Claudia Fitzherbert, reviewing Natasha Walter's *The New Feminism*, in *The Spectator*, Feb. 7, 1998.

[45] Othello, by William Shakespeare.

[46] *The Natural Law*, by Heinrich A. Rommen, pp. 5-6, quoting from *Source Book in Ancient Philosophy*, by Charles M. Bakewell.

[47] Id, p. xii.

[48] "We're talking about a revolution, not just reform. It's the deepest possible change there is." Gloria Steinem, circa 1972, as quoted in *Feminism and Freedom*, by Michael Levin, p. 18.

[49] *24 Years of House Work and the Place is Still a Mess*, by Pat Schroeder; *Representing Mom*, by Susan Molinari. Both are reviewed by Florence King in *The Weekly Standard*, Sept. 1998.

[50] "Casual: ... and Ladies of the Clubs," by Pia Nordlinger, *The Weekly Standard*, July 27, 1998.

[51] "Table Manners and Morals," by Elizabeth Powers, *Commentary*, May 1998.

[52] Steve Sailer, "The Nature of Nurture," reviewing Judith Rich Harris's *The Nurture Assumption: Why Children Turn Out the Way They Do*, in *National Review*, October, 1998.

[53] Linda Bowles, Conservative Chronicle, Nov. 11, 1998. Again, regarding female writers in general, the best seem to be guided by Christianity and/or an appreciation for the worth of marriage and parenting, which tends to focus their thought on areas they know best – families, children, education – that is, if we discount the failing of many female teachers in accepting the education establishment's misguided "child-oriented," "problem-solving," "value-free," "multicultural" ideas over the past fifty or more years. When lay women propound on public matters, it is too often biting, rancorous, angry, Eleanor-Cliftian arbitrarianism; they pretend to know morality but only on the surface – it is not their specialty – concepts differ from conceits unconcerned with right order. Aside from the few good female polemicists, one sees more and more striking cases of essentially valueless, freewheeling female writing.

    The supply is endless and continues daily. For instance, in the October 24, 1998, issue of *The Spectator*, Jennie Bristow reveals a tart, assertive irreverence as she goes to some lengths to deride the idea that women are vulnerable or should plan to avoid risks. As if unaware of the inconsistency, she boasts of her "particularly unfeminine dread of all things healthy and pampering." She adds, "I am instinctively wary of all women environments of any kind and I am sick and tired of sermons about how you should limit your social life to avoid being mugged." Life is indeed harsh for the eternal flapper, stamping her big foot and indulging in whims. This one shows all the signs of an emerging virago – a liberette who has not yet been mugged, for whom life boils down not to making the most of ones talents by enhancing the public good or following ones natural instincts to help build a thriving family but to enjoy ones selfish whims. No doubt, she even disdains the precaution of fire, auto or medical insurance and probably looks forward to government social security, as she girlishly exercises her "liberation" much like the little piggy who built his house of straw. It is rather surprising that her article was printed at all. ("They Protect Too Much," *The Spectator*, October 24, 1998)

In Chapter IX, we shall meet briefly a female who happens to disagree with Bristow as far as needing protection is concerned but who nevertheless displays the same assertive nastiness in making her essentially gynocratic case. Carol Siemens lives in Washington, D.C., and feels that, in criticizing abortion, *The American Spectator*'s Ben Stein is not sufficiently aware of the realities of a girl's living in a "typically sexually predatory Washington, D.C. neighborhood," which from recent reports, is not much different than Jennie's London neighborhood, so between the two, we see a prime example of women's assumption that, right or wrong, men should defer to them at all times. When one realizes that, instead of recommending other alternatives like moving, marrying, adoption or carrying a gun, Siemens's only thought is to defend the killing of a baby presumably conceived in "predatory sex," her input seems hardly conducive to either a virtuous citizenry or wise self-governance. Since these ladies are urging conflicting positions both of which are off base, it offers another case for sound male leadership.

Then, as if *The Spectator* editor has granted *carte blanche* to his distaff acolytes, Sheila Gunn contributes an even more forgettable bit of gossip; namely, her opinions on the female Tory Members of Parliament, which for her becomes an aimless stream-of- consciousness sortie of back-biting. (Sheila Gunn, *The Spectator*, October 24, 1998, "Tories Who Have Woman Trouble") If we recall all the talk about female brutalization or being mugged, this lady deserves a national Mugging Award of the top rank. No one comes off unscathed, which probably explains the irony that "women on selection committees are the ones who block women candidates," although this seems to evade Gunn. The remarkable thing about this piece is its almost science-fiction frame of reference, which renders it unintelligible until one grasps that she is talking about Parliament as if *men and women were identical creatures*. While one might take her criticisms as a general case against female Parliamentarians *per se*, such is not her intention. As with other such ventures, she reveals a defensive bias, expecting to see more female Parliament members and not very subtly assuming that their current paucity is unfair. There is no mention of maleness or femaleness, only an assumption that a woman is just as qualified to be a Pitt, Disraeli or Churchill, Gladstone or any other historical leader. She even equates a woman's hesitation to change her residence out of concern for her family with a "family man's as well," although professional and industrial men have always had to move regardless of family. For Gunn, life is to be transformed according to a woman's fancy regardless of the dead, the living and the yet unborn. "The unbought grace of life" yields to a melting pot of sexes, in which the Sheila Bristows and Carol Siemenses will hold sway with their conflicting, tyrannical confusions.

This is a minor nuance perhaps, yet nevertheless part of our picture. Gunn's acerbic tittle-tattle about a chance encounter on the subway is not the stuff of great nations. Again, without guidance in Christian lore, most women's writing is worth ignoring; almost subversive of common sense, civility and right order. Considering his subsequent defeat, it seems no small coincidence that Ms. Gunn served as John Major's political press secretary, which one suspects did little to enhance a vigorous manly message for his government. With their tendency to suffuse the reality of male leadership with overplayed visions of female rule, such women are not improving the process of self-government in either Great Britain or the United States. Is this laying the blame for male shortcomings on women? In a way, yes; since, if we acknowledge that women have the power for good or evil that we say they do, as women, when they misplay their roles, then, yes, they must share the blame when manhood declines.

As if to prove the point, Melanie Phillips provides an excellent essay in *The Sunday Telegraph*, reviewing six books about mothers, fathers and family, and in the process nicely encapsulating in a page-and-a-half the main themes of the present book. (Nov. 13, 1998, "Casualties in the dad-free zone") The usual authors who repeat the postmodern fancies of self-invented womanhood and befuddled manhood, she routs incisively; while those who reflect the wisdom of ages, she admirably reinforces, even though hers is an entirely contemporary, self-generated perspective – a woman's intuition, again. While, somewhat surprisingly, she only passes by Christianity as a sort of peripheral sub-plot, she nevertheless marshals much common sense from sociologists and various "studies" to portray a positive image of the family and its great value to society. For several examples relevant to our own study, we might start with this:

> Across the Atlantic, the sociologist David Popenhoe writes that the decline of fatherhood is the major force behind the most pressing problems of American society: crime, teenage pregnancies, educational failure, drug abuse and the growing number of women and children in poverty. Not, in other words, the "invention of tradition," but the destruction of tradition.

Here, she is dealing with a lady writer's argument that motherhood is only a recent "invention." We should point out, however, that despite Phillip's intelligent essay, she nevertheless shows all the signs of feminism herself in treating her subject as if it is more a matter of personal choice than common norms. She is aware of such things as "the breakdown of social cohesion" but only as rhetorical embellishment, not as a system of responsibilities in which both men and women endeavored to build worthwhile lives. For her,

> (M)others should be given the choice to work or not. Recent statistics show that although two-thirds of mothers now work outside the home, one-third of those don't want to but are forced to do so through economic circumstances. No one wants to force women back into the home. But nor should they be forced to leave their children.

There is no mention here of the common good. (Sparta's intransigent women come to mind.) Women's perennial defensive mechanism is at play, which views social issues only as cases of women being "forced" to abide by customs or serve as mothers, all of which is dealt with by the Church far more wisely as a matter of "service in Christ." In Melanie Phillip's tormented eyes, womanhood is only another example of women's "victimization," showing again the pervasive infamy of women's studies. To consider a mother's loving care as "forced" seems dysfunctional. For that matter, who does Phillips envision will be "giving" women "the choice to work or not"? Is not this somewhat naive? Or perhaps it results from decades of British socialism.

Nevertheless, Phillips's over-all treatment is worthwhile. She quotes from Christina Hardyman's *The Future of the Family* that the family "is five times more important a source of self-identification for women than their occupation is." She mentions "studies which show that where women try to straddle the separate spheres of work and family, levels of dissatisfaction and stress within the family are far higher than in households with a clear division of roles." As if again to reveal her feminist illusions, she sighs that "the New Man is sadly a phenomenon more to be located in the imagination than in the kitchen," somehow allowing us a moment of optimism that the situation in Britain is not as gray as many women writers would indicate. She quotes Edward Westermarck's remark in 1906 that "the maternal sentiment is universal in mankind" leaving one to wish people would return to such realities for guidance instead of present myths designed to create a unisex society in which there are no differences at all between the roles of men and women, in which masculinity is neutered and all the anxiety about the effects on children of family disintegration, fatherlessness and much substitute care can be safely sneered at as "nostalgia" for a "golden age."

Phillips reveals a touching frustration with her world, not quite yet realizing that the "masculinity" she quite rightly pines for (while assuming full feminine freedom) might be more complicated than a "woman's choice" could handle. She poignantly dismisses Robert Griswold's miscue on traditional absent fathers, noting the "great difference between the father who is away from home for long periods and the father who has left the family home completely. There is also a great difference for children between fathers who die and fathers who divorce their mothers." In the books she reviews, the usual postmodern misconceptions of men and women are apparent, this time from both sexes but mostly from the fair sex. But she closes her generally excellent article with this mention of the Institute of Economic Affairs (IEA) offering, *The Fragmenting Family,*

> As Patricia Morgan comments mordantly in her contribution to the IEA's essay, at any time in our past "even the prospect of developments so threatening to the cohesion of society and

its capacity to replace itself adequately would probably have caused no small consternation and triggered remedial action." Morgan's analysis of the "inescapable data", showing the advantages of marriage and stable family life as well as the "looking glass logic" which inverts them, stands as a robust corrective to the irrationality, ideology and ignorance which now passes for debate on the family. Not surprising, then, that the IEA pamphlet's editor Miriam David – who writes with approval of "father-free zones" – should refer to Morgan in her introduction with incredulous and supercilious disdain. Truth, it seems, really is the first casualty of war – especially a culture war.

For the eagle eye, the lurking question in Phillips's essay is whether these ladies realize that ultimately the standards of manhood must be revived to find true solutions to their dilemma. And this will take sapient women. Men must be allowed former arenas, perquisites, hierarchy, exclusivity, authority, respect, and responsibility. Schools and laws have done their damage, which means the people have slept while havoc ensued. Before women took over these writing jobs, radio and T.V. punditry, editorships of IEA pamphlets, chairmanships of this and that, professorships and whatnot, we enjoyed a modicum of orderly systems and folkways productive and preservative of the common good. Does the idea of "triggering remedial action" not ring alarm bells even at this late date after decades of disastrous "remedial action"? As mentioned, the ladies cannot have it both ways, acting the liberated female while enjoying the sense and substance of full-blooded *fatherly* males. It is a paradox we shall have to learn to live with, that men will not gravitate to activities in which women are proliferating; "equality" is a misleading lodestar. The hard truth is that we rear "fatherly males" in solid, traditional families graced by strong mothers and *fathers*.

Another telling example appears in the Autumn 1998 Heritage Foundation "Members News," in which Midge Decter's "Denver Discourse," a Heritage "Leadership for America Lecture," is summarized. She notes how "the women's movement has created disorder" and recalls how military mothers went off to the 1990 Persian Gulf War, which to her represents not "the achievement of women's equality; it was about the nuttiness ... that has overtaken all too many American families.... When you can't tell the soldier from the baby-tender, ... you've got profound disorder.... being the member of a family does not make you happy. It makes you *human*." The paradox arises when on the rear page, next to an item quoting former Attorney General Edwin Meese's warning that "We have a serious leadership crisis that is convulsing the nation. It is causing our government to become a laughing stock around the globe," there also appears a proud notice that "Becky Dunlap joins the Heritage team." It seems that this lady whose impressive résumé reflects decades of male deference to female public figures and inevitable diminishment of male leadership is now offered the leadership that Meese rightly misses. Again, we cannot have it both ways: It is *male* leadership we lack, and male leaders are forged over decades in male roles of responsibility and service unplagued by "sex equality and the rights of woman." As Decter might put it, "When you can't tell the vice president from the baby-tender, you've got profound disorder." (Heritage Members News, Autumn 1998)

[54] Alison Eadie, The Sunday Telegraph, Nov. 8, 1998. Still another example of our cultural Iron Mask – self-imposed by misguided governance – appears in an Associated Press item on a pending "employment-bias" case, which amounts in effect to our government's having thrown out all of Aristotle's, Saint Paul's, the most reliable recent scholarship, and even Rousseau's thought in order to construct a Big Sister hegemony. "The Supreme Court will help decide how much employers can be forced to pay when they discriminate against workers based on race, religion, national origin, or sex." (*Fresno Bee*, Nov. 3, 1998, "High court to decide employment-bias case." Italics supplied.) The human brain is apparently to be put on hold. In this case, one Carole Kolstad lost out on a high-ranking job in an office of the American Dental Association and a lower court ruled that the Association had illegally failed to promote her. However, an appeals court barred her from collecting punitive damages because the Association's conduct had not been "egregious," although other courts have apparently allowed such damages whenever "intentional discrimination" has been proven, whether or not "egregious." Kolstad took her case it to the U.S. Supreme Court, whose justices, apparently not having enough to do, will hear the case.

Kolstad's bemused lawyer, a University of Washington law professor and apparently an avid fan of the White Queen, earnestly contends that "this is an important issue that will affect many thousands of cases and is especially important in sexual-harassment cases." The suit alleges "sexual bias," and the lower court ruled in her favor because of our old friend Title VII of the Civil Rights Act of 1964, which the reader will recall Congress enacted while in a state of egregious hypnosis. Socratic sexual merge-mania has won out over Aristotlean common sense and men and women are now to be interchangeable. While law professors carve careers out of such cartoon chicanery, and the Associated Press takes it all seriously, the American and British people have only themselves to blame, for it is they who have allowed our regnant dystopia of which Judge Larry Stirling of San Diego writes, "During all these discussions on judges, I trust you will not forget that 95 percent of us are down here on the front line resolving thousands of cases annually while trying to make sense of tens of thousands of federal and state laws and as many precedents." *California Political Review*, Sept./October, 1998, "Correspondence." See also George Howell's comments of a century ago, Chapter X) Apparently Kolstad's lawyers miss Jeffrey D. Wallin's point regarding George Washington that "the deepest meaning of self-government is self-restraint, both individual and writ large." (Chap. X, Notes 14 and 15)

Feminists have made much of the "glass ceiling" as a supposed artificial, arbitrary male construct unfairly banning women from executive roles in industry and finance, when in fact it is merely their pejorative figure of speech contrived to disguise their essential unfitness for executive roles in the passion of full-blown solipsism. Their best service by far is in interior, functional, more personal roles in which the self is not immersed, whereas a male is best suited for immersion in the structural chores of leadership and direction characteristic of organizational endeavor. No matter how a female tries to adapt, her innate parameters of beauty and ornament persevere; her delightful voice on a telephone turns feral in a radio campaign and loses its primary value. As a virtual-reality conceit, the "glass ceiling" inartfully distracts from natural distinctions between male and female, like mixing red and green to get mud. What the imagination misconstrues, neither the heart nor the reason should ratify, yet the alarming aspect of this gimmick is that neither the press nor the people have yet seen through it.

[55] "Boyz II Men," by David Klinghoffer, *National Review*, Aug. 3, 1998, a review of Patricia Hersch's *Time Apart: A Journey into the Heart of American Adolescence.*

[56] *Crisis*, Jan. 1993, review by Robert P. Hunt of George Wiegel's *Century of Catholic Social Thought*. (Quoted in full above, in Introduction)

[57] E.g., *Losing Ground*, by Charles Murray.

[58] *Reflections On the Revolution in France*, p. 146.

[59] *Women in the Holocaust*, edited by Dalia Ofeo and Lenore J. Weitzman.

[60] Robert Francis Smith, "Love Divine: Remembering Gerhart Niemeyer," *The University Bookman*, Winter, 1997.

[61] *ex femina*, The Newsletter of the Independent Women's Forum, July 1998, p. 2.

[62] *The Women's Quarterly*, Summer 1997, rear cover.

[63] Id.

[64] *ex femina*, ibid.

[65] "The Madness of the American Family," by Midge Decter, *Policy Review*, Oct. 1998.

[66] *ex femina*, ibid.

[67] Id. See Chapter IV, Note 33.

[68] The Hotchkiss School Alumni Magazine, Fall, 1988.

[69] Id. Another women's group, the Ecumenical Coalition of Women and Society (ECWS), a project of the Washington-based Institute on Religion and Democracy, has issued "A Christian Women's Declaration," which was reproduced as "Women of Renewal: A Statement," in *First Things* (February, 1998). Institutes seem to abound these days, as do statements by women, as though self-defining pronouncements are the rage, even though somewhat un-marian and hardly "interior." It is as if certain energetic activists were determined to have their say and, as here, are able to enlist considerable help. However, as always, there is a sense of inferiority, as though these ladies were not very sure of themselves and need group reassurance that their menfolk might still be so naïve or patriarchal as to

give up their seats in the life boats, although strangely the statement makes small mention of menfolk other than in the usual defensive rubric! This ECWS endeavor apparently aiming to "lift women to higher levels of respect, dignity and freedom" unavoidably sounds either plaintive, wistful or pretentious. Seeking "more opportunities and greater respect" as if the law of nature did not already accord them precedence; advocating "women's rights and dignity" as if the worth of individual women needed lumping together in a promotional group; it is all so desperate.

Paying mere lip service to "the two complementary sexes" perhaps reveals the ultimate futility of this ostentatious effort, since men and women were destined to act together and, separating women out is like printing a car manual only on the chassis without mention of the pistons and cylinders. (Or, one can switch the roles, it doesn't matter!) It amounts to a thinly disguised feminist plunge into waters too deep and powerful for mere swimmers to handle. They do not realize there is something grotesque in women holding forth on theology or philosophy, aping doctors of the church in order to assert women's life role with precarious grasp and obscure motive. I shall not repeat the lengthy rhetoric here on "women of the medieval period enriching the Church" through all the "service, writing, prayer, contemplation, teaching," and so forth, or "effective advocates of women's rights and dignity," as they "affirm the Scriptures, the natural, created order, "the triune God," and "acknowledge human sinfulness." They reject the litany of "empty vessels shaped by patriarchy," "abuse and oppression," "victims," and the like, even as the tiresome inroads of feminism are obvious. It is all like applying icing to a cake already inches too thick.

Although I sense the hand of feminism in this exercise, there is also a sense that they mean well and are only misguided. If all they say is true, why not just go about their business of living, loving, nurturing, sustaining, educating themselves and their children, and service to God? Why gather to orchestrate this display? Are not Churches and pastors doing the job? Why offer platitudes against claims of "women's rights" while claiming them later, or seeking "leadership" and "advances for women" as if men must relinquish even more responsibilities to the fair sex? After all, when a mighty four-master loses its rudder, what was once a graceful ship soon "advances" into shoals and shallows. What further "advances" do they foresee? One can "advance" one's arms by walking on them but the legs soon grow weak.

A "renewal of Biblical orthodoxy" would require strong and wise husbands and patriarchs, along with a repeal of Titles VII and IX. Are the ladies ready for that, along with Ephesian headship? Are women trying after all to tell their menfolk to take charge? Instead of a phalanx of marching women, we need wise and loving wives, who open their mouths in wisdom and whose tongues are the law of kindness. Instead of endeavoring to "rejuvenate world-wide Christian witness," these women would better serve Christ by raising sons to be men – men who understand how to negotiate the choppy and serene waters of marriage with a woman – one woman – while pursuing manly, productive occupations for their themselves and their families. The little platoons are where it all begins.

[70] "Single," by Catherine Whelan, *National Review*, Sept. 14, 1998. See also "Blunkett to bring back single-sex education," by Joe Murphy and Martin Bentham, *The Sunday Telegraph*, August 20, 2000; "How Exams Are Fixed in Favor of Girls," by Madsen Pirie, *The Spectator*, January 20, 2001; *The Religion & Society Report*, February, 1995, Harold O.J Brown, editor (The Rockford Institute).

[71] *U.S. vs Commonwealth of Virginia*. See deposition of David Riesman, videotaped, Civil Action No. 90-0126-R, Feb. 21, 1991. Also, "How to Ruin an Institution," by Woody West, *The Weekly Standard*, March 4, 2002.

Educators could learn much from world-renown medical researcher, Alexis Carrel. While one can disagree with his radical positivist scientism, his scientific analysis of the human being was impressive (*Man the Unknown*, 1935). Contrary to most educators today, for instance, he realized (p. 321) that "(T)he things of this world are simple or complex, according to the techniques that we select for studying them. In fact, functional simplicity always corresponds to a complex substratum. This is a primary datum of observation, which must be accepted just as it is."

Discounting Carrel's own solutions for our "weakening civilization," we can learn from his probing analysis of "the secret mechanisms of our physiological and mental activities and the causes of our weakness" and acknowledge that, in ignoring the complexities of the sexes, "we have transgressed natural laws." While, for instance, the Founders understood much about human nature, civil society, and right order, more recent leaders have strayed into areas far beyond their comprehension without regard for human nature or higher values. Instead of wise direction, for them it is simply a matter of what the latest fancy calls for. Among the most important areas being short-changed is that of the two human sexes, where, to appease a self-centered ideology, feminism, fund-raising administrators ignore millennia of experience and hard-earned customs that were wisely based on an understanding of the complexities involved. In 1935, Carrel had already encountered this ideology and resisted emphatically the foolish feminist pretensions that "both sexes should have the same education, the same powers, and the same responsibilities."

He realized that, in reality "woman differs profoundly from man. Every one of the cells of her body bears the mark of her sex. The same is true of her organs and, above all, of her central nervous system. Physiological laws are as inexorable as those of the sidereal world. They cannot be replaced by human wishes. We are obliged to accept them just as they are. Women should develop their aptitudes in accordance with their own nature, without trying to imitate the males. Their part in the progress of civilization is higher than that of man. They should not abandon their specific functions…"(p. 90)

> "The importance to her of the generative function has not been sufficiently recognized. It is, therefore, absurd to turn women against maternity. The same intellectual and physical training, and the same ambitions, should not be given to young girls as to young boys. Educators should pay very close attention to the organic and mental peculiarities of the male and the female, and to their natural functions. Between the two sexes there are irrevocable differences. And it is imperative to take them into account in constructing the civilized world." (p. 92)

The West's so-called progress towards "women's liberation" and "leadership" has resulted not from common sense or natural progress but from craven obeisance to an irrational ideology – feminism. The misguided trend toward androgynous, co-ed education was the doing of an ignorant, confused people in a mindless age. More recent studies only corroborate Carrel's insights and it is time now for real educators to right the ship.

[72] "Classic column to order," *The Spectator*, Aug. 29, 1998.

[73] *The American Democrat*, by James Fenimore Cooper, p. 168.

[74] "The betrayal of liberalism, I," by Hilton Kramer, *The New Criterion*, Sept. 1998, quoting Arthur M. Schlesinger, Jr.

[75] Paraphrasing a letter from Michael Levin to *The Salisbury Review* on the subject of race, Aug. 29, 1998.

[76] "The betrayal of liberalism, I," ibid, drawn from Lionel Trilling's *The Liberal Imagination*, quoting John Stuart Mill's essay on Coleridge.

[77] Alison Weir, "The Queen Who Still Rules Us," *The Spectator*, October 17, 1998.

[78] David Hughes, "A perfectionist in the wilds of Bohemia," *The Spectator*, October 17, 1998.

[79] The Madness of the American Family," ibid.

[80] Mona Charen, *Conservative Chronicle*, October 21, 1998, "Are powerful women different?"

[81] Cal Thomas, *Conservative Chronicle*, October 28, 1998, "Women 'leaders.'"

[82] *Brain Sex*, by Anne Moir and David Jessel, p. 162.

[83] Ibid, p. 135.

[84] Ibid, pp. 12-13.

Chapter IX (pages 287–316)

[1] *The Professor at the Breakfast Table*, by Oliver Wendell Holmes (1860).

[2] John Knox, *The Fresno Bee*, @ 1972.

[3] Robert Louis Stevenson, *Selected Essays* (Regnery), p. 233. (RLS)

[4] Id, p. 187.

[5] *Deaconesses*, by Aimé Georges Martimort, pp. 71, 119, 181, 182.

[6] RLS, ibid, p. 191.

[7] Id, p. 187.

[8] Id, p. 188.

[9] Id, p. 193.

[10] Id, p. 207.

[11] Id, p. 162.

[12] RLS, ibid, p. 206.

[13] Although it serves a legitimate purpose for Stevenson to raise germane points, he crosses the boundary of worthwhile historical comment. His young Victorian distaste for the fifty-nine-year-old Knox's taking as his second wife a seventeen-year-old girl shows a degree of puritanism or naiveté that belies his qualifications to write on the subject at all. According to RLS, the marriage was arranged, although she was willing and, in fact, bore Knox happily three daughters and was extremely attentive to him. That this grates on RLS's conscience shows little grasp of the female mind and heart, especially since his own marriage was to a divorced woman ten years his senior. Perhaps he and Knox's other nosy judges forgot the various passages in Genesis that did not forbid such marriages, which, if legally performed "by custom and public consent," deserved no censure.

[14] Id, p. 234.

[15] G.K. Chesterton, *Collected Works*, Vol. XVIII, "Robert Louis Stevenson: The Limits of a Craft."

[16] *The Theory of Moral Sentiments*," by Adam Smith, front flyleaf (Conservative Leaders Series, Regnery).

[17] Ibid.

[18] Id, Vol. I, p. 116.

[19] Id, p. 117.

[20] Id, p. 114.

[21] Id, pp. 251-252.

[22] Id, Vol. II, pp. 205-206.

[23] "Reporting Nuremburg," by Carl Rollyson, *The New Criterion*, Sept. 1998.

[24] *What Women Say About Men* (*WWSM*), © Armand Eisen, published by Andrews & McMeel, Ariel Books, Kansas City, p. 10.

[25] Smith, id, p. 209.

[26] Id, pp. 209-210.

[27] Id, p. 211-212.

[28] Id, pp. 212-213.

[29] Id, p. 214. This thought was formerly basic to our patrimony. See *The American Cause*, by Russell Kirk, p. 43: "We do not try to make our law-code identical with the Christian code of ethics. We restrict the operation of our positive laws to those essential matters of public security that cannot be neglected without immediate danger to the whole fabric of civilized society." Numerous other thinkers reinforce this pillar of self-government.

[30] Id, pp. 9-10.

[31] Id, p. 11.

[32] Id.

[33] Id, Vol. I, pp. 249-250.

[34] Id, Vol. II, p. 14.

[35] Id, p. 15.

[36] Id, pp. 15-16.

[37] Id, p. 38 (see also Vol. II, pp. 185-187).

[38] Id, p. 24.

[39] Id, pp. 24-25.

[40] Id, p. 26.

[41] Smith, ibid, Vol. I, pp. 224-225.

[42] Jonathan Last, "What Einstein Did in 1905," reviewing John Stossel's *Einstein's Miraculous Year: Five Papers that Changed the Face of Physics,*" in *The Weekly Standard*, October 5, 1998.

[43] *The Theology of Karl Barth*, by Hans Urs von Balthasar, p. 48.

[44] Id.

[45] *The American Spectator*, "Correspondence," letter from Carol Siemens, October, 1998.

[46] Smith, id, p. 143.

[47] Id, p. 249.

[48] *WWSM*, ibid, Phyllis McGinley, p. 50.

[49] *Goddess Unmasked: The Rise Of Neopagan Spirituality*, by Philip G. Davis (*GU*).

[50] *Goddess Unmasked*, ibid, p. 168.

[51] Id, p. 328.

[52] Id, p. 7.

[53] Id, p. 9.

[54] Id, p. 262.

[55] Id, p. 89.

[56] Id, p. 87.

[57] Id, p. 163.

Chapter X (pages 317–362)

[1] *A Plea For Liberty*, edited by Thomas Mackay (Liberty Classics), "Liberty for Labour," by George Howell, M.P., p. 153, (*APFL*).

[2] *The Diversity Machine*, by Frederick R. Lynch, p. 365. (Free Press).

[3] *Metaphysics*, by Aristotle, Book X, 1058a29-b25, (Princeton, Bollinger Series LXXI, Vol. 2).

[4] Id, *Nichomachean Ethics*, Book VIII, 1162a16-26.

[5] Id, *Economics*, Book I, 1343a.

[6] Id, 1343b7-26.

[7] Id, 1343b26-1344a8.

[8] Kathleen Parker, *The Orlando Sentinel*, @ 1991.

[9] Aristotle, *Economics*, ibid, 1343a16.

[10] Id, *Politics*, Book II, 1269b22-37.

[11] Id, Book I, 1259a37-1259b12.

[12] Id, 1260a19-31.

[13] Jeffrey D. Wallin, "The Relevance of George Washington," *The*

University Bookman, Summer 1998, reviewing Patrick Garrity and Matthew Spalding's *A Sacred Union of Citizens: George Washington's Farewell Address and the American Character*.

Amidst the now familiar self-congratulation, animation to more power, and so forth, issuing from recurring "women's conferences" these days, one misses the depth of thought animating the Founders – i.e., that required for wise, long-term administration of ordered freedom. As Edmund Burke wrote, "to form a *free government* – that is, to temper together these opposite elements of liberty and restraint in one consistent work, requires much thought, deep reflection, a sagacious, powerful, and combining mind." (from Irving Babbitt's *Democracy and Leadership*, p. 161.)

[14] Id.

[15] Morgan N. Knull, "A Champion of Political Prudence," *The University Bookman*, Summer 1998, reviewing Robert Allen Rutland's *James Madison: The Founding Father*.

[16] *Democracy and Leadership*, by Irving Babbitt, p. 38.

[17] Id, p. 40.

[18] Id, pp. 40-41. This theme is frequent in James Fenimore Cooper's *The American Democrat* (1838) (Liberty Classics).

We have also heard Edwin Meese's warning of a "leadership crisis convulsing the nation." (The Heritage Foundation *Member News*, Autumn, 1998) It seems a common theme nowadays in concerned quarters. Morgan Knull discusses it in a review of Robert Allen Rutland's *James Madison; The Founding Father*: "The more perceptive or honest among us cannot help noticing that the real 'devolution' occurring in Congress is expressed not so much in a resurgence of state sovereignty ("O block grants") as the near absence of statesmen. This vacuum of leadership is one more respect in which the present has become disjointed from the past. The regime of civic republicanism that Madison trusted would fortify and sustain the United States seems distant from the avarice and hubris of our contemporary leaders." ("A Champion of Political Prudence," *The University Bookman*, Summer, 1998)

Michael Ledeen writes of the challenge for the U.S. of world terrorism and our need to fight back: "To make matters worse, to date there is no sign of any national leader in the Republic, on either side of the aisle, who is capable of giving voice to these truths and leading the nation in a successful struggle on our behalf. It was inevitable and proper that Republicans should rally round the president when he finally showed some sign of life, but their long silence on foreign policy debacles of this (Clinton) administration made it impossible for them to discuss the matter in its real context." ("Striking Out," *The American Spectator*, October, 1998)(In 2002, George W. Bush might be changing Ledeen's 1998 assessment.)

It is no different in Great Britain, where Philip Gretton criticizes various theories on why John Major was defeated on the issue of European Union: ".... the most important factor; the lack of leadership on the European issue. Why vote for a leader who can neither make up his own mind nor persuade his lieutenants to sing from one hymnsheet? Sleaze and staleness probably insured a Tory defeat. The lack of leadership turned it into a rout." (*The Spectator*, October 10, 1998, "Letters.") And, no, for all the reasons urged herein, this is no reason to recall Margaret Thatcher or a newer model iron lady to man the barricades. After all, what are males good for but leadership! And Thatcher's subtle legacy has been a dearth of male leaders. As a recent writer discloses, despite her superb role-playing, her feminine words did not always hang together with reliable impact. John Campbell discusses a chapter on Thatcher in a book by David Cannadine entitled *Class in Britain*:

> His most fascinating chapter (on impossible class boundaries) brings this all home to Mrs. Thatcher. From her memoirs, he shows that she unconsciously applies all three models to the Grantham of her youth. He quotes her rejection of class as "a communist concept," and her egalitarian belief in individuals as consumers, but contrasts it with her simultaneously fierce identification with the middle class ("our people"). One moment she could propound a Burkean view of hierarchy and natural subordination; the next – like Gladstone – she could be a populist raging against the Establishment. Here were contradictions aplenty. Small wonder that Thatcher never projected a fully coherent social vision. ("A triple vision," by John Campbell, *The Spectator*, November 14, 1998)

Again, while males also can resort to such confusing dialectic, especially in our less than principled or educated times, more is nevertheless expected of males, who at least have the greater potential for reasoned consistency. As Irving Babbitt commented, "Now the true leader is the man of character, and the ultimate root of character is humility," a Confucian conception. (*Democracy and Leadership*, p. 57) Women are not noted for humility, thus are not ideal for leadership. Still another aspect of our need for leadership is brought out by Thomas Fleming, in emphasizing that it involves not merely Horatios at the bridge although they are surely welcome) but a *communal awakening*. Warning against a "one-eyed perspective" that ignores the public ethos, Fleming suggests that

> (I)ndividual resistance is a gesture even more futile than a new pledge of allegiance to a rival gang. Most mom-and-pop grocers know what happens if they refuse to pay protection. Only a community that is coherent and unified can oppose the Mob, whether the *capo* is John Gotti or Bill Clinton (or Barbara Walters or Betty Friedan), and we are a long way, in this country, from the time when such communities existed. That is why the first task is not to get rid of Clinton, defeat Gore, or even lower taxes. Our first task is to begin building the communities of resistance that will some day say, "No" when the Mob (or female candidates) comes into your neighborhood asking for the votes that keep them in power. ("Mob Rules," by Thomas Fleming, *Chronicles*, October, 1998) (parens supplied, with license)

It will take a real leader to rise up and sway the community to this end and one suspects there will be great sacrifice and much vitriol before the people start coming around. It will also take a community of citizens who have the miraculous wisdom and self-control to start re-educating themselves in the vast storehouse of our intellectual inheritance. But, as unreal as they are, the present circumstances of the sexes in this free country cannot continue forever.

Aside from the Nineteenth and Twenty-sixth Amendments, an indicia of just how much this will take might be seen in the Seventeenth Amendment, another bit of effluvium rising from the noxious fumes of progressivism around the turn of the century (1913). Irving Babbitt believed this period ran into problems of standards and leadership because it yielded "traditional standards, humanistic and religious, to naturalism" (scientism and Darwinism). In so doing, instead of striving "to get at standards positively and critically," the progressives failed "to work out critical equivalents of traditional standards" and thus led us into "a series of violent oscillations between humanitarian idealism and a Machiavellian realism." (parenthesis supplied)

> Humanitarian idealism is still firmly entrenched in this country (1924), especially in academic circles, where it seems to be held more confidently, one is almost tempted to say, more smugly, with each succeeding year. …. The gap between what men do and what they ought to do is turning out to be even wider under the humanitarian dispensation than under that of medieval Christianity. Yet the Machiavellian solution is in itself impossible. If the Occident does not get beyond this type of realism, it will simply enact all the pagan stupidities and hasten once more to the pagan doom. (*Democracy and Leadership*, pp. 339-340)

Returning to the 17th Amendment, as former Senator Eugene McCarthy writes in his book, *No-Fault Politics: Modern Presidents, the Press, and Reformers*, "As an ideal, the Senate should be one part House of Lords, one part Greek chorus, and one part Platonic guardians. Instead, the one institution of national government that could (and was intended to) provide wisdom, detachment and balance is reduced to acting as a second House and/or presidential breeding ground." ("Clean Gene: The Forgotten Hero of 1968," a review by Steven Chapman of McCarthy's book, *The American Spectator*, August, 1998)

In itself, this transformation shows the lack of true, constitutional leadership back in the Roosevelt-Wilson era, when men were succumbing to Babbitt's Machiavellian realism (humanitarian idealism) or the siren sing of "equality, the rights of woman, and democracy," with which we are still afflicted. One can only hope that such a recovery will ensue, although, judging from the likes of Steven Chapman, it may take some doing. In his review of McCarthy's book, he shows a nagging dislike for the senator, perhaps misunderstanding his familiar bent for whimsical metaphor, and rather savagely misconstrues the above passage as though the senator were a total fool: "It apparently did not occur to (the senator) that the new role was inevitable once senators, originally elected by state legislatures, were subject to direct election … " In fact, it would take a fool not to see such an obvious connection, which subtlety Chapman misses, as well as the fact that by such careless tinkering we excised a key procedural mechanism for leadership formation – a local crucible of top leaders selecting the most capable for senatorial responsibility – traded in for a popularity contest, or an entertainment where attractive ladies can claim to be telling the "truth as I see it," while tergiversating at will.

Chapman goes on to criticize McCarthy also for labeling the vice-presidency as an anachronism and justifies his own somewhat middling views by mentioning "four reasons vice presidents have gotten more scrutiny over the past fifty years: Harry Truman, Lyndon Johnson, Gerald Ford, and George Bush ... ," each of whom, of course, went on to become president. However, if anything, his examples show that the men were not scrutinized *enough*. The V.P. job affords little opportunity for real public scrutiny on policy grounds, and the four men proved to be far from outstanding examples of male leadership in the classical sense. McCarthy is more right than Chapman and the reason I cite the example is that we shall have to rear more savvy males who at least recognize the problem before we can expect any correction.

[19] *The American Commonwealth*, by James Bryce, Vol. II, p. 1407, (*TAC*).

[20] Id, p. 1411.

[21] Id, p. 1403.

[22] Id, p. 1408.

[23] Id, Vol. I, pp. 432-433.

[24] Id, pp. 133, 1227, 1232 (Vols. I & II).

[25] Id, Vol. II, p. 1228.

[26] Id, p. 1233.

[27] Id, p. 1229.

[28] Id, p. 1408.

[29] Id, p. 1224.

[30] Id, p. 1233.

[31] Id, p. 1411.

[32] Id, p. 1411. The following additional excerpts may amplify the reader's understanding of Bryce's thinking on men and women in America:

> No one who observes America can doubt that whatever is deemed to be for the real benefit of women in the social and industrial sphere will be obtained for them from the goodwill and sympathy of men, without the agency of the political vote. It is on grounds of abstract right, it is because the exclusion from political power is deemed in itself unjust and degrading, and is thought to place woman on a lower level, that this exclusion is resented. .... Yet it must not be supposed that the sentimental arguments are all on one side. There is a widespread apprehension that to bring women into politics might lower their social position, diminish men's deference for them, harden and roughen them, and, as it is expressed, "brush the bloom off the flowers." This feeling is at least as strong among women as among men, and some judicious observers deem it stronger now than it was formerly. Of the many American ladies whose opinion I have from time to time during forty years inquired, the enormous majority expressed themselves hostile .... it is felt that "politics" are more likely to soil women than women to purify "politics." (pp. 1232-1233)

More specifically, Bryce listed the following causes tending to discourage women's suffrage – lurking uncertainties eventually swept aside in the rush to cater to the fair sex – mainly the less lovable, raucous variety: (1) Prohibitionism would be more possible. (2) The growth of the Socialist and Labor Parties, who correctly anticipated help from the women's vote. (3) The unfortunate tendency to exalt direct popular sovereignty and disparage representative government. (4) The hope for social reforms such as those promoted by the Progressive Party. Perhaps this is why Teddy Roosevelt unwisely backed the ladies. (5) The "woman movement." (1233-1234)

[33] *Introduction To the Study of the Law of the Constitution*, by Albert Venn Dicey; "Foreword," by Richard E. Michener, p. *xi*, (*TLC*).

[34] Id, p. *lxxxiv*.

[35] Id, pp. *lxxxiii-lxxxiv*.

[36] Id, p. *lxxxv*.

[37] Id. p. *lxxxvi-lxxxvii*.

[38] Id, p. *lxxxvii*. A.V. Dicey's thought reflects that of a great mind, whose wisdom would be valuable today in Great Britain where Tony Blair's

unrestrained tinkering deserves far more thought than current leaders appear capable of, as for instance, on the egalitarian impulse known as "proportional representation," Dicey considers it a pratfall for the gullible: "Unity of action" and the common good are "of more consequence than a variety of opinion." (p. *lxxxvii*)

[39] Wilfred M. McClay, "Is America an Experiment?" *The Public Interest*, Fall 1998.

[40] *APFL*, ibid, "Preface," by Thomas Mackay, p. *vii*.

[41] Id, "The Impracticability of Socialism," by Edward Stanley Robertson, p. 51.

[42] Id, "Liberty For Labour," by George Howell, pp. 178-179.

[43] Charley Reese, "Men becoming obsolete," *Conservative Chronicle*, October 14, 1998.

[44] Charley Reese, id, October 28, 1998.

[45] *Liberty, Equality, Fraternity*, by James Fitzjames Stephen, edited by Stuart D. Warner, rear cover comment by Stefan Collini, Cambridge University, (*LEF*).

[46] Id, p. 134, quoting from John Stuart Mill's *The Subjection Of Women*.

[47] Id, pp. 134-135.

[48] Id, p. 139.

[49] Id, p. 143.

[50] *Feminism and Freedom*, by Michael Levin, p. 17, quoting John Stuart Mill, 1869.

[51] *LEF*, Ibid, p. 142. James Fitzjames Stephen's views on the human sexes are quite pertinent and deserve careful scrutiny. For the sake of brevity, only a few will be offered here. In contrast to the United States Congress's enactment of the 1964 Civil Rights Bill and the 1972 Education Bill, measures which bulldozed away the very roots of our long customs of sexual order, Stephen agreed with John Stuart Mill on the proper approach to law-making and justice, although that is about all they did agree on:

> ... Mr. Mill proceeds to expound in a long and interesting chapter what I think is the true theory of justice. It may be thus stated: "Justice," like nearly every word which men use in

ethical discussions, is ambiguous, and is exceedingly likely to mislead those who use it unless its ambiguity is recognized and allowed for. It implies, first, the impartial application of a law to the particular cases which fall under it. It implies, secondly, that the law so to be administered shall either be for the general good, or at least shall have been enacted by the legislator with an honest intention to promote the good of those whom it is intended to benefit. (p. 126)

As for "sex equality" or "equality" in general, and Stephen and Mill are in complete disagreement:

... I think (Mr. Mill's doctrine of equality) is unsound in every respect. I think it rests upon an unsound view of history, an unsound view of morals, and a grotesquely distorted view of facts, and I believe that its practical application would be as injurious as its theory false. (p. 135)

Mr. Stephen then dissects Mill's views one by one, very carefully, and in my view demolishes them. He considers relative strength, rights and duties, human nature, natural inequalities, military service, and the like: "Are boys to learn to sew, to keep house, and to cook, and are girls to play cricket, to row, and be drilled like boys? I cannot argue with a person who says Yes. A person who says No admits an inequality between the sexes on which education must be founded, and which it must therefore perpetuate and perhaps increase." (p.141) Obviously, we have passed the bounds he laid down and, no less than Tocqueville, proved him right. Soccer girls or females playing out a role as Air Force pilots or brigade commanders are hardly paradigms for womanhood. Echoing Saint Paul, C.S. Lewis and Gilbert Meilaender on husbands and wives:

No one contends that a man ought to have power to order his wife about like a slave and beat her if she disobeys him. The question of obedience arises in quite another way. It may, and no doubt often does, arise between the very best and most affectionate married people, and it need no more interfere with their mutual affection than the absolute power of the captain of a ship need interfere with perfect friendship and confidence between himself and his first lieutenant.

Feminists will scoff at Stephen, of course, but their shrill voices will defeat their own arguments.

> My object at present is simply to establish the general proposition that men and women are not equals, and that the laws which affect their relations ought to recognize that fact. …. (pp. 144)
>
> I think that wise and good men ought to rule those who are foolish and bad. To say that the sole function of the wise and good is to preach to their neighbors, and that everyone indiscriminately should be left to do what he likes, and should be provided with a rateable share of the sovereign power in the shape of a vote, and that the result of this will be the direction of power by wisdom, seems to me to be the wildest romance that ever got possession of any considerable number of minds. (p. 156)

As if reinforcing my argument that "equality" is a geometric term not suitable for politics, Stephen has this to say:

> Equality, therefore, if not like liberty, a word of negation, is a word of relation. It tells us nothing definite unless we know what two or more things are affirmed to be equal and what they are in themselves, and when we are informed upon these points we get only statements about matters of fact, true or false, important or not, as it may be. (p. 163)

These brief excerpts cannot do full justice to his treatise, which I hope the reader will be able to study at his leisure.

[52] "John Stuart Mill and Liberalism – A Symposium – *The Political Science Reviewer*, 1995 (ISI).

[53] *The Diversity Machine*, by Frederick R. Lynch, ibid, p. 24, (*TDM*).

[54] Id, p. 335.

[55]

[56] Id, p. 362.

[57] Id, pp. 363-364.

[58] Id. Another example of our current addiction to "gender identity" or "race-class-politics" and sexual egalitarianism can be seen in the writing of former Assistant Secretary of the Treasury, Paul Craig Roberts, who, with Lawrence Stratton, authored *The New Color Line* (1995), a commendable treatise against racial quotas, as far as it goes. As a 1960s civil rights activist, Roberts regrets our resort to quotas but is not ready to root it out at the source, the 1964 Civil Rights Law. The

many like Lynch, Roberts and Stratton who adhere to America as an egalitarian society stripped of race-class-gender preferences must learn that such a goal is probably beyond any reasonable "theory of moral sentiments" and, in any case, *will not arise under laws setting race-class-gender criteria*. If I say, "You shall not use sex to judge appearance," I am forcing future judges to invent rules as to sex.

Roberts and Stratton seem to misconstrue various aspects of our system when they claim that, "Where the opportunity is open to them, as in California, with its public referendum system, citizens are moving to take back their sovereignty over the law. Momentum is building ... for a 1996 initiative, modeled on the 1964 Civil Rights Act, to prohibit the use of quotas by ... public institutions." (p. 2) In fact, the people did pass this peculiar initiative (Prop. 209) but, what Stratton and Roberts do not mention is that the people had little idea what they were doing other than to vote against quotas, even though the proposition made no mention of quotas, and the effect was not to regain "sovereignty" but to further empower the courts to rule their lives. Prattle and pecksniffery as to race and sex persist. (A tar baby.) While one senses their worthwhile goal, the authors' rhetoric on "race, class, and gender" reflects the inevitable brier patch resulting from their "liberal" desire to erase distinctions and any semblance of discriminating human judgment other than what conforms to their idea of democracy and so forth. They rightly abhor "polarization," "determinism," "materialistic basis of thought," and "group politics" but fail to see that their rather crude "civil rights" laws are the cause.

And to accentuate the error, in their loyalty to 1964 and "moral causes" that Adam Smith and others have warned against, Roberts and Stratton make no distinction as to sex. Men and women are to be as "equal" as "black and white," except where a court might otherwise find "bona fide qualifications based on sex." Despite their lofty suppositions, however, until we repeal all laws on sex other than in long-tested common and statutory law (marital, domestic, etc.) and the criminal law, we shall remain vulnerable to what the authors call "feminist hegemony." (p. 167)

Two other formidable graduates of the 1960s civil rights era are Peter Collier and David Horowitz, who have also written about "equality before the law" but have not yet seen fit to separate sex from race on the law books, although I suspect they would if pressed. All four of these gentlemen need to see the intricacies of the legislation involved. Since we are no more "equal" but much more sexist, racist and befuddled than fifty years ago, more laws are not the answer; Repeal is the answer. At the same time, Collier and Horowitz are very attuned to the ravages of feminism and offer an interesting sketch of another "disorderly" American woman in the person of Angela Davis of Marin-County shoot-out fame (acquitted by a bemused Marin County jury and, in 1997 elevated by a blinkered California University system as a full professor in the Women of Color Research Cluster, bloviating demurely within the History of Consciousness Department at the University of California, Santa Cruz). (*The Race Card*, by Peter Collier and David Horowitz, 1997)

As the authors put it, "The names themselves sound like something from the course catalogue of the University of Mars, and they speak to the vulgarization that has overtaken American higher education in the last thirty years." (p. 170) With her womanly wisdom, forever adding to the annals of higher thought, she describes one of her courses, "A survey of the principle (sic) ideological issues of the 20th century; attitudes toward sex, race, class, work, violence and knowledge viewed from the perspective of structuralism and semiological theories of culture." (pp. 176-177) That the Nineteenth Amendment taught us the value of such esoteric womanly wisdom! A remarkable misfit, shorn of the right order of the sexes and cut loose from ancient folkways, footloose on the path of progress without the benefit of patriarchal "moral sentiments," Ms. Davis is a symbol of our times of havoc and dysfunction.

[59] "The West Under Siege," by Roger Kimball, reviewing David Gress's *From Plato To NATO: The Idea Of the West and Its Opponents*, in *National Review*, Sept. 28, 1998.

[60] *The Education of Henry Adams* (*EHA*), by Henry Adams, p. 415. Perhaps like most civilized people through the ages, Adams appreciated women for their beauty but primarily their fecundity – their ineluctable destiny of immense import for mankind – and he wrote passionately of errant trends:

> Everyone, even among Puritans, knew that neither Diana of the Ephesians nor any of the oriental Goddesses was worshipped for her beauty. She was Goddess because of her force; she was

the animated dynamo; she was reproduction – the greatest and most mysterious of all energies; all she needed was to be fecund. (p. 356)

From the male, she could look for no help; his instinct of power was blind. The Church had known more about women than science will ever know, and the historian who studied the sources of Christianity felt sometimes convinced that the Church had been made by the woman chiefly as her protest against man. At times, the historian would have been almost willing to maintain that the man had overthrown the Church chiefly because it was feminine. After the overthrow of the Church, the woman had no refuge except such as the man created for himself. She was free; she had no illusions; she was sexless; she had discarded all that the male disliked; and although she secretly regretted the discard, she knew that she could not go backward. She must, like the man, marry machinery. (p. 414)

Adams has a sense of something wrong, although he has not sought the root causes, preferring instead to wax poetic or ironic. One hopes he wouldn't have become thoroughly postmodern in accepting trends as going "forward."

[61] *Visions of Order (VO)*, p. 63.

[62] *VO*, ibid, p. 15.

[63] Associated Press, *The Fresno Bee*, "Prejudice may be ingrained at a deeper, subconscious a level," regarding research by Dr. Anthony Greenwald of the University of Washington and Dr. Mahzarin Banaji of Yale University, developers of the Implicit Associations Test, Nov. 13, 1998.

[64] *VO*, ibid, p. 75.

[65] *Ideas Have Consequences (IHC)*, by Richard M. Weaver, p. 177.

[66] Id. Professor Weaver's insights are similar to those of Bryce and Adams, and somewhat like Santayana's:

At the source of the disorder there lies, I must repeat, an impiety toward nature, but we have seen how, when a perverse decision has been made, material factors begin to exert a disproportionate effect. Woman has increasingly gone into the world as an economic "equal" and therefore competitor of man (once again equality destroys fraternity). …. The ultimate reason lies in the world picture, for once woman has been degraded in that picture – and putting her on a level with the male is more truly a degradation than an elevation – she is more at the mercy of economic circumstances.

With her superior closeness to nature, her intuitive realism, her unfailing ability to detect sophistry in mere intellectuality, how was she cozened into the mistake of going modern? After the gentleman went, the lady had to go too. No longer protected, the woman now has her career, in which she makes a drab pilgrimage from two-room apartment to job to divorce court. ....

Well was it said that he who leaves his proper sphere shows that he is ignorant both of that which he quits and that which he enters. Women have been misled by the philosophy of activism into forgetting that for them, as custodians of the values, it is better to "be" than to "do."

If our society were minded to move resolutely toward an ideal, its women would find little appeal, I am sure, in lives of machine-tending and money-handling. And this is so just because woman will regain her superiority when again she finds privacy in the home and becomes, as it were, a priestess radiating the power of proper sentiment. Her life at its best is a ceremony. When William Butler Yeats in "A Prayer for My Daughter" says, "Let her think opinions are accursed," he indicts the modern displaced female, the nervous, hysterical, frustrated, unhappy female, who has lost all queenliness and obtained nothing. What has this act of impiety brought us except, in the mordant phrase of Henry James's The Bostonians, an era of "long-haired men and short-haired women"? (pp. 178-180)

These words recall Margaret Meade's vision of a happy woman: "When the role of wife and mother is exalted." It is possible that Weaver's assessment would be even more accurate were it not for Broadway-Hollywood ("show business"), which sedates the public (and women, especially) with images of unrealistic glamour and public display of female sexuality whose power formerly was properly centered in the home. Media approbation leaves them to believe that, contrary to Meade, the roles of showgirl, Voyager captain, vampire slayer, and stripteaser are "exalted." Also, knowing what we do about feminism, he would understand better how woman has been "cozened" into her new role of "independence."

[67] Id, p. 178.

[68] *Visions of Order* (*VO*), ibid, p. 5.

[69] Id, p. 5.

[70] Id, p. 6.

[71] Id, p. 6.

[72] Id, p. 16.

[73] Barbara Amiel, *National Review*, Nov. 24, 1998.

[74] Michael Ledeen, *The American Spectator*, @ 1990.

[75] Jane Larkin Crane, *National Review*, Oct. 28, 1998, reviewing *The War of the Words*, by Susan Gubar, Sandra M. Gilbert and Elaine Showalter.

[76] Carol Iannone, *Commentary*, @ 1988.

[77] Jeffrey Hart, *National Review*, Sept. 30, 1988.

[78] *What Will Happen to God?* By William Oddie, pp. 154-155.

[79] *VO*, ibid, p. 85.

[80] "Science and Design," by William Dembski, *First Things*, Oct. 1998, on Michael Behe's *Darwin's Black Box*.

[81] James Tunstead Burtchaell, "The Necessity of Community," reviewing George Dennis O'Brien's *All the Essential Half Truths About Higher Education*, in *First Things*, Oct. 1998, quoting Charles Hutchins.

[82] Tom Bethell, "The Ex-Gay Movement: Homosexuals can change, Anthony Falzarano says," *The American Spectator*, Oct, 1998.

[83] "Men want it all, too," by Gayle Vassar Melvin (Knight Ridder Newspapers), on Sonny Massey's *Working Fathers*, in *The Fresno Bee*, Oct. 19, 1998.

[84] *The Fresno Bee*, Oct. 22, 1998, on 17-year-old Bulgarian-American gymnast, Dominique Moceanu.

[85] John Lehman, "Our Military Condition," *The American Spectator*, Oct., 1998.

[86] John Richard Neuhaus, "The Public Square," *First Things*, Oct., 1998.

[87] *Selected Works Of Edmund Burke*, Vol. I, Liberty Fund, 1999. "Thoughts on the Cause of the Present Discontents," pp. 154-155.

[88] *Wanting a Child*, an anthology edited by Helen Schulman and Jill Bialosky (Farrar, Straus, & Giroux).

[89] This aspect, that women are more apt to be driven by "their own wanting" and their families' interests or perceptions than the common, long-term good is, of course, open to further research, although gender-gap statistics thus far are revealing. Another instance arises in Marianne Means's Hearst News item on "gender barriers" previously discussed. For one thing, her approach itself is single-minded, based on the assumption that it is just a matter of sexual equivalency – women are mere statistics, and damn sociology, biology, history, the common good – it's more a matter of her own wanting. She cites Congresswoman Jennifer Dunn's campaign for the position of House Majority Leader, which was apparently based in part on a contention that the GOP leadership needs a woman's voice to soften the party's image and present a more compassionate face to the world. Ironically, most female politicians these days flaunt their motherhood, although a century ago it was considered a distraction and a disadvantage for a public career. When Rep. Pat Schroeder, also a mother, arrived in Congress in 1973, a male veteran lawmaker told her that he preferred his women cuddly and sweet-smelling. She replied she preferred her men the same way. (*The Fresno Bee*, November 22, 1998)

The main points brought out here are [1] the feminist sassy, cutesy approach to Madisonian seriousness; [2] injecting sex into the corridors of power inevitably demeans the process; [3] a certain dystopia appears in promoting absentee mothers; [4] the entire process has been dumbed down; [5] the American people have only themselves to blame for electing people like Schroeder year in year out, even allowing her to retire voluntarily; and [6] men should not be so hamstrung by civility towards women to accommodate such obstruction of good governance. And, oh yes, womanly "compassion" is a two-edged sword which men have ordinarily applied reasonably and quite naturally in the constitutional process but now is being used as dishonest leverage for more state welfare, greater laxity, and rejection of traditions and the Constitution. It is merely a rehash of motherhood, apple pie, kissing babies and Senator Foghorn. The all-male franchise dealt with this much better than sanctimonious co-eds; and private charity once dished out ample compassion much more effectively *and morally* than the county welfare department. One can only hope that Marianne Means is right in finding that "the momentum and novelty" of female candidates "have passed."

A still further dubious example of womanly "compassion" is reported by Harold O.J. Brown regarding the current fancy of promoting homosexuality for the young under the guise of befuddled "love." It should alert us to the moral miasma characteristic of women's "unconditional love" when misapplied out of its familial purview, much like Eve's accommodation of the serpent. It seems that a recent Lambeth Conference of Anglican bishops struggled with the issue of homosexuality, that is, whether to endorse it or to reinforce biblical teachings against it. "With the Africans, a zealous concern for human suffering was combined with a determination to uphold the church's traditional understanding of sexual morality." (*The Religion & Society Report*, Nov. 1998, The Howard Center for Family, Religion and Society) Apparently, in contrast to more lax American and English bishops, Asians side with the Africans on this issue, and fortunately the latter carried the day. In the process, however, one Anglican Bishop Catherine Waynick, an American, had her compassionate, but less than profound say, likening the church's criticism of homosexuality to its long tolerance of slavery, saying, "Our call is not to correctness, but to love." Regarding which ringing indictment, Dr. Brown has this to say

> The centuries-old stand of the church against the ordination of women (not to mention their consecration as bishops) is supported, but not clearly mandated in Scripture; the condemnation of homosexuality is explicit. It is unfortunate that a female bishop, who embodies the church's rejection of tradition on an issue of church organization, should also seek to overturn its position on morality.

Dr. Brown is being very circumspect here, yet still discloses a serious flaw in present-day Anglican ecclesiology: Waynick's asseveration shows why she should not be a pastor, much less a bishop and, for that matter, serves as another reason why women should not be ordained at all, much less consecrated. Brown goes on to say,

> Where the Anglican churches are growing and thriving, they also promote evangelism and traditional morals; where they

are willing to go along with the latest trends and preferences in sexual matters, they're in decline, in some places almost moribund. A similar fate seems to be overtaking some of the other compromising mainline churches in the United States, where adoption of the "Anything Goes" morality seems to drive more people away than it attracts.

We see a final example of women's dubious public contribution in Barbara Walters, a veritable guru of the airwaves, whose sexual attraction has long since drifted into mere womanliness, without the semblance of wisdom to go with her Fourth Estate privileges. I do not watch her shows, catching only an occasional glimpse in passing, yet the fact she is still aired as a hostess or commentator seems to speak volumes on the level of intelligence and understanding of current media moguls. One can only wonder what influence such immense exposure to the public eye can have for the future of the republic, that is, if we are still allowed to think on such matters. My example goes back to ABC's 20/20 episode previously discussed, as reported by The Independent Women's Forum. (in their newsletter, *femina*, July, 1998) As already mentioned (Chapter VIII), in response to John Stossel's remark that the "logic" of sex equality (!) would lead to endless law suits, Walters apparently replied, "But on the other hand, if you didn't, you would not have women's sports. It was so unbalanced." One can picture a smiling Barbara uttering such a monstrous distortion for the viewing public, enjoying her "compassionate" woman's license to pontificate on matters beyond her grasp, actually getting paid enormous sums to misinform the once virtuous and savvy citizenry in our new world of pulchritudinous parlor punditry. Alice's wonderland has metamorphized as postmodern Anglo-America, with Walters as a bonafide herstorian diaphanously instructing a befuddled people on the malfunctioning of their republic as if it were merely a chatty bridal shower. The Nineteenth Amendment strikes again.

CONCLUSION (PAGES 363–372)

[1] *Summa Contra Gentiles*, by Thomas Aquinas, Book One, p. 63, quoting from Aristotle's *Nichomachean Ethics*, I 3 (1094b-24). As for those who suggest that Aquinas demeaned women, see Michael Nolan's

clarification in *First Things*, Nov. 1998, "What Aquinas Never Said About Women": "All in all, then, those searching for evidence that Christianity has viewed women as defective to man will have to look elsewhere than to Thomas Aquinas."

[2] *Democracy and Leadership*, by Irving Babbitt, p. 56.

[3] *History of Political Philosophy*, edited by Leo Strauss and Joseph Cropsey, on "Immanuel Kant," by Pierre Hassner, pp. 592-593.

[4] Brad Lowell Stone, "Vocation, Liberal Education, and Vocationalism," *Humanitas*, Vol. XI, No. 1, 1998, citing Cicero's *De Officiis*.

[5] *Summa Contra Gentiles*, ibid.

[6] Id, p. 70.

[7] Id, p. 71 (Eccles., 3.25).

[8] One man who understood Ben Franklin's advice was apparently John Wayne, the strapping, manly American movie hero after whom a Southern California airport is named. He was married three times, to little Latin women. As L.M. Boyd explains it in an item in *The Fresno Bee*, circa 1972,

> Why is it Hollywood hero John Wayne not just once nor twice but thrice married little Latin women? So inquires a client. That's pretty personal. Wayne ought not be called upon to explain it. However, that great French love and war expert Madame Dariaux once wrote: "The ideal formula must be an American husband and a Latin wife. The husband will find it bliss to be considered the master at last. And the wife will probably be overwhelmed by so much courtesy and respect." Might mention Madame Dariaux also contended the worst possible marriage was that of an American wife and a Latin husband.

This seems to suggest that American males are not as attentive to a congruous balance of the sexes as they should be.

An example of current misconceptions appears in a letter from Edward T. Oakes, S.J., to First Things, commenting on an article by J. Budziszewski on the natural law. Father Oakes writes,

> .... can conscience change? .... (T)his example occurred to me precisely because of the example of Aristotle: although his analysis of ethics is still far superior to most of his modern competitors, there can be no question that the conscience of mankind has

changed since Aristotle's day, most notoriously on the question of slavery and the equality of women. Simply put, can this evolution of the conscience of the human race be accounted for ... ?

Father Oakes is too intelligent to slip into such an innocent error so casually, reflecting the general male insouciance or carelessness regarding the sexes, as Nicholas Davidson, for one, has brought out. Without confronting Oakes's perception of the sexes, Professor Budziszewski nevertheless offers an excellent insight for our purposes:

> Like grammar, conscience has both an unchanging deep structure and a changing surface structure. The great Scholastic thinkers recognized this, speaking of both *synderesis*, which cannot err, and *conscientia*, which can. A phenomenon they knew about but did not analyze is that *conscientia* cannot only err but rationalize; we can either try to come to terms with first principles, or play tricks with them instead. Just as Father Oakes suggests, the *conscientia* of a society can either advance or regress, depending on which of these responses it chooses to make. The focus of my article is the perverse tribute that our rationalizations pay to the very principles they deny.

Here, the professor skirts around Oakes's assumption of an "evolution" in which "mankind's conscience has changed on the equality of women," but does offer an incisive dichotomy for our purposes, of gullible conscience *vs* perduring biological truth – the Eliot-Kirkian permanent things. A full discussion would require laying out the "unchanging deep structure" of the human sexes which Oakes ignores, and examining the more deceptive surface appearances which feminism has been allowed to rationalize and play tricks with. As usual with merely polemical abstractions, unless carefully handled, "equality" makes for a poor parameter for humanity, and Oakes is far too premature in declaring an impossible "equality of the sexes," or an "evolution" that has spanned all of about fifty years of revisionist, vindictive theory from malcontents. Our knowledge of women has surpassed Aristotle's in important but not all respects. Undistracted by the idea of "equality" and our own preoccupations with "she who must be obeyed," Aristotle's views are less obsequious, yet he showed no actual disrespect for women and circumstances in his day probably justified his views. The fact remains, however, as it did in James Fitzjames

Stephen's day, that men are the physically stronger sex and even the intervening romantic age did not change this or its miscellaneous side effects. While we know that women have their own valuable functions, Aristotle was simply not kowtowing to public women as men do today. Chivalry and romanticism have not transformed women into the male equivalents the public rhetoric tends to insinuate, or vice versa.

More to the point, however, such honors are again only exceptions proving the rule. No matter how good a speech a woman can give, she is still less an orator than a woman giving a speech. The ultimate problem remains that, even though they are capable (they have mouths, two legs, a tongue, two arms, and so forth), in public roles they still do not sound as "painterly," well-blended, integrated, natural, à propos, unbizarre, seemly, manly, leader like, substantial as men. Shrillness and beauty cannot mature a wine before its time no matter how clever and articulate.

9 Roger Scruton, "Rousseau and the origins of liberalism," *The New Criterion*, October, 1998. His thinking is similar to Professor Richard Epstein's, as expressed in his book, *Forbidden Grounds*, and elsewhere.

10 *Amo, Amas, Amat*, by Eugene Ehrlich. Forcing a drastic sex change on an unsuspecting society with "civil-rights-equality" edicts hardly brought the "advance" the ladies crow about. Women are certainly more visible in more ways than one – not only functionally but also quite physiologically (in the flesh) – and they are holding down jobs galore, but there is yet no sign of a real "advance" either for them or for society, psychologically, demographically, or individually. On top of that, with ever more women populating crucial opinion centers like publishing and media houses, their gender bias is blocking out Madisonian seriousness and objectivity while muffling the "refinement and enlargement of the public views" in ways not very salubrious for the republic. In effect, Big Sister has infiltrated the brain centers of civilization and civil apoplexy looms, as many men endure the discomfiture of an upside-down world in which women boss men.

Granted, again, if we discount the latent ladyness and the voices, there are many women who can do the job quite well, whether as judges, editors, office managers, even vice presidents or chairmen of activist conservative causes dealing with male pursuits like the military, the law, and so forth, but the masquerade persists. For the male subordinates, it is a job, and men can survive, even though such ladies are not the result of real, natural competition as much as of arbitrary social engineering that has diminished the number of strong, principled, knowledgeable males. But present-day trends in greater women's authority do not represent real power as much as a temporary, deferential perquisite ceded by men not yet attuned to ontological social currents, the "real tendency of Providential social forces" – daughters elevated by fathers for a day in time. While it would be wise now to consider putting the first team back in the game, the trouble is that, after so long, an inevitable distortion in perceptions has resulted, creating a dysfunctional wonderland that is considered by too many as normal "evolution" merely because too few have managed to question the odd pattern. Yet, while it is true that some quadrupeds see the female of the species playing powerful roles, such a reversal has never been true of the hominoids.

As if to dramatize the point that 1964's Titles VII and IX were ill-advised and should be repealed, Heinrich A. Rommen's offered analogous words of caution in 1936 with regards to the events in Germany, which eventually were published in the United States in 1947 as *The Natural Law* (and in 1998 by Liberty Fund), in which he expounds on principles similar to those discussed by J. Budziszewski. Rommen is "relentlessly critical of legal positivism" such as that giving rise to Titles VII and IX, finding that

> Law ... has its basis in nature. Man has an inborn notion of right and wrong, and law in its very essence rests not upon the arbitrary will of a ruler or upon the decree of a multitude, but upon nature, i.e., upon innate ideas (*non scripta sed nata lex*). Cicero (106-43 B.C.) was the interpreter and transmitter of the Stoic doctrine of natural law. The *lex nata*, the law within us, he regards as the foundation of law in general. It is not to be gathered, as a general concept by way of abstraction, from the law of the Twelve Tables or from the praetor's edict – that is, from the positive law – but *ex initima philosophia* . Since it is identical with right reason, it is universally valid, unchangeable and incapable of being abrogated; for its author is the divine reason itself – taken, of course, in a pantheistic, impersonal sense. It is also called eternal law. Cicero could thus write: "If the principles of Justice were founded on the decrees of peoples, the edicts of princes, or the decisions of judges, then Justice

would sanction robbery and adultery and forgery of wills, in case these acts were approved by the votes or decrees of the populace. But if so great a power belongs to the decisions of and decrees of fools that the laws of Nature can be changed by their votes, then why do they not ordain that what is bad and baneful shall be considered good and salutary? .... For since an intelligence common to us all makes things known to us and formulates them in our minds, honorable actions are ascribed by us to virtue, and dishonourable actions to vice; and only a madman would conclude that these judgments are matters of opinion.

As Russell Hittinger tells us in the Introduction, "the reader will appreciate that the book was written by a lawyer in response to a political and legal crisis" brought about by the Nazi Party as it "deftly used German legislative, administrative, and judicial institutions to impose totalitarian rule." "...(T)he philosophical inquiry leads the reader to the perennial questions." For one thing, as J. Budziszewiski makes clear, the natural law is not grounded solely in Paganism but also in Judeo-Christianity. Also, despite his distrust of usurpative positive law, Rommen quite definitely sees its value, properly managed, in perfecting the natural law and, as Hittinger tells us, it is only when "social, political, and legal institutions are challenged," that "it becomes necessary once again to inquire into first things," as, one should add, we are doing in the present book. As Robert Weissberg also realizes ("The Abduction of Tolerance," *Society*, Nov./Dec. 1998), the process of judgment is quite complicated "because," as Hittinger puts it, "the vindication (of natural law) depends upon an array of principles about the human person, the relation between intellect and will, and the nature of society. In a relatively healthy culture, these principles are given expression through (the above institutions) as well as through the judgments of common sense." As I hope the reader has surmised, it is my contention that feminism has caused a similar crisis in our society, such that with the ongoing cultural wars we can not honestly claim to be at the moment a "relatively healthy society" and thus need again to "inquire into first things" instead of only compassionate community concerns, sports, music, the weather, and raising money for public broadcasting that peppers its self-laudatory, non-commercial spiel with commercial advertising.

[11] *The Best of Burke*, edited by Peter J. Stanlis, p. 208. "Speech on Conciliation with the Colonies," March 22, 1775.

[12] Id, pp. 184-185.

[13] Id, pp. 215-216.

[14] *Little Dorrit*, by Charles Dickens, p. 162.

[15] Ibid.

Reminiscent of the rampaging Bastille mob, we see an up-to-date version of "destroying institutions" in the equally Jacobinic acts of the National Organization of Women (NOW), as reflected in their latest rampage directed against the University of Southern California (USC) and the University of California, Los Angeles (UCLA), under the Robespierrian edict of Title IX of the 1972 Civil Rights Act. As reported in *The Fresno Bee* (December 11, 1998), NOW is filing complaints with the U.S. Department of Education's Office of Civil Rights, alleging that USC and UCLA "favor men's athletic programs over women's sports." NOW's spokeswoman, Linda Joplin, claims that the two schools are not "in compliance" and should use this "opportunity to make the changes that should have been made 10, 15, 20 years ago." So much for American women as loving wives! We are all cuckolded King Arthurs now. Apparently, the main contention is that, for instance, while USC men's basketball one year received $809,570, women's basketball received only $129,626; at UCLA it was $552,241 to the men, and $295,684 to the women.

This kind of shenanigan is a blemish on our society that should stir sensible leaders to action. It is no "advance" for women to see Joplin uttering such nonsense, no sign of "power" when a foolish law long overdue for repeal allows such bullying. Are these the Chestertonian women who are "horrible in a herd, a nightmare, a Bacchic orgie, a Witches' Sabbath"? It would appear so. Would the suit have had standing under the common law? Not if knowledgeable attorneys aborted it at the start with sound reason, common sense and settled customs. It is based on "equity," yet equity requires a thorough balancing of facts, morality, and fairness, aspects circumvented by careless positive laws. As we have mentioned, statutes of "sex equality" were reductio-ad-absurdum reflexes that backfired, leaving us with unwarranted legal shackles allowing Cinderella's evil stepsisters to sue their brothers, attack, dismember, weaken, distract, and drain entire institutions, severing worthwhile customs on narrow feminist, chauvinist grounds. Jezebel has been given a leg up on a bamboozled society. Title IX allows women to sue an artist for not using their favorite colors, or for using the whole range of his palette instead of merely a few chosen drab tints. As Robert Weissberg put it so aptly, "a discrimination-free society is not a tolerant society."

Girls need instruction to become responsible adults, but not through sports like boys, for whom sports serve as an inherent rite of passage; a proving, testing ground; lessons in cooperation, teamwork, fellowship, humility, endurance, rules, tactics, style, discipline, physical courage; an outlet for young testosterone as its proprietor builds character. This is especially true for adolescents in primary and secondary education. As for higher education, although the subject is more controversial, still a better case can be made for men's sports than for women's (although the terms "men" and "women" for 20-year-olds remains questionable). Even in college and university, the young male physical urge remains strong and athletics provide a productive, valuable means to supplement an all-around education while building healthy bodies. While girls too need exercise, equating the two is like servicing an eighteen-wheeler as a Volkswagen bug. As L.M. Boyd reported in *The Fresno Bee* some years back,

> Highly athletic women do not tend to have a particularly easy time in childbirth. Seemingly weak and fragile girls do. A medico named Dr. V.R. Rhodes therefore concludes, "Muscular development is contrary to essential femininity."

In any case, in view of all these parameters (and more), to compare male and female college sports as if they shared the same frame of reference is sheer foolishness. *Yet Title IX ordains that it be so!*

Carrying it a step further, as the *Fresno Bee* item brings out quite clearly and simply, intercollegiate athletics cost money and women's sports don't match men's earning capacity. Thus, as a purely free market concern, Title IX is out of its depth, as are radical efforts like NOW's to level us down to a sterile mediocrity. When, as reported by USC's attorney, football and basketball teams earn the money to finance the entire athletic program for all sports, where is the equity that requires that women's programs receive equal amounts to men's football and basketball? And, if one surmises that a fair allocation is obviously necessary, who best should administer it, NOW, the courts, Congress, or the college administrations themselves who know best what the demands are and what their students need. After all, colleges are manned by educators whose job presumably still is to administer an education (one hopes, to include a healthy dose of the best that has been thought and said) to their charges – in *locus parentis* – so, what business is it of NOW's? One senses the wide chasm separating the world of reality and the disruptive world of NOW, when UCLA's spokeswoman remarks that UCLA "doesn't compare funding for the men's and women's basketball teams. We fund our programs to be competitive." Bless her heart! Competition brings out truth and excellence, where NOW only seeks "equality" or "equity" with unclean hands. Their "equity" has nothing to do with truth, excellence and competitiveness, especially when NOW spokeswomen assume desserts not earned and ignore wider, deeper concerns in the rush to their own selfish goals. Wise legislators representing a wise people would refine and enlarge their views to the point of repealing this insidious statute.

[16] As Burke advised, "We are too apt to consider things in the state in which we find them, without sufficiently adverting to the causes by which they have been produced, and possibly may be upheld." (*Reflections on the Revolution in France*, p. 172.) Which returns us to education, to books, to the written word on other than the Internet's "short remarks about current events and items of interest," to ancient folkways and Kirkean-Eliot permanent things. While we are not all that geared to the basics – the Constitution, our Anglo-Saxon heritage, our Indo-European civilization, honesty, prescriptions, permanent things, our communal morality, it is probably because we are not very well versed in any of them. Unless we are so geared – mainly the humanities – anything we manage to do will probably not turn out very worthwhile. Instead, perhaps it is best we not always "be doing something" to rearrange our polity according to the preferred vision of the Internet moment, in which talented writers vie with their peers over the most Jacobin reform or latest vote count. In view of the prevailing ignorance and misrepresentation of Western Civilization, one can reasonably conclude that our vaunted system of public education has seriously failed us, having for decades devolved into theories of diversity, problem-solving, multiculturalism, and historical revisionism.

Obviously, women's studies should be done away with, at least as any sort of higher education. Perhaps they could serve as a form of therapy for psychopathic young women. The national Department of Education should be dismantled and scattered at sea, to allow education to become a local challenge, motivated by families and parents rather than bureaucrats and public sophisters. The various theories of education should be allowed to engage the minds of intelligent, responsible teachers unfettered by modern politicians, which would be enough of a task by itself as it returned us to a rigorous dialectic rather than a politically immobilizing dyschezia. One important aspect should be kept in mind, however, namely, the deep origins, long history and significance of the U.S. Constitution, without which we would not be a nation and with which we must survive. This is where the common good germinates, along with our religious heritage. It need not be a contrived civic project as much as a motive for absorbing history and philosophy, their tributaries and adjuncts. Meanwhile, a symptom of the present faulty system persists in the mass-market textbook industry.

For our purposes, a helpful essay on the subject of textbooks is offered by Gilbert T. Sewall and Stapley W. Emberling (*Society*, Nov./Dec. 1998, "Review Essay: A New Generation of History Textbooks"), from which one gathers that nationalized and even state-centered education is leading to an inordinate influence of none too careful or conscientious textbook publishers whose mass productions reflect the political sentiment of the left or of the moment and are dumbing down the literature to our quick-byte, popular culture rather than a diligent engagement of established, proven disciplines. "Three states – California, Texas and Florida – are extremely powerful on account of their size and their state-level textbook adoption practices." Whatever revisionist fad these states favor ends up influencing the whole country. The reader has probably heard of the so-called "national history standards," reflecting the on-going fascination with multiculturalism – the regnant, socially suicidal educationalist notion that all cultures are equal except our own. For example, the authors tell of Houghton Mifflin's new pastiche, *To See a World*, a surrender of United States history to "world cultures," in which

> (C)overage of European history has been radically cut, supplanted by African, Caribbean, and Latin American studies.

The 700-page book wraps up the period from the so-called Columbian Exchange to the Industrial Revolution in six pages. Ancient Rome, Greece, and Early Christianity together merit a mere 30 pages. Twentieth-century Europe, including Russia and the Soviet Union to the end of the Cold War, is given a total of 20 pages. ... in the spirit of cultural equivalency, the study of Europe has been demoted to about one-seventh of the book. The following passage reflects its flawed historiography and a radical change in subject priorities in such an abbreviated treatment:

Unlike the Renaissance man, the Renaissance woman was not encouraged to develop her abilities. One male writer gave Renaissance woman this advice: "It does not befit (suit) women to handle weapons, to ride, to play tennis, to wrestle, and to do many other things that befit men ..." (Baldasare Castiglione, *The Book of the Courtier*, 1528)

"Some Renaissance women ignored this advice. Some became writers or artists. Others became skilled workers or shop owners. A few held political power."

This is not serious women's history but feminist propaganda. In the same lesson children meet Isabella d'Este and Christine de Pizan, who together merit about the same amount of space as Nicolaus Copernicus. As inclusion takes place, of course, editors must renounce older historical figures and subjects.

Here is another instance of "herstory," revising the past to suit the ladies' fancy. One could go on but space limitations forbid. Simply put, "the United States is reinvented as a 'land of diversity,' and a 'nation of many peoples.' What remains solely of America's civic being (what I have been trying to emphasize – the origins and meaning of the Constitution and the common good) is the immigrant experience, and in keeping with its view of the American past, the book stresses hardships late 19th and early 20th century migrants faced in a hard hearted land." (paren supplied) The anti-American bent is not very surprising when we know that "the chief architect of the proposed national history standards," Gary B. Nash, is the driving force, assisted by "a radical Hispanic anthropologist and a trendy historian of Africa." The present writer strongly believes that "sex equality" is a large part of the problem, since educators these days include many high-profile women and womanly ambivalence is the principle characteristic of multiculturalism. The educated ladies too often argue that "truth" is relative. And one wonders why Sewall and Emberling even suggest the credibility of "women's history" at all, much as if women were a separate species! Such comes from dysfunction. Otherwise, their report is exemplary and deserving of our attention. They close with this none too encouraging synopsis:

> The mass-market history textbooks that succeed in the market during the next few years will have a vast influence on social studies beyond the textbook cycle itself. They will reveal the kinds of civic knowledge and the literacy skills that educators expect of younger citizens. They will reflect how the nation intends to represent itself and its ideals to the youth of the early twenty-first century. They will be important indicators of "who we are" and "what we are" as a nation and people after a decade of exposure to multiculturalism.

> During the 1990s, publishers and editors apparently decided that we are all multiculturalists now and acted accordingly. They must be expecting California to endorse new histories and welcome new "world cultures" textbooks to the fold. Because of its size and money, the Golden State has the chance to demand textbooks that are more honest, rigorous and varied. Will it rise to the challenge?

> It should need no emphasis that this conglomeration of textbook supply on a centralized scale is a huge mistake that wouldn't be as likely under federalism, that is, if the national government removed its tentacles from the field of education. We managed reasonably well before Jimmy Carter's brainchild, and our only hope for recovery is to dump it and its progressive, deconstructive, suicidal anti-American influence. Let a free people educate themselves as did the Founders and their sons and daughters and their offspring for about a century. Nor was the Renaissance or the Enlightenment co-educational, or orchestrated from an Oval Office, state department of education or with socialistic tax dollars.

Another example of why we cannot expect the ladies to lead us back to excellence appears in the same issue of *Society*, in Howard L. Kaye's review of Julie Thompson Klein's *Crossing Boundaries: Knowledge, Disciplinarities, and Interdisciplinarities*, the title itself reflecting a woman's love of wordplay. Kaye finds Klein's book "an important work" because, "by being blind and indifferent herself to the distinctions between science and non-science, knowledge and ideology, objectivity and interested work, teaching and indoctrination, scholarship and entrepreneurship, intellectual work and political activism," Klein "has managed to demonstrate, however unintentionally, just how far 'the politicalization of the academy' and the commercialization of science have proceeded." Klein's dispassionate narration of various radicalisms, restructuring, politicizing, left culturalist theory, assaulting disciplinary structures, aiming to overthrow existing social and cultural order, and the involvement of government and industry in the academy, is "blithely indifferent" to the lurking disorder or "cultural and moral significance" and focuses more on "brown bag lunches and glossy brochures." Klein's is apparently a detailed though detached interest more in the appearance of usefulness in revising standards and customs than in preserving the integrity of higher education or any common good. All in all, another example of women's thought – interiorities, relationships, responsibilities, caring – rather than a knowledgeable male focus on rules, fundamentals, and order.

[17] *The Fresno Bee,* Dec. 4, 1998, "Weekend Life."

[18] Women may not excel as doctors, lawyers, beggarmen, thieves, or tinkers, tailors, soldiers and spies (pace Mata Hari), nor, all things considered, do they really improve the professions, so essentially they are adornments, adding a perfumed scent, loveliness and caring sustenance, all very felicitous. But, if we want lovable women, we should encourage them to be lovable and not professionally utilitarian. For, if they are not the latter, they're not benefiting the job, whatever it may be; and, if they stay on regardless, they are changing the workplace. Whether this is good or not should be up to the employer. And whether society should agree to absorb the additional costs of the market's accommodating women as workplace integers, is a question only time will answer. On the other hand, if they do become merely functional-utilitarian and thus peripheral to society, they are not as womanly and, along with society itself, are missing out on women's more central role.

True to Burke's "delayed action" theory, modern Americans seem always several decades behind the march of time. While assimilation of various nationalities and races is inevitable and proceeds apace, "assimilation of the sexes" is an impossibility, beyond the pale. The twain will meet between east and west before it ever meets between men and women except in marriage. Or at least, no one has ever come up with studies showing that the myriad nuances and distinctions are disappearing, even in Hollywood fabrications. Adam and Eve will remain the challenge for the ages.

[19] *Reflections on the Revolution in France,* by Edmund Burke, p. 120.

Bibliography

The following works have contributed to this book in some measure, although some more than others: and some, with only a quotation or two. A few with only one quotation do not appear here. Since myriad articles from periodicals would be profuse, titles for the latter are simply listed. Readers can find specific citations in Notes.

Adams, Henry, *The Education of Henry Adams*. Vintage Books/The Library of America, 1990.

Anderson, Kristi, *After Suffrage: Women in Partisan and Electoral Politics Before the New Deal*. University of Chicago Press, 1996.

Aquinas, Thomas, *Summa Contra Gentiles*, Book One. University of Notre Dame Press, 1975.

Aristotle, *Politics*, Book II; *Metaphysics*, Book X; *Nichomachean Ethics*, Book VIII; and *Economics*, Book I. Princeton, 1991.

Armand Eisen, *What Women Say About Men*, Andrews & McMeel, Kansas City, 1993.

The Bible. Authorized King James Version.

Babbitt Irving, *Democracy and Leadership*. Liberty Fund, 1979.

Blanchard, Paul Adam, "Insert the Word 'sex' – How Segregationists Handed Feminists a 1964 'Civil Rights' Victory Against the Family."

March, 1998, *The Family in America*, The Howard Center for Family, Religion & Society, Rockford, IL.

Blankenhorn, David, *Fatherless America*. Basic Books, 1995.

Bloom, Allan, *The Closing of the American Mind*. Simon & Schuster, 1987.

Brown, Harold O.J., *The Religion & Society Report*. August, 1998.

Bryce, James, *The American Commonwealth*. Liberty Fund, 1995.

Budziszewski, J., *Written on the Heart: The Case For Natural Law*. InterVarsity Press, 1997.

Burke, Edmund, *Reflections on the Revolution in France*. Penguin, 1986.

— . *Selected Works of Edmund Burke*, Vol. I, "Thoughts on the Cause of Our Present Discontents." The Liberty Fund, 1999.

Canavan, Francis, *The Pluralist Game*. Rowman and Littlefield, 1995.

Carey, George W., and Kendall, Willmore, *The Basic Symbols of the American Political Tradition*. The Catholic University of America Press, 1995.

Carrel, Alexis, *Man the Unknown*. Harper & Brothers, 1935.

Carroll, Lewis, *Through the Looking Glass* and *Alice in Wonderland*. Bantam, 1981.

Catholic Church. *The Church and Women*, compendium. Ignatius, 1988.

— . Pope John Paul II, *On the Dignity & Vocation of Women*. (*Mulieris Dignitatem*) St. Paul Books, 1988.

— . *Strengthening the Bonds of Peace: A Pastoral Reflection on Women in the Church and Society*. National Council of Catholic Bishops, 1994.

— . *One In Christ Jesus: Toward a Pastoral Response to the Concerns of Women in the Church and Society*. National Council of Bishops, 1992.

Chesterton, G.K., *Heritics*, "On Mr. Rudyard Kipling and Making the

World Small." Ignatius, 1986.

— . With Holbrook Jackson, *Platitudes Undone*. Ignatius, 1997.

— . *What's Wrong With the World*: "The Higher Anarchy," and "The Queen and the Suffragettes." Ignatius, 1997. Collected works, Vol. IV.

— . "Robert Louis Stevenson: The Limits of a Craft." Collected Works, Vol. XVIII.

Conrad, Joseph, *The Nigger of the Narcissus*. Harper & Row, 1967.

Cooper, James Fenimore, *The American Democrat*. Liberty Fund.

Davidson, Nicholas, *The Failure of Feminism*. Prometheus, 1998.

Davis, Philip G., *Goddess Unmasked: The Rise of Neopagan Feminist Spirituality*. Spence, 1998.

Dawson, Christopher, *Dynamics of World History*.

— . *Religion and Culture*. ISI Books.

Decter, Midge, *The New Chastity and Other Arguments Against Women's Liberation*. 1973.

Dicey, Albert Venn, *Introduction to the Law of the Constitution*. Liberty Fund, 1982.

Donnelly, Elaine, *CMR Notes*, the Center of Military Readiness. June, 1998.

Eliot, T.S., *Christianity and Culture*. Harcourt Brace, 1988.

Epstein, Richard, *Forbidden Grounds: The Case Against Employment Discrimination Laws* (Harvard, 1992).

Federici, Michael P., *Eric Voegelin*. ISI Books, 2002.

Franklin, Benjamin, *Poor Richard's Almanac*. Excerpts from his "Wit and Wisdom," Peter Pauper Press.

Gilder, George, *Men and Marriage*. Pelican, 1986.

Goldberg, Steven, *Why Men Rule*. Open Court, 1993.

Graglia, F. Caroline, *Domestic Tranquility: A Brief Against Feminism*. Spence, 1998.

Hauke, Manfred, *Gods or Goddesses?* Ignatius, 1995.

Henri, Robert, *The Art Spirit*. Lippincott, 1930. Violet Organ, 1951.

Horowitz, David, *The Feminist Assault on the Military*, a pamphlet. The Center for the Study of Popular Culture, circa 1998.

Jefferson, Thomas, *The Life and Selected Writings of Thomas Jefferson*, edited by Adrienne Koch and William Peden. Random House. Also, Library of America.

Joyce, James, *A Portrait of the Artist as a Young Man*. Viking, 1965.

Kipling, Rudyard, *Gunga Din and Other Favorite Poems*. Dover, 1990.

Kirk, Russell, *Edmund Burke: A Genius Reconsidered*. Sherwood Sugden, 1998.

— . *The Conservative Mind*. Regnery Gateway, 1987.

— . *The American Cause*. Independent Studies Institute. First Edition, Regnery, 1957.

Knight, Robert H., *The Age of Consent: The Rise of Relativism and the Corruption of Popular Culture*. Spence, 1998.

Lawrence, D.H., *Women In Love*. Penguin, 1987.

Levin, Michael, *Feminism and Freedom*. Transaction , 1987.

Lewis, C.S., *Surprised By Joy*. Harcourt Brace Jovanovich, 1984.

— . *Mere Christianity*. 1952. As quoted in *First Things*, June/July 1992.

Lorenz, Konrad, *On Aggression*. Bantam, 1969.

Mackay, Thomas, editor, *A Plea For Liberty*. Liberty Classics, 1981.

Mackey, Wade. C., "Demographic Implications of the Declining Role of the Father in Western Society." *The Journal of Social, Political and Economic Studies*, Fall, 1999. The Council For Social & Economic

Studies, Washington, D.C.

Madison, James, Federalist No. 51. Bantam, 1982.

Maier, Pauline, *American Scripture: The Making of the Declaration of Independence*. Knopf, 1997.

Martimort, Aimé Georges, *Deaconesses*. Ignatius, 1986.

Mitchell, Brian, *Women in the Military: Flirting With Disaster*. Regnery, 1998.

Moir, Anne, and Jessel, David, *Brain Sex: The Real Difference Between Men and Women*. Delta, 1991.

Morris, Desmond, *The Naked Ape*. Dell, 1969.

Newman, John Henry, *The Heart of Newman*, edited by Erich Przywara. Ignatius, 1997.

— . *Discourse to Mixed Congregations*. Ignatius.

Nietzsche, Friedrich, *Thus Spake Zarathustra*. Penguin, 1985.

Nock, Albert Jay, *Memoirs of a Superfluous Man*. Hallberg, 1994.

Oddie, William, *What Will Happen To God?* Ignatius, 1998.

Ozouf, Mona, *Women's Words: Essays on French Singularity*. Univ. of Chicago Press, 1997.

Panichas, George A., *The Burden of Vision*. Regnery Gateway, 1985.

Passno, Diane, *feminism: mystique of mistake?* Tyndale, Focus on the Family, 2000.

Pearce, Joseph, *Wisdom and Innocence: A Life of G.K. Chesterton*. Ignatius, 1996.

Pernoud, Régine, *Women in the Days of the Cathedrals*. Ignatius, 1998.

Pieper, Josef, *Josef Pieper: An Anthology*. Ignatius, 1989.

Plato, *The Republic*. Modern library paperback, Benjamin Jowett.

Podles, Leon J., *The Church Impotent: The Feminization of Christianity*,

Spence, 1999.

Roepke, Wilhelm, *The Moral Foundations of Civil Society*. Transaction Publishers, 1996.

— . *The Social Crisis of Our Times*. Transaction Publishers, 1992.

Rommen, Heinrich A., *The Natural Law*. Liberty Fund, 1998.

Ryn, Claes G., *The New Jacobinism: Can Democracy Survive?* National Humanities Institute, 1991.

Shils, Edward, *The Virtue of Civility*. Liberty Fund, 1997.

Shklar, Judith N., *Redeeming American Political Thought*, Chicago, 1998.

Smith, Adam, *The Theory of Moral Sentiments*. Regnery, 1997.

Stephen, James Fitzjames, *Liberty, Equality, Fraternity*. Liberty Fund, 1993.

Stevenson, Robert Louis, *Selected Essays*. Regnery Gateway, 1988.

Strauss, Leo, and Cropsey, Joseph, *History of Political Philosophy*. University of Chicago, 1987.

Tocqueville, Alexis de, *Democracy in America*. Vintage Books, Alfred A. Knopf, 1959.

Tolstoy, Leo, *What is Art?* The Liberal Arts Press, 1960, Bobbs Merrill.

Tooley, James, *The Miseducation of Women*, Ivan R. Dee, 2002–03.

United States Military Academy, *Report on Women at West Point*. 1992. Prepared for the Department of the Army Committee on Women in the Armed Forces (DACOWITS).

Voegelin, Eric, *Order and History*, Volume II. Louisiana State University Press.

— . *The New Science of Politics*. University of Chicago Press, 1987.

— . *Science, Politics and Gnosticism*. Regnery Gateway, 1990.

Von Balthasar, Hans Urs, *Tragedy Under Grace: Reinhold Schneider and the Experience of the West*. Ignatius, 1997.

—. *The Theology of Karl Barth*. Ignatius, 1992.

Von Hildebrand, Dietrich, *Man And Woman: Love and the Meaning of Intimacy*. Sophia Institute, 1992.

Weaver, Richard M., *Ideas Have Consequences*. University of Chicago, 1984.

—. *Visions of Order*. Intercollegiate Studies Institute, 1995.

West, Thomas G., *Vindicating the Founders*. Rowman and Littlefield, 1997.

Wilson, Glenn, *The Great Sex* Divide. Scott-Townsend, 1992.

Wilson, James Q., *The Marriage Problem: How Our Culture Has Weakened Families*. Harper Collins, 2002.

Zubaty, Rich, *Surviving the Feminization of America*. Panther Press, 1993.

Periodicals

Academic Questions

California Political Review

Commentary

Contact, Public Information Newsletter, Cal. State. Univ. Fressno.

Conservative Chronicle

Crisis

First Things

Heterodoxy

Humanitas

Modern Age

National Review

Partisan Review

Society

The Freeman

The Free Market, Ludwig von Mises Institute

The Fresno Bee

The Intercollegiate Review

The Journal of Social, Political, and Economic Studies

The Latin Mass

The New Criterion

The Political Science Reviewer

The Public Interest

The Religion & Society Report

The Salisbury Review

The Spectator

The Sunday Telegraph

The Times Literary Supplement

The University Bookman

The Weekly Standard

Index

A

Abortion culture, 307-09, 359,
Accuracy in Academia, 229
Adam & Eve, *vii*, 1,16, 48, 50, 51, 53, 54, 60
    63, 66, 70, 127, 159, 165, 233, 444n.18
Adams, Brooks, 52
Adams, Henry, 14, 34, 52, 67, 345-46, 354
    Education of Henry Adams, 67, 345-46
Aeschylus
    Oresteia (humility before God), 227
Affirmative action, *ii*, 344
Alby, Barbara, 10
Albrecht, Barbara, 92-93, 102-06, 111-12, 125-26
    223
Albright, Madeleine, 134, 224-25
Allen, Wayne (re liberalism), 226
American Civil Liberties Union (ACLU), 223
Amiel, Barbara (re "fascist tinge" of "women's
    movement"), 350
Anderson, Kristi, 164, 169, 171, 175
*After Suffrage: Women in Partisan & Electoral
Politics Before the New Deal* (Chicago), 164-68
Androgyny, in military, 356

see also West Point
Aquinas, Thomas, St., 5, 42, 80, 354, 363, 364-65, 431n.1
Arendt, Hannah
Aristotle, 5, 14, 318-325, 346, 354, 433-34n.8
    classical balance of men & women; natural law
Arnold, Matthew, 35, 361
Arpad, Susan, 50
Arthur, King, 48
Astor, Lady Nancy, 68
Augustine, Saint, *i*, 42, 130, 152
Austen, Jane, 14, 202, 229-30

B

Babbitt, Irving, 41-43, 68, 326-27, 363, 393n.32, 417n.18
    Democracy and Leadership, 41-42
    ultimate roots of leadership, character, requires humility
Babcock, Chris (research on male & female brains), 118
Bachofen, Jakob, 315
    gynocentric worship
Bagehot, Walter, 394n.41
Barrett, David, 85-86
Barth, Karl, 77, 116, 123-24, 126, 130, 150, 310
Barton, Clara, 26
Beecher, Henry Ward, 92
Behe, Michael, *vi*, 352
Berger, Brigitte, 351
"bitter harvest of division, anger, suspicion and all uncharitableness."
Berger, Raoul, 200
Berke, Matthew, 56, 65
Berlinski, David, 9, 4
Bethell, Tom, 355
    need for masculine presence in family

Bible (scripture), 13-14, 170-71, 227, 357
Bible vs the Romantic Age, 288-296
Biological sex differences, 149-51
    (see also "sex differences")
Bischof, N. (Swiss scientist), 93
Blair, Cherie, British First Lady, 98-99, 104
Blair, Tony, 85, 143-44, 234
Blanchard, Paul Adam, 384n.33 (on careless enactment of 1964 Civil Rights Act)
Blankenhorn, David, 48, 74, 383n.12
Bloom, Allan, 63, 66, 95, 187-90, 203
    Closing of the American Mind, 187
Blogg, Frances, (Mrs. G.K. Chesterton), 30-31
Blunkett, David, 409n.70
    British Education Secretary
    bringing back single-sex education
Boas, Franz, 92
Bobby-soxers (Beatle concerts), 182
Bouyer, L. (French theologian), 122
Bowles, Linda, 255
Boxer, Barbara, 391-92n.32
Boyd, L.M., 432n.8, 438n15
Bradford, Melville E., 200
Bradley, Ed, 265
Brains, male and female (types of cognition), 118
Bristow, Jennie, 218, 393n.32, 399n.53
Brontës, Charlotte & Emily, 202-04, 230
    Jane Eyre
    Wuthering Heights
Brooks, Cleanth, 35
Brooks, Van Wyck, 14-15
Brophy, Brigid, 67
Brothers, Dr. Joyce, 47, 68
Brown, Andrew, 84-85
Brown, Harold O.J., 77, 229-31, 409n.70 (re single-sex schools), 430n.89 (sexual morality and a confused Anglican Church)
Brownmiller, Susan, 129

Brownson, Orestes, 14
Bryce, James, 156
   The American Commonwealth, 156-57, 327-33
   American women made much of, debate over co-education, female franchise, sex differences, diluting the wisdom of the electorate,
Budziszewski, J., 5, 50, 432-33n.8
Bultmann, Rudolph, 35
Bunyon, John, 231
   Pilgrim's Progress
Burggraf, Jutta, 78, 117-18, 125, 128
Burk, Martha, 325
Burke, Edmund, 30, 39, 49, 62, 68, 115, 198, 223, 257, 267, 314, 357, 367, 371, 415n.13, 439n.16
Burnham, James, 364
Burtchaell, James Tunstead, 428n.81
Burton, Richard & Isabel, 240-41, 398n.38
   biography by Mary Lovell
   male explorer, loving wife
Bush, George H.W. & George W., Presidents, 208
Byron, George Gordon, Lord, 34

C

California Judicial Council, *ii*
California Civil Rights Initiative (Prop. 209), 424n.58
California Political Review, 392n.32, 406n.54
Campbell, William F., 51
Camelot, Lerner & Loewe, 48
Campbell, John, 416n.18
   discussing David Cannadine's *Class in Britain*, with chapter on contradictions of Margaret Thatcher
Campus Report (AIA), 397n.25
Canavan, Francis, 62, 75
Carr, Anne, 105
Catholic Church, 3-4, 24, 122, 163
   Ad Hoc Committee for a Pastoral Response to Women's

Concerns, 136-39
  Catholic Society of America, 105
  Catechism of the Catholic Church, 101, 112
  National Conference of Catholic Bishops (NCCB), 132
  Ordinatio Sacerdotalis (re male priests), 135, 144
  "Strengthening the Bonds of Peace" (pastoral letter), 133
  U.S. Catholic Conference, 132
  "Women: Educators for Peace" (1995 World Day of Peace), 134
Carignan, Dean M., 8,
Carey, George W., 13, 200, 377n.17
Carrel, Alexis, 16, 349, 409n.71
  Man the Unknown
Carroll, Lewis (Dobson), 143-44
  Alice in Wonderland
  Through the Looking Glass
  Humpty Dumpty, 143-44
  White Queen, 143-44, 192, 206
Catherine of Siena, 245
Center for the American Women in Politics (Rutgers), 172
Chanel, Coco, 67
Chapman, John Jay, 14-15
Chapman, Steven, 418-19n.18
Charlotte's Web, 48
Charen, Mona, 59, 278-79
Chaucer, Geoffrey, 35
Cher, 67
Chesterton, Gilbert K., 30-31, 46, 67, 84, 107, 295-96
China, female genital mutilation, 225
Chosen Women (Orange County, CA), 109
Christ, Carol P., 106
Christianity, 7, 225, 399, 402 (see also "Bible")
Church and Women, (Ignatius Press), 109-30
Citadel, 213
Civil Rights Act, 1964, Title VII, *iii*, *v*, 25, 226, 272, 351, 366-68, 371, 406n.54, 421n.51
Civil Rights Act (Education), 1972, Title IX, *ii*, *iii*, *v*, 371, 421n.51, 431n.89, 437-39n.15

Clark, Marcia (O.J. Simpson prosecutor), 224
Classicism, 316, 317-52
Clift, Eleanor, 399n.53
Clinton, William J., President, 142, 144, 172-73,
   180-82, 208, 234, 296
   Browning, Dolly Kyle, 180-81
      Purposes of the Heart, 181
   Nina Burleigh (writing in *Mirabella*), 180-81
   Jones, Paula, 181
   Lewinsky, Monica, 180
Co-ed sports, 242-43
Co-education, 322, 324, 439n.16
Coleridge, Samuel, 35
Collini, Stefan, 421n.45
Commentary, 20, 258-63
Collier, Peter, 424-45n.58
Color wheel, 64
Common good, 11, 25, 172, 235, 341, 402n.53,
   440n.16
   order of being, common law, etc., 249-50
Conforti, Sister Pascal, 358
   blurry theology
Congress, U.S., *iii*, 18
Connell, Desmond, Bishop, 127
Conrad, Joseph, 30, 35, 38-39
   Nigger of the Narcissus, 30, 38
Constitution, U.S., 172
Coons, John E., 375n.17
Cooper, James Fenimore
   The American Democrat, 167, 275, 415n.18
Coolidge, Cal, *ii*
Corinthians, 81, 150
Corliss, William J., 215
Crabtree, Charlotte, 155
Crane, Jane Larkin, 351
   review of book by Susan Gubar, Sandra M. Gilbert,
   and Elaine Showalter: "private psychiatric
   distresses," "infantilizing" their sex, etc.

Crisis, 215
Crittenden, Danielle, 59
Croly, Herbert (liberal democracy), 168-70, 172, 175,179, 200
Cross, Nancy M., 95, 231-33

D

DACOWITS (Dept. of the Army Committee on Women in the Service), 139
Daly, Mary, 102
Dante, Alighieri, 58, 98
Darwin, Charles, *vi*, 9, 40
David, Miriam, 404n.53
    IEA editor-feminist disdains family, rebutted by Melanie Phillips
Davies, Stevie, 245
    Unbridled Spirit, on women of the English Revolution: Margaret Fell, Elizabeth Pool, Anna Trapnel, Lucy Hutchinson, husbands Ralph Josselin & Nehemiah Wallington, 245-47
    reviewed by Anthony Fletcher
Davidson, Nicholas, 17, 91-92, 192, 208, 232, 246; 433n.8
    The Failure of Feminism
Davis, Angela, 425n.58
Davis, Philip G., 192, 197, 209
    Goddess Unmasked: The Rise of Neopagan Feminist Spirituality, 312-16
Dawson, Christopher, 205-06, 374n.5, 378n.9
Declaration of Independence, 23, 200
Decter, Midge, 14, 96, 193, 208, 210, 267, 277-78, 404n.53
    The New Chastity and Other Arguments Against Women's Liberation, 97, 208
        Women change with childbirth; male exteriority, female interiority
        telling the soldier from the baby tender

Dembski, William A., 349, 353-54
Democratic Party, 142
Dicey, Albert Venn, 333-36
   Introduction to the Study of the Law of the Constitution,
     confusion of government by women's vote, sex differences,
     goal of wise leadership, quality vs quantity
Dickens, Charles, 368
   Little Dorrit, Office of Circumlocution
Discrimination as to sex, 138, 174, 349, 352, 358,
   405-06n.54, 434n.10 to 444n.18
   "bona fide qualifications," the new, statutory,
     judiciable paradigm for sex, *vi*
Dobson, Reverend Dr. James, 63, 66, 74
Domestic crime, 306
Donnelly, Elaine (Center for Military Readiness), 139, 268
Dostoevsky, Fyodor, 157
Duffy, Eamon, 86, 182-83
Dunn, Ross E., 155
Dworkin, Andrea, 12

E

Eadie, Alison, 255 (re "putting women on top")
Ecumenical Coalition of Women and Society, 407n.69
   Christian Women of Renewal: their statement
Eddy, Mary Baker, 184
Edwards, Jonathan, 52
Eisler, Riane (quoted by Philip Davis)
   The Chalice and the Blade, 197
Eliot, George, 16, 61, 92, 203-04, 229
   Adam Bede, 204
Eliot, T.S., 3, 5, 6, 7, 8, 35, 52-53, 349
Elizabeth I, 276
   lauded by Alison Weir, 276
Elshtain, Jean, 207
Emberling, Stapley W., 440-42n.16
Emerson, Ralph Waldo, 14-15, 52
Emily's List, 172, 212

Employment bias, 405n.54
Enda, Jodi (Knight Ridder), 171-73
Engels, Friedrich, 92
Enlightenment, the, 163, 313-14
    reinventing history, 314
Ephesians, 72-73, 75-76, 137
Episcopal Church USA, 102-03
Epstein, Richard, 434n.9
    Forbidden Grounds
Equal Employment Opportunities Commission, 267
Equal Rights Amendment, 115
Ericson, Edward E., 140
Evans, Stanton, 201
Everson v. Board of Education, 396n.11
    revisionist judicial tampering with religion
    modern secularism

F

Family, 356-57, 403-05n.53
Faulkner, William
    The Town, 207
Federalist Papers, iv
Federalist No. 10, 23
Founders, 10, 201
Female priests, 430-31n.89
Feminism, ii, 9, 12, 26, 35, 42-43, 54, 92, 112,
    156-59, 171, 177-79, 225, 228-29, 241, 247,
    315, 327, 365, 433n.8
Feminist theology, 4, 104, 107, 121
Fermat's Proof, 10
Fessio, Father Joseph D. (on deaconesses), 122-25
Finn, Chester E. Jr., 55
Finn, Widget, 43
Fiorenza, Elisabeth Schüssler, 158, 197
First Things, 357-61
Fleming, Thomas, 417n.18
    need communities of resistance

Florovsky, Father, 389n.3
Fong, Matthew, 391-92n.32
Forrest, Thomas, 102
Fox-Genovese, Elizabeth, 180-81, 216-20, 228
Franklin, Ben, 49, 365
Fresno Bee, (McClatchy), 142, 163, 171, 296, 370, 432n.8
Friedan, Betty, 12, 60, 152, 160, 191, 351
Frink, Elisabeth (Lis), sculptress, 277
    "I need men for my work"; book reviewed by David Hughes
Fukuyama, Francis, 19-20
Fulenwider, Claire, *i*

G

Gaisford, Sue (letter to *The Spectator*), 194
Gardner, Gerald B., 313-14
    first modern witch
Garrity, Patrick, 415n.13
Gelernter, David, 161-62, 212, 214-15
Gender Bias Committee, *ii*
    "gender bias", *ii*, 56-57, 67-70
Gender Gap, *iii*, 22, 279, 367, 368
"Gender" issues, 43, 171, 247, 429n.89
Genesis, 13, 72, 73, 91, 92, 104, 112
Genovese, Kitty, 77
Gilder, George, 17, 26, 34, 61, 72, 188, 208, 219
Gilligan, Carol, 47, 49
Ginsburg, Ruth Bader, 215, 272
    United States v. Virginia
"Girl in a Million" (British film), 178-79
Glass Ceiling Act, *v*, 406n.54
Glyn-Jones, Ann, 234-35
God, the ultimate wisdom, 227
    fear of, 227
Goddess movement, 312-16
    Wicca, 213

Goethe, Johann Wolfgang von, 75, 316
Goldberg, Steven, *ii*, 15-17, 22, 47, 188, 192, 208
    210, 228
    Why Men Rule
Goodman, Ellen, 54, 55, 60
Gore, Al, 10
Gospel According to St. John, 1
Gottschalk, Chet, letter on Fukuyama's report, 19-20
Graglia, F. Carolyn, 59, 180, 209-19, 269
    Domestic Tranquility: A Brief Against Feminism,
        59, 180
Grazia, Sebastian de (reviewing Maier's *American
    Scripture*), 201
Greer, Germaine, 12, 60, 98
Gress, David, 344
    *From Plato to NATO: The Idea of the West and
    Its Opponents* (a dynamic order of competing powers)
Gretton, Philip, 416n.18 (re lack of Tory leadership)
Griswold, Robert, 403n.53
Guinier, Lani, 54-56, 60
Gunn, Sheila, 400-01n.53

H

Habermas, Jürgen (re the common good), 235
Halkin, Hillel, 20-21
Halkes, Catherina, 93, 102, 104, 129
Hardyman, Christina, 403n.53
    The Future of the Family
Harris, Judith Rich, 254-55
    *The Nurture Assumption: Why Children Turn Out
    the Way they Do*, reviewed by Steve Sailer in
    National Review.
Hart, Jeffrey, 37, 58, 351 ("feminist bowdlerists,"
    the "new Stalinists in the Academy")
Hassner, Pierre, 363-64
    On Immanuel Kant, duty & virtue from above
Hauke, Manfred, 4, 95-96, 101-09, 119-20,

192, 208
God or Goddesses, 101
Haynes, Ray, 391-92n.32
Husband's headship, 323
    see also Chapters IV & V
Healy, Gene, 240
    re murder of Amy Biehl in Africa
Hefner, Robert, 77
Hegel, 16, 46, 170
Heidigger, 170
Henri, Robert, 32-34
    Art Spirit, 32-33
Herbert, Mary Sydney, Countess of Pembroke, 230
Heritage Foundation, 405n.53
Herman, Arthur, 234, 238
    The Idea of Decline in Western History, 234
    How the Scots Invented the Modern World, 238
Hersch, Patricia, 256-58
    A Tribe Apart; A Journey into the Heart of American Adolescence, reviewed by David Klinghoffer
"Herstory," Chapter VII, 440-41n.16
Himmelfarb, Gertrude, 198
Hittinger, Russell, 436n.10
Hobbes, Thomas, 170
Hofstadter, Richard, 92
Holmes, Oliver Wendell, 287
Homosexuality, 243-45, 355, 358
Horowitz, David, 424-25n.58
Hotchkiss School, female Dean of Faculty, 270
    on "whether Frye's literary structures are sexually biased"
Hotz, Robert Lee, 397n.19
    motherhood makes women smarter
Howard, Donald, 35
Howell, George, 317, 337, 406n.54
    Interference with liberties of grown men
Hubbard, Ron, 184
Hudson, Deal (Editor of *Crisis*), 190-91

Huffington, Arianna Stassinopoulos, 151-52
Humanitarian idealism, 418n.18
Humanitas, 393n.32
Humility, 226-27
    "The fear of the Lord is the instruction of wisdom; and before honor is humility," 227
    feminist attributes? 227
Hunt, Robert P., 5, 256
Hurston, Zora Neale, 204
Hutson, James H., 396n.11
    Founders intended no "wall of separation"

I

Iannone, Carol, 351
    female scholars: "Bogus scholars make a bogus case."
Icarus, 17
Idealization of women, 58
Independent Women's Forum (IWF), 196, 263-71
    board member Diana Furchgott-Roth, 196
    "individual responsibility, strong families, limited government, and opportunity"
    The Women's Quarterly, 266
    Former President Ricky Silberman, 367, 270
    Ann Northrup, judged for her hard work & talents, 271
Inevitability of Patriarchy (Steven Goldberg), 381n.6
Institute of Economic Affairs (IEA), 403n.53
    The Fragmenting Family
Intelligent Design, vii, 310 (Einstein & relativity), 352-354 (for the human species)
Invisible hand, 366, 371, see also Adam Smith.
Irreducible complexity, 352-54
    or irreducible simplicity, 354
Isaiah, 81

J

Jackson, Holbrook, 46, 57, 67
Japan, 20
Jefferson, Thomas, 31, 46, 396n.11
Jellyby, Mrs. 240
Jewish studies, 20-21
Joan of Arc, 134, 163, 184, 245
John Paul II, Pope, *iii*, 71, 87-90, 92-94, 95, 102, 106, 118, 144
Johnson, Paul, 147-48, 193-94
Johnson, Dr. Samuel, 46, 90, 136
Johnson, George Sim, 71
Jong, Erica, 51
Joyce, James, 34
    Ulysses, 214
    Molly Bloom, 214
Judeo-Christian heritage, 236

K

Kant, Immanuel, 18, 363-64
Kasper, Walter, 113
Kaye, Howard L., 442-43n.16
Keller, Helen, 26
Kendall, Willmore, 13, 200
Kennedy, John F., 85
Kenny, Mary, 273-75
    tailor-made news columns
Kentenich, J. (metaphysician), 111
Kerr, Jean, 69
Kimball Roger, 7, 17-18, 39-40, 60, 107, 344, 394n.41
King, Florence, 14, 57, 92, 399n.49
Kipling, Rudyard, 46, 47, 68
    "The Female of the Species," 162
Kirk, Russell, 175-76, 200, 226, 344, 413n.29
    re limits of statutory law
Klein, Julie Thompson, 442-43n.16
    Crossing Boundaries: Knowledge, Disciplinarities,

And Interdisciplinarities
Kleinheyer, Bruno (on deaconesses), 120
Knight, Robert H. (re sexual revolution), 222-23
Knox, John, 14, 287-96
    The First Trumpet Blast Against the Monstrous Regiment of Women (Calvin, Paul, Tertullian, Augustine, Ambrose, Basil, Chrysostom, & the Pandects)
Knull, Morgan, 415n.18
    the near absence of Madisonian statesmen
Koch, Adrienne, 378n.6
Kochlin, Michael, 374n.1
Kolakowski, Leszek, 60
Korea, 20
Kristol, William, 211
Kramer, Hilton, 7, 215

L

Labash, Matt
La Haye, Beverly (Concerned Women of America), 109, 232, 263-64
Lança, Patricia, 54, 233
Landes, Paula Fredrikson, 96
Latin Mass, 30
Latina Women's Conference, 142
Lawler, Peter Augustine, 21
Lawrence, D.H., 63-64
    Women in Love, 63-64
Leadership, 136, 326, 415-18n.18
Lear's daughters, 180, 216
Leary, Timothy, 107
LeCarre, John
    The Spy That Came in From the Cold, 188
Ledeen, Michael (on women authors), 350-51, 415-16n.18 (re lack of leadership)
Lehman, John, 356
    androgyny for the military?

Lehmann, Bishop Karl, 110-11
Lenzner, Steve, 374n.1
Leo, John, 56-57
Levin, Michael, *ii*, 17, 22, 45-46, 159, 192
    208, 228, 275-76
    Feminism and Freedom
Lewis, C.S., 5, 48, 64, 72-75, 149, 238, 322
    A Grief Observed, 64
Lewis, Michael, 139
    Poisoning the Ivy, 140
Liberalism, 113, 369
    classical, 225
Libertarianism, 220-21
Lightroller, Charles H., 26
Linker, Damon, 383n.21
Little, Rod (in *The Spectator*), 118
    "Why women can't read maps"
Lopata, Helen (see Gilder), 219
Lovell, Mary S., 240-41, 398n.38
    A Rage to Live, re Richard & Isabel Burton
Luce, Claire Boothe, 67
Lycurgus and the Spartan women, 110
Lucy, prehistoric, 78
Lynch, Frederick R., 317, 342-44
    "diversity management"
    Gottfredson, Linda, sociologist,
    casuistry of sex-integration & "gender" talk;
    influence of J.S. Mill; autocracy
Lynch, Jessica, PFC, 104

M

Mackay, Thomas (on the advancing interference by
    government), 336-37
    A Plea for Liberty, essays by Edward Stanley
    Robinson (women needed in the family); George
    Howell (too many new statutes)
Mackey, Wade C., 27, 137, 383n.12

population replacement, need for fathers & mothers
MacKinnon, Catherine, 237-39
 Sexual Harassment of Working Women:
 A Case of Sexual Discrimination
Madison, James, 11, 23, 56, 325-56 (re Allen Rutland's
 James Madison: The Founding Father, reviewed by
 Morgan N. Knull)
Madisonian factions, *iv*, 55
Maier, Pauline, 200
 American Scripture, 200-02
Male clubs, 213
Male objectivity, 315
Manet, Édouard, 33
Mansfield, Jane, 236
Maritain, Jacques, 35, 191
Marrin, Minette, 243-45
 on women being lovable
Marryat, Captain Frederick, 27
Mark, Gospel According to, 120
Marshner, Connaught (National Pro-Family
 Coalition), 109
Martimort, Aimé Georges, 4, 86, 131, 192, 208
 Deaconesses, 86, 120, 130-32
Marxism, 26, 170, 315
Mary, Saint, 4, 59, 80, 91, 96, 106, 114-18,
 122-23, 128, 136, 364
Masculine roles, value of, 27, 137, 355, 383n.12
Mason, Ian Garrick, 7
Masquerade, 274, 371, 434-435n.10
McCarthy, Eugene, 418n.18
McClay, Wilfred M., 80, 335-36 (re ordered liberty)
McDonagh, Eileen L., 165
McDougall, Walter A., 215
McElroy, Wendy ("individualist feminism"), 172
 220-23, 228, 230, 279
 re Moses Harman's "self-ownership in marriage"
McGinley, Phyllis, 61, 312
McInerny, Ralph, 86

Mead, Lawrence M., 173
    "The Politics of the Disadvantaged," 173
Means, Marianne, 429n.89
    Hearst news item on "gender barriers"
Meese, Edwin, 405n.53
Meilaender, Gilbert, 73-75, 77, 84, 323
Merikoski, Ingrid, 238
    re responsibility & reverence for the past
Meves, C. (quoted by B. Albrecht), 112
Meyer-Wilmes, Hedwig, 102
Michelet, Jules, 313
    "Woman is a religion"
Midgley, Mary, 8
Mill, John Stuart, 92, 178, 335-36, 339-42
Millett, Kate, 147
Mitchell, Brian, 215
Modern Age, 5
Moir, Bill & Anne, 192-93
    Why Men Don't Iron
Moir, Anne and David Jessel, 221, 281-85
Brain Sex: The Real Difference Between Men & Women
Molinari, Susan, 251
Moll, Helmut (on deaconesses), 121-22, 129
Moltmann-Wendel, Elizabeth, 102
Monroe, Marilyn, 391n.31
Moore, Charlotte, 192-93
Moore, Paul. J., Bishop (Anglican), 126
Moral equivalence, 224-25
Morgan, Patricia, 403-04n.53
    advantage of marriage and stable family is inescapable
Morisot, Berthe, 33-34
Mormon women, 230
Morris, Gouverneur, 11
Morris, Joan, 85
Motherhood, effect on women, 223-24
    See also Midge Decter, 278

Mottram, Buster, 176, 218
Muggeridge, Malcolm, 148
Mulack, Christa, 102, 108
Mulloy, John J., 374n.5
Murray, John Courtney, 5, 256

N

Nash, Gary B., 155, 441n.16
National Organization for Women, 172, 437n.11
National Masters News (re female competition), 219
National Review, 231-33, 235-36
Natural law, 434-36n.10
    See also Aristotle, 318-325
Nazi propaganda (atonal music), 190-91
    Joseph Goebbels
    Anton Weber
    Arnold Schoenberg
    Pierre Boulet
Need for nurses, 104
Neuchterlein, James, *iv*
Neuhaus, Richard John, 87-88, 94, 95, 224, 357-61
New Criterion, 135, 394n.41
Newman, John Henry, 79, 84, 133
Niemeyer, Gerhart, 265
    Between Nothingness & Paradise
Niebuhr, Reinhold, *iv*
Nietzsche, Friedrich Wilhelm, 49, 63, 170
    Zarathustra, 48, 63
Nightingale, Florence, 26, 184
Nineteenth Amendment, *iii*, 22, 164-68, 173, 230, 251, 264, 273, 311 (against theory of mutual happiness), 325, 339 (Damoclean sword), 367, 371, 392n.32, 417n.18, 425n.58
Nock, Albert Jay, 14-16, 18
Nolan, Michael, 431n.1
Nordlinger, Pia (on women's reading habits), 251-52
Notre Dame University, 86

Nussbaum, Martha, 86

O

Oakes, Edward T., S.J., 432n.8
Oakeshott, Michael, 161
O'Brien, George Dennis, 428n.81
O'Connor, Flannery, 95, 198, 204
Oddie, William, 25-26, 106, 157-9, 192, 205, 208
    What Will Happen to God? 25–26, 73, 75,
        96, 101, 102-03, 124, 126, 145-53, 351
O'Leary, Dale, 53-54, 234
Orwell, George, 34, 148
Ozouf, Mona, 176
    Women's Words: An Essay on French Singularity, 176-79

P

Paglia, Camille, 22-23, 180
Panichas, George, 5
Pannenberg, Wolfhart, 15, 18
Pascal, 115
Parris, Matthew, 143-44
Patriarchy, 43, 228
Paul, Saint, 15, 82, 84, 90-91, 107, 133
Pearson, Maryon, 67
Pearson, Sidney A., Jr., 168-70
    "Herbert Croly and Liberal Democracy"
Pease, Allan, 380n.39
    Why Men Don't Listen & Women Can't Read Maps
Peden, William, 378n.6
Pelling, Rev. John, 97-98, 102
Pernoud, Régine, 159, 169, 171, 214, 245
    Women in the Days of the Cathedrals, 159-64
"Personal is the political," 175
Peter, Saint, 81, 82
Peterson, Marilyn, 70

Phillips, Melanie, 401-02n.53
    almost a family advocate, rebuts Miriam David,
    approves Patricia Morgan's views (IEA pamphlet)
Pieper, Josef, *i*
Pirie, Madsen, 409n.70
    how exams are fixed in favor of girls
Plaskow, Judith, 106
Plato, 1, 14, 30, 37
    Republic, The, 37-38
Podhoretz, Norman, 129, 215
Podles, Leon J., 385n.2 (*Church Impotent: The Feminization of Christianity*)
Political correctness, *vi*, 1, 174, 344
Pope Joan, by Lawrence Durrell, 85
Popenhoe, David, 402n.53
    decline of fatherhood
Posner, Richard, Judge, 268
Powers, Elizabeth, 70-71, 253-54, 257
    re a liberated woman's versatility
Prejudice (natural & worthwhile), 347-48
Price, Richard, 49
Progressivism, 168-70, 179, 327, 335, 369, 418n.18
Proportionate representation, 334-35, 420-21n.38
Proudie, Mrs., wife of Bishop of Barchester, 342 (Anthony Trollope)
Proverbs, 73, 82-83

Q

Quinn, Dermot (on Christopher Dawson), 205
Quixote, Don, 253

R

Rasmussen, David M., 53, 235
Ratzinger, Joseph, Cardinal, 114-16, 121, 144
Ravel, Maurice (composed pieces for female pianists), 306

Reading, Marchioness of (*The Spectator*), 134
Reagan, Ronald, *v*
Reese, Charley, 215, 337-39 (women's perspective self-centered rather than on ordered freedoms)
Reik, Theodore, 47, 68
Reist, John S. Jr., 35
Religion, 17, 226, 357, 440n.16
Rice, Condoleezza, 180
Right order, 352, Introduction, Chapters I, II, etc.
Ripperger, Father Chad, 30
Roberts, Paul Craig, 423-24n.58
  The New Color Line
Robertson, Edward Stanley, 336-37
Rockwell, Llewellyn H., Jr. 37
Roepke, Wilhelm, *iii*, 6, 51-52
Rogers, Byron, 97
Rollyson, Carl, 300
  "Reporting Nuremburg," on Rebecca West
Rommen, Heinrich A., 249-50, 435-36n.10
  The Natural Law
Roman Catholic Bishops of the U.S., 87
Roosevelt, Theodore, 16, 168, 179, 420n.32
Rousseau, Jean Jacques, 32, 177, 366, 369
  Emile, 369
Ruether, Rosemary Radford, 102, 232
Rush, Benjamin, 23-24
Russo, John Paul, 42, 361
Ryn, Claes G., 37, 187

S

Sagan, Françoise, 67
Sailer, Steve, 215
Sanger, Margaret (Planned Parenthood), 223
Santayana, George, 189, 201, 314, 344, 394n.41
Sappho, 14
Sauerbrey, Ellen ("Maryland's Thatcher"), 236
Schaub, Diana (reviewing Ozouf), 176-79

Scheffczyk, Leo, 116-17
Schiller, 316
Schlafly, Phyllis (Eagle Forum), 14, 109, 173,
    180, 193, 232, 263-64
Schlesinger, Arthur M., Jr., 275
    The Vital Center, the need for accountability
Schneider, Reinhold, 36
Schoenfeld, Gabriel, 258-63
    responding to arguments on Holocaust feminism
Scholarship, importance of, 354, 440-41n.16
Schroeder, Pat, 251, 429n.89
Schulman, Margaret, 171
Scruton, Roger, 60, 366, 369
Secular humanism, 314-15
Seiler, Stephen, 215
Seventeenth Amendment, 418n.18
Sewall, Gilbert T., 440-42n.16
Sex differences, Chapter III, 275, 279, 284, 318, 340-41,
    346, 370, 380n.39, 422-23n.51
    see also Davidson, Gilder, Goldberg, Levin
Sexual harassment, *ii*, 247, 266-67
Sex integration, 32, 37, 429n.89
Sex equality in sports, 431n.89, 437-39n.15
Shakespeare, William, 35, 40, 51, 66, 150, 229
    Troilus & Cressida, 51
    Merchant of Venice, 191
Shalit, Wendy, 237-39
    re sexual harassment, etc.
Shelley, Percy Bysshe, 35
Siemens, Carol, 310 (angry gynocentricism),
    400-01n.53
Single-sex schools, 271-73, 409n.70
    Whelan, Christine B. (in *National Review*), 271,
    in favor of single-sex schools (for girls only?)
    Riesman, David, in favor, 272
Sixties (60s), decade of the, 18
Shils, Edward, 11-12
Shklar, Judith, 395n.57

Redeeming American Political Thought
    revisionist history
Small Business Administration, 142
Smith, Adam
    The Theory of Moral Sentiments, 297-312
        Art, nature, need to uphold existing morals, over-all design, common good, healthy balance, breach of chastity, sexual decorum, order & harmony, avoid legislating scrupulosity of conscience leading to political correctness & casuistry; positive laws must not stifle natural justice; priesthood too solemn, and military too dangerous or women; infanticide barbarous & gross; Titles VII & IX shackle the invisible hand
Society (Transaction Periodicals Consortium - Rutgers), 171, 203
    Women in Austria, by Erika Turner, 203
    Letters to a Young Feminist, by Dr. Phyllis Chesler;
    Women and Madness, ditto;
        Lauded by Adrienne Rich & Gloria Steinem respectively, 203
Socrates, 37-38
Sommers, Christina Hoff, 57, 227-29, 314
Sorokin, Ptirim, *iii*, 157
    The Crisis of Our Age, 157
Spalding, Matthew, 396n.11, 415n.13
    no "wall of separation"
Spartan women, 322-23, 325
Spectator, 399-401n.53
Spencer, Herbert, 69
Spender, Stephen, 147
Spong, Bishop John Shelby, 103
Stanford, Peter, 85, 182-83
Star Trek, 391n.31
    "Voyager," 391n.31
Steichen, Donna, 160
Stein, Edith, 95, 232-32
Steinem, Gloria, 67-68, 232, 399n.48
    "revolution, not just reform"
Stephen, James Fitzjames, 14, 339-41
    Liberty, Equality, Fraternity, rebuttal of

J.S. Mill's *On Liberty*
Stevenson, Robert Louis, 287-96
    Romantic opposition to Knox; Adam-like obeisance to the opposite sex; (Aylmer, Mary Queen of Scots); critique by G.K. Chesterton.
Steyn, Mark (re sex discrimination law), 224
Stirling, Larry, Judge, 406n.54
    too many statutes
Stone, Brad Lowell, 364
    vocation based on ones talents
Stossel, John (ABC news), 268, 413n.42
    on sex discrimination in sports
    on Einstein's discoveries
Stowe, Harriet Beecher, 188
Stratton, Lawrence, 423-24n.58
    The New Color Line
Strong, Anna Louise, 148
Suffragettes, 173
Susan B. Anthony list, 211

T

Tannen, Deborah, 54
Ten Commandments, 15, 165
Teresa, Mother, 8, 9, 122
Terwilliger, Bishop, 102
Textbooks, public education, 440-41n.16 (revisionist)
Thatcher, Margaret, 134
    girlish nature more than Burke/Smith, 301, 416n.18 (without a fully coherent social vision)
Thielicke, Helmut, 74, 84
Thomas, Cal, 280
    re *Vanity Fair*'s "most influential women":
    traditional women more influential.
Tillis, Pam, 370
Times Literary Supplement, 182-87
    Barbara Leigh Smith Bodichon, 186-87, 190,
        by Pam Hirsch, reviewed by Kate Chisholm, 186-87

Le Quesne, Mary, 183-84
    "Women of Spirit"
    Christina of Markyate
    Perpetua
Mary Sydney Herbert, Countess of Pembroke, Collected Works,
    edited by Margaret P. Hannay, et al, reviewed by
    Katherine Duncan-Jones, 199-200
Visionary Women Series, 183
Walker, Nicola, 185-86
    reviewing *Amazonian: the Penguin book of women's new
    travel writing*
Women of the Twelfth Century, by George Duby,
    reviewed by Elisabeth Van Houts, 204
see also Natasha Walter, 248-49
Timothy, 81-83
Titanic, (the ship), 26, 76, 115, 218
Title VII, *iii*, *v*, 39, 213 (see also "Civil Rights Law")
Title IX, *ii*, *iii*, *iv*, *v*, 213, 268-269 (ditto)
Titus, 81
Tocqueville, Alexis de, 14, 24, 72, 75, 327
    Democracy in America (re realistic sex relations),
    decadence of manhood
Tolstoy, Leo, 35-37
Torrey, Morrison, 50
Tresmontant, Claude, 156
Twain, Mark (Clemens), 105
Twain, Mrs., 172
Twenty-sixth Amendment, 361

U

University Bookman, 140, 238

V

Valadon, Suzanne (mother of Utrillo), 195-96
    biography by June Rose

reviewed by Richard Shone
Valuinas, Algis, (re Job's humility before God), 226-27
Vander Elst, Philip, 153
Victorian Age (ideal of the Lady & the Gentleman), 94, 163, 238
V.M.I., 213
Voegelin, Eric, 2, 3, 161, 170
   The New Science of Politics, 170
   Science, Politics, and Gnosticism, 170
Von Balthasar, Hans Urs, 36, 84, 116, 120-21, 123-24, 130
Von Hildebrand, Dietrich, 84, 114
Von Mises, Ludwig, 37

W

Wain, John, 219
Walter, Natasha, 248-49
   The New Feminism, reviewed by Claudia Fitzherbert, re "equality feminism" (*Spectator*); also reviewed by Mary Margaret McCabe, *Times Literary Supplement*
Walters, Barbara, 269, 431n.89
   on Title IX
Washington, D.C., *vi*
Washington, George, 11, 406n.54
   Wallin, Jeffrey, reviewing Matthew Spaulding's & Patrick Garrity's *A Sacred Union of Citizens: George Washington's Farewell Address and the National Character*, 325
Wayne, John, 432n.8
Wax, Amy (see Gelernter & Graglia), 214
Weaver, Richard M., 14, 346-350
   The Ethics of Rhetoric, 346
   Visions of Order, 346
   dialectic, rhetoric & enthymemes
The Weekly Standard, 181
Weill, Simone, 198

Weiss, Michael, 49-50, 107
Weissberg, Robert, 436n.10
Welty, Eudora, 204
West Point (United States Military Academy), *iii*, 118
West, Thomas G., 10-12, 21-25, 26
    Vindicating the Founders
West, Woody, 409n.71 (on the Supreme Court's androgynizing V.M.I.)
Westermarck, Edward, 403n.53
    maternal sentiment universal to mankind
Western Civilization, 2, 58-59
What Women Say About Men (Andrews & McMeel), 56, 67
Whetstone, Trevor, 397n.25
"Why Women Can't Read Maps," 118-19, 380n.39
    Rod Little, Chris Babcock, *The Spectator*
    Allan Pease, *Sunday Telegraph*
Wiegel, George, 256
    A Century of Catholic Social Thought
Will, George, *ii*
Williams, Charles, 64
Wills, Garry, 200
Wilson, A.N., 218-19
Wilson, James Q., 62, 67-68, 356-57
Wilson, Woodrow, 16
    Congressional Government, 168
Windschuttle, Keith, 156, 389n.1
Wittig, Monique (quoted by Philip Davis), 197
Wollstonecraft, Mary, 314
    Vindication of the Rights of Women
Women as leaders of men, 18, 32, 224, 366, 370, 392n.32, 405n.53, 429n.89, 434-45n.10
Women, idealization of, 313, 315, 345
Women's central role ("interiority"), 102-128, 243-45, 443-44n.18
"Women's issues," *ii*
    Sex equality, 22-23, 43, 137, 139, 203, 220-21, 245, 311, 340-41, 348-49, 422-23n.51, 433n.8
Women's lib, 18, 26, 30, 138, 146, 152, 239-40,

285, 365, 366, 403-04n.53, 427n.66
Women's morality, 53, 188, 234-35, 358-59, 394n.41
Women's rights, 24, 146
Women's sexuality, 346, 370
    See also Gilder, Goldberg, Levin, Davidson
Women's studies, 50, 135, 140, 146, 160, 164, 216, 222, 359-51, 440n.16
Women's voices, 105-06, 125
Women's vulnerability to violence, 237, 239-43
Wood, Ralph C. (writing on Flannery O'Connor), 198
Woodhull, Victoria, 92
Woollcombe, Kenneth, Anglican Bishop, 148
Working mothers, 359-60
    Susan Chira's *Mother's Place: Taking the Debate About Working Mothers Beyond Guilt and Blame* discussed by Richard John Neuhaus
Wurtzel, Elizabeth, 171
Wuthnow, Robert, 7

X

Xanthippe, 38, 246

HQ 1154 .C59 2005
Chynoweth, W. Edward.
Masquerade

JAN 3 1 2006